Praise for *Reinforcement Learning*

"Reinforcement learning is one of the most exciting areas of machine learning and, unfortunately, also one of the most complex. Reinforcement Learning does a terrific job of laying out the background, landscape and opportunities to take advantage of this ground-breaking technique in ways that will significantly advance the way data scientists can impact their businesses."

—*David Aronchick, Cofounder of Kubeflow*

"Dr. Phil Winder's book on reinforcement learning is a breath of fresh air. He has distilled a topic that is incredibly dynamic into an easy-to-follow book that focuses on the reader's understanding and insights. This book is exciting because of how relevant reinforcement learning is to learning under uncertain environments."

—*Founder of Your Chief Scientist, Trainer, and Author of* Thoughtful Machine Learning

"A must-have book for anyone wanting to apply reinforcement learning techniques to real-world problems. It takes the reader from first principles to state-of-the-art with a wealth of practical examples and detailed explanations."

—*David Foster, Partner at Applied Data Science Partners and Author of* Generative Deep Learning

"Great book by Phil Winder. Nature's proven method of learning by doing finally finds its way into the software developer's standard toolbox. Reinforcement learning is the flywheel of artificial intelligence, and this book aims to bring that perspective to applications in industry and business."

—*Danny Lange, SVP of AI, Unity*

Reinforcement Learning
Industrial Applications of Intelligent Agents

Phil Winder, Ph.D.

Beijing · Boston · Farnham · Sebastopol · Tokyo  O'REILLY®

Reinforcement Learning

by Phil Winder, Ph.D.

Copyright © 2021 Winder Research and Development Ltd. All rights reserved.

Published by O'Reilly Media, Inc., 1005 Gravenstein Highway North, Sebastopol, CA 95472.

O'Reilly books may be purchased for educational, business, or sales promotional use. Online editions are also available for most titles (*http://oreilly.com*). For more information, contact our corporate/institutional sales department: 800-998-9938 or *corporate@oreilly.com*.

Acquisitions Editor: Jonathan Hassell
Developmental Editor: Corbin Collins
Production Editor: Beth Kelly
Copyeditor: Charles Roumeliotis
Proofreader: Kim Cofer

Indexer: Judy McConville
Interior Designer: David Futato
Cover Designer: Karen Montgomery
Illustrator: Kate Dullea

December 2020:   First Edition

Revision History for the First Edition
2020-11-06:   First Release
2023-01-13:   Second Release

See *http://oreilly.com/catalog/errata.csp?isbn=9781098114831* for release details.

978-1-098-11483-1

[LSI]

For Emma, Eva, and Cora

Table of Contents

Preface

Reinforcement learning (RL) is a machine learning (ML) paradigm that is capable of optimizing sequential decisions. RL is interesting because it mimics how we, as humans, learn. We are instinctively capable of learning strategies that help us master complex tasks like riding a bike or taking a mathematics exam. RL attempts to copy this process by interacting with the environment to learn strategies.

Recently, businesses have been applying ML algorithms to make one-shot decisions. These are trained upon data to make the best decision at the time. But often, the right decision at the time may not be the best decision in the long term. Yes, that full tub of ice cream will make you happy in the short term, but you'll have to do more exercise next week. Similarly, click-bait recommendations might have the highest click-through rates, but in the long term these articles feel like a scam and hurt long-term engagement or retention.

RL is exciting because it is possible to learn long-term strategies and apply them to complex industrial problems. Businesses and practitioners alike can use goals that directly relate to the business like profit, number of users, and retention, not technical evaluation metrics like accuracy or F1-score. Put simply, many challenges depend on sequential decision making. ML is not designed to solve these problems, RL is.

Objective

I wrote this book because I have read about so many amazing examples of using RL to solve seemingly impossible tasks. But all of these examples were from academic research papers and the books I subsequently read were either targeted toward academia or were glorified code listings. Hardly any had an industrial perspective or explained how to use RL in production settings. I knew how powerful this technology could be, so I set out to write a book about using RL in industry.

When I started writing, I wanted to concentrate on the operational aspects, but I quickly realized that hardly anyone in industry had heard of RL, let alone running RL in production. Also, throughout my reader research, I found that many engineers and data scientists had never even seen a lot of the underlying algorithms. So this book morphed into part fundamental explanation and part practical implementation advice. My hope is that this book will inspire and encourage the use of RL in industrial settings.

I believe that this is the first book to discuss operational RL concerns and certainly the only book that has combined algorithmic and operational developments into a coherent picture of the RL development process.

Who Should Read This Book?

The aim of this book is to promote the use of RL in production systems. If you are (now or in the future) building RL products, whether in research, development, or operations, then this book is for you. This also means that I have tailored this book more toward industry than academia.

Guiding Principles and Style

I decided on a few guiding principles that I thought were important for a book like this, based upon my own experience with other books.

The first is that I entirely avoid code listings. I believe that in most cases books are not an appropriate place for code listings— software engineering books are an obvious exception. This goes against conventional wisdom but personally, I'm sick of skipping over pages and pages of code. I buy books to hear the thoughts of the author, the way they explain the concepts, the insights. Another reason for not printing code is that many of the implementations, especially in later chapters, are really quite complex, with a lot of optimization detail in the implementation that detracts from the main ideas that I want to teach. You would typically use a library implementation anyway. And then there are the algorithms that don't have implementations yet because they are too new or too complex to be merged into the standard libraries. For all these reasons and more, this is not a typical "show-me-the-code" book.

But don't worry, this doesn't mean there is no code at all. There is, but it's in an accompanying repository, along with lots of other practical examples, how-to guides, reviews, collections of papers, and lots more content (see "Supplementary Materials" on page xix).

And what this does mean is that there is more room for insight, explanations, and, occasionally, a few bad jokes. You will walk away from reading this book appreciating the amount and density of the content, the breadth of coverage, and the fact that you have not had to skip over pages of code.

The second principle I had was about the math. RL is a highly mathematical topic, because it is usually much easier to explain an algorithm with a few lines of mathematics, rather than 20 lines of code. But I totally appreciate how mathematics can seem like an alien language sometimes. Like any other programming language, mathematics has its own syntax, assumed knowledge, and built-in functions that you have to know before you can fully appreciate it.

So throughout this book I don't shy away from the mathematics, especially during the explanations of the algorithms fundamental to RL, because they are an important part. However, I do try to limit the mathematics where I can and provide long explanations where I can't. I generally try to follow the notation provided by Thomas and Okal's Markov Decision Process Notation, Version 1.[1] But I often abuse the notation to make it even simpler.

The third principle, which you might find different to other technical books that focus more on best practices and the art of engineering, relate to the fact that RL development has been driven by research, not by experience. So this book is chock-full of references to research papers. I attempt to collate and summarize all of this research to provide you with a broad understanding of the state-of-the-art. I also try to balance the depth that I go into.

As a teacher, this is a really hard thing to do, because you might be an expert already, or you might be a complete novice that has just learned how to code. I can't please everyone, but I can aim for the middle. On average, I hope you will feel that there is a good balance between giving you enough information to feel confident, but simplifying enough to prevent you from being overwhelmed. If you do want to go into more depth in particular subjects, then please refer to the research papers, references, and other academic books. If you are feeling overwhelmed, take your time, there's no rush. I've provided lots of links to other resources that will help you along your way.

The fourth principle is that I always attempt to point out pitfalls or things that can go wrong. I have spoken to some people who take this to mean that RL isn't ready or I don't believe in it; it is ready and I do believe in it. But it is vitally important to understand the unknowns and the difficulties so you are not overpromising or allocating enough time to do the work. This is certainly not "normal" software engineering. So wherever you see "challenges" or explanations of "how to improve," this is vital and important information. Failure is the best teacher.

Prerequisites

This all means that RL is quite an advanced topic, before you even get started. To enjoy this book the most, you would benefit from some exposure to data science and machine learning and you will need a little mathematics knowledge.

But don't worry if you don't have this. You can always learn it later. I provide lots of references and links to further reading and explain ancillary concepts where it makes sense. I promise that you will still take away a huge amount of knowledge.

Scope and Outline

The scope of the book spans your journey of trying to move RL products into production. First, you need to learn the basic framework that RL is built around. Next you move on to simple algorithms that exploit this framework. Then you can learn about more and more advanced algorithms that are capable of greater feats. Then you need to think about how to apply this knowledge to your industrial problem. And finally, you need to design a robust system to make it operationally viable.

This is the path that the book follows and I recommend that you read it linearly, from start to finish. Later chapters build upon ideas in the early chapters, so you may miss out on something if you skip it. However, feel free to skip to specific chapters or sections that interest you. Whenever necessary, I link back to previous sections.

Here is an overview to whet your appetite:

Chapter 1, "Why Reinforcement Learning?"
The book begins with a gentle introduction into the history and background of RL, with inspiration from other scientific disciplines to provide inspiration. It sets the groundwork and gives you an overview of all the different types of algorithms in RL.

Chapter 2, "Markov Decision Processes, Dynamic Programming, and Monte Carlo Methods"
The hard work begins with a chapter defining the fundamental concepts in RL including Markov decision processes, dynamic programming, and Monte Carlo methods.

Chapter 3, "Temporal-Difference Learning, Q-Learning, and n-Step Algorithms"
In this chapter you graduate to so-called *value methods*, which attempt to quantify the value of being in a particular state, the basic algorithm that dominates all modern RL.

Chapter 4, "Deep Q-Networks"
Much of the recent excitement has been due to the combination of value methods with deep learning. You will dive into this concoction and I promise you will be surprised by the performance of these algorithms.

Chapter 5, "Policy Gradient Methods"
Now you'll learn about the second most popular form of RL algorithms—policy gradient methods—which attempt to nudge a parameterized strategy toward better performance. The primary benefit is that they can handle continuous actions.

Chapter 6, "Beyond Policy Gradients"

Basic policy gradient algorithms have a range of issues, but this chapter considers and fixes many of the problems that they suffer from. And the promise of off-policy training is introduced to improve efficiency.

Chapter 7, "Learning All Possible Policies with Entropy Methods"

Entropy methods have proven to be robust and capable of learning strategies for complex activities such as driving cars or controlling traffic flow.

Chapter 8, "Improving How an Agent Learns"

Taking a step back from the core RL algorithms, this chapter investigates how ancillary components can help solve difficult problems. Here I focus on different RL paradigms and alternative ways to formulate the Markov decision process.

Chapter 9, "Practical Reinforcement Learning"

This is the first of two chapters on building production RL systems. This chapter walks you through the process of designing and implementing industrial RL algorithms. It describes the process, design decisions, and implementation practicalities.

Chapter 10, "Operational Reinforcement Learning"

If you want advice on how to run RL products in production, then this chapter is for you. Here I delve into the architectural design that you should consider to make your solution scale and be more robust, then detail the key aspects you need to watch out for.

Chapter 11, "Conclusions and the Future"

The final chapter is not just another summary. It contains a wealth of practical tips and tricks that you will find useful during your RL journey and presents suggestions for future research.

Supplementary Materials

I have created the website *https://rl-book.com* to organize all of the extra materials that accompany this book. Here you will find accompanying code, in-depth articles and worksheets, comparisons and reviews of RL technology, databases of current RL case studies, and much more. See "Guiding Principles and Style" on page xvi to find out why there is no code printed in this book.

The reason for creating a whole website, rather than just a code repository, was because I believe that RL is more than just code. It's a paradigm-changing way of thinking about how decisions can have long-term effects. It's a new set of technology and it needs a totally different architecture. For all of these reasons and more, this supplementary information does not fit in a repository. It doesn't suit being printed, because it might change rapidly or is just inefficient. So I created this ecosystem that I am sure you will find valuable. Make sure you check it out and if there's anything missing, let me know.

Conventions Used in This Book

The following typographical conventions are used in this book:

Italic
> Indicates new terms and is occasionally used for emphasis.

`Constant width`
> Used to refer to specific classes or RL environments.

 This element signifies a tip or suggestion.

 This element signifies a general note.

 This element indicates a warning or caution.

Acronyms

Reinforcement learning is full of acronyms, especially when talking about algorithm implementations. I have provided a full list of these and a description of key terms in the Glossary.

Mathematical Notation

In general, I tend toward using Thomas and Okal's Markov Decision Process Notation, Version 1. However, I have attempted to simplify it even further by removing formalities like the time demarcation and expanding the use of the apostrophe to mean the current and the next. For full mathematical rigor, please refer to the academic textbooks and papers.

In general, curly letters represent a set and lowercase letters denote an element of the set. An apostrophe denotes the next time step. Uppercase characters represent a function or a constant.

I forgo the formality of sampling a specific state from a random variable and instead use a specific instantiation of a variable, s for example, to help the readability of equations.

In the literature you will typically find an uppercase character representing a stochastic variable.

Some of the algorithms are heavily indexed, which means that you have to buffer data and access specific points within that buffer. When I derive these algorithms I have to resort to using a subscript to denote the index; a_t would mean the action at time or position t, for example.

If you are new to reading equations, go slowly. First look to understand what each symbol represents, then establish what the equation is trying to do. Like any skill, the more you do it, the easier it will become. The dot-equals sign, $\doteq$, can be read as "is defined as."

When reading the algorithms, read them procedurally. Where possible, I use text but on many occasions it is much more succinct to use the equation. The $\leftarrow$ symbol in the algorithms reads "update"; this is preferred because technically an equals sign means mathematical equality, like a == in your software. Most software languages abuse this notation and use an equals sign to mean both define and update.

I have chosen to present the algorithms in academic pseudocode, rather than in a software engineering style. I thought long and hard about this, but in the end there are three key reasons for this decision. First, all of the academic literature presents it in this way. I wanted this book to be a bridge between industry and academia and I think that having yet another representation will make this divide bigger. The second is that these algorithms are more succinct in academic form, because of the mathematics. If you had to convert the mathematics to software pseudocode, it would result in a sea of for loops and temporary variables. The final reason is that it would have been too easy to make a mistake. Even though I have simplified the mathematics, the pseudocode is representative of a real implementation. Converting the paper implementations into software pseudocode would have introduced too many errors.

Fair Use Policy

This book is here to help you get your job done. In general, if example code is offered with this book, you may use it in your programs and documentation. You do not need to contact us for permission unless you're reproducing a significant portion of the code. For example, writing a program that uses several chunks of code from this book does not require permission. Selling or distributing a CD-ROM of examples from O'Reilly books does require permission. Answering a question by citing this book and quoting example code does not require permission. Incorporating a significant amount of example code from this book into your product's documentation does require permission.

We appreciate, but do not require, attribution. An attribution usually includes the title, author, publisher, and ISBN. For example: "*Reinforcement Learning* by Phil Winder, Ph.D. (O'Reilly). Copyright 2021 Winder Research and Development Ltd., 978-1-098-11483-1."

If you feel your use of code examples falls outside fair use or the permission given above, feel free to contact us at *permissions@oreilly.com*.

O'Reilly Online Learning

 For more than 40 years, *O'Reilly Media* has provided technology and business training, knowledge, and insight to help companies succeed.

Our unique network of experts and innovators share their knowledge and expertise through books, articles, and our online learning platform. O'Reilly's online learning platform gives you on-demand access to live training courses, in-depth learning paths, interactive coding environments, and a vast collection of text and video from O'Reilly and 200+ other publishers. For more information, visit *http://oreilly.com*.

How to Contact Us

For any RL support or advice, please get in touch with Phil using the details in About the Author.

Please address comments and questions concerning this book to the publisher:

O'Reilly Media, Inc.
1005 Gravenstein Highway North
Sebastopol, CA 95472
800-998-9938 (in the United States or Canada)
707-829-0515 (international or local)
707-829-0104 (fax)

We have a web page for this book, where we list errata, examples, and any additional information. You can access this page at *https://oreil.ly/ReinforceLearn*.

To comment or ask technical questions about this book, send email to *bookquestions@oreilly.com*.

For more news and information about our books and courses, see our website at *http://www.oreilly.com*.

Find us on Facebook: *http://facebook.com/oreilly*

Follow us on Twitter: *http://twitter.com/oreillymedia*

Watch us on YouTube: *http://youtube.com/oreillymedia*

Acknowledgments

This section is dedicated to all the people who helped me write this book.

First, I would like to thank all of the people who helped proof, review, and provide advice for this book. Without you this book would have looked like it was written by an eight-year-old. Thank you to Eric Ma, Josh Starmer, Nick Winder, Ben Henson, David Foster, Catalin Jora, Matt Hobby, Kim Falk, Vladimir Blagojevic, and Matthew Pettis.

And thank you to the fantastic O'Reilly team for their encouragement, advice, reviews, and edits. I owe a lot of thanks to Corbin Collins, Gary O'Brien, Jon Hassel, and Nick Adams. Without you this wouldn't exist.

To my wonderful wife and children. Thank you Cora for your humor, Eva for your love, and Emma for your strength and support. You make me who I am.

And to my family, Dot and Richard, Carol and Paul, Nick and Ashley, Sarah, Richard, Oliver, and Charlotte, Steve and Aaron, Lucy, Jamie, Oliver, and Emily. Thank you for your support.

And finally, to all of our friends. Thank you for the good times!

References

[1] Thomas, Philip S., and Billy Okal. 2016. "A Notation for Markov Decision Processes" (*https://oreil.ly/VT7np*). ArXiv:1512.09075, September.

CHAPTER 1

Why Reinforcement Learning?

How do humans learn? This deceivingly simple question has baffled thinkers for millennia. The Greek philosopher Plato and his student Aristotle asked themselves: are truth and knowledge found within us (rationalism) or are they experienced (empiricism)? Even today, 2,500 years later, humans are still trying to answer this perpetual question.

If humans already knew everything, then they would not need to experience any more of life. Humans could spend the rest of their time on Earth improving lives by making good decisions and pondering big questions like "Where are my keys?" and "Did I lock the front door?" But how do humans gain that knowledge in the first place? You can teach knowledge. And higher levels of average education lead to a better society. But you cannot teach everything. Both in the classroom and in life, the student must *experience*.

Young children inspire this process. They need to experience a range of situations and outcomes. In the long term, they begin to seek rewarding experiences and avoid detrimental ones (you hope). They actively make decisions and assess the results. But a child's life is puzzling and the rewards are often misleading. The immediate reward of climbing into a cupboard and eating a cookie is great, but the punishment is greater.

Learning by *reinforcement* combines two tasks. The first is exploring new situations. The second is using that experience to make better decisions. Given time, this results in a plan to achieve a task. For example, a child learns to walk, after standing up, by leaning forward and falling into the arms of a loving parent. But this is only after many hours of hand holding, wobbles, and falls. Eventually, the baby's leg muscles operate in unison using a multistep strategy that tells them what to move when. You can't teach every plan that the child will ever need, so instead life provides a framework that allows them a way to learn.

This book shows how you can perform the reinforcement process inside a computer. But why do this? It enables a machine to learn, by itself. To paraphrase my wife's favorite TV show: you are providing the machine the capability to seek out new experiences, to boldly go where no machine has gone before.

This chapter presents an introduction to learning by reinforcement. (I defer a formal definition of reinforcement learning until Chapter 2.) First, I describe why engineers need this and why now. By the end of the chapter you will know which industries can use reinforcement learning and will develop your first mathematical model. You will also get an overview of the types of algorithms you will encounter later in the book.

  I use the word *engineer* throughout this book to talk abstractly about anyone who uses their skill to design a solution to solve a problem. So I mean software engineers, data engineers, data scientists, researchers, and so on.

Why Now?

Two reasons have precipitated the need and ability to perform reinforcement learning: access to large amounts of data and faster data processing speeds.

Up to the year 2000, human knowledge was stored on analog devices like books, newspapers, and magnetic tapes. If you compressed this knowledge, then in 1993 you would have needed 15.8 exabytes of space (one exabyte is one billion gigabytes). In 2018 that had increased to 33 zettabytes (one zettabyte is one thousand billion gigabytes).[1] Cloud vendors even have to resort to shipping container-sized hard disk drives to upload large amounts of data.[2]

You also need the necessary computational power to analyze all that data. To show this, consider the case of one of the earliest reinforcement learning implementations.

In 1947, Dietrich Prinz worked for Ferranti in Manchester, UK. There he helped to design and build the first production version of the Manchester computer called the Ferranti Mark 1.[3] He learned to program the Mark 1 under the tutelage of Alan Turing and Cicely Popplewell. Influenced by Turing's paper on the subject, in 1952 Prinz released a chess program that could solve a single set of problems called "mate-in-2." These are puzzles where you pick the two moves that cause a checkmate in chess. Prinz's algorithm exhaustively searched through all possible positions to generate a solution in 15—20 minutes, on average. This is an implementation of the Monte Carlo algorithm described in Chapter 2. Prinz came to see chess programming as "a clue to methods that could be used to deal with structural or logistical problems in other areas, through electronic computers." He was right.[4]

The confluence of the volume of data and the increasing computational performance of the hardware meant that in around 2010 it became both possible and necessary to teach machines to learn.

Machine Learning

 A full summary of machine learning is outside the scope of this book. But reinforcement learning depends upon it. Read as much as you can about machine learning, especially the books I recommend in "Further Reading" on page 20.

The ubiquity of data and the availability of cheap, high-performance computation has allowed researchers to revisit the algorithms of the 1950s. They chose the name *machine learning* (ML), which is a misnomer, because ML is simultaneously accepted as a discipline and a set of techniques. I consider ML a child of *data science*, which is an overarching scientific field that investigates the data generated by phenomena. I dislike the term *artificial intelligence* (AI) for a similar reason; it is hard enough to define what intelligence is, let alone specify how it is achieved.

ML starts with lots of information in the form of *observational* data. An observation represents a collection of attributes, at a single point, that describe an entity. For example, in an election poll one observation represents the prospective vote of a single person. For a recommendation task, an observation might be a click on a particular product. Engineers use ML algorithms to interpret and make decisions upon this information.

In *supervised* learning, *labels* represent the answer to the problem, for that particular observation. The algorithm then attempts to use the information to guess the correct result. *Unsupervised* learning works without labels and you make decisions based upon the characteristics of the data. I always recommend that my clients at Winder Research aim for supervised learning—by paying for or running experiments to find labels, for example—because if you don't have any ground truth, then you will find it hard to quantify performance.

The process of finding an algorithm to solve a problem is called *modeling*. Engineers design models to simplify and represent the underlying phenomena. They use a model to make educated guesses about new observations. For example, a model might tell you that a new customer has provided false information in their application, or it might convert your speech into text.

Given these descriptions, consider trying to teach your child how to ride a bike. What is the best way of doing this? According to the ML paradigm, you should provide lots of observations with labels. You might tell your child to watch videos of professional cyclists. Once they have seen enough videos, ignoring any protests of boredom, you might test their ability according to some arbitrary, technical success criteria. Would this work? No.

Despite ML being fundamental to many applications, some problems do not fit. A better solution, to continue the previous example, is to let your child try. Sometimes they will try and fail. Other times they will succeed. Each decision will alter their judgment. After enough tries and some guidance, they will learn strategies to maximize their own definition of success. This is the promise of learning by reinforcement, rather than by supervision.

Reinforcement Learning

Reinforcement learning (RL) tells you how to make the best decisions, sequentially, within a context, to maximize a real-life measure of success. The decision-making entity learns this through trial and error. It is not told which decisions to make, but instead it must learn by itself, by trying them. Figure 1-1 introduces the four components of RL, and Chapter 2 delves deeper.

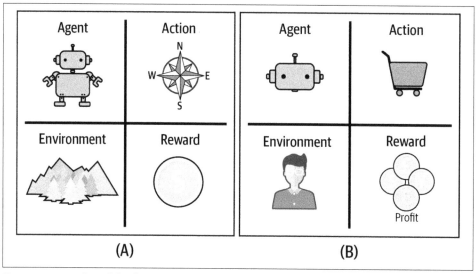

Figure 1-1. A plot of the four components required for RL: an agent, to present actions, to an environment, for the greatest reward. Example (A) shows a robot that intends to move through a maze to collect a coin. Example (B) shows an ecommerce application that automatically adds products to users' baskets, to maximize profit.

Each decision is an *action*. For example, when you ride a bike the actions are the steering direction, how much to pedal, and whether to brake. If you try to automatically add items to a shopping basket, then the actions are a decision to add certain products.

The context, although it could represent any real-life situation, is often constrained to make the problem solvable. RL practitioners create an interface to interact with the *environment*. This could be a simulation, real life, or a combination of both. The environment accepts actions and responds with the result and a new set of observations.

The *agent* is the entity that makes decisions. This could be your child, some software, or a robot, for example.

The *reward* encodes the challenge. This feedback mechanism tells the agent which actions led to success (or failure). The reward signal is typically numeric but only needs to reinforce behavior; genetic learning strategies delete underperforming agents, rather than providing no reward, for example.

Continuing the examples, you could reward a robot for reaching a goal or the agent for adding the right product to a basket. Simple, right? But what if the robot takes three days to solve a simple maze because it spends most of the time spinning in circles? Or what if the agent starts adding all products to the basket?

This process occurs in animals, too. They must maximize the chance of survival to pass on their genes. For example, like most herbivores, moose need to eat a lot to survive. But in 2011 a moose near Gothenburg, Sweden, was found stuck in a tree after eating fermented apples.[5] The moose reward system, which tells them to eat, has broken down because the goal is too generic. You can't eat anything and everything to maximize your chances of survival. It's more complicated than that.

These examples begin to highlight a major problem in RL, one that has existed since Ada Lovelace first wrote an algorithm to produce Bernoulli numbers. How do you tell a machine what you want it to do? RL agents suffer because they often optimize for the wrong thing. For now, I recommend you keep the reward as simple as you can. Problems often have a natural reward. Chapter 9 discusses this in more detail.

These four components represent a *Markov decision process* (MDP). You use MDPs to frame your problems, even nonengineering problems. Chapter 2 presents these ideas in more detail.

When Should You Use RL?

Some RL examples you find on the internet look forced. They take an ML example and attempt to apply RL despite the lack of a clear agent or action. Look at a few examples trying to incorporate RL into stock market prediction, for example. There is a possibility of using an automated agent to make trades, but in many examples this isn't the focus; the focus is still on the predictive model. This is not appropriate and is best left to ML.

RL works best when decisions are sequential and actions lead to exploration in the environment. Take robotics, a classic RL application. The goal of a robot is to learn how to perform unknown tasks. You shouldn't tell the robot how to succeed because this is either too difficult (how do you tell a robot to build a house) or you may be biased by your own experience (you are not a robot), so you don't know the best way to move as a robot. If instead you allow the robot to explore, it can iterate toward an optimal solution. This is a good fit for RL.

You should always choose the simplest solution that solves your immediate problem to a satisfactory level.

RL's primary advantage is that it optimizes for long-term, multistep rewards. A secondary benefit is that it is very easy to incorporate metrics used by the business. For example, advertising solutions are typically optimized to promote the best click-through rates for an individual advertisement. This is suboptimal, because viewers often see multiple advertisements and the goal is not a click, but something bigger like retention, a sign-up, or a purchase. The combination of advertisements shown, in what order, with what content, can all be optimized automatically by RL utilizing an easy-to-use goal that matches the business' needs.

You can forgo some of the four components presented in the previous section to make development easier. If you don't have a natural reward signal, like a robot reaching a goal, then it is possible to engineer an artificial reward. It is also common to create a simulation of an environment. You can quantize or truncate actions. But these are all compromises. A simulation can never replace real-life experience.

RL actively searches for the optimal model. You don't have to generate a random sample and fit offline. Rapid, online learning can work wonders when it is important to maximize performance as quickly as possible. For example, in profit-based A/B tests, like deciding what marketing copy to use, you don't want to waste time collecting a random sample if one underperforms. RL does this for free. You can learn more about how A/B testing relates to RL in Chapter 2.

In summary, RL is best suited to applications that need sequential, complex decisions and have a long-term goal (in the context of a single decision). ML might get you halfway there, but RL excels in environments with direct feedback. I have spoken to some practitioners that have used RL to replace teams of data scientists tweaking performance out of ML solutions.

RL Applications

Throughout this book I present a range of examples for two reasons. First, I want to illustrate the theoretical aspects, like how algorithms work. These examples are simple and abstract. Personally, I find that seeing examples helps me learn. I also recommend that you try to replicate the examples to help you learn. Second, I want to show how to use RL in industry.

The media has tended to focus on examples where agents defeat humans at games. They love a good story about humans becoming obsolete. And academics continue to find games useful because of the complex simulated environments. But I have decided not to talk about DeepMind's AlphaGo Zero, a version of the agent that defeated the Go world champion, nor OpenAI Five, which beat the Dota 2 world champions, and instead focus on applications and examples across a broad range of industries. I am not saying that gaming examples are a waste of time. Gaming companies can use RL for many practical purposes, like helping them test or optimizing in-game "AIs" to maximize revenue. I am saying that I want to help you look past the hype and show you all the different places where RL is applicable. To show you what is possible, I present a broad selection of experiments that I personally find interesting:

- The field of robotics has many applications, including improving the movement and manufacturing, playing ball-in-a-cup, and flipping pancakes.[6] Autonomous vehicles are also an active topic of research.[7]

- You can use RL to improve cloud computing. One paper optimizes applications for latency,[8] another power efficiency/usage.[9] Datacenter cooling, CPU cooling, and network routing are all RL applications in use today.[10,11,12]

- The financial industry uses RL to make trades and to perform portfolio allocation.[13,14] And there is significant interest in optimizing pricing in real time.[15]

- The amount of energy used by buildings (through heating, water, light, and so on) can be significantly reduced with RL.[16] And electric grids can leverage RL to deal with situations where demand is complex; homes are both producers and consumers.[17]

- RL is improving traffic light control and active lane management.[18,19] Smart cities also benefit.[20]

- Recent papers suggest many applications of RL in healthcare, especially in the areas of dosing and treatment schedules.[21,22] RL can be used to design better prosthetics and prosthetic controllers.[23]

- The education system and e-learning can benefit from highly individualized RL-driven curriculums.[24]

No business sector is left untouched: gaming, technology, transport, finance, science and nature, industry, manufacturing, and civil services all have cited RL applications.

I don't want to lose you in an infinite list, so instead I refer you to the accompanying website (*https://rl-book.com/applications/?utm_source=oreilly&utm_medium=book&utm_campaign=rl*) where I have a comprehensive catalog of RL applications.

Any technology is hazardous in the wrong hands. And like the populist arguments against AI, you could interpret RL as being dangerous. I ask that as an engineer, as a human, consider what you are building. How will it affect other people? What are the risks? Does it conflict with your morals? Always justify your work to yourself. If you can't do that, then you probably shouldn't be doing it. The following are three more documented nefarious applications. Each one has a different ethical boundary. Where is your boundary? Which applications are acceptable to you?

- Pwnagotchi is a device powered by RL that actively scans, sniffs, and hacks WPA/WPA2 WiFi networks by decrypting handshakes.[25]

- Researchers showed that you can train agents to evade static malware models in virus scanners.[26]

- The US Army is developing warfare simulations to demonstrate how autonomous robots can help in the battlefield.[27]

I discuss safety and ethics in more depth in Chapter 10.

Taxonomy of RL Approaches

Several themes have evolved throughout the development of RL. You can use these themes to group algorithms together. This book details many of these algorithms, but it helps to provide an overview now.

Model-Free or Model-Based

The first major decision that you have to make is whether you have an accurate model of the environment. *Model-based* algorithms use definitive knowledge of the environment they are operating in to improve learning. For example, board games often limit the moves that you can make, and you can use this knowledge to (a) constrain the algorithm so that it does not provide invalid actions and (b) improve performance by projecting forward in time (for example, if I move here and if the opponent moves there, I can win). Human-beating algorithms for games like Go and poker can take advantage of the game's fixed rules. You and your opponent can make a limited set of moves. This limits the number of strategies the algorithms have to search through. Like expert systems, model-based solutions learn efficiently because they don't waste time searching improper paths.[28, 29]

Model-free algorithms can, in theory, apply to any problem. They learn strategies through interaction, absorbing any environmental rules in the process.

This is not the end of the story, however. Some algorithms can learn models of the environment at the same time as learning optimal strategies. Several new algorithms can also leverage the potential, but unknown actions of other agents (or other players). In other words, these agents can learn to counteract another agent's strategies.

Algorithms such as these tend to blur the distinction between model-based and model-free, because ultimately you need a model of the environment somewhere. The difference is whether you can statically define it, whether you can learn it, or whether you can assume the model from the strategy.

I dedicate this book to model-free algorithms because you can apply them to any industrial problem. But if you have a situation where your environment has strict, static rules, consider developing a bespoke model-based RL algorithm that is able to take advantage.

How Agents Use and Update Their Strategy

The goal of any agent is to learn a strategy that maximizes a reward. I use the word *strategy*, because the word is easier to understand, but the correct term is *policy*. Chapter 2 introduces policies in more detail.

Precisely how and when an algorithm updates the strategy is the defining factor between the majority of model-free RL algorithms. There are two key forms of strategy that dominate the performance and functionality of the agent, but they are very easy to confuse.

The first is the difference between online and offline updates to the strategy. Online agents improve their strategies using only the data they have just observed and then immediately throw it away. They don't store or reuse old data. All RL agents need to update their strategy when they encounter a new experience to some extent, but most state-of-the-art algorithms agree that retaining and reusing past experience is useful.

Offline agents are able to learn from offline datasets or old logs. This can be a major benefit because sometimes it is difficult or expensive to interact with the real world. However, RL tends to be most useful when agents learn online, so most algorithms aim for a mix of online and offline learning.

The second, sometimes subtle, difference depends on how agents select the action defined by its strategy. *On-policy* agents learn to predict the reward of being in particular states after choosing actions according to the current strategy. *Off-policy* agents learn to predict the reward after choosing *any* action.

I appreciate this subtlety is difficult to understand, so let me present a quick example. Imagine you are a baby and about ready to try new food. Evolution was kind enough to provide sweet sensors on your tongue that make you feel happy, so you love your mother's milk. An on-policy baby would attempt to learn a new policy using the current policy as a starting point. They would likely tend toward other sweet things that taste like milk. On-policy baby would have a "sweet tooth." Off-policy baby, however, still uses the current policy as a starting point, but is allowed to explore other, possibly random choices, while still being given milk. Off-policy baby would still like sweet milk, but might also find that they like other pleasing tastes.

The distinction may seem small at this point, but this early discovery enabled the amazing RL-driven feats you see today. Most state-of-the-art algorithms are off-policy, to encourage or improve exploration. They allow for the use of a planning mechanism to direct the agent and tend to work better on tasks with delayed rewards. However, on-policy policy algorithms tend to learn quicker, because they can instantly exploit new strategies. Modern algorithms try to form a balance between these qualities for the best of both worlds.

Discrete or Continuous Actions

Actions within an environment can take many forms: you could vary the amount of torque to apply to a motor controller, decide whether to add a banana to a shopping basket, or buy millions of dollars of stock on a trade.

Some actions are binary: a stop/go road sign has precisely two classes. Other times you might have categories that you can encode into binary actions. For example, you could quantize the throttle control of a vehicle into three binary actions: none, half-power, and full power.

But often actions require more finesse. When you drive a car you rotate the steering wheel over an infinite number of angles. If you made it discrete, pain would ensue. How would you like it if your bus driver turned the steering wheel in 90-degree increments?

The weight or length of time of an action might also be important. In *Super Mario Bros.* the longer you hold the jump button the higher Mario jumps. You could make time part of the problem and have a continuous action that represents the amount of time to hold a button, for example. Or you could make it discrete and ensure you repeatedly poll the agent to see if it should continue to perform the action. If you can argue that the length of time of the action is decoupled from performing the action, they could be separate variables.

RL algorithms should handle both binary and continuously variable actions. But many algorithms are limited to one.

Optimization Methods

Somewhere around 14 to 16 years old, you probably learned how to solve linear equations by hand when given data and lots of paper. But the examples you worked with were probably very simple, using a single unknown variable. In the real world you will often work with hundreds, thousands, or even millions of independent variables. At this point it becomes infeasible to use the same methods you learned at school because of the computational complexity.

In general, you build models (which may or may not contain linear equations) and train them using an optimization method. RL has the same problem. You want to build an agent that is able to produce a solution given a goal. Precisely how it does this creates another fundamental theme in RL.

One way is to try as many actions as possible and record the results. In the future you can guide the agent by following the strategy that led to the best result. These are called *value-based* algorithms, and I introduce you to them shortly.

Another way is to maintain a model and tweak the parameters of the model to tend toward the actions that produced the best result. These are called *policy-based* algorithms. You can read more about them in Chapter 5.

To help you understand this, imagine a two-dimensional grid with a cliff toward the south. Your task is to design a robot that will repeatedly test each square and learn that there is a cost associated with falling off the cliff. If you used a value-based algorithm, and if you converted the strategy into words, it would say "do not step off a cliff." A policy-based algorithm would say "move away from the cliff." A subtle but important difference.

Value- and policy-based algorithms are currently the most studied and therefore the most popular. But *imitation-based* algorithms, where you optimize the agent to mimic the actions of an expert, can work well when you are trying to incorporate human guidance. Any other algorithms that don't fit into any of these classes may spawn new methodologies in the future.

Policy Evaluation and Improvement

Another way of interpreting how an algorithm improves its strategy is to view it in terms of *policy evaluation* and *policy improvement*, shown in Figure 1-2.

First, an agent follows a strategy (the policy) to make decisions, which generates new data that describes the state of the environment.

From this new data, the agent attempts to predict the reward from the current state of the environment; it evaluates the current policy.

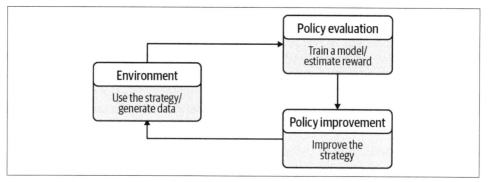

Figure 1-2. An interpretation of how algorithms update their strategy.

Next, the agent uses this prediction to decide what to do next. In general it tries to change the strategy to improve the policy. It might suggest to move to a state of higher predicted reward, or it might choose to explore more. Either way, the action is presented back to the environment and the merry-go-round starts again.

The vast majority of algorithms follow this pattern. It is such a fundamental structure that if I ever get the opportunity to rewrite this book, I would consider presenting the content in this way.

Fundamental Concepts in Reinforcement Learning

The idea of learning by reinforcement through trial and error, the fundamental basis for all RL algorithms, originated in early work on the psychology of animal learning. The celebrated Russian physiologist Ivan Pavlov first reported in 1927 that you can trigger an animal's digestive system using stimuli that are irrelevant to the task of eating. In one famous experiment he measured the amount of saliva produced by dogs when presented with food. At the same time, he introduced a sound. After several repetitions, the dog salivated in response to the sound alone.[30]

Sound is not a natural precursor to food, nor does it aid eating. The connection between innate reflexes, such as eye blinking or saliva generation, and new stimuli is now called classical, or Pavlovian, conditioning.

The First RL Algorithm

In 1972 Robert Rescorla and Allan Wagner found another interesting phenomenon that Pavlovian conditioning couldn't explain. They first blew a puff of air into a rabbit's eye, which caused it to blink. They then trained the rabbit to associate an external stimulus, a sound, with the puff of air. The rabbit blinked when it heard the sound, even if there was no puff of air. They then retrained the rabbit to blink when exposed to both a sound and a light. Again, when the rabbit heard the sound and saw the light with no puff of air, it blinked. But next, when the researchers only flashed the light, the rabbit did not blink.[31]

The rabbit had developed a hierarchy of expectations; sound and light equals blink. When the rabbit did not observe the base expectation (the sound), this *blocked* all subsequent conditioning. You may have experienced this sensation yourself. Occasionally you learn something so incredible, so fundamental, you might feel that any derivative beliefs are also invalid. Your lower-level conditioning has been violated and your higher-order expectations have been blocked. The result of this work was the Rescorla–Wagner model. Their research was never presented this way, but this describes a method called *value estimation*.

Value estimation

Imagine yourself trying to simulate the Rescorla–Wagner rabbit trial. The goal is to predict when the rabbit blinks. You can create a model of that experiment by describing the inputs and the expected output. The inputs represent the actions under your control and the output is a prediction of whether the rabbit blinks.

You can represent the inputs as a vector $s = (s_0, s_1, ..., s_{n-1})$ where $s_i = 1$ if the *i*th stimulus is present in a trial and zero otherwise. These are binary actions.

For example, imagine that the feature s_0 represents the sound and s_1 represents the light. Then the vector $s = [0, 1]$ represents the situation where the sound is not present and the light is.

You can write the estimated output as V, which represents the prediction of whether the rabbit blinks or not. The states are then mapped to the correct prediction using a function, $V(s)$.

 I have made an active decision to simplify the mathematics as much as possible, to improve readability and understanding. This means that it loses mathematical formality, like denoting an estimate with a *hat*, to improve readability. See the academic papers for full mathematical rigor.

Now comes the hard part: defining the mapping function. One common solution is to multiply the inputs by *parameters* under your control. You can alter these parameters to produce an output that depends on the inputs. These parameters are called *weights* and the model you have just built is *linear*.

The weights are defined by another vector, *w*, which is the same shape as the features. For example, the data may show that the light did not cause the rabbit to blink; it blinked only when it heard the sound. This results in a model with a weight of value 1 for the sound feature and a weight of value 0 for the light.

Formally, the function is a sum of the inputs multiplied by the weights. This operation is called a *dot product*. The result, which is shown in Equation 1-1, is a prediction of whether the rabbit blinks.

Equation 1-1. Value estimate

$$V(s, w) \doteq w_0 s_0 + w_1 s_1 + \dots + w_n s_n$$
$$= w \cdot s = w^\mathsf{T} s$$

But, in general, how do you decide on the values for the weights?

Prediction error

You can use an optimization method to find the optimal parameters. The most common method is to quantify how wrong your estimate is compared to the ground truth (the correct answer). Then you can try lots of different weights to minimize the error.

The error in your prediction, δ, is the difference between the actual outcome of the experiment, E, and the prediction (the value estimate). The prediction is based upon the current state of the environment (an observation of the rabbit), s, and the current weights. All variables change over time and are often denoted with the subscript t, but I ignore that to reduce the amount of notation. You can see this defined in Equation 1-2.

Equation 1-2. Prediction error

$$\delta \doteq E - V(s, w)$$

One way to think of Equation 1-2 is that δ is a form of surprise. If you make a prediction that the rabbit will definitely blink and it does not, then the difference between what you predicted and what happened will be large; you'd be surprised by the result.

Given a quantitative definition of surprise, how should the weights be altered? One way is to nudge the weights in proportion to the prediction error. For example, consider the situation where the expectation was that the sound (index zero) and the light (index one) had equal importance. The set of weights is $w = [1, 1]$.

This time the experiment is to shine only the light, not sound. So the observed state of the experiment is $x(s) = [0, 1]$. To make a prediction, $V(s, w)$, calculate the result of performing a dot product on the previous vectors. The result is 1 (blink).

When you ran your simulation, the rabbit did not blink. The value was actually 0. The value of Equation 1-2, δ, is equal to -1.

Knowledge of the previous state and the prediction error helps alter the weights. Multiplying these together, the result is $\delta x(s) = [0, -1]$. Adding this to the current weights yields $w = [1, 0]$.

Note how the new weights would have correctly predicted the actual outcome, 0 (not blink) ($w^\mathsf{T} x(s) = [1, 0]^\mathsf{T}[0, 1] = 0$).

Weight update rule

If you have any experience with ML, you know that you should not try to jump straight to the correct, *optimal* result. One reason is that the experimental outcome might be noisy. Always move toward the correct result gradually and repeat the experiment multiple times. Then, due to the *law of large numbers*, you converge toward the best average answer, which is also the optimal one. One caveat is that this is only true if the underlying mathematics proves that convergence is inevitable; in many algorithms, like those with nonlinear approximators, it is not guaranteed.

This is formalized as an *update rule* for the weights. In Equation 1-3, you can control the speed at which the weights update using the hyperparameter α, which must be between zero and one. Equation 1-3 *updates* the weights inline, which means that the weights in the next time step derive from the weights in the current time step. Again, I ignore the subscripts to simplify the notation.

> *Equation 1-3. Weight update rule*
>
> $w \leftarrow w - \alpha \delta x(s)$

Is RL the Same as ML?

The mathematics presented in Equation 1-1 and Equation 1-3 provide one psychological model of how animals learn. You could easily apply the same approach to software-controlled agents. But the real reason for going into such depth was to provide a mathematical warm-up exercise for the rest of the book. Here I used mathematical symbols that are used in later chapters (the original paper used different symbols and terminology from psychology).

If you ignore the mathematics for a moment, the idea of updating the weights to produce a better fit might sound familiar. You are right; this is regression from ML. The objective is to predict a numerical outcome (the total reward) from a given set of inputs (the observations). Practitioners call this the the *prediction* problem. In order to make good decisions, you need to be able to predict which actions are optimal.

The main thing that differentiates ML from RL is that you are giving agents the freedom of choice. This is the *control* part of the problem and at first glance looks like a simple addition on top of the ML *prediction* problem. But don't underestimate this challenge. You might think that the best policy is to pick the action with the highest prediction. No, because there may be other states that are even more rewarding.

Control endows autonomy; super-machines can learn from their own mistakes. This skill opens a range of new opportunities. Many challenges are so complicated—teaching a robot to take pictures of a specific object, for example—that engineers have to resort to constraints, rules, and splitting the challenge into micro-problems. Similarly, I work with clients who have to retrain their models on a daily or hourly basis to incorporate new data. No more. Relinquish control and use RL.

RL algorithms attempt to balance these two concerns, exploration and exploitation, in different ways. One common difference is how algorithms alter the rate at which they explore. Some explore at a fixed rate, others set a rate that is proportional to the prediction of the value. Some even attempt the probability of attaining the maximum reward for a given state. This is discussed throughout the book.

Reward and Feedback

ML researchers have taken inspiration from neuroscience. The most commonly cited example of this is the development of the *artificial neuron*, the basis of *neural networks* and *deep learning*, which is a model of the constituent unit in your brain, much like how the atomic model summarizes an elemental unit of matter. RL, in particular, has been influenced by how the brain communicates.

A neurotransmitter, dopamine, is produced by special cells in the brain. It is involved in major brain processes, including motivation and learning and, therefore, decision making. It can also have negative aspects such as addiction and a range of medical disorders. Although there is still much unknown about dopamine, it is known to be fundamental in processing rewards.

Traditional theories about the presence of dopamine relied upon the reinforcing and pleasurable effect of the chemical. But studies in the early 1990s showed a number of startling facts. Researchers were able to quantitatively measure the activity of dopamine in monkeys. Their results showed that there was a background level of constant dopamine release. They then trained each monkey in a traditional conditioning task, like the one you saw in "Value estimation" on page 13, where the monkeys expected food a few minutes after they were shown a light. When the training started, there was a significant increase over background dopamine levels when the reward was given. Over time, the researchers observed that the dopamine release in the monkeys shifted toward the onset of the light. Eventually, each monkey produced a dopamine spike whenever they saw a light.[32] If you excuse the leap to human experiences, I can attest that my children are more excited about the prospect of getting ice cream than actually eating the ice cream.

An even more fascinating follow-up study used the same conditioning training and observed the same dopamine spike when a monkey predicted the reward due to the conditioned stimulus. However, when the researchers showed the stimulus but did not give the monkey a reward at the expected time, there was a significant decrease in background dopamine levels. There was a negative dopamine effect (if compared to the baseline) when the monkey did not receive a reward.[33]

Like in "Prediction error" on page 14, these experiences can be well modeled by a corrective process. The dopamine neurons are not signaling a reward in itself. The dopamine is the signal representing the reward prediction errors. In other words, dopamine is the brain's δ.

Delayed rewards

A reward simulates the idea of motivation in agents. What motivates you to get up in the morning? Are you instantly rewarded? Probably not. This is why delayed gratification is such an important, and difficult, life skill to master. The reward for getting out of bed in the morning, eating a healthy breakfast, working hard, and being nice to people is different for all of us.

The delayed reward problem is also difficult to solve in RL. Often an agent needs to wait a long time to observe the reward. Algorithmic tricks can help here, but fundamentally, altering the reward signal so it provides more frequent updates helps guide the agent toward the solution. Altering the reward this way is called *reward shaping*, but I like to think of it as *reward engineering*, akin to feature engineering in ML.

Related to this problem is the attribution of a reward. For example, which decisions caused you to end up in the situation you are in now? How can you know? An early decision may have made the difference between success and failure. But given all the possible states and actions in a complex system, solving this problem is difficult. In general it is only possible to say that the decisions are optimal on average, given a set of assumptions and constraints.

Hindsight

The idiom *trust your gut* means that you should trust your instinctive reaction when observing a new situation. These heuristic shortcuts have been learned through years of experience and generally lead to good results. Critical thinking, the process where you logically and methodically work through a problem, takes much more energy and concentration.

These two processes in the brain, often called the system 1 and 2 models, are an energy-saving mechanism. Why waste precious mental resources dealing with the tasks that you perform on a daily basis? You would find it difficult to have to consciously think about how to walk. But Alzheimer's sufferers have to deal with this horrendously debilitating situation every day.[34]

Researchers propose that neurological differences within the brain account for these systems.[35] The job of the "instinctive" part of the brain is to quickly decide upon actions. The task of the other is to audit those actions and take corrective measures if necessary.

This structure led to the development of the *actor-critic* family of algorithms. The *actor* has the responsibility of making important decisions to maximize reward. The *critic* is there for future planning and to correct the actor when it gets the answer wrong. This discovery was vital for many advanced RL algorithms.

Reinforcement Learning as a Discipline

RL developed as two independent disciplines up until around the 1980s. Psychology studied animal behavior. Mechanical and electrical engineers developed the theory to describe the optimal control of systems.

The term *optimal control* originated in the 1950s to describe how to tune a system to maintain a goal. This culminated in 1957 when Richard Bellman developed the *Markov decision process* (MDP), a set of requirements for a mathematically tractable environment, and *dynamic programming*, a method of solving MDPs.[36]

According to one source, studies in animal behavior go back as far as the 19th century where experiments involving "groping and experimenting" were observed.[37] Edward Thorndike locked cats in "puzzle boxes" and timed how long it took the cats to escape.[38] He found that the time to escape decreased with repeated experiences, from 5 minutes down to 6 seconds. The result of this work was the "law of effect," which is more generally known as learning by trial and error.

The term *reinforcement* first appeared in the translations from Pavlov's manuscripts on conditioned reflexes in 1927. But RL was popularized by the grandfather of computing, Alan Turing, when he penned his earliest thoughts on artificial intelligence in 1948. In the following quote he is talking about how to "organize" a physical collection of electronic circuits he called "machines" into doing something practical:

> This may be done simply by allowing the machine to wander at random through a sequence of situations, and applying pain stimuli when the wrong choice is made, pleasure stimuli when the right one is made. It is best also to apply pain stimuli when irrelevant choices are made. This is to prevent getting isolated in a ring of irrelevant situations. The machine is now "ready for use".[39]
>
> —Alan Turing (1948)

I find it remarkable how much of Turing's work is still relevant today. In his time researchers were building robotic machines to achieve mundane tasks. One particularly ingenious researcher called William Grey Walter built a "mechanical tortoise" in 1951. In 1953 he unveiled a "tortoise" called CORA (Conditioned Reflex Analogue) that was capable of "learning" from its environment. The robot contained circuits that could simulate Pavlovian conditioning experiments. Even then, the public was fascinated with such machines that could "learn":

> In England a police whistle has two notes which sound together and make a particularly disagreeable sound. I tried to teach [CORA], therefore, that one note meant obstacle, and that the other note meant food. I tried to make this differential reflex by having two tuned circuits, one of which was associated with the appetitive response and the other with the avoidance response. It was arranged that one side of the whistle was blown before the machine touched an object so that it learned to avoid that, while the other side of the whistle was blown before it was supposed to see the light. The effect of giving both notes was almost always disastrous; it went right off into the darkness on the right-hand side of the room and hovered round there for five minutes in a sort of sulk. It became irresponsive to stimulation and ran round in circles.[40]
>
> —William Grey Walter (1956)

Towards the end of the 1950s researchers' interests were shifting away from pure trial and error learning and toward supervised learning. In fact, in the early days people used to use these two terms interchangeably. The early neural network pioneers including Frank Rosenblatt, Bernard Widrow, and Ted Hoff used the terms *reward* and *punishment* in their papers. This caused confusion because supervised, unsupervised, and RL were all used to denote the same idea.

At the same time the overselling of AI in the 1950s and 1960s caused widespread dissatisfaction at the slow progress. In 1973, the *Lighthill report* on the state of AI research in the UK criticized the utter failure to achieve its "grandiose objectives."[41] Based upon this report, most of the public research funding in the UK was cut and the rest of the world followed. The 1970s became known as the "AI winter" and progress stalled.

The resurgence of RL in the 1980s is acknowledged to be due to Harry Klopf declaring throughout the 1970s that the knowledge and use of key learning behaviors was being lost. He reiterated that control over the environment, to achieve some desired result, was the key to intelligent systems. Richard Sutton and Andrew Barto worked in the 1980s and 1990s to advance Klopf's ideas to unite the fields of psychology and control theory (see "Fundamental Concepts in Reinforcement Learning" on page 12) through *temporal-difference* (TD) learning. In 1989 Chris Watkins integrated all previous threads of RL research and created *Q-learning*.

I end my very brief look at the history of RL here because the results of the next 30 years of research is the content of this book. You can learn more about the history of RL from the references in "Further Reading" on page 20.

Summary

The market research firm Gartner suggests that in the US, AI augmentation is worth trillions of dollars per year to businesses.[42] RL has a big part to play in this market, because many of today's business problems are strategic. From the shop floor to the C-level, businesses are full of unoptimized multistep decisions like adding items to shopping baskets or defining a go-to-market strategy. Alone, ML is suboptimal, because it has a myopic view of the problem. But the explosion of data, computational power, and improved simulations all enable software-driven, ML-powered, RL agents that can learn optimal strategies that outperform humans.

Biological processes continue to inspire RL implementations. Early psychological experiments highlighted the importance of exploration and reward. Researchers have proposed different ways of emulating learning by reinforcement, which has led to several common themes. As an engineer, you must decide which of these themes suit your problem; for example, how you optimize your RL algorithm, what form the actions take, whether the agent requires a formal planning mechanism, and whether the policy should be updated online. You will gain more experience throughout this book, and in the final chapters I will show you how to apply them. With the careful definition of actions and rewards, you can design agents to operate within environments to solve a range of industrial tasks. But first you need to learn about the algorithms that allow the agents to learn optimal policies. The main purpose of this book, then, is to teach you how they work and how to apply them.

Further Reading

- Introduction to RL:
    - There are many resources, but Sergey Levine's (*https://oreil.ly/wgxnk*) is one of the best.
- History of RL:
    - Sutton, Richard S., and Andrew G. Barto. 2018. *Reinforcement Learning: An Introduction*. MIT Press.
    - A historical survey of RL from 1996, but still relevant today.[43]

References

[1] Reinsel, David, John Gantz, and John Rydning. 2018. "The Digitization of the World from Edge to Core" (*https://oreil.ly/96vhZ*). IDC.

[2] AWS Snowmobile (*https://oreil.ly/O5-K9*) is a service that allows you to use a shipping container to snail-mail your data to its datacenters.

[3] "Papers of Dr Dietrich G. Prinz-Archives Hub" (*https://oreil.ly/XCG9g*). n.d. Accessed 2 July 2019.

[4] Copeland, B. Jack. 2004. *The Essential Turing*. Clarendon Press.

[5] BBC News. "Drunk Swedish Elk Found in Apple Tree Near Gothenburg" (*https://oreil.ly/zr3Da*). 8 September 2011.

[6] Kormushev, Petar, et al. 2013. "Reinforcement Learning in Robotics: Applications and Real-World Challenges" (*https://oreil.ly/juf15*). *Robotics* 2(3): 122–48.

[7] Huang, Wenhui, Francesco Braghin, and Zhuo Wang. 2020. "Learning to Drive via Apprenticeship Learning and Deep Reinforcement Learning" (*https://oreil.ly/pqtHi*). ArXiv:2001.03864, January.

[8] Dutreilh, Xavier, et al. 2011. "Using Reinforcement Learning for Autonomic Resource Allocation in Clouds: Towards a Fully Automated Workflow." ICAS 2011, The Seventh International Conference on Autonomic and Autonomous Systems, 67–74.

[9] Liu, Ning, et al. 2017. "A Hierarchical Framework of Cloud Resource Allocation and Power Management Using Deep Reinforcement Learning" (*https://oreil.ly/N2wL7*). ArXiv:1703.04221, August.

[10] "DeepMind AI Reduces Google Data Centre Cooling Bill by 40%" (*https://oreil.ly/rjAae*). n.d. DeepMind. Accessed 3 July 2019.

[11] Das, Anup, et al. 2014. "Reinforcement Learning-Based Inter- and Intra-Application Thermal Optimization for Lifetime Improvement of Multicore Systems" (*https://doi.org/10.1145*). In *Proceedings of the 51st Annual Design Automation Conference*, 170:1–170:6. DAC '14. New York, NY, USA: ACM.

[12] Littman, M., and J. Boyan. 2013. "A Distributed Reinforcement Learning Scheme for Network Routing" (*https://oreil.ly/543Qz*). *Proceedings of the International Workshop on Applications of Neural Networks to Telecommunications*. 17 June.

[13] Wang, Haoran. 2019. "Large Scale Continuous-Time Mean-Variance Portfolio Allocation via Reinforcement Learning" (*https://oreil.ly/5J5qV*). ArXiv:1907.11718, August.

[14] Wang, Jingyuan, Yang Zhang, Ke Tang, Junjie Wu, and Zhang Xiong. 2019. "AlphaStock: A Buying-Winners-and-Selling-Losers Investment Strategy Using Interpretable Deep Reinforcement Attention Networks" (*https://oreil.ly/c0HA2*). *Proceedings of the 25th ACM SIGKDD International Conference on Knowledge Discovery & Data Mining—KDD '19*, 1900–1908.

[15] Maestre, Roberto, et al. 2019. "Reinforcement Learning for Fair Dynamic Pricing." In *Intelligent Systems and Applications*, edited by Kohei Arai, Supriya Kapoor,

and Rahul Bhatia, 120–35. *Advances in Intelligent Systems and Computing.* Springer International Publishing.

[16] Mason, Karl, and Santiago Grijalva. 2019. "A Review of Reinforcement Learning for Autonomous Building Energy Management" (*https://oreil.ly/lSfBf*). ArXiv: 1903.05196, March.

[17] Rolnick, David, et al. 2019. "Tackling Climate Change with Machine Learning" (*https://oreil.ly/eUDYX*). ArXiv:1906.05433, June.

[18] LA, P., and S. Bhatnagar. 2011. "Reinforcement Learning With Function Approximation for Traffic Signal Control" (*https://oreil.ly/1tBej*). *IEEE Transactions on Intelligent Transportation Systems* 12(2): 412–21.

[19] Rezaee, K., B. Abdulhai, and H. Abdelgawad. 2012. "Application of Reinforcement Learning with Continuous State Space to Ramp Metering in Real-World Conditions" (*https://oreil.ly/G60Wu*). In *2012 15th International IEEE Conference on Intelligent Transportation Systems*, 1590–95.

[20] Mohammadi, M., A. Al-Fuqaha, M. Guizani, and J. Oh. 2018. "Semisupervised Deep Reinforcement Learning in Support of IoT and Smart City Services" (*https://oreil.ly/orzkT*). *IEEE Internet of Things Journal* 5(2): 624–35.

[21] Shah, Pratik. n.d. "Reinforcement Learning with Action-Derived Rewards for Chemotherapy and Clinical Trial Dosing Regimen Selection" (*https://oreil.ly/p3sBr*). MIT Media Lab. Accessed 4 July 2019.

[22] Liu, Ying, et al. 2017. "Deep Reinforcement Learning for Dynamic Treatment Regimes on Medical Registry Data" (*https://oreil.ly/BftR5*). *Healthcare Informatics: The Business Magazine for Information and Communication Systems* (August): 380–85.

[23] Mohammedalamen, Montaser, et al. 2019. "Transfer Learning for Prosthetics Using Imitation Learning" (*https://oreil.ly/hTpsA*). ArXiv:1901.04772, January.

[24] Chi, Min, et al. 2011. "Empirically Evaluating the Application of Reinforcement Learning to the Induction of Effective and Adaptive Pedagogical Strategies" (*https://oreil.ly/XyKdy*). *User Modeling and User-Adapted Interaction* 21(1): 137–80.

[25] Pwnagotchi. "Pwnagotchi: Deep Reinforcement Learning for Wifi Pwning!" (*https://oreil.ly/olVVt*).

[26] Anderson, Hyrum S., et al. 2018. "Learning to Evade Static PE Machine Learning Malware Models via Reinforcement Learning" (*https://oreil.ly/X2n4W*). ArXiv: 1801.08917, January.

[27] Sydney J. Freedberg, Jr. "AI & Robots Crush Foes In Army Wargame" (*https://oreil.ly/4UA9Z*). Breaking Defense. December 2019.

[28] Silver, David, et al. 2017. "Mastering the Game of Go without Human Knowledge" (*https://oreil.ly/LJROD*). *Nature* 550(7676): 354–59.

[29] Zha, Daochen, Kwei-Herng Lai, Yuanpu Cao, Songyi Huang, Ruzhe Wei, Junyu Guo, and Xia Hu. 2019. "RLCard: A Toolkit for Reinforcement Learning in Card Games" (*https://oreil.ly/YbLGv*). ArXiv:1910.04376, October.

[30] Pavlov, I. P. 1927. *Conditioned Reflexes: An Investigation of the Physiological Activity of the Cerebral Cortex*. Oxford, England: Oxford Univ. Press.

[31] Rescorla, R.A and Wagner, A.R. 1972. "A Theory of Pavlovian Conditioning: Variations in the Effectiveness of Reinforcement and Nonreinforcement." In *Classical Conditioning II: Current Research and Theory*, 64–99. New York, NY: Appleton-Century-Crofts.

[32] Schultz, Wolfram, Ranulfo Romo, Tomas Ljungberg, Jacques Mirenowicz, Jeffrey R. Hollerman, and Anthony Dickinson. 1995. "Reward-Related Signals Carried by Dopamine Neurons." In *Models of Information Processing in the Basal Ganglia*, 233–48. Computational Neuroscience. Cambridge, MA: The MIT Press.

[33] Schultz, Wolfram, Peter Dayan, and P. Read Montague. 1997. "A Neural Substrate of Prediction and Reward" (*https://oreil.ly/6KztR*). *Science* 275(5306): 1593–99.

[34] Kahneman, Daniel. 2012. *Thinking, Fast and Slow*. Penguin UK.

[35] Takahashi, Yuji, Geoffrey Schoenbaum, and Yael Niv. 2008. "Silencing the Critics: Understanding the Effects of Cocaine Sensitization on Dorsolateral and Ventral Striatum in the Context of an Actor/Critic Model" (*https://oreil.ly/fXxaf*). *Frontiers in Neuroscience* 2.

[36] Bellman, Richard. 1957. "A Markovian Decision Process." *Journal of Mathematics and Mechanics* 6(5): 679–84.

[37] Newman, Edwin B. 1954. "Experimental Psychology" (*https://oreil.ly/qC3Ne*). *Psychological Bulletin* 51(6): 591–93.

[38] Thorndike, Edward L. 1898. "Animal Intelligence: An Experimental Study of the Associative Processes in Animals" (*https://oreil.ly/VLNEN*). *The Psychological Review: Monograph Supplements* 2(4): i–109.

[39] Turing, A. M. 1948. "Intelligent Machinery." In Copeland, B. Jack. 2004. *The Essential Turing*, 428. Clarendon Press.

[40] Grey Walter, W. (1956). Presentation: Dr. Grey Walter. In J.M. Tanner and B. Inhelder (Eds.), *Discussions on Child Development: Volume 2*, 21–74. London: Tavistock Publications.

[41] Lighthill, J. 1973. "Artificial intelligence: A paper symposium." Science Research Council, London.

[42] "Gartner Says AI Augmentation Will Create $2.9 Trillion of Business Value in 2021" (*https://oreil.ly/n6kP7*). n.d. Gartner. Accessed 17 August 2020.

[43] Kaelbling, L. P., M. L. Littman, and A. W. Moore. 1996. "Reinforcement Learning: A Survey" (*https://oreil.ly/xmhsX*). ArXiv:Cs/9605103, April.

CHAPTER 2

Markov Decision Processes, Dynamic Programming, and Monte Carlo Methods

The foundation of reinforcement learning (RL) is based upon three topics. The most important is the *Markov decision process* (MDP), a framework that helps you describe your problem. *Dynamic programming* (DP) and *Monte Carlo* methods lie at the heart of all algorithms that intend to solve MDPs. But first, let me discuss an application that you have probably heard of, but didn't consider to be RL.

Multi-Arm Bandit Testing

Imagine you work for an online ecommerce company. Given your role in engineering, you will be expected to develop new features and maintain existing ones. For example, you might be asked to improve the checkout process or migrate to a new library.

But how can you be certain that your changes have the desired effect? Monitoring key performance indicators (KPIs) is one possible solution. For new features you want to positively impact the KPIs. For maintenance tasks you want no impact.

As an example, take the classic scenario of establishing the best color for a button. Which is better, red or green? How do you quantify the difference? To approach this using RL you must define the three core elements of the problem: the reward, the actions, and the environment.

 In-depth practical advice on the development of RL solutions is provided in Chapter 9.

Reward Engineering

To quantify performance, the result of an action must be measurable. In RL, this is the purpose of the reward. It provides evidence of an outcome, which can be good or bad. Practitioners typically encode good outcomes as positive values (but this is not strictly necessary).

What reward signal should you choose for the website button example? You could say that clicks are a positive outcome. And a sale is a strongly positive outcome. Often you will have limited access to metrics and have to compromise. For example, rather than use the sale as the KPI, you could calculate the average sale for everyone who clicks the button and assign that single value to every click. That way you would not need to integrate with another system.

For the related problem of testing that new software doesn't have a significant detrimental effect, you might be able to get away with something as simple as button clicks with a simple +1 reward. If the metrics show a similar number of clicks then you can be happy you haven't broken anything—a successful day of engineering.

Either way, the reward must be quantitative and, ideally, it should be as simple as possible. If you use an overly complex reward signal then the proposed algorithms might overfit and learn to take advantage of a flaw in the reward signal, rather than solving the intended problem. For example, distance-to-goal–based rewards are often used and are usually quite robust, but an agent trying to navigate a maze using this reward is likely to get stuck in a dead end near the goal, because being close to the goal provides *nearly* optimal rewards.

Next, how can you use the reward to quantify the best outcome?

Policy Evaluation: The Value Function

In an environment, an agent takes a specific action, a, which is a member of the mathematical set $\mathcal{A}$. In other words, the agent could have taken one of many actions from the set $\mathcal{A}$, but on this occasion it chose a. This is written as $a \in \mathcal{A}$.

The environment rewarded the agent with a specific reward, r, which comes from a wide range of potential rewards defined by the set $\mathcal{R}$. This moved the environment into a new state, $s \in \mathcal{S}$.

All of these variables could be stochastic, meaning that if your agent requested exactly the same action in precisely the same situation, the environment may return a slightly different reward or state. In the literature you will see these denoted as uppercase letters, but in this book I only use the lowercase terminology to simplify the notation, even thought it might not be strictly accurate.

In the previous website button example, the action is to choose whether to show the red button or the green button to a visitor, which in mathematical form would be $\mathcal{A} \doteq \{a_{red}, a_{green}\}$. Whenever a user visits your website your agent will decide which action to choose, as defined by the current strategy. The user then clicks the button or doesn't and a reward is sent back to your agent. It's easiest to imagine the reward being one for a click and zero for no click, for example. But it could easily be the profit made from that customer or any other business metric.

So back to the original question, which is best? One way of quantifying performance is to calculate the average reward, r^{avg}, for a certain number of customers, N, for each action, a, shown in Equation 2-1.

 Remember that presenting a single button and waiting for a single click is not a sequential task; there is only a single decision. This is the primary difference between bandits and RL. I will demonstrate sequential decisions shortly.

Equation 2-1. Average reward calculation

$$r^{avg}(a) \doteq \frac{1}{N(a)} \sum_{i=1}^{N(a)} r(a)_i = \frac{r_1 + r_2 + \cdots + r_{N(a)}}{N(a)}$$

Equation 2-1 explains that to calculate the average reward for each action, you sum the observed rewards and divide by the number of customers.

This works, but is not computationally efficient in terms of storage. More importantly, you'd have to wait until lots of customers have interacted with your button before you can compute this.

Instead you can reformulate Equation 2-1 as an *online* algorithm. This means that the parameters of the algorithm are updated in place, rather than waiting until the end of all the experiments. Equation 2-2 derives this explicitly, because it is important for many subsequent RL algorithms.

Equation 2-2. Online value function

$$r_N^{avg} \leftarrow \frac{1}{N} \sum_{i=1}^{N} r_i \qquad (1)$$

$$\leftarrow \frac{1}{N} \left(r_N + \sum_{i=1}^{N-1} r_i \right) \qquad (2)$$

$$\leftarrow \frac{1}{N} \left(r_N + (N-1) \frac{1}{N-1} \sum_{i=1}^{N-1} r_i \right) \quad (3)$$

$$\leftarrow \frac{1}{N} \left(r_N + (N-1) r_{N-1}^{avg} \right) \qquad (4)$$

$$\leftarrow \frac{1}{N} \left(r_N + N r_{N-1}^{avg} - r_{N-1}^{avg} \right) \qquad (5)$$

$$\leftarrow r_{N-1}^{avg} + \frac{1}{N} \left(r_N - r_{N-1}^{avg} \right) \qquad (6)$$

This is one of those mathematical manipulations that is only obvious in hindsight. The goal is to convert a static average calculation into an online version using mathematical tricks. If you do not concentrate, the tricks are easy to miss.

I begin in step (1) by reusing Equation 2-1, but this time I have removed the notation stating that the reward is a function of the action. Remember that this is the same for each action. I also use the assignment operator, $\leftarrow$, to denote that I am updating the variable in place. It is not an equality.

In step (2) I start to extract the most recent reward from the sum, so that the summation operator ends at the second-to-last customer, $N-1$.

In (3), I use my mathematical trickery to multiply the sum by $1 = (N-1)/(N-1)$. This move requires the foresight to see that $\frac{1}{N-1} \sum_{i=1}^{N-1} r_i$ is in the same form as step (1), which makes it equivalent to r_{N-1}^{avg}. Hence, in step (4), I can replace the expansion from the previous step with r_{N-1}^{avg}.

Between (4) and (5) I perform some multiplication to expand the $(N-1)$ and you can see that there is a $1/N$ and an N that cancel each other out.

In (6), after multiplying by 1/N, the result looks like an exponentially weighted moving average (also known as exponential smoothing), a common form of online algorithm to estimate the mean.

In fact, most RL algorithms operate in this way. You can clean up the notation in Equation 2-2 to result in the common form of the exponentially weighted moving average algorithm, shown in Equation 2-3.

Equation 2-3. General form of an exponentially weighted moving average

$$r = r + \alpha(r' - r)$$

This might sound familiar. This is the same as Equation 1-3, except here I have not used matrix mathematics. Calculating the error and updating the predictions accordingly is a common theme across machine learning and RL.

Now that you know how to calculate the reward and how to update it online, the next challenge is to decide which action to take, based upon the these average rewards.

Policy Improvement: Choosing the Best Action

Allowing an agent full control over the choices it makes distinguishes RL from ML. You need to decide how the agent makes those decisions. Let me start with the simplest solution first, then expand from there.

Using the same website button example, assume that you have already decided that the agent receives a fixed reward for every button click.

You could show the new version of the website 50% of the time. Later, you can sum the reward (the number of clicks) to find the preferred button. This is precisely what A/B testing does. But this solution has a major flaw: 50% of customers see a suboptimal button. Your company loses sales.

In a second approach, you could show the new version 50% of the time to begin with, but shift the split toward the preferred option over time. This is the idea behind bandit algorithms.

This strategy highlights an important problem in RL. You need to observe the rewards from all of the actions multiple times before you know which is best. But you also want the agent to exploit the best known actions to maximize your reward now. This is the compromise between *exploration* and *exploitation*.

A generalized version of this algorithm devotes some time to exploration and some to exploitation. Upon every action there is some probability that the action will be a random choice, specified by the parameter ϵ. This is called the ϵ-greedy algorithm and is shown in Algorithm 2-1. r^{avg} and N have the same meaning as before.

Algorithm 2-1. ϵ-greedy bandit algorithm

1: **input**: a exploration probability $0 \le \epsilon \le 1$,

2: Initialize $r^{avg}(a) \leftarrow 0, N(a) \leftarrow 0$, for each $a \in \mathscr{A}$

3: **loop** for ever:

4: $a \leftarrow \begin{cases} \underset{a_s \in \mathscr{A}(s)}{\operatorname{argmax}} \ r^{avg}(a_s) \ \text{with probability } 1 - \epsilon, \text{ breaking ties randomly} \\ \\ \text{random } a \qquad \text{with probability } \epsilon \end{cases}$

5: Present action a in the environment and receive reward r

6: $N(a) \leftarrow N(a) + 1$

7: $r^{avg}(a) \leftarrow r^{avg}(a) + \dfrac{1}{N(a)}\left[r - r^{avg}(a)\right]$

Step (1) states that you need to pass in a value for ϵ between zero and one. Higher values will explore. Lower values will exploit. Step (2) creates arrays to store the results. Step (3) tells you to loop forever.

The algorithm gets interesting in step (4). With a probability of $1 - \epsilon$, the agent should choose the action that produces the current highest average reward. Similarly, the agent should select a random action with probability ϵ.

Step (5) runs the chosen action in the environment and returns the reward, which I define shortly. For example, if the algorithm chose the red button, your UI should present that and inform you if the user clicked. This is the interaction with the environment.

Step (6) increments a counter for this action for use next. And finally, step (7) updates the online average reward function (Equation 2-2) based upon the instantaneous reward, the action, and the number of times the agent has chosen that action. Over time this value estimate will become more accurate, assuming the rewards don't change.

Algorithm 2-1 is a bandit algorithm, named after the one-armed slot machines. Over time this algorithm allows you to automatically pick the "arm" on the bandit machine that provides the highest reward. If you wanted to perform automated bandit testing, a process of comparing two or more competing solutions, Algorithm 2-1 allows you to automatically tend toward the version that produces the highest reward.

Simulating the Environment

When you work on an industrial project, the best environment is real life. However, your environment may be too expensive, dangerous, or complicated to develop against. Instead, you can build a simulation, which could be a simplified version of a domain (like a three-dimensional gaming engine), or modeled from collected data.

Pretend that the notional website visitors do not click the button every time, only some proportion of the time. Also, they prefer the red button over the green button. In this example, I assume that a whopping 40% of users click the red button, but only 5% of users click the green. But these numbers could come from prior experimentation or a published model. You can use this information to create a simple simulator to test your RL algorithm, as shown in Algorithm 2-2.

Algorithm 2-2. Website simulator

function $\textsc{Environment}(a, p(a))$

input: The action, a, and its probability, $p(a)$

output: $r \leftarrow 1$ with probability $p(a)$, else 0.

I know this is simple, but I thought it was useful to spell out that simulations don't have to be complex to be useful. It accepts an action and the probability of an action and outputs a reward of 1 with probability $p(a)$. I provide a reward of 1 here, but you could return a number that makes more sense in your context. For example, the total value of the sale (in which case you will need to simulate order values as well).

Running the Experiment

Now you can run your first experiment. Figure 2-1 illustrates the workflow of a typical bandit test on a website. This image might differ from what you expect, because I explicitly include the following RL components: the agent, the action, and the reward. First the user browses to your URL and the agent decides which button to show. Then the user views the page and may click the button. The result passes back to the agent so it can learn which action to choose in the future.

All code is available for you to use online on the accompanying website (*https://rl-book.com*) (see "Supplementary Materials" on page xix for more information).

I implemented Algorithm 2-2 using two Bernoulli distributions, which represent the two buttons, with the probability of being selected set to 40% for the red button and

5% for the green. I then implemented Algorithm 2-1 to learn which button was pre-fered by these simulated users automatically.

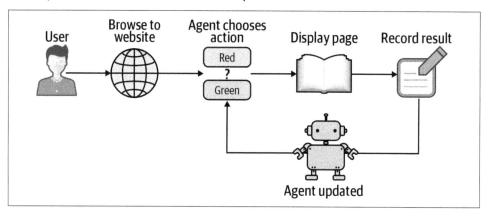

Figure 2-1. A depiction of the bandit testing workflow.

Figure 2-2 compares three different values of the hyperparameter ϵ, which I pass into Algorithm 2-1. Each simulation ran for 250 steps, which means that the algorithm had 250 opportunities to learn the underlying button-color preferences (that is, the simulated customer prefers the red button) and extract the most value. Each line rep-resents the percentage of time that the agent chose the optimal button to show to the visitor, on average, over 1,000 repeats to reduce the noise due to random sampling.

Looking at the start of the experiment, you can see that it took some time for each run to learn the optimal button. The rate of this learning depends on the following factors. When ϵ is high, the agent chooses random actions most of the time and the agent has many opportunities to stumble accross the best action. When ϵ is low, the agent has fewer opportunities to explore and you will have to wait for a long time. In other words, ϵ affects the learning speed.

Looking toward the end of the experiment, different values of ϵ affect the eventual optimal reward percentage. I say eventual because each curve is asymptotic, which means tending toward some final value. Imagine you are the algorithm with an ϵ of 1. This means that you always select a random action (show a random button). This means the maximum reward you could ever get is 50%. If you start to reduce ϵ, then you do get to choose the optimal action, some of the time. The asymptote of the opti-mal action is $\epsilon / n + (1 - \epsilon)$, where n is the number of actions. When $\epsilon = 1$, the agent always picks a random action and the result is an optimal action of 0.5. When $\epsilon = 0.1$, the result is an optimal action of 0.95. ϵ affects the final rate at which the algorithm chooses the optimal action.

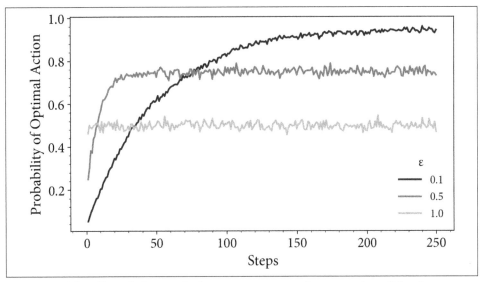

Figure 2-2. The effect of altering the hyperparameter ε, the proportion of the time you want the agent to explore. High values of ε lead to greater exploration, but less exploitation of the optimal action and vice versa.

Improving the ε-greedy Algorithm

All algorithms are fundamentally limited by how effectively they explore and how quickly they exploit. The best algorithms are able to do both at the same time, but defining how to explore is largely problem dependent. For example, a maze and an optimal healthcare schedule would require different exploration strategies.

The previous section showed that the hyperparameter ε controls this trade-off. Too high and the agent does too much searching, which results in choosing bad actions. Too low and the agent does too little searching and takes a long time to find new optimal actions.

 I want provide some intuition on other simple exploration methods here. See the literature in "Further Reading" on page 57 for more details.

The simulation also factors into this discussion. If the difference between the rewards of two actions is small, the agent has to sample these two outcomes a lot. According to the law of large numbers, the agent's confidence bound on the reward becomes smaller with more observations.

It is often better to choose the action based upon the current estimates of the distribution of rewards. In other words, rather than returning a single action, the agent returns the probabilities of each action, weighted by expected rewards of each state. This is called a *softmax* function. This provides a natural exploration function defined by the current reward estimates.

If the eventual aim is to extract as much reward as possible, then there is no point continuing to explore. You could remove the ϵ-greedy action. But it is more common to reduce the value of ϵ over time. This is called *annealing*. The word annealing comes from metallurgy. It means to heat and cool metals slowly, to strengthen and remove stresses.

A third popular improvement revolves around the idea that it doesn't make sense to explore randomly, especially in simple simulations. The agent will learn more by exploring states that it hasn't seen before. These algorithms add a *bonus* to each action for inadequately sampled states and are called *upper-confidence-bound* (UCB) methods. UCB algorithms are useful because they have no hyperparameters like ϵ (or the rate at which ϵ decreases, for annealing).

Figure 2-3 compares these three methods. I chose the value of ϵ to approximate the same final performance as the other methods. You can see that the annealing-softmax and the UCB strategies learn an optimal action far quicker than the ϵ-greedy method. UCB also benefits from having no tunable parameters.

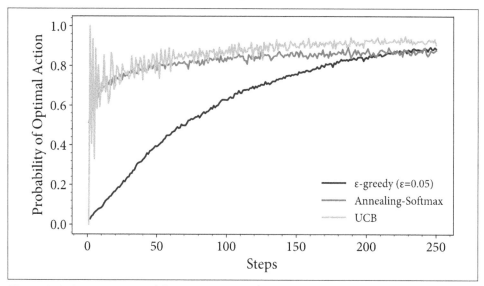

Figure 2-3. A comparison of three common exploration strategies: ϵ-greedy, annealing-softmax, and UCB.

Increasing the rate at which algorithms learn is a common goal of new RL algorithms.

Markov Decision Processes

A Markov decision process (MDP) is a mathematical formalism of many of the ideas introduced in Chapter 1. An *agent* influences the observed behavior of a stochastic system (the *environment*) by choosing *actions*. The goal is to choose the set of actions that allow the system to behave in an optimal way, as defined by some success criterion (the *reward*).

The agent can never fully appreciate the environment. The agent receives a limited set of *observations* that represent the current *state* of the system. These two words mean exactly what they are. The state is the condition that the environment is in at a particular time. The observation is the occluded view of that state. In many environments the state can be directly observed.

Digital agents perform actions at discrete times. This gives rise to the idea of a *step* in time. Note that this does not prevent the use of continuous actions, like the angle of a steering wheel. The opposite of a digital agent, an analog agent, much like a mechanically damped system, is technically possible but I have never seen one. An interesting hobby project perhaps?

As such, the agent and environment interact in a sequence of discrete time steps, t. At each time step the agent receives a representation of the state, s. Based upon the state of the environment the agent can suggest an action, a, and one time step later receives a value representing the reward, r, and a new set of states, s'. Here, the apostrophe above the s is used to represent the *next* state. You will often see subscripts with t and $t + 1$ that mean the same thing. Figure 2-4 visualizes these elements.

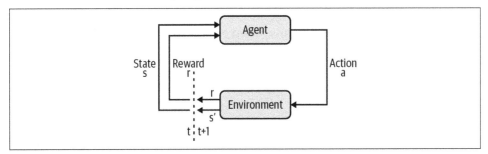

Figure 2-4. A representation of the interface and feedback loop between the environment and the agent in an MDP. The agent accepts the current state and reward from the environment and based upon this information performs an action. The environment takes the action and produces a new reward and state for the next time step.

Remember that the states and rewards are random variables, not definite values, because most environments are stochastic. For example, your agent could choose to turn the steering wheel in a self-driving car, but there is no guarantee that the car will actually turn; it might be on ice. To cater for this, the concept of a *transition model* is used. This is also called the *dynamics* of the MDP in some books. The transition model, shown in Equation 2-4, is the probability of landing in a new state with a reward given a previous state and performed action. The notation has been simplified to emphasize the causal effect of the action.

Equation 2-4. Transition model of an MDP

$$p(s', r \mid s, a)$$

Equation 2-4 is the key to the MDP. In a Markov decision process, the transition model describes the dynamics of the environment. The next state and reward depend only on the previous state and the action. And the only difference between an MDP and a traditional Markov chain, which is also called a *Markov process*, is the addition of the action and reward parameters. The action is a *decision*, which is the "D" in MDP.

 I like to think of the MDP as an interface. It is a contract between the agent and the environment. The agent can only observe the states and suggest an action. In return the environment will give you a new state and some value that represents how well you are doing. This might sound constrictive, but it allows for a remarkable amount of flexibility on both sides of the interface. The environment can be as complex as it needs to be. It could be a simulation of users clicking a button, an Atari game, or even real life. The agent also can be as complex as it needs to be. It could be deciding to show a green or red button, whether to move left or right in a game, or if it is a good idea to move to the countryside.

I use the apostrophe to denote a step forward in time. But that time does not have to be of a fixed interval. It only serves to make actions distinct. In other words, whenever you feel the need to make a decision, that is when you step. Think of actions as course corrections and time as a record of the timestamp.

Inventory Control

Defining a problem in RL terms is a common issue for people who have a background in data science. Gaining more experience in the problem definition phase is worthwhile before you move on to other ways of solving MDPs.

Inventory control is a good example to start with because it is both useful and easy to understand. This example has direct analogies with pricing, optimal stopping (selling an asset), maintenance, and more. I start with a very simple example and then expand it to a more complex version.

Imagine you own a small shop. This shop is so small you only have a single product. Each day customers buy your product so you need to restock. If you run out of stock, then you can't sell your product and make any money; you don't want to run out of stock. You rent your shop and it costs you a certain amount of money per square meter. You don't want to stock millions of items because you would need a larger premises. I could define many high-level problems, like the optimal size for the premises, or minimizing the delivery charges, but to start simply, I define the problem as deciding the best point to restock.

Let s represent the number of items in stock on a particular day. This is the state of the environment. In an attempt to keep things as simple as possible, I assume three possible states: no stock, one item in stock, or two items in stock, $\mathscr{S} \doteq \{0, 1, 2\}$ (the curly font here means that it represents a set).

Given the current state, the agent can perform an action. Keeping it simple, assume that the agent can take one of two actions. Either restock, which orders 1 new product, or do nothing: $\mathscr{A} \doteq \{\text{restock}, \text{none}\}$. If the current state was 1 and the agent performs the action, the next state will be 2. Also assume that you cannot order any stock when you are at full capacity.

The next thing missing from Equation 2-4 is the transition probabilities. What are the probabilities that the agent shifts from one state to another? Since you are simulating the environment, you have to choose those, but they could come from observations of your shop. Say that the probability of a single sale during a day, $p(\text{sale})$, is 0.7. In the future you could predict the number of items sold. But for now, I use a Bernoulli distribution again. This means that in each state there is a 70% probability of a sale and a 30% probability of no sale.

This is a purely hypothetical example. Of course it takes time to restock in real life. Simplifications are a necessary part of engineering, especially in early phases of development. Once you have a working prototype, then you can work on removing some of those simplifications.

The final thing you need is a reward, r. Your shop needs to make money, so you can reward yourself every time you sell a product. But sales are possible only if the product is in stock at the time, or if you restocked just in time. This means the reward is conditional on the current state and on a sale; no sale means no reward. You can see this definition in mathematical form in Equation 2-5.

Equation 2-5. Inventory control reward definition

$$r \doteq \begin{cases} 1 & \text{if } s > 0 \text{ and a sale} \\ 1 & \text{if } a = \text{restock and a sale} \\ 0 & \text{otherwise} \end{cases}$$

Transition table

The next job is to define all the possible state transitions in the system and you can do this in three different ways. The first way is to present all possible combinations as a table, known as the *transition table*, shown in Table 2-1.

Table 2-1. MDP transition table

s	a	s'	$p(s'|s,a)$	r
0	none	0	$1 - p(\text{sale})$	0
0	none	0	$p(\text{sale})$	0
0	restock	1	$1 - p(\text{sale})$	0
0	restock	0	$p(\text{sale})$	1
1	none	1	$1 - p(\text{sale})$	0
1	none	0	$p(\text{sale})$	1
1	restock	2	$1 - p(\text{sale})$	0
1	restock	1	$p(\text{sale})$	1
2	none	2	$1 - p(\text{sale})$	0
2	none	1	$p(\text{sale})$	1
2	restock	2	$p(\text{sale})$	1

In Table 2-1 there is a row for each possible combination of the current state, s, action, a, next state, s', and probability of the transition into a state given a previous state and action, $p(s'|s,a)$; the reward for making that transition is in the final column, r. You can use this table to trace the *trajectory* of the agent.

State 2 (two items) has only three possible transitions, because I have left off the final restock with no sale eventuality. I am saying that restocking when full is impossible.

Transition graph

Another way to represent this information is through a directed graph, known as a *transition graph*, shown in Figure 2-5.

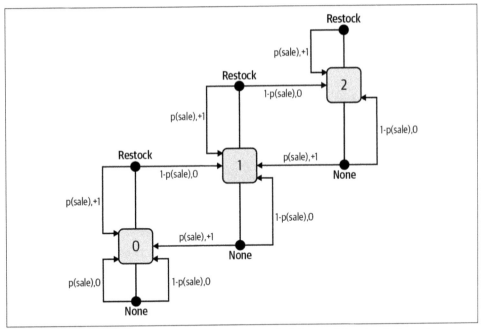

Figure 2-5. A graph representing the transition probabilities of the simple inventory problem.

The graph has two types of nodes (called vertices): one for the state, represented by a circle with the name of that state inside, and another for the action, represented by a solid circle. These connect through links (called edges), labeled with the probability of following that link after the action (the transition probability) and the reward obtained after following that link.

Transition matrix

The final way to represent the transition probabilities is with a matrix for each action, known as the *transition matrix*. You can construct the matrix in the same way as in Table 2-1.

$$p(s', a = \text{none}) = \begin{bmatrix} 1 & 0 & 0 \\ p(\text{sale}) & 1 - p(\text{sale}) & 0 \\ 0 & p(\text{sale}) & 1 - p(\text{sale}) \end{bmatrix}$$

$$p(s', a = \text{restock}) = \begin{bmatrix} p(\text{sale}) & 1 - p(\text{sale}) & 0 \\ 0 & p(\text{sale}) & 1 - p(\text{sale}) \\ 0 & 0 & 1 \end{bmatrix}$$

Each cell represents the probability of transitioning from the current state (0, 1, or 2 in rows) into the new state (0, 1, or 2 in columns). Note that each row must sum to 1. For example, if the agent chooses not to restock, action a = none, you use the top transition matrix. If the shop has one item in stock, so the state is 1 (the second row), you can see that there is a probability of p(sale) of transitioning into state 0, you've sold the item, and 1 − p(sale) of staying in the same state after no sale. Also note that you need a separate function or matrix for the obtained rewards as well.

I prefer the transition graph because it allows you to trace the trajectory taken by the agent with your finger. But you can only visualize the graph up to a small number of states and actions. Computational capacity is the only thing that limits the transition matrix, but it is difficult to interpret by eye.

Inventory Control Simulation

The previous sections presented all the ingredients required to build a simulation (the environment). But what about the agent? When should you restock?

You already placed a constraint that you cannot restock if the stockroom is full. That is one hard rule. But after that, what is the best action to take? If you look purely at the rewards, which represent the goal, then there is only a positive reward on making sales. Crucially, there is no negative reward for placing orders. In other words, according to the reward matrix, it doesn't cost anything to keep stock and it is free to order new stock. Given this reward structure, the best strategy is to keep ordering as much as you can.

Even though the strategy is obvious in this case, you should always test your idea— the scientific method. It is always a good idea to compare your theory against other baselines.

Figure 2-6 compares three different restocking strategies, or *policies*. Policies tell the agent which actions to take and in general the best ones maximize the total reward. The policies are keep restocking as much as possible, restock only when the stock levels drop to zero, or restock at random. The lines represent the cumulative rewards for each of the policies. The proportion of sales made is presented in brackets in the legend.

It is clear in this case that restocking at random is not a good idea, because quite often people wanted to buy but there was no stock. This was because the probability of a sale (0.7) was greater than the probability of restocking (0.5). The constant-restock policy managed to keep up with demand because you reordered at each time step. So the stock level (the state) bounced between 2 and 1. The reorder when zero stock policy bounced around the 0–1 level, because it only restocked when it hit zero. Effectively there is no performance difference between these two, but note that you might

---

consider the keep buying policy to be wasteful, because you are using more space than you need, or safe, in case there's a rush. It depends on your high-level perspective and goal.

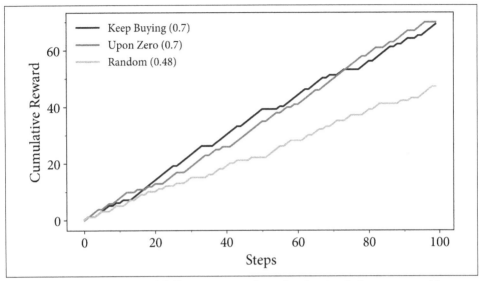

Figure 2-6. A comparison of different agent policies for the simple inventory problem. The proportion of sales made per day are in brackets. 0.7 is the maximum due to the problem definition.

 This is an interesting example of how exactly the same data can mean different things to different people. Your boss might hate the waste, or they might love the buffer. Neither position is wrong.

You have just derived your first set of policies. And I haven't yet discussed how to learn an optimal policy—that will take the rest of the book. But this is an important result to take in; an optimal policy is dependent on all components of an MDP.

Changing the environment to include more stock, or allowing people to buy more than one item at a time, affects the best restocking strategy. Altering the reward function by introducing a penalty for ordering—a charge for delivery, for example—also alters the best strategy. In these cases it might be better to wait until you have zero stock then order a full 2 units worth of product. The reward function defines what problem you want solved, not how to achieve it.

Standard MDPs require the state to be fully observable. If the agent cannot observe the true state of the system, then how can it pick an optimal action? There is an extension to the MDP model called partially observable MDPs (POMDPs). Here, you can introduce an extra mapping between the observations and the actual state. In other words, the agent would need to learn how to map actions to observations that are mapped to states that it cannot observe, a double mapping. As you can imagine, this is tricky to solve, because of more unknowns. In many applications, engineers trick the system back into a standard MDP by feeding more information from previous time steps into the current time step. Knowledge of the past can help the agent figure out how the actions altered the perceived states over a longer period of time.

I also want to stress that the important thing here is the observation of the state, not the environment. Agents do not concern themselves about what is happening behind the MDP interface. You can alter the simulation as much as you want, so long as you do not change the interface. In the inventory example, if you altered the customer's buying behavior, it only affects the optimal policy. It does not change *how* the agent learns.

Bear these points in mind when you read the rest of this book.

Policies and Value Functions

A policy is like a strategy. For example, you can't be entirely sure what the other football team is going to do (the other team's activities are stochastic), but you can approximate their actions and tell your players to act accordingly. A policy is a mapping from states to potential actions. Precisely how you do that mapping is the major difference between a large number of RL algorithms. But why should you build a mapping in the first place? And how can you evaluate different policies?

Discounted Rewards

In many problems, including the inventory and website button examples, the reward at each step is straightforward to reason about. At each time step the agent may or may not receive a reward. Through multiple steps (in the inventory example), the agent may receive multiple rewards. In general the challenge is to maximize the total reward that you expect to receive.

The *return*, G, is the total reward from this current step up to the final time step (or infinity). The first dot-equals sign can be read as "I define G to be." Note that the agent receives the reward after transitioning into the next step. Most practical implementations return the state and the reward at the same time, so they set the initial reward to zero.

Equation 2-6 sums all the future rewards up until a final time step, T. This final state is called a *terminal state* and only occurs in *episodic* tasks. An episode represents one full run through all steps that end at a natural termination point. This could be when your robot falls off a cliff, or if your character in a game dies. But of course, there may be tasks that continue forever, like the inventory example— if you allow me to be optimistic about the state of the retail market. In this case the terminal state is $T = \infty$ and the expected return could also be infinite.

Equation 2-6. Return

$$G \doteq r + r' + \cdots + r_T$$

To mitigate against the explosive power of infinity, Equation 2-7 adds a discounting factor that exponentially reduces future rewards.

Equation 2-7. Discounted return

$$G \doteq r + \gamma r' + \gamma^2 r'' + \cdots = \sum_{k=0}^{T} \gamma^k r_k$$

In Equation 2-7, T represents the terminal state and could be infinity. γ is called the *discount rate* or *factor*. It controls how soon future rewards are ignored and should be be a value between 0 and 1, inclusive. In other words, if $\gamma = 0$ then only the present reward is taken into consideration. If $\gamma = 1$ then this is the same as Equation 2-6. Typically you want to take the future rewards into account to be able to solve problems where the reward is far into the future. But precise values will differ depending on the problem at hand. In most nontrivial examples the discount rate is set between 0.9 and 0.99.

Therefore, you want to build an agent that can generate the largest *expected return*. One question you might have is how to calculate the expected return, given that it depends on future rewards. The answer is through iteration and learning which states and actions map to the best rewards. In other words, you should iterate to find the best policy.

Predicting Rewards with the State-Value Function

In the inventory example of "Inventory Control Simulation" on page 40, I arbitrarily chose three restocking strategies. But I want to optimize the choice of action to maximize the expected return automatically. This is the purpose of the *policy*; it maps states to actions. Formally, it is the probability of choosing an action given a state, $p(a|s)$, and is denoted by π.

Policies can be improved by nudging the gradient of the policy with respect to the expected return. I will return to this in Chapter 5.

You can calculate the expected return from the return, G, expected from your current policy, π, starting from the current state, s. This is called the *state-value function* for the policy and is shown in Equation 2-8.

Equation 2-8. State-value function

$$V_\pi(s) \doteq \mathbb{E}_\pi[G|s] = \mathbb{E}_\pi\left[\sum_{k=0}^{T} \gamma^k r_k \middle| s\right]$$

I appreciate on first glance that this equation looks complex, so let me walk you through it. There are three parts to the equation, separated by the equals signs. On the left, V is the symbol used to denote the value function.

 For those who aren't math-native, I find that imagining the mathematical functions as functions in software helps.

The second part, the definition of the function, is saying that the value function is the expected value of the return, given a current state, following the policy π. The symbol $\mathbb{E}$ is the expectation operator (more about this in a moment). This instructs you to calculate the expected value of the term in the brackets. And the π subscript tells you that the agent should follow the policy to calculate that expectation.

The third part of the equation on the right is an expansion of the term in the brackets. You know how G is defined from Equation 2-7. And you know you need to start from the current state. At this point the math inside the brackets is basically saying "sum all the rewards from this point forward."

Equation 2-8 has two important points. The first is the expectation operator. Most RL algorithms assume rewards are characterized by a normal distribution and the expectation can be calculated as the sample mean. In other words, the result of the expectation operator is the average discounted reward from that given state. Rewards in some applications may not be normally distributed. For example, what would you choose: one single big reward or many small rewards? In both situations the mean is the same, but the distribution of rewards isn't. Reward nuances can be hidden by the expectation operator. In fact, a lot of research has recently focused on trying to evaluate and use the distribution of rewards instead (see "Distributional RL" on page 100).

The second important part is the policy. You can only calculate the expected return if you already have a policy. But this equation is meant to help you quantify the performance of a policy. This is a classic chicken and egg problem that RL solves by starting randomly and iterating to find an improvement.

Simulation using the state-value function

I find that my intuition of an equation is improved through a simple simulation. I developed a program that simulates positions on five squares (the states). The agent starts on the lefthand side. In each time step the agent can move left or right. The simulation ends if the agent reaches the goal state of square 5, on the righthand side, or if the agent moves left on square 0, off an imaginary cliff. To keep things as simple as possible, the policy is a random one, in which it randomly chooses either left or right on every time step.

 You should continuously consider different environments. *Overfitting* is the process of accidentally building a model or an algorithm that works with very specific data or circumstances. It is easy to improve an algorithm to the point where it overfits your simulation and find it does not work in real life, for example. Industrial RL algorithms should be robust, and considering different environments is one way to help your algorithm *generalize*. Also, using different environments is an important way of gaining experience. Hence, I intentionally keep switching environments throughout these examples.

The goal of Equation 2-8 is to calculate the expected reward for each state. You can do this by recording the position of the agent through each *epoch*, which is a continuous loop of the environment until the agent reaches a terminal state. Eventually, you will obtain a reward and you can go back and look at all the states visited along the way. You then add the reward to a cumulative sum and keep a counter to calculate the average return observed after visiting all of those states.

 Whenever you perform an experiment, it is prudent to imagine some theoretical expectations, or priors—defining a hypothesis is the heart of the scientific method.

Imagine you are on square 1, on the lefthand side. Imagine how to get to each of the terminal states. You can move one square to the left and fall off the cliff. Or you can move four squares to the right and reach the end. Your first policy is a random one; it randomly chooses a new direction uniformly. It randomly picks to move one square left more often than four squares right. On average, only 1 out of 5 attempts reach the righthand side; the rest fall off the cliff. If you set the the reward to 5 (to match the number of squares) and you do not penalize for falling off the board, then the expected reward of each state should be the same as the position of the square.

In this example, the expected return from square 1 should be 1. The expected reward in the terminal state should be 5, because there is no need to move. In intermediary states, because the agent is moving randomly, there is still a chance that the agent might randomly move back toward the cliff. So even when on the fourth square, one step away from the reward, the random agent 1 out of 5 times will stumble back to the cliff, on average.

If this doesn't make sense, imagine two squares where a single move to the right reaches the goal state. Now increase the number of squares.

Note that in this example you are setting the discount factor to 1. In more complicated environments you should set this to less than 1 because early moves in an episode are typically less important than those close to a terminating state. But the precise value depends on the reward and whether the problem is continuous or not.

When I run this simulation it takes a large number of iterations to stabilize. After the first iteration, the agent jumped immediately to the left and died. So the expected return at iteration 0 is [0.00, NaN, NaN, NaN], where positions in this array represent the squares 1 through 4. Square 5 isn't recorded because there is no action to take in the terminal state. After ten iterations the agent has reached the goal state a couple of times: [0.77, 3.00, 5.00, 5.00]. After a thousand iterations the expected returns begin to get close to the previous estimate: [1.04, 2.09, 2.93, 3.83]. After ten thousand random experiments the result is very close: [1.00, 1.97, 2.92, 3.92]. The more iterations I run the closer it will get to the true expected value. The result of this simulation can be seen in Figure 2-7.

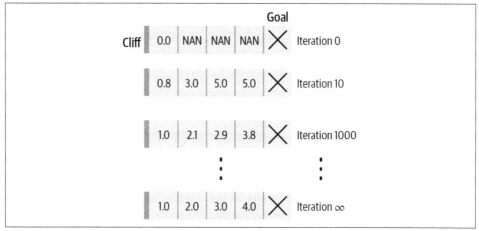

Figure 2-7. The result of simulating the calculation of the state-value function in a simple environment. Each square represents a state. The value inside each square represents the expected return starting from that state and following the random policy. After repeated iterations the expected return from each state approaches the theoretical expectation.

Another interesting experiment to try is to change the starting position. After ten thousand iterations the results are the same (within the range of random fluctuations). You could try adding discounting or penalize for falling off the cliff to see what happens. I encourage you to develop your own code to gain intuition, but of course you can refer to the practical examples on the accompanying website (see "Supplementary Materials" on page xix).

Predicting Rewards with the Action-Value Function

The previous example shows you how to predict the expected return from a given state, which is the average reward observed after previous visits to that state. But actions are not all created equal. What if taking one action led you closer toward rewarding states? Many algorithms use this information to help decide which is the best action to choose. This requires an expected return for any action in any state and is shown in Equation 2-9.

Equation 2-9. Action-value function

$$Q_\pi(s, a) \doteq \mathbb{E}_\pi[G|s, a] = \mathbb{E}_\pi\left[\sum_{k=0}^{T} \gamma^k r_k|s, a\right]$$

Equation 2-9 is the *action-value function* for a policy π. You can see that it is virtually the same as Equation 2-8 except for the fact that there are two parameters to the function: the state and the action. You can imagine this being implemented as a two-dimensional lookup table to store the rewards for states and their actions. This function is often called the Q-function, for brevity.

Figure 2-8 shows the result of the same simulation from "Simulation using the state-value function" on page 45, but with the action-value function instead. Equation 2-9 brings the addition of storing the expected return for both the state and action. One result is that moving left from square 0 will always return a reward of zero. Moving right from square 4 will always result in a reward of 5.0.

Another interesting result is that the expected value for all the right actions are higher than the corresponding left actions. This is because the further the agent moves to the right, the better the chances of actually reaching the goal state. To finish, let me ask you a question. Given these states, actions, and expected returns, can you think of a policy, or a strategy, that is optimal for this environment? Can you imagine yourself as an agent, making a decision at each square? How do you choose which direction to take?

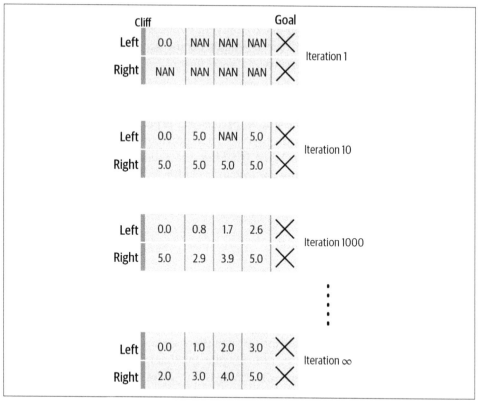

Figure 2-8. The result of simulating the calculation of the action-value function in a simple environment. The setup is the same as in Figure 2-7. The difference here is that I am recording the result of the action as well as the state.

Optimal Policies

An optimal policy is one that when followed generates the highest possible expected return. This means that there is at least one policy that provides the greatest return, which I denote as π_*. The equivalent optimal state-value and action-value functions are $V_*(s)$ and $Q_*(s, a)$, respectively.

The state-value functions and the action-value functions are related. They both represent the same information but at different levels of granularity. The state-value function is the expected reward averaged over all actions, which provides a low-resolution view of which states valued highly. The action-value function provides a high-resolution picture of which actions and states are the best.

Imagine you have good estimates for the expected values, because you have been randomly moving around the environment for a long time, for example. Then an optimal policy would suggest actions that move the agent toward higher expected

---

returns. In other words, an optimal policy is one that chooses the action with the maximum return.

 Most RL problems are framed to maximize the return, but this isn't strictly necessary. I recommend sticking to maximization though, to avoid confusion.

Now that you have an optimal policy, imagine calculating the state-value and action-value functions again, when following this policy. Both values will be exactly the same. The state-value function is equal to picking the best action in the action-value function. Equation 2-10 represents this idea in mathematical form and is called the *Bellman optimality equation*.

 The official Bellman optimality equation is more formal, aggregating over the transition probabilities and the probability of a policy selecting an action. For more information see "Further Reading" on page 57.

Equation 2-10. Optimal value function

$$V_*(s) \doteq \operatorname*{argmax}_{a_s \in \mathcal{A}(s)} Q_{\pi_*}(s, a_s)$$
$$= \operatorname*{argmax}_{a_s \in \mathcal{A}(s)} \mathbb{E}_{\pi_*}[G \mid s, a_s]$$

Equation 2-10 reuses the definition of the action-value function, Q, from Equation 2-9, using the return G. It states that choosing the action that maximizes the action-value function at every step is the same as the optimal value function. Let me restate that, because it is important. You obtain the highest total reward if you repeatedly choose the action with the highest expected return.

This might not make sense at first, because you can imagine that there may be greater rewards elsewhere. But remember that equations have full knowledge about all future rewards (look at the return, G, in the equations). So the action-value function (or state-value function) has already accounted for the fact that the agent is going to visit that rewarding state in its estimate.

So to answer the question from the end of "Predicting Rewards with the Action-Value Function" on page 47, the optimal policy is one that repeatedly chooses the action with the highest reward. In that example, the action with the highest reward was always on the righthand side, so the optimal policy is to choose "right" every time.

Monte Carlo Policy Generation

The example in "Simulation using the state-value function" on page 45 randomly selected actions and recorded the reward, but you don't have to. Instead you can exhaustively search every possible permutation of moves and store the trajectory. Then the optimal policy is the trajectory that achieved the highest reward.

But this strategy is impractical in most cases. Even for the simple example in Figure 2-7, you could imagine a strategy that repeatedly picks right then left and never terminates. You could help the agent by constraining the exhaustive search, but in general, you need to use something else.

Formally, the issue is the high dimensionality of the problem. The go-to algorithm that happily digests high-dimensional sampling problems is *Monte Carlo* (MC). Imagine a black-box environment, illustrated in Figure 2-9, in which you have no visibility. You control the actions presented to the environment, so you know the distribution of the inputs. But you have no idea of the distribution of the outputs, because the environment is not under your control. Characterizing the output distribution helps you pick the action that delivers the highest return (on average).

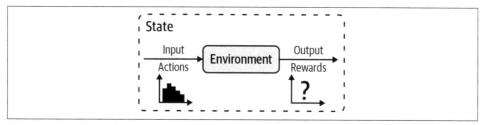

Figure 2-9. A black-box description of the Monte Carlo technique. Inputs are known, outputs are not. By randomly stimulating the inputs you can observe and characterize the output.

MC techniques randomly sample the input to observe what happens at the output. After adequately sampling actions you can characterize the output and therefore determine the reward. The term is used broadly to include any estimation method that includes a significant random component. But in RL it denotes techniques that average the reward returned over entire trajectories. You can find out more about MC techniques in "Further Reading" on page 57.

Now I can turn this idea into an algorithm, one that first generates an entire trajectory then updates the action-value function according to the observed reward. Given time the policy will tend toward the optimal one. Algorithm 2-3 is called an on-policy MC algorithm because it (a) samples full trajectories and (b) is estimating the value of the policy and using it to select actions at the same time.

Algorithm 2-3. On-policy MC algorithm

1: **input**: a policy function, $\pi\big(a\,|\,s,Q_\pi(s,a)\big)$

2: Initialize $Q(s,a) \leftarrow 0$, for all $s \in \mathcal{S}, a \in \mathcal{A}(s)$,
$Returns(s,a) \leftarrow [\,]$, for all $s \in \mathcal{S}, a \in \mathcal{A}(s)$

3: **loop**:

4:     Generate full episode trajectory following π

5:     Initialize $G \leftarrow 0$

6:     **loop** for each step of episode, $t \doteq T-1, T-2, \cdots, t_0$:

7:         $G \leftarrow \gamma G + r$

8:         **if** (s,a) not in $\big(s_0,a_0\big), \big(s_1,a_1\big), \cdots, \big(s_{t-1},a_{t-1}\big)$:

9:             Append G to $Returns(s,a)$

10:             $Q(s,a) \leftarrow average(Returns(s,a))$

Algorithm 2-3 begins in step (1) by passing in an implementation of a policy. This algorithm is typically presented with the policy built in, but I find it simpler to ignore the details of the policy and instead inject it as a dependency. The policy, $\pi\big(a\,|\,s,Q_\pi(s,a)\big)$, returns an action for a given state using the action-value function populated in this algorithm. Step (2) initializes the action-value function and creates a buffer for all the interactions with the environment.

Step (4) generates a trajectory for a full episode using the current policy. In my code I created a policy that picks the action with the highest expected return, like in Equation 2-10, with an ϵ-greedy search.

Step (6) iterates over every step in the episode in reverse. This is an important distinction; the agent chooses actions based upon *future* rewards. So step (6) starts at the end and iterates backward, summing rewards as it goes. Eventually it will end up at the first state and then you have one prediction of the expected return from that state.

Step (7) adds the reward discounting to the expected return from Equation 2-7. If the current state-action pair was not visited earlier in the trajectory [step (8)] then step (9) appends the pair to the buffer. This *first-visit* implementation estimates $V_\pi(s)$ as the average of the returns from the first visit to the state. *Every-visit* implementations estimate $V_\pi(s)$ as the average returns from every visit to a state. Both implementations lead to the same estimate but researchers have studied the first-visit algorithm in more depth and found it slightly less erroneous (every-visit action value estimates are more noisy—see "Further Reading" on page 57 for more information).

Finally, in step (10), the current action-value prediction is updated. This provides the policy with an estimate of the expected return for any state-action pair. This estimate is the average discounted return observed over all trajectories. Using an average makes the assumption that the expected return is normally distributed; it may not be, but this assumption works well in practice.

The results from Algorithm 2-3 are the same as in Figure 2-8 if you set the ϵ-greedy parameter to explore-only and the discount factor to 1.

Value Iteration with Dynamic Programming

In the previous sections I propagated the reward backward through a trajectory at the end of an episode. But there is another way.

Imagine an algorithm that scans one step ahead. Given a state, the agent can peek one step ahead to observe the next expected return. In environments where the terminal state provides the reward, like in Figure 2-10, in iteration (1) the agent will look one state ahead and see the terminal state, so it knows which action to take. In iteration (2) the agent sees the state before the terminal state, and knows which action to take again. This continues until the policy stabilizes.

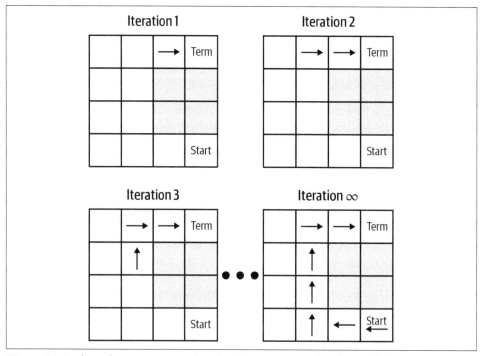

Figure 2-10. The policy generated when looking one state ahead over different iterations of the algorithm.

The literature often creates two abstractions based upon this process: policy evaluation and policy improvement. *Policy evaluation* provides the estimate of the expected value. *Policy improvement* updates the policy to take advantage of new knowledge coming from the value function, like a new promising path to explore.

When you combine evaluation and improvement, this is called *generalized policy iteration* (GPI). Implementations differ depending on at what level you interleave improvement and evaluation. For example, you could wait until the end of an episode to perform an improvement using MC methods, like in "Monte Carlo Policy Generation" on page 50.

Alternatively, you could update your value estimates after each step. *Dynamic programming* methods look one step ahead and iterate over all actions. Contrast this with MC techniques that choose a single action, but have to simulate a full episode.

Figure 2-11 illustrates the difference through something called a *backup diagram* for the state-value function. Open circles represent states and filled circles represent actions. In DP, in a given state, it searches across all possible actions. This makes it possible to update the policy after a single step. MC first generates a full episode by following a policy, then it updates the policy.

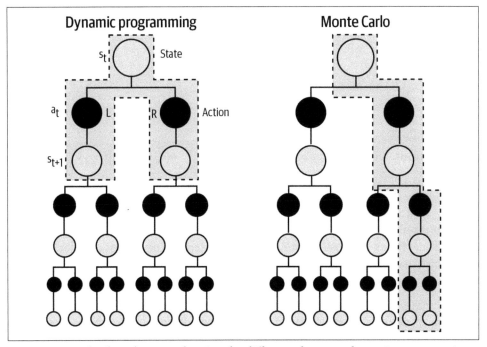

Figure 2-11. A backup diagram showing the difference between dynamic programming and Monte Carlo policy update techniques (for the value-state function).

Implementing Value Iteration

A technique called *value iteration* implements DP, but there is a problem. Value iteration depends on knowing the transition probabilities in full; you need a model of your environment. This is because the agent needs to know which actions it is allowed to try. In a two-dimensional grid, for example, you need to tell the agent that it cannot move outside of the boundaries by setting those probabilities to zero.

If you have control over the design of the environment and the problem is simple enough, then you can specify the transition probabilities in advance, like in the examples of "Inventory Control" on page 36 or "Simulation using the state-value function" on page 45. Chapter 3 develops generic algorithms for use when you don't have a full model of the environment. For now, assume you do and you can pass it into Algorithm 2-4.

Algorithm 2-4. Value iteration for generating an optimal policy

1: **input**: transition probabilities, $p(s', r \mid s, a)$, stopping threshold, $\theta > 0$

2: Initialize $V(s)$, for all $s \in \mathscr{S}$

3: **do**:

3a: $\nabla \leftarrow 0$

4:     **loop** for each $s \in \mathscr{S}$:

5:       $v \leftarrow V(s)$

6:       $V(s) \leftarrow \max_{a} \sum_{s', r} p(s', r \mid s, a)[r + \gamma V(s')]$

7:       $\nabla \leftarrow \max (\nabla, \mid v - V(s) \mid)$

8: **while** $\nabla > \theta$

9: **output**: an optimal policy, $\pi(s) \doteq \operatorname*{argmax}_{a_s \in \mathscr{A}(s)} \sum_{s', r} p(s', r \mid s, a_s)[r + \gamma V(s')]$

In step (1) of Algorithm 2-4, you need to specify the transition probabilities and a stopping threshold. In a toy grid environment, for example, the transition probabilities are equal for all actions except for those that step off the grid or are blocked by a wall, which have a transition probability of zero. The stopping threshold controls how long to keep refining the value estimate.

Step (2) initializes the state-value buffer for all states and a variable for maintaining the current amount of error. Step (3) enters a do-while loop and step (4) loops over every state in the environment. Step (5) stores a local copy of the state-value estimate for the current state for use later.

Step (6) is where the action happens. Starting from the lefthand side, it finds the largest expected return after trying all actions. The sum is summing over all potential next states and rewards for an action (because even though you select action left, you might end up going straight on). Then the probability represents the chances of landing in a next state with a reward given a current state and action. And finally the value of this series of events is the reward from the action plus the value of the next state.

I recommend that you reread the equation and the description again because step (6) squeezes a lot into one line. Now that you have reread it, let me give you a hand-worked example that I visualize in Figure 2-12.

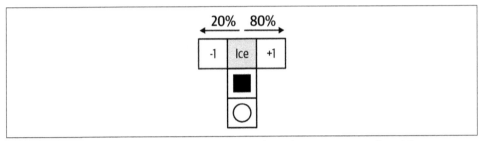

Figure 2-12. A stylized example demonstrating the value iteration update. The square represents your current position. The values represent the rewards. The expected value for the current state is 0.6.

Imagine you are standing in a grid, represented by the square, where you can only move forward or backward and all state-value estimates are zero. If you step back the movement is certain but you receive a reward of 0. If you step forward you will slip on ice and there is a 20% chance that you will fall to the left with a value of −1 and an 80% chance that you fall to the right with a value of 1.

Step (6) from Algorithm 2-4 aims to find the highest value for any action. This environment has two actions: up and down. The probability of transitioning down when actioning down is 1. The reward is 0 and since all the value estimates are zero the total sum for the down action is $1 \times 0 = 0$. For the up action, the two outcomes have two rewards. This sum becomes $0.2 \times -1 + 0.8 \times 1 = 0.6$. Hence, the maximum value over all actions for the current state is 0.6.

The previous example was for a single state, but that calculation depends on other states. This is why Algorithm 2-4 needs to iterate over all states to fill in the gaps. After the first pass of all states, it is likely that you need to update them all again because the values have changed. Step (7) records the maximum error to allow step (8) to decide whether to keep iterating. If you are interested, you can look up the convergence proof from the references in "Further Reading" on page 57.

Finally, in step (9), the algorithm outputs a deterministic policy that chooses the action with the highest expected return.

Results of Value Iteration

The results of an implementation of Algorithm 2-4 are shown in Figure 2-13. A discount factor of 0.9 was used to find the optimal policy for the simple cliff problem encountered earlier.

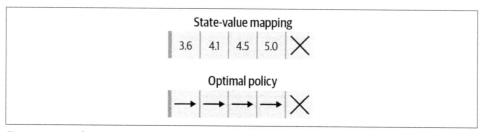

Figure 2-13. The result of training an agent using value iteration with a discount factor of 0.9. This image shows the state-value estimates and the optimal policy.

Like the MC version, the state-value map is simple to interpret. The closer the agent is to the goal, the greater the expected return. The slight difference is that the value is not dependent on randomly reaching the goal state. It is a discounted version of the reward if you were to follow a policy. The resulting policy is the same, however. And I could have used the same policy evaluation technique in the MC algorithm, too.

If I were to insert Algorithm 2-4 (the policy improvement algorithm) into an agent's interaction loop (policy evaluation), then you could improve the policy on every time step. Contrast this to MC techniques that have to wait until the end of an episode. DP can improve a policy much faster than MC, which is very important when dealing with problems with long (or infinite) episodes.

But four caveats prevent you from using DP in all but the simplest of environments. The first thing to watch out for is that you have to use discounting. If you didn't, all states would have a value equal to the reward. You must use discounting to direct the agent and suppress long trajectories. This is a common theme throughout all RL: prefer shorter trajectories.

Secondly, Algorithm 2-4 finishes when the agent has updated all states. That is fine in the toy examples seen so far, because they all have few states. But once the number of states or actions increases, then it becomes computationally prohibitive to use DP.

A third point, related to the previous, is the *sampling efficiency* of an algorithm. DP needs to visit all states and actions. This requires at least as many samples from the environment as states multiplied by actions. This might be a problem for environments you cannot simulate. Other model-based RL algorithms may be more efficient because they can interpolate a policy with fewer simulations. MC techniques are also more sample efficient because it is likely that they will not have to visit every single state to find a region of states that produce the best return.

Finally, and probably the biggest problem of all, is that you need the transition probabilities. You either need a model of the dynamics of the environment or you can learn a model via sampling methods. If you perform an action multiple times, you can estimate the probability of landing in any states. You can look forward to this in the next chapter.

Summary

This chapter began by demonstrating that bandit testing, something that you might have used before, is a form of RL. It is limited though, because most industrial applications have many more states and delayed rewards.

Markov decision processes (MDPs) are the framework upon which all problems are built. You can reframe many problems to fit into the MDP paradigm. The key elements of an MDP are an environment that exposes an observation of its state, a reward to denote success or failure, and actions that mutate the internal state of the environment.

By calculating the expected value of next states, algorithms can choose an action that maximizes the total reward. You saw this in the inventory control simulation. I constrained the problem to make it simpler, but you can find examples of more complex scenarios in the literature.

An optimal policy is something that the agent can follow to obtain a high reward. Finding the optimal policy is difficult and the algorithms presented in this book try to achieve this in different ways.

Finally, you discovered two ways of searching through an environment's states to estimate the return: Monte Carlo (MC) and dynamic programming (DP). MC methods work well for small state spaces and when learning performance isn't important. But DP is more efficient in the sense that it can learn prospective policies immediately, as opposed to MC, which has to wait until the end of an episode.

The next chapter expands upon DP and presents one of the most common RL algorithms used in industry today.

Further Reading

- Statistics:
  - Downey, Allen. 2014. *Think Stats: Exploratory Data Analysis*. O'Reilly Media.
- A/B testing and bandit algorithms:
  - White, John. 2012. *Bandit Algorithms for Website Optimization*. O'Reilly Media.

— My Python implementation of the Bandit simulation library. (*https:// gitlab.com/winderresearch/rl/BanditsBook/*)

— A thorough tutorial on sampling methods for bandits.[1]

- MDPs:

— Puterman, Martin L. 2014. *Markov Decision Processes: Discrete Stochastic Dynamic Programming.* John Wiley & Sons.

- Bellman equations, DP and MC:

— Sutton, Richard S., and Andrew G. Barto. 2018. *Reinforcement Learning: An Introduction.* MIT Press.

- MC techniques in other domains:

— Hilpisch, Yves. 2018. *Python for Finance: Mastering Data-Driven Finance.* O'Reilly Media.

References

[1] Russo, Daniel, Benjamin Van Roy, Abbas Kazerouni, Ian Osband, and Zheng Wen. 2020. "A Tutorial on Thompson Sampling" (*https://oreil.ly/N947v*). ArXiv: 1707.02038, July.

CHAPTER 3

Temporal-Difference Learning, Q-Learning, and n-Step Algorithms

Chapter 2 introduced two key concepts for solving Markov decision processes (MDPs). Monte Carlo (MC) techniques attempt to sample their way to an estimation of a value function. They can do this without explicit knowledge of the transition probabilities and can efficiently sample large state spaces. But they need to run for an entire episode before the agent can update the policy.

Conversely, dynamic programming (DP) methods *bootstrap* by updating the policy after a single time step. But DP algorithms must have complete knowledge of the transition probabilities and visit every possible state and action before they can find an optimal policy.

A wide range of disciplines use the term *bootstrapping* to mean the entity can "lift itself up." Businesses bootstrap by raising cash without any loans. Electronic transistor circuits use bootstrapping to raise the input impedance or raise the operating voltage. In statistics and RL, bootstrapping is a sampling method that uses individual observations to estimate the statistics of the population.

Temporal-difference (TD) learning is a combination of these two approaches. It learns directly from experience by sampling, but also bootstraps. This represents a breakthrough in capability that allows agents to learn optimal strategies in any environment. Prior to this point learning was so slow it made problems intractable or you needed a full model of the environment. Do not underestimate these methods; with the tools presented in this chapter you can design sophisticated automated systems. This chapter derives TD learning and uses it to define a variety of implementations.

Formulation of Temporal-Difference Learning

Recall that policies are dependent on predicting the state-value (or action-value) function. Once the agent has a prediction of the expected return, it then needs to pick the action that maximizes the reward.

 Remember than an "expected" value is the arithmetic mean (the average) of a large number of observations of that value. For now, you can compute an average of all of the returns observed when you have visited that state in the past. And an online version of an average is an exponentially decaying moving average. But later in the book we will be using models to predict the expected return.

Equation 2-8 defined the state-value function as the expected return starting from a given state and you saw how to convert to an online algorithm in Equation 2-2. Equation 3-1 is an online realization of of the MC estimate of the state-value function. The key part is the exponentially weighted moving average estimate of the return, G. Over time, you update the state-value estimate to get closer to the true expected return and α controls the rate at which you update.

Equation 3-1. Online Monte Carlo state-value function

$$V_\pi(s) \doteq \mathbb{E}_\pi[G \,|\, s]$$
$$\leftarrow \mathbb{E}_\pi\big[V_\pi(s) + \alpha\big(G - V_\pi(s)\big)\big|s\big]$$

Recall that G is the total return from the entire trajectory. So the problem with Equation 3-1 is that you need to wait until the end of an episode before you have a value for G. So yes, it's online in the sense that it updates one step at a time, but you still have to wait until the end of the episode.

The value estimate from "Value Iteration with Dynamic Programming" on page 52 presented a slightly different interpretation of the state-value function. Instead of waiting until the end of an episode to observe the return, you can iteratively update the current state-value estimate using the discounted estimate from the next step. Equation 3-2 shows an online version of DP. It is online, by definition, because it looks one step ahead all the time. Note that this equation starts from the same definition of the state-value function as the MC version.

Equation 3-2. Online dynamic programming state-value function

$$V_\pi(s) \doteq \mathbb{E}_\pi[G|s]$$
$$\leftarrow \max_a \sum_{s',r} p(s',r \mid s,a)[r + \gamma V(s')]$$

You already know that the issue here is that you don't know the transition probabilities. But notice in the final line of Equation 3-2 that the DP version is using an interesting definition for G, $r + \gamma V(s')$. This is saying the return is equal to the current reward plus the discounted prediction of the next state. In other words, the return is the current reward, plus the estimate of all future rewards. Is it possible to use this definition of G in the Monte Carlo algorithm so you don't have to wait until the end of an episode? Yes! Look at Equation 3-3.

Equation 3-3. Temporal-difference state-value function

$$V_\pi(s) \doteq \mathbb{E}_\pi\big[V_\pi(s) + \alpha\big(r + \gamma V_\pi(s') - V_\pi(s)\big)|s\big]$$

Equation 3-3 is the TD estimate of the expected return. It combines the benefits of bootstrapping with the sampling efficiency of the MC rolling average. Note that you could reformulate this equation to estimate the action-value function as well.

Finally, I can convert this to an online algorithm, which assumes that an exponentially weighted average is a suitable estimate for the expectation operator, and results in the online TD state-value estimate in Equation 3-4.

Equation 3-4. Online temporal-difference state-value function

$$V_\pi(s) \leftarrow V_\pi(s) + \alpha\big(r + \gamma V_\pi(s') - V_\pi(s)\big)$$

Take a moment to let these equations sink in; try to interpret the equations in your own words. They say that you can learn an optimal policy, according to an arbitrary definition of reward, by dancing around an environment and iteratively updating the state-value function according to Equation 3-3. The updates to the state-value function, and therefore the policy, are immediate, which means your next action should be better than the previous.

Q-Learning

In 1989, an implementation of TD learning called *Q-learning* made it easier for mathematicians to prove convergence. This algorithm is credited with kick-starting the excitement in RL. You can reformulate Equation 3-3 to provide the action-value function (Equation 2-9). In addition, Equation 3-5 implements a simple policy by intentionally choosing the best action for a given state (in the same way as in Equation 2-10).

Equation 3-5. Q-learning online update rule to estimate the expected return

$$Q(s, a) \leftarrow Q(s, a) + \alpha \left[r + \gamma \max_{a_s \in \mathscr{A}(s)} Q(s', a_s) - Q(s, a) \right]$$

Recall that $Q(s, a)$ is the action-value function, the one from Equation 2-9 that tells you the expected return of each action. Equation 3-5 is implemented as an online update rule, which means you should iterate to refine the estimate of $Q(s, a)$ by overwriting the previous estimate. Think of everything to the right of the α as a *delta*, a measure of how wrong the estimate is compared to what actually happened. And the TD one-step look-ahead implemented in the delta allows the algorithm to project one step forward. This allows the agent to ask, "Which is the best action?"

This is the most important improvement. Previous attempts estimated the expected return for each state using only knowledge of that state. Equation 3-5 allows the agent to look ahead to see which future trajectories are optimal. This is called a *rollout*. The agent rolls out the states and actions in the trajectory (up to a maximum of the end of an episode, like for MC methods). The agent can create policies that are not only locally optimal, but optimal in the future as well. The agent can create policies that can predict the future.

This implementation of the action-value function is particularly special, though, for one simple addition. The argmax from Equation 3-5 is telling the algorithm to scan over all possible actions for that state, and pick the one with the best expected return.

This active direction of the agent is called Q-learning and is implemented in Algorithm 3-1.

Algorithm 3-1. Q-learning (off-policy TD)

1: **input:** a policy that uses the action-value function, $\pi(a \mid s, Q(s, a))$

2: Initialize $Q(s, a) \leftarrow 0$, for all $s \in \mathscr{S}, a \in \mathscr{A}(s)$

3: **loop:** for each episode

4:    Initialize environment to provide s

5:    **do:**

6:       Choose a from s using π, breaking ties randomly

7:       Take action, a, and observe r, s'

8:       $Q(s, a) \leftarrow Q(s, a) + \alpha \left[r + \gamma \max_{a_s \in \mathscr{A}(s)} Q(s', a_s) - Q(s, a) \right]$

9:       $s \leftarrow s'$

10:    **while** s is not terminal

Algorithm 3-1 shows an implementation of Q-learning. You should recognize most of this algorithm as it is closely related to Algorithm 2-3 and Algorithm 2-4. As before, step (1) begins by passing in a policy that is used to decide the probability of which action to take (which might implement ϵ-greedy exploration from Algorithm 2-1, for example). Step (2) initializes an array to store all the action-value estimates. This can be efficiently implemented with a map that automatically defaults to a set value.

Step (3) iterates over all episodes and step (5) iterates over each step in an episode. Step (4) initializes the starting state. Environments typically provide a function to "reset" the agent to a default state.

Step (6) uses the external policy function to decide which action to take. The chosen action is that with the highest probability. I have made this more explicit than it is typically presented in the literature because I want to make it clear that there is never a single optimal action. Instead, a range of actions have some probability of being optimal. Q-learning picks the action with the highest probability, which is often derived from the largest value of $Q(s, a)$. And you can implement ϵ-greedy by setting all actions to the same probability, for some proportion of the time, for example.

Step (7) uses the chosen action in the environment and observes the reward and next state. Step (8) updates the current action-value estimate for the given state and action based upon the new behavior observed in the environment. Remember that the expected return is calculated as the sum of the current reward and the expected value of the next state. So the delta is this minus the expected value of the current state. Step (8) also exponentially decays the delta using the α parameter, which helps to average over noisy updates.

Step (9) sets the next state and finally step (10) repeats this process until the environment signals that the state is terminal. With enough episodes [step (3)], the action-value estimate approaches the correct expected return.

Look at the end of Algorithm 3-1, in step (8). Notice the TD error term on the right. $\max_{a_s \in \mathscr{A}(s)} Q(s', a_s)$ looks over all possible actions for that next state and chooses the one with the highest expected return. This has nothing to do with the action chosen in step (6). Instead, the agent is planning a route using future actions.

This is the first practical example of an *off-policy* agent. The algorithm is off-policy because the update only affects the current policy. It does not use the update to direct the agent. The agent still has to derive the action from the current policy. This is a subtle, but crucial improvement that has only recently been exploited. You can find more examples of off-policy algorithms later in the book.

Another thing to note is the use of the array in step (2). It stores the expected value estimate for each state-action pair in a table, so this is often called a *tabular* method. This distinction is important because it means you cannot use Algorithm 3-1 when you have continuous states or actions, which would lead to an array of infinite length. You will see methods that can natively handle continuous states in Chapter 4 or actions in Chapter 5. You can learn how to map continuous to discrete values in Chapter 9.

SARSA

SARSA was developed shortly after Q-learning to provide a more general solution to TD learning. The main difference from Q-learning is the lack of argmax in the delta. Instead it calculates the expected return by averaging over all runs (in an online manner).

You can observe from Equation 3-6 that the name of this particular implementation of TD learning comes from the state, action, and reward requirements to calculate the action-value function. The algorithm for SARSA is shown in Algorithm 3-2.

Equation 3-6. SARSA online estimate of the action-value function

$$Q(s, a) \leftarrow Q(s, a) + \alpha(r + \gamma Q(s', a') - Q(s, a))$$

Both Algorithm 3-2 and Algorithm 3-1 have hyperparameters. The first is γ, the factor that discounts the expected return, introduced in Equation 2-7. The second is the action-value learning rate, α, which should be between 0 and 1. High values learn faster but perform less averaging.

Algorithm 3-2. SARSA (on-policy TD)

1: **input**: a policy that uses the action-value function, $\pi(a \mid s, Q(s,a))$

2: Initialize $Q(s,a) \leftarrow 0$, for all $s \in \mathscr{S}, a \in \mathscr{A}(s)$

3: **loop**: for each episode

4:     $s, a \leftarrow$ Initialize s from the environment and choose a using π

5:     **do**:

6:        Take action, a, and observe r, s'

7:        Choose a' from s' using π, breaking ties randomly

8:        $Q(s,a) \leftarrow Q(s,a) + \alpha[r + \gamma Q(s',a') - Q(s,a)]$

9:        $s \leftarrow s', a \leftarrow a'$

10:     **while** s is not terminal

Algorithm 3-2 is almost the same as Algorithm 3-1, so I won't repeat the explanation in full. One difference is that the algorithm chooses the next action, a', in step (7), before it updates the action-value function in step (8). a' updates the policy and directs the agent on the next step, which makes this an *on-policy* algorithm.

The differences between on-policy and off-policy algorithms magnify when applying function approximation, which I use in Chapter 4. But do these subtleties actually make any difference? Let me test these algorithms to show you what happens.

Q-Learning Versus SARSA

One classic environment in the RL literature is the Gridworld, a two-dimensional grid of squares. You can place various obstacles in a square. In the first example I place a deep hole along one edge of the grid. This is simulating a cliff. The goal is to train an agent to navigate around the cliff from the starting point to the goal state.

I design the rewards to promote a shortest path to the goal. Each step has a reward of −1, falling off the cliff has a reward of −100, and the goal state has a reward of 0. The cliff and the goal state are terminal states (this is where the episode ends). You can see a visualization of this environment in Figure 3-1.

To demonstrate the differences I have implemented Q-learning and SARSA on the accompanying website. There you will also find an up-to-date list of current RL frameworks. And I talk more about the practicalities of implementing RL in Chapter 9.

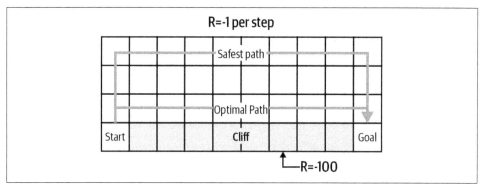

Figure 3-1. A depiction of the grid environment with a cliff along one side.[1]

If I train these agents on the environment described in Figure 3-1, I can record the episode rewards for each time step. Because of the random exploration of the agent, I need to repeat the experiment many times to average out the noise. You can see the results in Figure 3-2, in which the plots show the average sum of rewards over 100 parallel experiments.

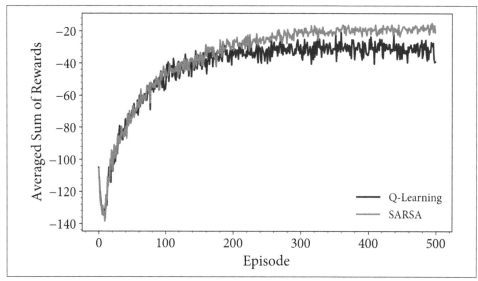

Figure 3-2. A comparison of Q-learning against SARSA for a simple grid problem. The agents were trained upon the environment in Figure 3-1. I used $\gamma \doteq 1.0$, $\epsilon \doteq 0.1$, and $\alpha \doteq 0.5$. The rewards for each episode were captured and averaged over 100 trials.

Recall that an episode is one full experiment, from the starting point to a terminal node, which in this case is falling off the cliff or reaching the end. The x-axis in Figure 3-2 is the episode number. 500 episodes mean 500 terminal events.

Figure 3-2 has two interesting regions. The first is the dip at the start of the learning. The performance of the first episode was better than the fifth. In other words, a random agent has better performance than one trained for five episodes. The reason for this is the reward structure. I specified a reward of −100 for falling off the cliff. Using a completely random agent, with the start so close to the cliff, you should expect the agent to fall off pretty much immediately. This accounts for the near −100 reward at the start. However, after a few trials, the agent has learned that falling off the cliff is not particularly enjoyable, so it attempts to steer away. Moving away results in a −1 reward per step, and because the cliff is quite long and the agent does not have much experience of reaching the goal state yet, it wastes steps then falls off the cliff anyway—a tough life. The sum of the negative reward due to the wasted steps and the eventual cliff dive results in a lower reward than when the agent started (approximately −125).

This is an interesting result. Sometimes you need to accept a lower reward in the short term to find a better reward in the long run. This is an extension of the exploitation versus exploration problem.

The second interesting result is that the SARSA result tends to have a greater reward and be less noisy than Q-learning. The reason for this can be best described by the resulting policies.

Figure 3-3 shows example policies for Q-learning and SARSA. Note that the specific policy may change between trials due to the random exploration. The SARSA agent tends to prefer the "safe" path, far away from the cliff. This is because occasionally, the ϵ-greedy action will randomly kick the agent over the cliff. Recall that SARSA is calculating the *average* expected return. Hence, on average, the expected return is better far away from the cliff because the chances of receiving three random kicks toward the cliff are slim.

However, the Q-learning algorithm does not predict the expected return. It predicts the best possible return from that state. And the best one, when there is no random kick, is straight along the cliff edge. A risky but, according to the definition of the reward, optimal policy.

This also explains the difference in variance. Because Q-learning is metaphorically on a knife edge, it sometimes falls off. This causes a massive but sporadic loss. The SARSA policy is far away from the cliff edge and rarely falls, so the rewards are more stable.

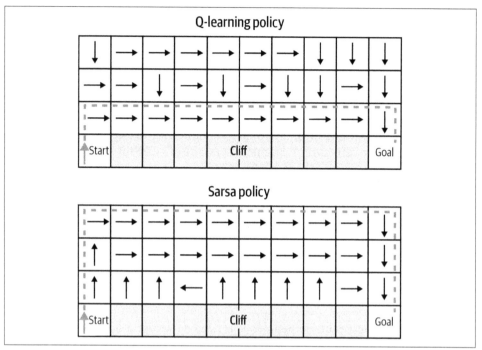

Figure 3-3. The policies derived by Q-learning and SARSA agents. Q-learning tends to prefer the optimal route. SARSA prefers the safe route.

Case Study: Automatically Scaling Application Containers to Reduce Cost

Software *containers* are changing the way that distributed applications are deployed and orchestrated in the cloud. Their primary benefit is the encapsulation of all runtime dependencies and the atomicity of the deployable unit. This means that applications can be dynamically scaled both horizontally, through duplication, and vertically, by increasing the allocated resources. Traditional scaling strategies rely on fixed, threshold-based heuristics like utilized CPU or memory usage and are likely to be suboptimal. Using RL to provide a scaling policy can reduce cost and improve performance.

Rossi, Nardelli, and Cardellini proposed an experiment to use both Q-learning and a model-based approach to provide optimal policies for scaling both vertically and horizontally.[2] They then implemented these algorithms in a live Docker Swarm environment.

Rossi et al. begin by using a generic black-box container that performs an arbitrary task. The agent interacts with the application through the confines of a Markov decision process.

The state is defined as the number of containers, the CPU utilization, and the CPU allocation to each container. They quantize the continuous variables into a fixed number of bins.

The action is defined as a change to the horizontal or vertical scale of the application. They can add or remove a replica, add or remove allocated CPUs, or both. They perform two experiments: the first simplifies the action space to only allow a single vertical or horizontal change, while the second allows both.

The reward is quite a complex function to balance the number of deployment changes, the latency, and utilization. These metrics have arbitrary weightings to allow the user to specify what is important to their application.

Although Rossi et al. initially used a simulator to develop their approach, they thankfully tested their algorithm in real life using Docker Swarm. They implemented a controller to monitor, analyze, plan, and execute changes to the application. Then they simulated user requests using a varying demand pattern to stress the application and train the algorithms to maximize the reward.

There are several interesting results from this experiment. First, they found that the algorithms were quicker to learn when they used a smaller action space in the experiment where the agent had to choose to scale vertically or horizontally, not both. This is a common result; smaller state and action spaces mean that the agent has to explore less and can find an optimal policy faster. During the simple experiment both the Q-learning and model-based approaches performed similarly. With the more complex action space, the model-based approach learned quicker and the results were much better.

The second interesting result is that using a model, bespoke to this challenge, improves learning and final performance. Their model-based approach incorporates transition probabilities into the value approximation, much like you did in "Inventory Control" on page 36, so the algorithm has prior knowledge of the effect of an action. However, their model implicitly biases the results toward that model. This is shown in the results when the model-based approach prefers to scale vertically more than horizontally. In most modern orchestrators it is much easier to scale horizontally, so this would be a detriment. The moral of this is that yes, model-based approaches introduce prior knowledge and significantly speed up learning, but you have to be sure that the model represents the true dynamics of the system and there is no implicit bias toward a certain policy.

The net result in either case is a significant improvement over static, threshold-based policies. Both algorithms improved utilization by an order of magnitude (which should translate into costs savings of an order of magnitude) while maintaining similar levels of latency.

You could improve this work in a number of ways. I would love to see this example implemented on Kubernetes and I would also like to see rewards using the real cost of the resources being used, rather than some measure of utilization. I would improve the state and action representations, too: using function approximation would remove the need to discretize the state, and a continuous action could choose better vertical scaling parameters. I would also be tempted to split the problem as well, because scaling vertically and horizontally has very different costs; in Kubernetes at least, it is much easier to scale horizontally.

Industrial Example: Real-Time Bidding in Advertising

Contrary to sponsored advertising, where advertisers set fixed bids, in real-time bidding (RTB) you can set a bid for every individual impression. When a user visits a website that supports ads, this triggers an auction where advertisers bid for an *impression*. Advertisers must submit bids within a period of time, where 100 ms is a common limit.

The advertising platform provides contextual and behavioral information to the advertiser for evaluation. The advertiser uses an automated algorithm to decide how much to bid based upon the context. In the long term, the platform's products must deliver a satisfying experience to maintain the advertising revenue stream. But advertisers want to maximize some key performance indicator (KPI)—for example, the number of impressions or click-through rate (CTR)—for the least cost.

RTB presents a clear action (the bid), state (the information provided by the platform), and agent (the bidding algorithm). Both platforms and advertisers can use RL to optimize for their definition of reward. As you can imagine, the raw bid-level impression data is valuable. But in 2013 a Chinese marketing company called iPinYou released a dataset hoping that researchers could improve the state of the art in bidding algorithms.[3]

Defining the MDP

I will show how simple RL algorithms, like Q-learning and SARSA, are able to provide a solution to the RTB problem. The major limitation of these algorithms is that they need a simple state space. Large or continuous states are not well suited because agents need many samples to form a reasonable estimate of the expected value (according to the law of large numbers). Continuous states cause further problems because of the discrete sampling. For tabular algorithms, you have to simplify and constrain the state to make it tractable.

I propose to create an RTB algorithm that maximizes the number of impressions for a given budget. I split the data into batches and each batch has a budget. The state consists of the average bid that the agent can make given the number of auctions remaining. For example, if the budget is 100 and the batch size is 10, then at the first auction the state is $100/10 = 10$. The purpose of this feature is to inform the agent that I want to spread the bids throughout the batch. I don't want the agent to spend the budget all at once. The agent will receive a reward of one if they win the auction and zero otherwise. To further reduce the number of states I round and truncate the real number to an integer. Later you will see examples of agents that are able to fit a function to the state to allow it to capture far more complex data.

This highlights an important lesson. The formulation of the MDP is arbitrary. You can imagine many different pieces of information to include in the state or create another reward. You have to design the MDP according to the problem you are trying to solve, within the constraints of the algorithm. Industrial data scientists rarely alter the implementation details of a machine learning algorithm; they are off-the-shelf. RL practitioners spend most of the time improving the representation of the state (typically called feature engineering) and refining the definition of reward. Industrial ML is similar, where a data scientist spends the majority of their time improving data or reformulating problems.

Results of the Real-Time Bidding Environments

I created two new environments. The first is a static RTB environment I built for testing. Each episode is a batch of 100 auctions and I fix the budget at 10,000. If the agent bids a value of greater than or equal to 100, it will win the auction. Hence, the optimal policy for this environment is to bid 100 at each auction to receive a reward of 100. The agent can increase or decrease the current bid by 50%, 10% or 0%. You can see the results in Figure 3-4.

This isn't very realistic but demonstrates that the algorithm implementations are working as expected. Despite learning the optimal policy, this plot does not reach a reward of 100 because of the high ϵ. That is, while obtaining these rewards the agent is still taking random (often incorrect) actions. There is also a subtle difference between SARSA and Q-learning, because SARSA prefers the safer path of slightly overbidding, which means it runs out of budget quicker than Q-learning; this is the same as what you saw in "Q-Learning Versus SARSA" on page 65.

The second environment uses real bidding data. If you follow the instructions from the make-ipinyou-data (*https://oreil.ly/uZ-xk*) repository, you will have directories that represent advertisers. Inside, these files contain the predicted CTR, whether a user actually clicked the ad, and the price of the winning bid. The batch size and the agent's actions are the same as before. The main difference is that the cost of winning the auction is now variable. The goal, as before, is to train an agent to win the most impressions for the given budget. I also make the situation more difficult by setting the agent's initial bid too low. The agent will have to learn to increase its bid. You can see the results in Figure 3-5.

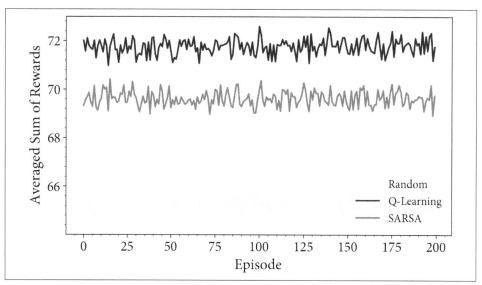

Figure 3-4. The average reward obtained by SARSA, Q-learning, and random agents in a simple, static, real-time bidding environment.

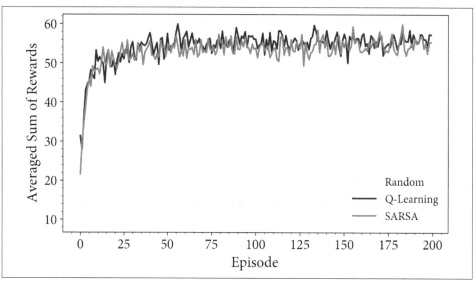

Figure 3-5. The average reward obtained by SARSA, Q-learning, and random agents in an environment based upon real data. The agent obtains a greater reward as episodes pass. The reason is that the agent has learned, through random exploration, that increasing the bid leads to greater rewards. Allowing the agent to continue learning is likely to increase the reward further.

Further Improvements

The previous example constrained the RTB problem because I needed to simplify the state space. Tabular methods, such as Q-learning and SARSA, struggle when the state space is large; an agent would have to sample a huge, possibly infinite, number of states. Later in the book you will see methods that build a model of the state space, rather than a lookup table.

Another concern is the choice of reward. I chose to use the impression count because this led to learning on each time step and therefore speeds up learning. It might be beneficial to instead use user clicks as a reward signal, since advertisers are often only interested if a user actually clicks their ad.

I also limited the amount of data used in training to allow the learning to complete in a matter of seconds; otherwise it takes hours to run. In an industrial setting you should use as much data as you can to help the agent generalize to new examples.

The initial bid setting is inappropriate because I am forcing the agent to learn from an extreme. I did this to show that the agent can learn to cope with new situations, like when a new, well-funded advertiser attempts to capture the market by outbidding you. A more realistic scenario might be to not reset the initial bid and carry it through from the previous episode.

To improve the resiliency and stability of the agent you should always apply constraints. For example, you could use *error clipping* to prevent outliers from shifting the expected return estimates too far in one go (see "PPO's clipped objective" on page 170 for an example of an algorithm that does this).

One paper takes batching one step further by merging a set of auctions into a single aggregate auction. The agent sets the bid level at the start and keeps it the same throughout the batch. The benefit is that this reduces the underlying volatility in the data through averaging.

The data exhibits temporal differences, too. At 3 A.M. fewer auctions take place and fewer advertisers are available compared to at 3 P.M. These two time periods require fundamentally different agents. Including the user's time in the agent state allows the agent to learn time-dependent policies.

The actions used within this environment were discrete alterations to the bid. This reduces the size of the state-action lookup table. Allowing the agent to set the value of the alteration is preferable. It is even possible to allow the agent to set the bid directly using algorithms that can output a continuously variable action.

That was a long list of improvements and I'm sure you can think of a lot more. But let me be clear that choosing the RL algorithm is often one of the easiest steps. This example demonstrates that in industry you will spend most of your time formulating an appropriate MDP or improving the features represented in the state.

Extensions to Q-Learning

Researchers can improve upon TD algorithms in a wide variety of ways. This section investigates some of the most important improvements specifically related to SARSA and Q-learning. Some improvements are better left until later chapters.

Double Q-Learning

Equation 3-5 updates $Q(s, a)$ using a notion of the best action, which in this case is the action that produces the highest expected reward. The problem with this is that the current maximum may be a statistical anomaly. Consider the case where the agent has just started learning. The first time the agent receives a positive reward, it will update the action-value estimate. Subsequent episodes will repeatedly choose the same set of actions. This could create a loop where the agent keeps making suboptimal decisions, because of that initial bad update.

One way to solve this problem is by using two action-value functions, in other words, two lookup tables.[4] The agent then uses one to update the other and vice versa. This produces an unbiased estimate of $Q(s, a)$, because it is not feeding back into itself. Typically the choice of which combination to update, for example updating Q_1 with the action-value estimate of Q_2, is random.

Delayed Q-Learning

In probably the best named computational theory of all time, *probably approximately correct* (PAC) learning states that for a given hypothesis, you need a specific number of samples to solve the problem within an acceptable error bound. In 2006 mathematicians developed a Q-learning-based algorithm based on this principle called *delayed Q-learning*.[5]

Rather than update the action-value function every time the agent visits that state-action pair, it buffers the rewards. Once the agent has visited a certain number of times, it then updates the main action-value function in one big hurrah.

The idea, due to the law of large numbers again, is that one estimate of the expected return could be noisy. Therefore, you should not update the main action-value table with potentially erroneous values, because the agent uses this to direct future agents. You should wait for a while and update only when there is a representative sample.

The downside of this approach is that it leads to a certain amount of delay before you begin to get good results. But once you do, learning is very quick, because the agent is not blighted by noise.

In a sense, this is just a way to prolong the exploration period. You get a similar effect if you anneal the ϵ in ϵ-greedy or use UCB (see "Improving the ϵ-greedy Algorithm" on page 33). A similar implementation called directed delayed Q-learning also integrates an exploration bonus for action-state pairs that have not been well sampled.[6]

Comparing Standard, Double, and Delayed Q-learning

Figure 3-6 compares the performance of standard, double, and delayed Q-learning on the grid environment. The double Q-learning implementation results in a better policy than standard Q-learning as shown in the higher average result (it will keep on improving if you give it more time; compare with Figure 3-2). For the delayed Q-learning implementation, the apparent discontinuities are worrying with respect to robustness, but the end result is very impressive. This is because the aggregation of many updates provides a more robust estimate of the action-value function. The flat region at the top is because delayed Q-learning intentionally stops learning after a certain number of updates.

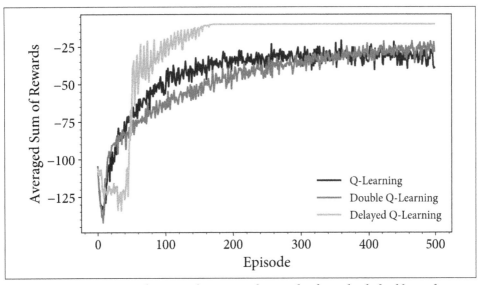

Figure 3-6. A comparison between the averaged rewards of standard, double, and delayed Q-learning on the grid environment.

Opposition Learning

In an interesting addition, Tizhoosh attempted to improve learning performance by intentionally sampling the opposite of whatever the policy chooses.[7] Known as Opposition-Based RL, the Q-learning inspired implementation intentionally samples and updates the opposite action as well as the action chosen by the current policy.

The gist of this idea is that an opposite action can reveal a revolutionary or counter-factual move, an action that the policy would never have recommended.

If a natural opposite exists then this is likely to yield faster learning in the early stages, because it prevents the worst-case scenario. However, if none exists then you might as well sample randomly, which amounts to a normal update and a random one. If that is acceptable, I could cheat and sample all actions.

The main issue with this is that in many environments you can't test multiple actions at the same time. For example, imagine you tried to use this algorithm on a robot. It would have to take the opposite (or random) action, move back, then take the policy action. The act of moving back may be imprecise and introduce errors. This also doesn't map well to continuous domains. A better approach is to prefer using multiple agents or separate critical policies to generate counteractions.

n-Step Algorithms

This chapter has considered a one-step lookahead. But why stop there? Why not have a two-step lookahead? Or more? That is precisely what *n*-step algorithms are all about. They provide a generalization of *unrolling* the expected value estimate to any number of steps. This is beneficial because it bridges the gap between dynamic programming and Monte Carlo.

For some applications it makes sense to look several steps ahead before making a choice. In the grid example, if the agent can see that the current trajectory is leading the agent to fall off the cliff, the agent can take avoiding action now, before it becomes too late. In a sense, the agent is looking further into the future.

The essence of the idea is to extend one of the TD implementations, Equation 3-3 for example, to iterate over any number of future states. Recall that the lookahead functionality came from DP (Equation 3-3), which combined the current reward with the prediction of the next state. I can extend this to look at the next two rewards and the expected return of the state after, as shown in Equation 3-7.

Equation 3-7. 2-step expected return

$$G_{t:t+2} \doteq r + \gamma r' + \gamma^2 Q(s'', a'')$$

I have added extra notation, $t + 2$, to denote that Equation 3-7 is looking two steps ahead. Equation 3-3 is equivalent to $G_{t:t+1}$. The key is that Equation 3-7 is using not just the next reward, but the reward after that. Similarly, it is not using the next action-value estimate, but the one after. You can generalize this into Equation 3-8.

Equation 3-8. n-step expected return

$$G_{t:t+n} \doteq r + \gamma r' + \cdots + \gamma^{n-1} r_{n-1} + \gamma^n Q(s_n, a_n)$$

You can augment the various TD update rules (Equation 3-6, for example) to use this new DP update. Equation 3-9 shows the equation for the action-value update function.

Equation 3-9. n-step TD update rule to estimate the expected return using the action-value function

$$Q(s, a) \leftarrow Q(s, a) + \alpha\left(G_{t:t+n} - Q(s, a)\right)$$

Equation 3-9 shows the n-step update for the action-value function. You can rewrite this to present the state-value function or make it Q-learning by adding $\mathrm{argmax}_{a_s \in \mathcal{A}(s)}$ inside $G_{t:t+n}$. In some references you will see further mathematical notation to denote that the new value of the action-value estimate, Q, is dependent on the previous estimate. For example, you should update Q before you use Q'. I have left these out to simplify the equation.

But this idea does cause a problem. The rewards are available *after* the agent has transitioned into the state. So the agent has to follow the trajectory, buffer the rewards, and then go back and update the original state t steps ago.

When my daughters are asleep and dreaming, you can hear them reliving the past day. They are retrieving their experience, reprocessing it with the benefit of hindsight, and learning from it. RL agents can do the same. Some algorithms use an *experience replay* buffer, to allow the agent to cogitate over its previous actions and learn from them. This is a store of the trajectory of the current episode. The agent can look back to calculate Equation 3-8.

The n-step algorithm in Algorithm 3-3 is functionally the same as Algorithm 3-2, but looks more complicated because it needs to iterate backward over the replay buffer and can only do so once you have enough samples. For example, in 2-step SARSA, you need to wait until the third step before you can go back and update the first, because you need to observe the second reward.

Algorithm 3-3. n-step SARSA

1: **input**: a policy that uses the action-value function, $\pi(a \mid s, Q(s, a))$,
   step size $0 < \alpha < 1$, a positive integer n

2: Initialize $Q(s, a) \leftarrow 0$, for all $s \in \mathscr{S}, a \in \mathscr{A}(s)$

3: **loop** for each episode:

4:     Initialize $T \leftarrow \infty$, $t \leftarrow 0$, replay buffers for S and A, and initial state s

5:     Choose a from s using π, breaking ties randomly

6:     **do**:

7:       **if** $t < T$:

8:         Take action, a, and observe r, s'

9:         **if** s' is terminal:

10:           $T \leftarrow t + 1$

11:         **else**:

12:           Choose a' from s' using π, breaking ties randomly

13:       $\tau \leftarrow t - n + 1$

14:       **if** $\tau \geq 0$:

15:         $G \leftarrow \sum\limits_{i \leftarrow \tau + 1}^{\min\,(\tau + n,\, T)} \gamma^{i - \tau - 1} r_i$

16:         **if** $\tau + n < T$:

17:           $G \leftarrow G + \gamma^n Q(s_{\tau + n}, a_{\tau + n})$

18:         $Q(s_\tau, a_\tau) \leftarrow Q(s_\tau, a_\tau) + \alpha[G - Q(s_\tau, a_\tau)]$

19:       $t \leftarrow t + 1, s \leftarrow s', a \leftarrow a'$

20:     **while** $\tau \neq T - 1$

Algorithm 3-3 looks scary, but I promise that the extra pseudocode is to iterate over the replay buffers. The idea is exactly the same as SARSA, except it is looking forward over multiple time steps, which means you have to buffer the experience. The apostrophe notation breaks down a little too, because you have to index over previous actions, states, and rewards. I think this algorithm highlights how much implementation complexity goes into some of these algorithms—and this is a simple algorithm.

Step (1) begins as usual, where you must pass in a policy and settings that control the number of steps in the n-step and the action-value step size. Step (2) initializes the action-value table. Step (3) iterates over each loop and step (4) initializes the T variable that represents the step number at the end of the episode, t, which represents the current step number, the replay buffers, and s, the default episode state. Step (5) selects the first action based upon the default state and the current policy and step (6) is the beginning of the main loop.

Most of that is the same as before. Step (7) differs by checking to see if the episode has already ended. If it has, you don't want to take any more actions. Until then, step (8) performs the action in the environment. Steps (9) and (10) check to see if that action led to the end of the episode. If yes, then set the variable T to denote the step at which the episode came to an end. Otherwise step (12) chooses the next action.

Step (13) updates a variable that points to the state-action pair that was n steps ago. Initially, this will be before $t = 0$, so it checks to prevent index-out-of-bound errors in step (14). If $\tau > = 0$ then Algorithm 3-3 begins to update the action-value functions with the expected return.

Step (15) calculates the reward part of the n-step expected return defined in Equation 3-7. Step (16) checks to see if the algorithm is past the end of the episode, plus n. If not, add the prediction of the next state to the expected return, as defined on the righthand side of Equation 3-7.

Step (18) is the same as before; it updates the action-value function using the n-step expected value estimate. Finally, step (19) increments the step counter. The algorithm returns to the main loop in step (20) after updating all steps up to termination.

n-Step Algorithms on Grid Environments

I implemented an n-step SARSA agent on the grid environment and set the number of steps to 2 and 4. All other settings are the same as the standard SARSA implementation. You can see the difference between standard and n-step SARSA in Figure 3-7.

The one thing that is obvious from Figure 3-7 is that the n-step algorithms are capable of learning optimal policies faster than their 1-step counterparts. This intuitively makes sense. If you are able to observe into the "future" (in quotes because the reality is that you are delaying updates) then you can learn optimal trajectories earlier. The optimal value for n depends on the problem and should be treated as a hyperparameter that requires tuning. The main drawback of these methods is the extra computational and memory burden.

This section focused upon on-policy SARSA. Of course, you can implement off-policy and non-SARSA implementations of n-step TD learning, too. You can read more about this in the books listed in "Further Reading" on page 85.

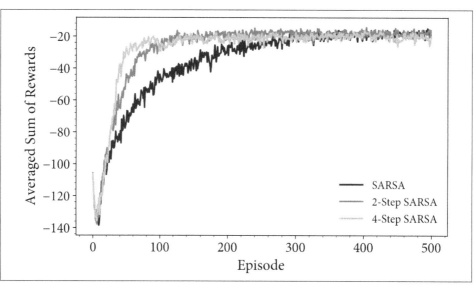

Figure 3-7. A comparison between the averaged rewards of standard and n-step SARSA agents on the grid environment. Note how the agents that use multiple steps learn optimal trajectories faster.

Eligibility Traces

"n-Step Algorithms" on page 76 developed a method to provide the benefits of both bootstrapping and forward planning. An extension to this idea is to average over different values of *n*, an average of 2-step and 4-step SARSA, for example. You can take this idea to the extreme and average over all values of *n*.

Of course, iterating over different *n*-step updates (Equation 3-9) adds a significant amount of computational complexity. Also, as you increase *n* the agent will have to wait for longer and longer before it can start updating the first time step. In the extreme this will be as bad as waiting until the end of the episode before the agent can make any updates (like MC methods).

The problem with the algorithms seen so far is that they attempt to look forward in time, which is impossible, so instead they delay updates and pretend like they are looking forward. One solution is to look backward in time, rather than forward. If you attempt to hike up a mountain in the fastest time possible, you can try several routes, then contemplate your actions to find the best trajectory.

In other words, the agent requires a new mechanism to mark a state-action pair as tainted so that it can come back and update that state with future updates. You can use *tracers* to mark the location of something of interest. Radioactive tracers help to diagnose illnesses and direct medicine. Geophysicists inject them into rock during hydraulic fracturing to provide evidence of the size and location of cracks. You can use a virtual tracer to remind the agent of which state-action estimates need updating in the future.

Next, you need to update state-action function with an average of all the n-step returns. A one-step update is the TD error update (Equation 3-6). You can approximate an average using an exponentially weighted moving average, which is the online equivalent of an average (as shown in "Policy Evaluation: The Value Function" on page 26). Interested readers can find a proof that this is equivalent to averaging many n-step returns and that it converges in "Further Reading" on page 85.

Combining the one-step update with the moving average, coupled with the idea of a tracer, provides an online SARSA that has zero delay (no direct n-step lookahead) but all the benefits of forward planning and bootstrapping. Since you have seen the mathematics before, let me dive into the algorithm in Algorithm 3-4.

Algorithm 3-4. SARSA(λ)

1: **input**: a policy that uses the action-value function, $\pi(a \mid s, Q(s, a))$,

    step size $0 < \alpha < 1$, a tracer decay rate $0 \leq \lambda \leq 1$

2: Initialize $Q(s, a) \leftarrow 0$, for all $s \in \mathcal{S}, a \in \mathcal{A}(s)$

3: **loop** for each episode:

4:     Initialize $z(s, a) \leftarrow 0$, for all $s \in \mathcal{S}, a \in \mathcal{A}(s)$, and default state s

5:     Choose a from s using π, breaking ties randomly

6:     **do**:

7:         Take action, a, and observe r, s'

8:         Choose a' from s' using π, breaking ties randomly

10:         $\delta \leftarrow r + \gamma Q(s', a') - Q(s, a)$

11:         $z(s, a) \leftarrow z(s, a) + 1$

12:         **for** each $s \in \mathcal{S}$:

13:             **for** each $a \in \mathcal{A}(s)$:

14:                 $Q(s, a) \leftarrow Q(s, a) + \alpha \delta z(s, a)$

15:                 $z(s, a) \leftarrow \gamma \lambda z(s, a)$

16:         $s \leftarrow s', a \leftarrow a'$

17:     **while** s is not terminal

Most of the code in Algorithm 3-4 is repeating Algorithm 3-2 so I won't repeat myself. The differences begin in step (10), where it temporarily calculates the one-step TD error for use later. Step (11) implements a tracer by incrementing a cell in a table that represents the current state-action pair. This is how the algorithm "remembers" which states and actions it touched during the trajectory.

Steps (12) and (13) loop over all states and actions to update the action-value function in step (14). Here, the addition is that it weights the TD error by the current tracer value, which exponentially decays in step (15). In other words, if the agent touched the state-action pair a long time ago there is a negligible update. If it touched it in the last time step, there is a large update.

Think about this. If you went to university a long time ago, how much does that contribute to what you are doing at work today? It probably influenced you a little, but not a lot. You can control the amount of influence with the λ parameter.

Figure 3-8 shows the results of this implementation in comparison to standard SARSA. Note how the λ parameter has a similar effect to altering the n in n-step SARSA. Higher values tend toward an MC regime, where the number of steps averaged over increases. Lower values tend toward pure TD, which is equivalent to the original SARSA implementation.

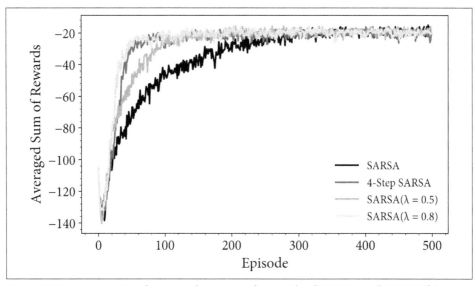

Figure 3-8. A comparison between the averaged rewards of SARSA and SARSA(λ) agents on the grid environment. All settings are the same as in Figure 3-7.

In case you were wondering, the term *eligibility* comes from the idea that the tracer decides whether a specific state-action pair in the action-value function is eligible for an update. If the tracer for a pair has a nonzero value, then it will receive some proportion of the reward.

Eligibility traces provide a computationally efficient, controllable hyperparameter that smoothly varies the learning regime between TD and MC. But it does raise the problem of where to place this parameter. Researchers have not found a theoretical basis for the choice of λ but experience provides empirical rules of thumb. In tasks with many steps per episode it makes sense to update not only the current step, but all the steps that led to that point. Like bowling lane bumpers that guide the ball toward the pins, updating the action-value estimates based upon the previous trajectory helps guide the movement of future agents. In general then, for nontrivial tasks, it pays to use $\lambda > 0$.

However, high values of λ mean that early state-action pairs receive updates even though it is unlikely they contributed to the current result. Consider the grid example with $\lambda \doteq 1$, which makes it equivalent to an MC agent. The first step will always receive an update, because that is the single direction in which it can move. This means that no matter where the agent ends up, all of the actions in the first state will converge to roughly the same value, because they are all affected by any future movement. This prevents it from learning any viable policy. In nontrivial problems you should keep $\lambda < 1$.

The one downside is the extra computational complexity. The traces require another buffer. You also need to iterate over all states and actions on each step to see if there is an eligible update for them. You can mitigate this issue by using a much smaller eligibility list, since the majority of state-action pairs will have a near-zero value. In general, the benefits outweigh the minor computational burden.

Extensions to Eligibility Traces

At risk of laboring the point, researchers have developed many tweaks to the basic algorithm. Some have gained more notoriety than others and of course, deciding which improvements are important is open to interpretation. You could take any of the previous tweaks and apply them here. For instance, you can generate a Q-learning equivalent and apply all the tweaks in "Extensions to Q-Learning" on page 74. But let me present a selection of the more publicized extensions that specifically relate to eligibility traces.

Watkins's Q(λ)

 Much of the literature implements Q(λ) as an off-policy algorithm with importance sampling. So far in this book I have only considered standard, noncorrected off-policy versions. This is discussed later in "Importance Sampling" on page 146.

One simple empirical improvement to the standard Q(λ), which implements an argmax on the TD update, is to reset the eligibility trace when the agent encounters the first nongreedy action. This makes sense, because you do not want to penalize previous steps for a wrong turn when that turn was part of the exploration of new states. Note that this doesn't make sense in a SARSA setting because SARSA's whole goal is to explore all states and average over them. If you implemented this it would perform slightly worse than standard SARSA(λ) because you are limiting the opportunities to update.

Fuzzy Wipes in Watkins's Q(λ)

Consider what would happen if you wiped all your memories right before you tried something new. Do you think that this would result in optimal learning? Probably not. Wiping the memory of all traces whenever the agent performs an exploratory move, like in Watkins's Q(λ), is extreme.

Fuzzy learning instead tries to decide whether wiping is a good idea.[8] This recent work proposes the use of decision rules to ascertain whether the eligibility trace for that state-action pair should be wiped. This feels a little arbitrary, so I expect researchers to discover new, simpler alternatives soon. Despite the heavy handed approach, it does appear to speed up learning.

Speedy Q-Learning

Speedy Q-learning is like eligibility traces, but is implemented in a slightly different way.[9] It updates the action-value function by exponentially decaying a sum of the previous and current TD update. The result is an averaging over one-step TD updates. But it does not update previously visited states with future rewards. In other words, it provides improvements over standard Q-learning, but will not learn as quickly as methods that can adaptively bootstrap all previous state-action pairs.

Accumulating Versus Replacing Eligibility Traces

Research suggests that the method of accumulating eligibility traces, rather than replacing, can have some impact on learning performance.[10] An accumulating tracer is like that implemented in Algorithm 3-4. The tracer for a state-action pair is incremented by some value. If an agent were to repeatedly visit the state, like if this state-action pair was on the optimal trajectory, then the tracer becomes very large. This represents a feedback loop that biases future learning toward the same state. This is good in some sense, since it will learn very quickly, but bad in another because it will suppress exploration.

But consider the situation where the environment is not an MDP, for example, a partially observable MDP, where the state is not fully observable like when your agent can't see around corners, or a *semi-MDP*, where transitions are stochastic. I will come back to these in Chapter 8. In these situations, it might not be optimal to blindly follow the same path, because the trajectory could have been noisy. Instead, it makes sense to trust the exploration and therefore replace the trace, rather than accumulate it. With that said, the experimental results show that the difference in performance is small and is likely to be inconsequential for most applications. In practice, hyperparameter tuning has a much greater influence.

Summary

This chapter summarized the most important research that happened throughout the 1990s and 2000s. Q-learning, in particular, is an algorithm that is used extensively within industry today. It has proven itself to be robust, easy to implement, and fast to learn.

Eligibility traces perform well, better than Q-learning in most cases, and will see extensive use in the future. Recent research suggests that humans also use eligibility traces as a way of solving the credit assignment problem.[11]

Remember that you can combine any number of these or the previous tweaks to create a new algorithm. For example, there is double delayed Q-learning, which as you can imagine, is a combination of double and delayed Q-learning.[12] You could add eligibility traces and fuzzy wipes to generate a better performing algorithm.

The downside of the algorithms in this chapter is that they use a table to store the action-value or state-value estimates. This means that they only work in discrete state spaces. You can work around this problem using feature engineering (see "Policy Engineering" on page 268), but the next chapter investigates how to handle continuous state spaces via function approximation.

Further Reading

- *n*-step TD-learning implementations and eligibility traces proof:
  - Sutton, Richard S., and Andrew G. Barto. 2018. *Reinforcement Learning: An Introduction*. MIT Press.

References

[1] Example adapted from Sutton, Richard S., and Andrew G. Barto. 2018. *Reinforcement Learning: An Introduction*. MIT Press.

[2] Rossi, Fabiana, Matteo Nardelli, and Valeria Cardellini. 2019. "Horizontal and Vertical Scaling of Container-Based Applications Using Reinforcement Learning" (*https://oreil.ly/tGvuN*). In *2019 IEEE 12th International Conference on Cloud Computing (CLOUD)*, 329–38.

[3] Zhang, Weinan, et al. 2014. "Real-Time Bidding Benchmarking with IPinYou Dataset" (*https://oreil.ly/l9O_v*). ArXiv:1407.7073, July.

[4] Hasselt, Hado V. 2010. "Double Q-Learning" (*https://oreil.ly/akRzg*).

[5] Strehl, et al. 2006. "PAC Model-Free Reinforcement Learning" (*https://oreil.ly/Z0mxa*). *ICML '06: Proceedings of the 23rd International Conference on Machine Learning*, 881–88.

[6] Oh, Min-hwan, and Garud Iyengar. 2018. "Directed Exploration in PAC Model-Free Reinforcement Learning" (*https://oreil.ly/zM1E7*). ArXiv:1808.10552, August.

[7] Tizhoosh, Hamid. 2006. "Opposition-Based Reinforcement Learning." JACIII 10 (January): 578–85.

[8] Shokri, Matin, et al. 2019. "Adaptive Fuzzy Watkins: A New Adaptive Approach for Eligibility Traces in Reinforcement Learning" (*https://oreil.ly/8nW3P*). *International Journal of Fuzzy Systems*.

[9] Ghavamzadeh, Mohammad, et al. 2011. "Speedy Q-Learning" (*https://oreil.ly/oyIAo*). In *Advances in Neural Information Processing Systems* 24.

[10] Leng, Jinsong, et al. 2008. "Experimental Analysis of Eligibility Traces Strategies in Temporal-Difference Learning" (*https://oreil.ly/OOEF0*). *IJKESDP* 1: 26–39.

[11] Lehmann, Marco, He Xu, Vasiliki Liakoni, Michael Herzog, Wulfram Gerstner, and Kerstin Preuschoff. 2017. "One-Shot Learning and Behavioral Eligibility Traces in Sequential Decision Making" (*https://oreil.ly/syD_E*). ArXiv:1707.04192, July.

[12] Abed-alguni, Bilal H., and Mohammad Ashraf Ottom. 2018. "Double delayed Q-learning." *International Journal of Artificial Intelligence* 16(2): 41–59.

CHAPTER 4

Deep Q-Networks

Tabular reinforcement learning (RL) algorithms, such as Q-learning or SARSA, represent the expected value estimates of a state, or state-action pair, in a lookup table (also known as a Q-table or Q-values). You have seen that this approach works well for small, discrete states. But when the number of states increases the size of the table increases exponentially. The state space becomes infinitely large with continuous variables.

Actions have a similar problem. In an action-value version of Q-learning or SARSA the number of actions increases the table size. And again, if the actions are continuous then the table becomes infinite. But continuous actions are desirable in many applications. In the advertisement bidding example in "Industrial Example: Real-Time Bidding in Advertising" on page 70, it is better if the agent could suggest a bid value directly, rather than rely on a predefined set of discrete alterations.

The most common solution to these problems is to replace the table with an approximation function. Rather than attempting to store a map of how states and actions alter the expected return, you can build a function that approximates it. At each time step the agent looks at the current state-action pair and predicts the expected value. This is a regression problem.

You can choose from the wide variety of regression algorithms to solve this. But state-action pairs tend to be highly nonlinear and often discontinuous. For example, imagine the state space of the cliff environment. The expected values should converge so that states near the goal are high and states further away decrease in proportion to the discounting and reward scheme. But there will be a large discontinuity next to the cliff. If the agent uses a linear model to approximate the state-value function, then the large negative reward of the cliff acts like an outlier when compared to the rest of the state space and biases the model.

However, simple models are often preferred in industry because they are well understood, robust, and easy to interpret. If you wish to use a simple model, you must take steps to ensure your state space is representative. To achieve this you could randomly sample your environment and store the states. You can then perform regression offline to evaluate how well your model fits the data.

The most commonly used model is a *deep artificial neural network*. The network uses the state of the environment as an input and the output is the expected value of each action. The approximation is capable of handling huge and complex state spaces. I delay discussing continuous actions until later in the book.

Deep Learning Architectures

To create an *artificial neural network* (ANN, or NN for short) you can create a stack of linear approximators and mutate each with a nonlinear activation function. Then you train the network to find the optimal weights via regression. The result is a model that is capable of approximating any arbitrary function.

This is the promise of deep learning (DL), which is the moniker for "deep" stacks of ANNs. Alan Turing might have described them as one of his "universal computing machines." By altering the structure and hyperparameters of the ANN, agents can model an arbitrary state space.

I will briefly review DL to set the context for deep RL. But this is not a book on deep learning or machine learning; if you wish to learn more please refer to the references in "Further Reading" on page 112.

Fundamentals

NNs are comprised of many interconnected functions, called *neurons*, that act in unison to solve classification or regression problems. A layer is a set of neurons with inputs and outputs. You can stack layers on top of each other to allow the ANN to learn abstractions of the data. The layer connected to the data is the *input layer*. The layer producing the outputs is the *output layer*. All layers in between are *hidden layers*.

The value of each connection, where a connection is between inputs, other neurons, or outputs, is multiplied by a *weight*. The neuron sums the products of the inputs and the weights (a dot product). You then train the weights to optimize an error function, which is the difference between the output of the ANN and the ground truth. Presented this way, ANNs are entirely linear. If you were performing classification then a simple ANN is a linear classifier. The same is true for regression.

The output of each neuron passes through a nonlinear *activation* function. The choice of function is a hyperparameter, but all activation functions are, by definition, nonlinear or discontinuous. This enables the ANN to approximate nonlinear functions or classify nonlinearly.

ANNs "learn" by changing the values of the weights. On each update, the training routine nudges the weights in proportion to the gradient of the error function. A key idea is that you update the weights iteratively by repeatedly stimulating the black box and correcting its estimate. Given enough data and time, the ANN will predict accurate values or classes.

Common Neural Network Architectures

Deep ANNs come in all shapes and sizes. All are fundamentally based on the idea of stacking neurons. *Deep* is a reference to large numbers of hidden layers that are required to model abstract concepts. But the specific architecture tends to be domain dependent.

Multilayer perceptrons (MLPs) are the simplest and traditional architecture for DL. Multiple layers of NNs are *fully connected* and *feed-forward*; the output of each neuron in the layer above is directed to every neuron in the layer below. The number of neurons in the input layer is the same as the size of the data. The size of the output layer is set to the number of classes and often provides a probability distribution over the classes by passing the neurons through a *softmax* function.

Deep belief networks (DBNs) are like MLPs, except that the connections between the top two (or more) layers are undirected; the information can pass back up from the second layer to the first. The undirected layers are restricted Boltzmann machines (RBMs). RBMs allow you to model the data and the MLP layers enable classification, based upon the model. This is beneficial because the model is capable of extracting *latent* information; information that is not directly observable. However, RBMs become more difficult to train in proportion to the network size.

Autoencoders have an architecture that tapers toward the middle, like an hourglass. The goal is to reproduce some input data as best as it can, given the constraint of the taper. For example, if there were two neurons in the middle and the corresponding reproduction was acceptable, then you could use the outputs of the two neurons to represent your data, instead of the raw data. In other words, it is a form of compression. Many architectures incorporate autoencoders as a form of automated feature extraction.

Convolutional NNs (CNNs) work well in domains where individual observations are locally correlated. For example, if one pixel in an image is black, then surrounding pixels are also likely to be black. This means that CNNs are well suited to images, natural language, and time series. The basic premise is that the CNN pre-processes the data through a set of filters, called convolutions. After going through several layers of filters the result is fed into an MLP. The training process optimizes the filters and the

MLP for the problem at hand. The major benefit is that the filters allow the architecture as a whole to be time, rotation, and skew dependent, so long as those examples exist in the training data.

Recurrent NNs (RNNs) are a class of architectures that feed back the result of one time step into the input of the next. Given data that is temporally correlated, like text or time series, RNNs are able to "remember" the past and leverage this information to make decisions. RNNs are notoriously hard to train because of the feedback loop. Long short-term memory (LSTM) and gated recurrent units (GRUs) improve upon RNNs by incorporating *gates* to dump the previous "history" and cut the destructive feedback loop, like a blowoff valve in a turbocharged engine.

Echo state networks (ESNs) use a randomly initialized "pool" of RNNs to transform inputs into a higher number of dimensions. The major benefit of ESNs is that you don't need to train the RNNs; you train the conversion back from the high dimensional space to your problem, possibly using something as simple as a logistic classifier. This removes all the issues relating to training RNNs and NNs.

Deep Learning Frameworks

I always recommend writing your own simple neural network library to help understanding, but for all industrial applications you should use a library. Intel, Mathworks, Wolfram, and others all have proprietary libraries. But I will focus on open source.

Open source DL libraries take two forms: implementation and wrapper. Implementation libraries are responsible for defining the NN (often as a *directed acyclic graph* [DAG]), optimizing the execution and abstracting the computation. Wrapper libraries introduce another layer of abstraction that allow you to define NNs in high-level concepts.

After years of intense competition, the most popular, actively maintained DL implementation frameworks include TensorFlow, PyTorch, and MXNet. TensorFlow is flexible enough to handle all NN architectures and use cases, but it is low-level, opinionated, and complex. It has a high barrier to entry, but is well supported and works everywhere you can think of. PyTorch has a lower barrier to entry and has a cool feature of being able to change the computation graph at any point during training. The API is reasonably high level, which makes it easier to use. MXNet is part of the Apache Foundation, unlike the previous two, which are backed by companies (Google and Facebook, respectively). MXNet has bindings in a range of languages and reportedly scales better than any other library.

Keras is probably the most famous wrapper library. You can write in a high-level API, where each line of code represents a layer in your NN, which you can then deploy to TensorFlow, Theano, or CNTK (the latter two are now defunct). A separate library allows you to use MXNet, too. PyTorch has its own set of wrapper libraries, Ignite and

Skorch being the most popular general-purpose high-level APIs. Gluon is a wrapper for MXNet. Finally, ONNX is a different type of wrapper that aims to be a standardized format for NN models. It is capable of converting trained models from one framework into another for prediction. For example, you could train in PyTorch and serve in MXNet.

 If you forced me to make a recommendation, I suggest starting with a wrapper like Keras or Gluon first then graduating to PyTorch (because it too has a high-level API). But TensorFlow has strong industrial credentials, so that is a good choice, too. And MXNet is becoming increasingly popular for performance reasons. Any library will do, then. ONNX could become a standard for models in the future due to this reason.

Deep Reinforcement Learning

How does deep learning fit into RL? Recall from the beginning of Chapter 4 that you need models to cope with complex state spaces (*complex* in the sense of being continuous or having a high number of dimensions).

Simple models, like linear models, can cope with simple environments where the expected value mapping varies linearly. But many environments are far more complicated. For example, consider the advertisement bidding environment in "Industrial Example: Real-Time Bidding in Advertising" on page 70 again. If our state was the rate of spend over time, as it was in the example, then a linear model should be able to fit that well. But if you added a feature that was highly nonlinear, like information about the age of the person viewing the ads if your ad appealed to a very specific age range, then a linear model would fit poorly.

Using DL allows the agents to accept any form of information and delegate the modeling to the NN. What about if you have a state based upon an image? Not a problem for a model using CNNs. Time-series data? Some kind of RNN. High-dimensional multisensor data? MLP. DL effectively becomes a tool used to translate raw observations into actions. RL doesn't replace machine learning, it augments it.

Using DL in RL is more difficult than using it for ML. In supervised machine learning you improve a model by optimizing a measure of performance against the ground truth. In RL, the agent often has to wait a long time to receive any feedback at all. DL is already notorious because it takes a lot of data to train a good model, but combine this with the fact that the agent has to randomly stumble across a reward and it could take forever. For this and many more reasons, researchers have developed a bag of tricks to help DL learn in a reasonable amount of time.

Deep Q-Learning

Before 2013, researchers realized that they needed function approximation to solve problems with large or complex state spaces. They had proven that using a linear approximation retained the same convergence guarantees as tabular methods. But they warned that using nonlinear function approximators may in fact diverge, rather than converge.[1] So, much of the research focused on improving linear approximation methods.

Eventually the forbidden fruit that is DL proved too tempting for researchers and they designed a *deep Q-network* (DQN).[2] They realized that the main problem was the moving goalpost. Imagine trying to swat a fly. The fly's motion is so random and reactions so quick that only the Karate Kid could hope to catch it midair. If you wait until the fly is stationary, you have a much greater chance of predicting where the fly is going to be in 500 milliseconds and therefore have a better chance of hitting it. The agent has the same problem. Unless the data is stationary, it can find it very hard to converge. In some cases it can actually diverge because like in a destructive feedback loop, the next action might make matters worse.

In general, model optimizers like stochastic gradient descent assume that your data is independent and identically distributed (IID) random variables. When you sample close in time, the data is likely to be correlated. For example, the definition of the MDP says that the next observation is dependent on the previous state and the action taken. This violates the IID assumption and models can fail to converge.

Experience Replay

The initial solution to this problem was to use *experience replay*. This is a buffer of observations, actions, rewards, and subsequent observations that can be used to train the DL model. This allows you to use old data to train your model, making training more sample efficient, much like in "Eligibility Traces" on page 80. By taking a random subset when training, you break the correlation between consecutive observations.

The size of the experience replay buffer is important. Zhang and Sutton observed that a poorly tuned buffer size can have a large impact on performance.[3] In the worst case, agents can "catastrophically forget" experiences when observations drop off the end of a *first in, first out* (FIFO) buffer, which can lead to a large change in policy. Ideally, the distribution of the training data should match that observed by the agent.[4]

Q-Network Clones

In an update to the original DQN algorithm, the same researchers proposed cloning the Q-network. This leads to two NNs: one *online network* that produces actions and one *target network* that continues to learn. After some number of iterations the prediction network copies the current weights from the target network. The researchers found that this made the algorithm more stable and less likely to oscillate or diverge. The reason is the same as before. The data obtained by the agent is then stationary for a limited time. The trick is to set this period small enough so that you can improve the model quickly, but long enough to keep the data stationary.[5] You will also notice that this is the same as the idea presented in "Double Q-Learning" on page 74; two estimates are more stable than one.

Neural Network Architecture

Using randomly sampled experience replay and a target Q-network, DQN is stable enough to perform well in complex tasks. The primary driver is the choice of NN that models and maps the observations into actions. The original DQN paper played Atari games from video frames, so using a CNN is an obvious choice. But this does not prevent you from using other NN architectures. Choose an architecture that performs well in your domain.

Another interesting feature of DQN is the choice to predict the state-value function. Recall standard Q-learning (or SARSA) uses the action-value function; the Q-values hold both the state and the actions as parameters. The result is an expected value estimate for a state and a single action. You could train a single NN for each action. Instead, NNs can have several *heads* that predict the values of all actions at the same time. When training you can set the desired action to 1 and the undesired actions to 0, a one-hot encoding of the actions.

Implementing DQN

The equation representing the update rule for DQN is like "Q-Learning" on page 62. The major difference is that the Q-value is aproximated by a function, and that function has a set of parameters. For example, to choose the optimal action, pick the action that has the highest expected value like in Equation 4-1.

Equation 4-1. Choosing an action with DQN

$$a \leftarrow \operatorname*{argmax}_{a_s \in \mathcal{A}(s)} Q(s, a_s; \theta)$$

In Equation 4-1, Q represents the function used to predict the action values from the NN and θ represents the parameters of the function. All other symbols are the same as in Equation 3-5.

To train the NN you need to provide a loss function. Remember that the goal is to predict the action-value function. So a natural choice of loss function is the squared difference between the actual action-value function and the prediction, as shown in

Equation 4-2. This is typically implemented as the *mean squared error* (MSE), but any loss function is possible.

Equation 4-2. DQN loss function

$$L(\theta) \doteq \mathbb{E}_\pi\Big[\big(y - Q(s, a; \theta)\big)^2\Big]$$

NN optimizers use gradient descent to update the estimates of the parameters of the NN. They use knowledge of the gradient of the loss function to nudge the parameters in a direction that minimizes the loss function. The underlying DL framework handles the calculation of the gradient for you. But you could write it out by differentiating Equation 4-2 with respect to θ.

The implementation of DQN is much Q-learning from Algorithm 3-1. The differences are that the action is delivered directly from the NN, the experiences need buffering, and occasionally you need to transfer or train the target NN's parameters. The devil is in the detail. Precisely how you implement experience replay, what NN architecture and hyperparameters you choose, and when you do the training can make the difference between super-human performance and an algorithmic blowup.

For the rest of this chapter I have chosen to use a library called Coach (*https://oreil.ly/ HLkqv*) by Intel's Nervana Systems. I like it for three reasons: I find the abstractions intuitive, it implements many algorithms, and it supports lots of environments.

Example: DQN on the CartPole Environment

To gain some experience with DQN I recommend you use a simple "toy" environment, like the CartPole environment from OpenAI Gym (*https://oreil.ly/YGpj0*).

The environment simulates balancing a pole on a cart. The agent can nudge the cart left or right; these are the actions. It represents the state with a position on the x-axis, the velocity of the cart, the velocity of the tip of the pole, and the angle of the pole (0° is straight up). The agent receives a reward of 1 for every step taken. The episode ends when the pole angle is more than ±12°, the cart position is more than ±2.4 (the edge of the display), or the episode length is greater than 200 steps. To solve the environment you need an average reward greater than or equal to 195 over 100 consecutive trials.

Coach has a concept of presets (*https://oreil.ly/wDeC3*), which are settings for algorithms that are known to work. The CartPole_DQN (*https://oreil.ly/KTjRB*) preset has a solution to solve the CartPole environment with a DQN. I took this preset and made a few alterations to leave the following parameters:

- It copies the target weights to the online weights every 100 steps of the environment.
- The discount factor is set to 0.99.
- The maximum size of the memory is 40,000 experiences.
- It uses a constant ϵ-greedy schedule of 0.05 (to make the plots consistent).
- The NN uses an MSE-based loss, rather than the default Huber loss.
- No environment "warmup" to prepopulate the memory (to obtain a result from the beginning).

Of all of these settings, it is the use of MSE loss (Equation 4-2) that makes the biggest difference. Huber loss clips the loss to be a linear error above a threshold and zero otherwise. In more complex environments absolute losses like the Huber loss help mitigate against outliers. If you are using MSE, then outliers get squared and the huge error overwhelms all other data. But in this case the environment is simple and there is no noise, so MSE, because of the squaring, helps the NN learn faster, because the errors really are large to begin with. For this reason Huber loss tends to be the default loss function used in RL.

> In general I recommend that you should use an absolute loss in noisy environments and a squared loss for simpler, noise-free environments.

To provide a baseline for the DQN algorithm, I have implemented two new agents in Coach. The random agent picks a random action on every step. The Q-learning agent implements Q-learning as described in "Q-Learning" on page 62. Recall that tabular Q-learning cannot handle continuous states. I was able to solve the CartPole environment with Q-learning by multiplying all states by 10, rounding to the nearest whole number, and casting to an integer. I also only use the angle and the angular velocity of the pole (the third and fourth elements in the observation array, respectively). This results in approximately 150 states in the Q-value lookup table.

Figure 4-1 shows the episode rewards for the three agents. Both DQN and Q-learning are capable of finding an optimal policy. The random policy is able to achieve an average reward of approximately 25 steps. This is due to the environment physics. It takes that long for the pole to fall. The Q-learning agent initially performs better than the DQN. This is because the DQN needs a certain amount of data before it can train a reasonable model of the Q-values. The precise amount of data required depends on the complexity of the deep neural network and the size of the state space. The Q-learning agent sometimes performs poorly due to the ϵ-greedy random action. In contrast, DQN is capable of generalizing to states that it hasn't seen before, so performance is more stable.

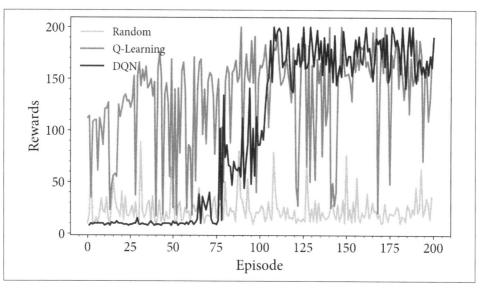

Figure 4-1. A plot of the episode rewards for random, Q-learning, and DQN agents. The results are noisy because they are not averaged.

Figures 4-2–4-4 show an example episode from the random, Q-learning, and DQN agents, respectively. Both the Q-learning and DQN examples last for 200 steps, which is the maximum for an episode.

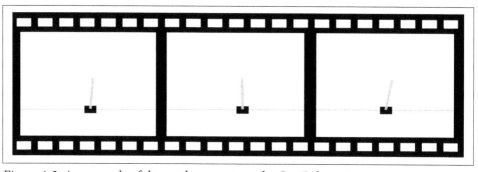

Figure 4-2. An example of the random agent on the CartPole environment.

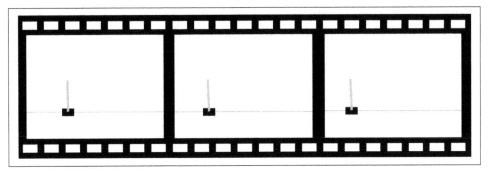

Figure 4-3. An example of the Q-learning agent on the CartPole environment.

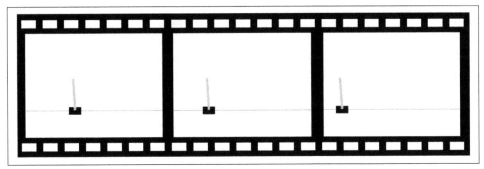

Figure 4-4. An example of the DQN agent on the CartPole environment.

Why train online?

At this point you might ask why you need to train online at all. You could generate and store 200 episodes' worth of data from the environment and train a model offline in a supervised way. For simple environments this can work, albeit inefficiently. To generate the data the agent still needs to follow a policy. You could choose a random policy but this is unlikely to generate long episodes. Consider the `CartPole` environment. How many attempts do you think it will take a random policy to achieve 200 time steps? A lot. In most applications the agent needs to learn online so it can observe later states.

The second reason is that the agent must produce *counterfactual* actions (actions that might not be good) to confirm that it does have the best policy. This is at the heart of exploration. Actions produce new, unseen trajectories. One of them will be optimal. If you don't have a sequential environment or you don't need to explore to find optimal policies, then use standard machine learning. I discuss this further in "Learning from Offline Data" on page 109.

Which is better? DQN versus Q-learning

The results show that standard Q-learning is as good as DQN. And I haven't applied any of the improvements to Q-learning seen in "Extensions to Q-Learning" on page 74. Why use DQN, given the complexities of adding an NN?

To make Q-learning work, I had to drastically reduce the amount of information. I removed half of the features and quantized the remaining to leave around 150 discrete values. To find those settings I had to perform feature engineering, which included trying many other combinations of features and quantization levels—effort that would take a book in itself. This might be worth the effort if you want to run models like this in production, because the simplicity will make decisions easier to explain, and the models will be more robust, more efficient, more stable, and so on.

With DQN I didn't change anything. The NN was able to take the raw information, figure out which features were important, and tell me which action was optimal. The model can incorporate continuous values, making the result more fine-grained when compared to tabular methods. If your domain is more complex and feature engineering becomes difficult, NNs can be an efficient solution. But beware that all the usual NN caveats apply: they need a lot of data, are prone to overfitting, are sensitive to initial conditions and hyperparameters, are not resilient or robust, and are open to adversarial attack (see "Secure RL" on page 327).

Case Study: Reducing Energy Usage in Buildings

Around 40% of the European Union's energy is spent on powering and heating buildings and this represents about 25% of the greenhouse gas emissions.[6] There are a range of technologies that can help reduce building energy requirements, but many of them are invasive and expensive. However, fine-tuning the control of building heating, ventilation, and air conditioning (HVAC) is applicable to buildings of any age. Marantos et al. propose using RL inside a smart thermostat to improve the comfort and efficiency of building heating systems.[7]

They begin by defining the Markov decision process. The state is represented by a concatenation of outdoor weather sensors like the temperature and the amount of sunlight, indoor sensors like humidity and temperature, energy sensors to quantify usage, and an indication of thermal comfort.

The agent is able to choose from three actions: maintain temperature, increase temperature by one degree, or reduce temperature by one degree.

The reward is quantified through a combination of thermal comfort and energy usage that is scaled using a rolling mean and standard deviation, to negate the need for using arbitrary scaling parameters. Since this is largely a continuous problem, Marantos et al. introduce a terminal state to prevent the agent from going out of bounds: if the agent attempts to go outside of a predefined operating window then it is penalized.

Marantos et al. chose to use the neural fitted Q-iteration (NFQ) algorithm, which was a forerunner of DQN. DQN has the same ideas as NFQ, except that it also includes experience replay and the target network. They use a feed-forward multilayer perceptron as the state representation function to predict binary actions.

They evaluate their implementation using a simulation that is used in a variety of similar work. The simulation corresponds to an actual building located in Crete, Greece, using public weather information. Compared to a standard threshold-based thermostat, the agent is able to reduce average energy usage by up to 59%, depending on the level of comfort chosen.

One interesting idea that you don't often see is that Marantos et al. implemented this algorithm in a Raspberry Pi Zero and demonstrated that even with the neural network, they have more than enough computational resources to train the model.

If I were to help improve this project the first thing I would consider is switching to DQN, or one of its derivatives, to improve algorithmic performance. NFQ is demonstrably weaker than DQN due to the experience replay and target network. This change would result in better sample efficiency and benefit from using an industry standard technique. I love the use of the embedded device to perform the computation and I would extend this by considering multiple agents throughout the building. In this multi-agent setting, agents could cooperate to optimize temperature comfort for different areas, like being cooler in bedrooms or turned off entirely overnight in living rooms.

Finally, this doesn't just have to apply to heating. An agent could easily improve lighting efficiency, hot-water use, and electrical efficiency, all of which have documented case studies. You can find more on the accompanying website (*https://rl-book.com/ applications/?utm_source=oreilly&utm_medium=book&utm_campaign=rl*).

Rainbow DQN

Being a derivation of Q-learning, you can improve DQN using the extensions seen in "Extensions to Q-Learning" on page 74. In 2017, researchers created Rainbow DQN using six extensions that each addressed fundamental concerns with Q-learning and DQN. The researchers also ran experiments to see which improved performance most.[8]

You have already seen the first two improvements: double Q-learning (see "Double Q-Learning" on page 74), to mitigate the maximization bias and *n*-step returns (see "n-Step Algorithms" on page 76), to accumulate the reward for multiple future steps.

Distributional RL

The most fundamental deviation from standard DQN is the reintroduction of probability into the agents. All Q-learning agents derive from the Bellman equation (Equation 2-10), which defines the optimal trajectory as the action that maximizes the expected reward. The key word here is *expected*. Q-learning implements this as an exponentially decaying average. Whenever you use a summary statistic you are implying assumptions about the underlying distribution. Usually, if you choose to use the mean as a summary statistic, you place an implicit assumption that the data is distributed according to a normal distribution. Is this correct?

For example, imagine you are balancing on the cliff in the Cliffworld environment. There is a large negative reward if you fall off the cliff. But there is also a much greater (but near zero) reward of walking along the cliff edge. "Q-Learning Versus SARSA" on page 65 showed that SARSA followed the average "safe" path far away from the cliff. Q-learning took the risky path next to the cliff because the fewer number of steps to the goal resulted in a slightly greater expected return. All states in the Cliff world environment lead to two outcomes. Both outcomes have their own distribution representing a small chance that some exploration may lead the agent to an alternative outcome. The expected return is not normally distributed. In general, rewards are *multimodal*.

Now imagine a Cliffworld-like environment where the difference between success and failure is not as dramatic. Imagine that the reward upon success is +1 and failure is –1. Then the expected return, for at least some states, will be close to zero. In these states, the average expected value yields actions that make no difference. This can lead to agents randomly wandering around meaningless states (compare this with gradient descent algorithms that plateau when the loss functions become too flat). This is shown in Figure 4-5. In general, reward distributions are much more complex.

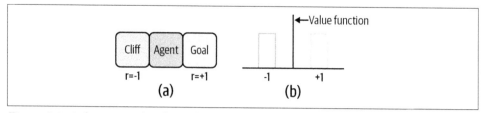

Figure 4-5. A depiction of multimodal rewards for a state. (a) presents a simple grid environment with a penalizing cliff on one side and a rewarding goal on the other. The reward distribution, shown in (b), has two opposite rewards and the mean, which is the same as the value function for that state, is zero.

In practice, this leads to convergence issues. The worst-case scenario is that the agent never converges. When it does, researchers often describe the agent as "chattering."

This is where the agent converges but never stabilizes. It can oscillate like in Figure 4-6 or can be more complex. Note that this is not the only cause of chattering.

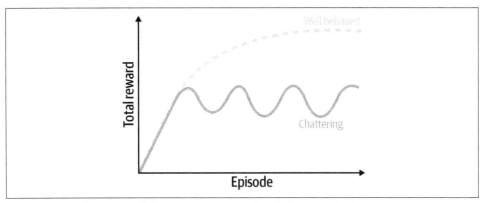

Figure 4-6. A depiction of chattering using a plot of the rewards during training.

Learning the *distribution of rewards* can lead to more stable learning.[9] Bellemare et al. reformulate the Bellman equation to account for random rewards that you can see in Equation 4-3, where y is the discount factor, and R is a stochastic reward that depends on a state and action.

Equation 4-3. Distributional Bellman equation

$$Z(s, a) \sim R(s, a) + \gamma Z(S', A')$$

Here I temporarily break from this book's convention and use capital letters to denote stochastic variables. Z represents the distribution of rewards. The expectation of Z is the Q-value. Like the Q-value, Z should be updated recursively according to the received reward. The key difference is the emphasis that the expected return, Z, is a random variable distributed over all future states, S, and future actions, A. In other words, the policy Z^π is a mapping of state-action pairs to a distribution of expected returns. This representation preserves multimodality and Bellemare et al. suggest that this leads to more stable learning. I recommend that you watch this video (*https:// oreil.ly/vTVHj*) to see an example of the distribution of rewards learned during a game of *Space Invaders*.

The first incarnation of this idea is an algorithm called C51. It asks two key questions. How do you represent the distribution? How do you create the update rule for Equation 4-3? The choice of distribution or function used to model the returns is important. C51 uses a discrete parametric distribution, in other words a histogram of returns. The "51" in C51 refers to the number of histogram bins chosen in the researchers' implementation and suggests that performance is proportional to the numbers of bins, albeit with diminishing returns.

To produce an estimate of the distribution, Bellemare et al. built an NN with 51 output "bins." When the environment produces a reward, which falls into one of the bins, the agent can train the NN to predict that bin. This is now a supervised classification problem and the agent can be trained using cross-entropy loss. The "C" in C51 refers to the fact that the agent is predicting classes, or categories.

Prioritized Experience Replay

The next set of improvements relate to the neural network. In DQN, transitions are sampled uniformly from the replay buffer (see "Deep Q-Learning" on page 92). The batch is likely to contain transitions that the agent has seen many times. It is better to include transitions from areas in which there is much to learn. *Prioritized experience replay* samples the replay buffer with a probability proportional to the absolute error of the temporal-difference update (see Equation 3-6).[10] Schaul et al. alter this idea to incorporate the *n*-step absolute error, instead of a single step.

Noisy Nets

In complex environments it may be difficult for the ϵ-greedy algorithm to stumble across a successful result. One idea, called *noisy nets*, is to augment the ϵ-greedy search by adding noise in the NN.[11] Recall that the NN is a model of prospective actions for a given state: a policy. Applying noise directly to the NN enables a random search in the context of the current policy. The model will learn to ignore the noise (because it is random) when it experiences enough transitions for a given state. But new states will continue to be noisy, allowing context-aware exploration and automatic annealing (see "Improving the ϵ-greedy Algorithm" on page 33).

Dueling Networks

In Q-learning algorithms, the expected value estimates (the Q-values) are often very similar. It is often unnecessary to even calculate the expected value because both choices can lead to the same result. For example, in the `CartPole` environment, the first action won't make much difference if it has learned to save the pole before it falls. Therefore, it makes sense to learn the state-value function, as opposed to the action-value function that I have been using since "Predicting Rewards with the Action-Value Function" on page 47. Then each observation can update an entire state, which should lead to faster learning. However, the agent still needs to choose an action.

Imagine for a second that you are able to accurately predict the state-value function. Recall that this is the expectation (the average) over all actions for that state. Therefore, I can represent the individual actions relative to that average. Researchers call this the *advantage function* and it is defined in Equation 4-4. To recover the action-value function required by Q-learning, you need to estimate the advantage function and the state-value function.

Equation 4-4. Advantage function

$$A^{\pi}(s, a) \doteq Q^{\pi}(s, a) - V^{\pi}(s)$$

Dueling networks achieve this by creating a single NN with two *heads*, which are predictive outputs. One head is responsible for estimating the state-value function and the other the advantage function. The NN recombines these two heads to generate the required action-value function.[12] The novelty is the special aggregator on the output of the two heads that allows the whole NN to be trained as one. The benefit is that the state-value function is quicker and easier to learn, which leads to faster convergence. Also, the effect of subtracting of the baseline in the advantage estimate improves stability. This is because the Q-learning maximization bias can cause large changes in individual action-value estimates.

Example: Rainbow DQN on Atari Games

The DQN paper popularized using the rewards of Atari games as a measure of agent performance. In this section I have re-created some of those results by training an agent to play two Atari games: *Pong* and *Ms Pac-Man*. I again use the Coach (*https://oreil.ly/HLkqv*) framework and its Atari presets.

The Atari environment is part of OpenAI Gym (*https://oreil.ly/DAe39*) and exposes raw Atari 2600 frames. Each frame is a 210×160 pixel image with an RGB 128-bit color palette. To reduce the computational complexity introduced by the large number of inputs, a pre-processing method converts the $210 \times 160 \times 3$ array by decimating, cropping, and converting it to grayscale. This reduces the number of input dimensions to 84×84. The agent clips the rewards at +/– 1 to unify the return of the Atari games.

The Atari games have lots of moving entities: bullets or ghosts, for example. The agent needs to be aware of the trajectory of these entities to react appropriately, to dodge a bullet or run away from a ghost. More advanced agents incorporate a time-dependent memory, often using recurrent neural networks. DQN and its derivatives do not, so instead agents typically stack multiple frames into a single observation by flattening the image and concatenating into one big array. This implementation merges four frames and the agent reuses the same action for the subsequent four frames.

Results

I chose to run two experiments due to the amount of time it took to train an agent. I used the default hyperparameter settings in the Coach library presets. These include annealing ϵ-greedy exploration for 250,000 frames and low ANN learning rates. I trained the agents on the Google Cloud Platform using `n1-standard-4` virtual machines connected to a single Nvidia Tesla P4 GPU in the Netherlands.

The training times and approximate costs are described in Table 4-1. The DQN agent, on average, takes 4.8 hours and costs $5.80 to train upon one million frames. The Rainbow agent takes 7.6 hours and costs $8.50 to achieve a similar result. Note that these values are indicators. They are heavily affected by hyperparameters, which are different for the two agents. Research shows that Rainbow far exceeds the performance of DQN when looking at performance over all Atari games.

Table 4-1. The time and cost to train the Atari games Pong and Ms Pac-Man to similar levels using DQN and Rainbow agents in the Coach framework

Agent	Game	Millions of Frames	Time (hours)	Cost (approximate USD)
DQN	Pong	2	10	12
DQN	Ms. Pac-Man	3	14	17
Rainbow	Pong	2.5	19	22
Rainbow	Ms. Pac-Man	3	23	26

These results highlight the exponential increase in complexity, which results in long training times. Despite proof that Rainbow results in better policies is less time, the context and circumstances are important. You must design the solution to fit within your specific requirements. For example, the improvement in performance obtained by using Rainbow may not justify the near doubling in computational cost. However, the training of the underlying ANN represents the bulk of the cost. If you can simplify, tune, or speed up the ANN architecture, the prices will drop dramatically.

Figure 4-7 shows the rewards obtained when training to play *Pong*. The Rainbow agent takes an extra 0.5 million frames to obtain a similar result to DQN. This could be due to the differing hyperparameter settings. The learning rate, α, is set to 1e-4 for DQN. Rainbow is two-thirds of that value at 6.25e-5. DQN uses ϵ-greedy exploration, but Rainbow uses parameter noise exploration. I am confident that with similar hyperparameters Rainbow will perform at least as well as DQN in this example.

Figure 4-8 shows the rewards for the Ms. Pac-Man game. I have smoothed the reward with a moving average of 100 frames. This is because the reward is much noisier due to the random starting positions of the ghosts. For example, a single game could have a low reward because on that occasion the ghosts started in dangerous positions. On other games it might be high because the ghosts start in safe positions. I recommend that you consider the distributions of rewards when working in a stochastic environment.

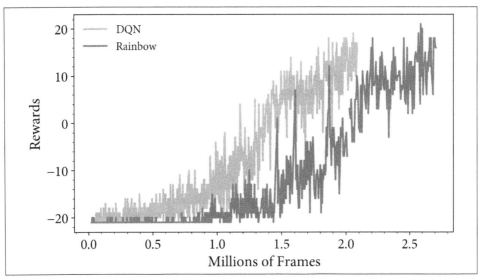

Figure 4-7. A plot of the rewards for DQN and Rainbow agents on the Atari game Pong.

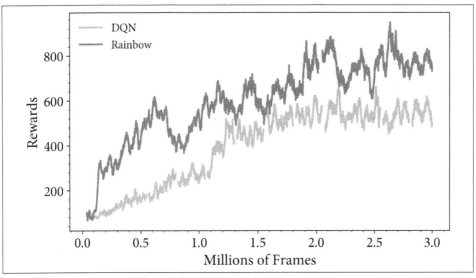

Figure 4-8. A plot of the rewards for DQN and Rainbow agents on the Atari game Ms. Pac-Man. The rewards have been smoothed using a 100-frame moving average.

Discussion

Figures 4-9 and 4-10 show a full episode from *Pong* for the DQN and Rainbow agents, respectively. Since these are single episodes and the hyperparameters used to train each agent differ, you must not to draw any firm conclusions from the result. But you can comment on the policy, from a human perspective.

Figure 4-9. An example of the trained DQN agent playing the Atari game Pong.

Figure 4-10. An example of the trained Rainbow agent playing the Atari game Pong.

When I first showed these videos to my wife, her initial reaction was "work, yeah right!" But after I explained that this was serious business, she noticed that the movement of the paddle was "agitated" when the ball wasn't near. This is because the actions make no difference to the result; the Q-values are almost all the same and result in random movement. The agent responds quickly when the ball is close to the paddle because it has learned that it will lose if it is not close to the ball.

The two agents have subtle distinctions. DQN tends to bounce the ball on the corner of the paddle, whereas Rainbow tends to swipe at the ball. I suspect that these actions are artifacts of the early stopping of the training. If I ran these experiments for 20 million frames, I predict that the techniques would tend to converge, but that would be expensive, so I leave that as a reader exercise.

Figures 4-11 and 4-12 show a full episode from Ms. Pac-Man for the DQN and Rainbow agents, respectively. Both agents do a commendable job at avoiding ghosts, collecting pellets, and using the teleports that warp Ms. Pac-Man to the other side of the screen. But in general Rainbow seems to perform better than DQN. It has also learned to look for power pellets so it can eat the ghosts. Rainbow almost completes the first level and given more training time I'm certain it can. Neither agent has yet learned to eat fruits to gain extra points or actively hunt down ghosts after eating a power pellet, if indeed that is an optimal policy.

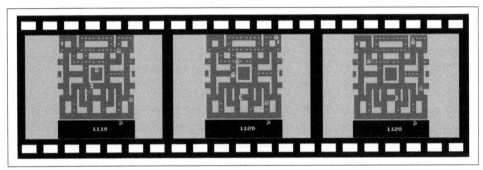

Figure 4-11. An example of the trained DQN agent playing the Atari game Ms. Pac-Man.

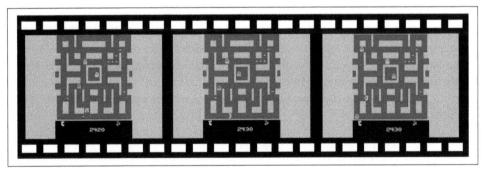

Figure 4-12. An example of the trained Rainbow agent playing the Atari game Ms. Pac-Man.

Other DQN Improvements

"Rainbow DQN" on page 99 introduced six improvements to DQN. Each algorithm tackles a single impediment and generalizes three themes of research. (1) Neural networks should learn faster and produce results that are more informative. (2) Q-learning should not be unstable or biased. (3) RL should find an optimal policy efficiently. You can see that these refer to three different levels of abstraction. In Rainbow DQN, for example, prioritized experience replay attempts to improve the learning of the neural network, dual double Q-learning helps prevent the maximization bias in Q-learning, and distributional RL helps learn more realistic rewards in RL. In this section I will introduce other recent improvements that focus on DQN.

Improving Exploration

The ϵ-greedy exploration strategy is ubiquitous, designed to randomly sample small, finite state spaces. But dithering methods, where you randomly perturb the agent, are not practical in complex environments; they require exponentially increasing amounts of data. One way of describing this problem is to imagine the surface represented by the Q-values. If a Q-learning agent repeatedly chooses a suboptimal state-action pair, subsequent episodes will also choose this pair, like the agent is stuck in a local maxima. One alternative is to consider other sampling methods.

"Improving the ϵ-greedy Algorithm" on page 33 introduced upper-confidence-bound (UCB) sampling, which biases actions toward undersampled states. This prevents the oversampling of initial optimal trajectories. Thompson sampling, often used in A/B testing (see "Multi-Arm Bandit Testing" on page 25), maintains distributions that represent the expected values. For Q-learning, this means each Q-value is a distribution, not an expectation. This is the same idea behind distributional RL (see "Distributional RL" on page 100). Bootstrapped DQN (BDQN) uses this idea and trains a neural network with multiple heads to simulate the distribution of Q-values, an *ensemble* of action-value estimates.[13] This was superseded by distributional RL, which efficiently predicts the actual distribution, not a crude approximation. But Osband et al. cleverly continued to reuse the randomly selected policy to drive exploration in the future as well. This led to the idea of "deep exploration." In complex environments, ϵ-greedy moves like a fly, often returning to states it has previously observed. It makes sense to push deeper to find new, unobserved states. You can see similarities here with noisy nets, too.

From a Bayesian perspective, modeling the Q-values as distributions is arguably the right way, but often computationally complex. If you treat each head of the neural network as independent estimates of the same policy, then you can combine them into an ensemble and obtain similar performance. To recap, an ensemble is a combination of algorithms that generates multiple hypotheses. The combination is generally more robust and less prone to overfitting. Following independent policies in a more efficient way, like via UCB sampling for example, is another way to achieve "deep exploration."[14,15] Another major benefit is that you can follow the policy offered by one head to obtain the benefits of searching a deep, unexplored area in the state space, but then later share this learning to the other heads.[16] More recent research has shown that although sharing speeds up learning, ultimate performance improves with more diverse heads.[17]

Improving Rewards

The previous section used separate policy estimates as a proxy for estimating the reward distribution. C51 (see "Distributional RL" on page 100) predicts a histogram of the distribution. Neither of these is as efficient as directly approximating the distribution, for example, picking the histogram bounds and the number of bins in C51.

A more elegant solution is to estimate the quantiles of the target distribution. After selecting the number of quantiles, which defines the resolution of the estimate and the number of heads in the neural network, the loss function minimizes the error between the predicted and actual quantiles. The major difference between bootstrapped DQN, C51, ensemble DQN, and this is the loss function. In Distributional RL with Quantile Regression, Dabney et al. replace the standard loss function used in RL (Huber loss) with a quantile equivalent. This results in higher performance on all the standard Atari games but, importantly, provides you with a high-resolution estimate of the reward distribution.[18]

Recent research is tending to agree that learning reward distributions is beneficial, but not for the reason you expect. Learning distributions should provide more information, which should lead to better policies. But researchers found that it has a regularizing effect on the neural network. In other words, distributional techniques may help to stabilize learning not because learning distributions is more data-efficient, but because it constrains the unwieldy neural network.[19]

Learning from Offline Data

Many industrial applications of RL need to learn from data that has already been collected. *Batch* RL is the task of learning a policy from a fixed dataset without further interaction from the environment. This is common in situations where interaction is costly, risky, or time consuming. Using a library of data can also speed up development. This problem is closely related to learning by example, which is also called imitation learning, and discussed in "Imitation RL" on page 236.

Most RL algorithms generate observations through interaction with an environment. The observations are then stored in buffers for later reuse. Could these algorithms also work without interaction and learn completely offline?

In one experiment, researchers trained two agents, one learning from interaction and another that only used the buffer of the first. In a surprising result, the buffer-trained agent performed significantly worse when trained with the same algorithm on the same dataset.

The reason for this, which comes from statistical learning theory, is that the training data does not match the testing data. The data generated by an agent is dependent on its policy at the time. The collected data is not necessarily representative of the entire state-action space. The first agent is capable of good performance because it has the power to self-correct through interaction. The buffer-trained agent cannot and requires truly representative data.

Prioritized experience replay, double Q-learning, and dueling Q-networks all help to mitigate this problem by making the data more representative in the first place, but they don't tackle the core problem. *Batch-constrained* deep Q-learning (BCQ) provides a more direct solution. The implementation is quite complicated, but the key addition is a different way to provide experience. Rather than feeding the raw observations to the buffer-trained agent, the researchers train another neural network to generate prospective actions using a *conditional variational autoencoder*. This is a type of autoencoder that allows you to generate observations from specific classes. This has the effect of constraining the policy by only generating actions that lead to states in the buffer. They also include the ability to tune the model to generate random actions by adding noise to the actions, if desired. This helps to make the resulting policy more robust, by filling in the gaps left after sampling.

One final alteration is that they train two networks, like in double Q-learning, to obtain two independent estimates. They then clip these estimates to generate low variance Q-value updates, weighted by a hyperparameter.[20]

Figure 4-13 compares the results of two experiments on the `CartPole` environment, using Coach. First, I generate a buffer of transitions using a standard DQN agent. This buffer is then passed into a second agent that never explores. This simulates the situation where you have an algorithm running in production and you want to leverage logged data. When you train a second agent you will not be able to explore, because you cannot perform an action.

In the first experiment, I trained a DQN agent on the buffer data (the gray line). Note how the reward is poor in plot (a). The reason for this is that the agent is unstable, demonstrated by the diverging Q-values in plot (b). The agent will attempt to follow a policy to states that are not in the buffer. The maximization step in Q-learning will lead to an overly optimistic estimate of a Q-value. Because the agent cannot interact with the environment, it cannot retrieve evidence to suggest otherwise. The agent will keep following the bad Q-value and the value will keep on increasing. Recall that in an online environment, the agent can sample that state to verify the expected return. This constrains the Q-values.

In the second experiment, I trained a BCQ agent on the buffer data (the black line). Note the reward convergence in plot (a) and the stable Q-values in plot (b). This is primarily due to the generative model, which provides realistic return estimates via a simulation of the environment (a simulation of a simulation), but also, to a lesser extent, because of the low-variance sampling of independent Q-value estimates.

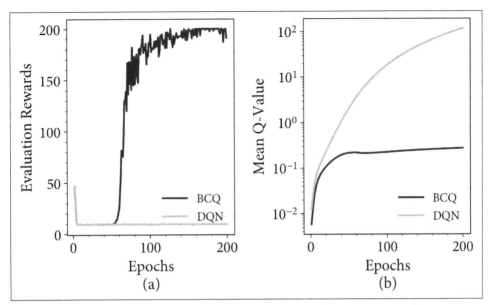

Figure 4-13. Results from an experiment to train BCQ and DQN agents with no interaction with the environment. (a) shows the rewards when evaluating inside the environment. (b) shows the mean Q-values (note the logarithmic y-axis).

Note that the use of the autoencoder adds complexity. In simpler agents like linear Q-learning, you could leverage simpler generative models, like *k-nearest neighbors*.[21]

Summary

In this whistle-stop tour, you can see how using deep neural networks as function approximators has revolutionized and reinvigorated Q-learning, the algorithm published in 1991. I thought it was useful to include a very brief overview of the main neural network architectures, but please refer yourself to a book on the subject in "Further Reading" on page 112.

Deep Q-networks was the breakthrough paper, but neural networks have been used in RL for a long time.[22] Given the flexibility of neural networks, you can find as many improvements to DQN as the number of papers on deep learning. The key insight is that although nonlinear function approximators are unruly and may not converge, they have the incredible ability to approximate any function. This opens the door to applications that were previously deemed too complex.

This power was demonstrated by playing Atari games, but you can see more examples of industrial use cases every day. This chapter marks the end of your journey through basic tabular methods. In the next chapter I reformulate the problem of finding an optimal policy.

Further Reading

- Machine learning:

  — Provost, Foster, and Tom Fawcett. 2013. *Data Science for Business: What You Need to Know about Data Mining and Data-Analytic Thinking* (*https://oreil.ly/gcJ09*). O'Reilly Media.

  — Raschka, Sebastian. 2015. *Python Machine Learning*. Packt Publishing Ltd.

- Deep learning:

  — Goodfellow, Ian, Yoshua Bengio, and Aaron Courville. 2016. *Deep Learning*. MIT Press.

  — Chollet, François. 2017. *Deep Learning with Python*. Manning Publications Company.

- Generative models (autoencoders and such):

  — Foster, David. 2019. *Generative Deep Learning: Teaching Machines to Paint, Write, Compose, and Play*. O'Reilly Media.

References

[1] Tsitsiklis, J. N., and B. Van Roy. 1997. "An Analysis of Temporal-Difference Learning with Function Approximation" (*https://oreil.ly/aK17s*). *IEEE Transactions on Automatic Control* 42 (5): 674–90.

[2] Mnih, Volodymyr, Koray Kavukcuoglu, David Silver, Alex Graves, Ioannis Antonoglou, Daan Wierstra, and Martin Riedmiller. 2013. "Playing Atari with Deep Reinforcement Learning" (*https://oreil.ly/HOqeN*). ArXiv:1312.5602, December.

[3] Zhang, Shangtong, and Richard S. Sutton. 2018. "A Deeper Look at Experience Replay" (*https://oreil.ly/qnRKD*). ArXiv:1712.01275, April.

[4] Isele, David, and Akansel Cosgun. 2018. "Selective Experience Replay for Lifelong Learning" (*https://oreil.ly/Wsk1d*). ArXiv:1802.10269, February.

[5] Mnih, Volodymyr, et. al 2018. "Human-Level Control through Deep Reinforcement Learning" (*https://oreil.ly/AU1td*). *Nature* 518, 529–533.

[6] "Shedding Light on Energy on the EU: How Are Emissions of Greenhouse Gases by the EU Evolving?" (*https://oreil.ly/yLgeU*). n.d. Shedding Light on Energy on the EU. Accessed 12 September 2020.

[7] Marantos, Charalampos, Christos P. Lamprakos, Vasileios Tsoutsouras, Kostas Siozios, and Dimitrios Soudris. 2018. "Towards Plug&Play Smart Thermostats Inspired by Reinforcement Learning" (*https://oreil.ly/ozLFF*). *In Proceedings of the*

Workshop on INTelligent Embedded Systems Architectures and Applications, 39–44. INTESA 2018. New York, NY, USA: Association for Computing Machinery.

[8] Hessel, Matteo, Joseph Modayil, Hado van Hasselt, Tom Schaul, Georg Ostrovski, Will Dabney, Dan Horgan, Bilal Piot, Mohammad Azar, and David Silver. 2017. "Rainbow: Combining Improvements in Deep Reinforcement Learning" (*https://oreil.ly/wKDL4*). ArXiv:1710.02298, October.

[9] Bellemare, Marc G., Will Dabney, and Rémi Munos. 2017. "A Distributional Perspective on Reinforcement Learning" (*https://oreil.ly/ODa3y*). ArXiv:1707.06887, July.

[10] Schaul, Tom, John Quan, Ioannis Antonoglou, and David Silver. 2015. "Prioritized Experience Replay" (*https://oreil.ly/0NPIN*). ArXiv:1511.05952, November.

[11] Fortunato, Meire, Mohammad Gheshlaghi Azar, Bilal Piot, Jacob Menick, Ian Osband, Alex Graves, Vlad Mnih, et al. 2017. "Noisy Networks for Exploration" (*https://oreil.ly/TNcdO*). ArXiv:1706.10295, June.

[12] Wang, Ziyu, Tom Schaul, Matteo Hessel, Hado van Hasselt, Marc Lanctot, and Nando de Freitas. 2015. "Dueling Network Architectures for Deep Reinforcement Learning" (*https://oreil.ly/w4xRr*). ArXiv:1511.06581, November.

[13] Osband, Ian, Charles Blundell, Alexander Pritzel, and Benjamin Van Roy. 2016. "Deep Exploration via Bootstrapped DQN" (*https://oreil.ly/RmkiV*). ArXiv:1602.04621, July.

[14] Lu, Xiuyuan, and Benjamin Van Roy. 2017. "Ensemble Sampling" (*https://oreil.ly/7Bo99*). ArXiv:1705.07347, November.

[15] Chen, Richard Y., Szymon Sidor, Pieter Abbeel, and John Schulman. 2017. "UCB Exploration via Q-Ensembles" (*https://oreil.ly/c2e4v*). ArXiv:1706.01502, November.

[16] Menon, Rakesh R., and Balaraman Ravindran. 2017. "Shared Learning: Enhancing Reinforcement in Q-Ensembles" (*https://oreil.ly/dYjc7*). ArXiv:1709.04909, September.

[17] Jain, Siddhartha, Ge Liu, Jonas Mueller, and David Gifford. 2019. "Maximizing Overall Diversity for Improved Uncertainty Estimates in Deep Ensembles" (*https://oreil.ly/Ounz8*). ArXiv:1906.07380, June.

[18] Dabney, Will, Mark Rowland, Marc G. Bellemare, and Rémi Munos. 2017. "Distributional Reinforcement Learning with Quantile Regression" (*https://oreil.ly/pLAuN*). ArXiv:1710.10044, October.

[19] Lyle, Clare, Pablo Samuel Castro, and Marc G. Bellemare. 2019. "A Comparative Analysis of Expected and Distributional Reinforcement Learning" (*https://oreil.ly/jY6-f*). ArXiv:1901.11084, February.

[20] Fujimoto, Scott, David Meger, and Doina Precup. 2019. "Off-Policy Deep Reinforcement Learning without Exploration" (*https://oreil.ly/6EdcI*). ArXiv:1812.02900, August.

[21] Shah, Devavrat, and Qiaomin Xie. 2018. "Q-Learning with Nearest Neighbors" (*https://oreil.ly/1VJH5*). ArXiv:1802.03900, October.

[22] Gaskett, Chris, David Wettergreen, and Alexander Zelinsky. 1999. "Q-Learning in Continuous State and Action Spaces" (*https://oreil.ly/jMjWm*). In *Advanced Topics in Artificial Intelligence*, edited by Norman Foo, 417–28. Lecture Notes in Computer Science. Berlin, Heidelberg: Springer.

CHAPTER 5

Policy Gradient Methods

Chapter 2 introduced value methods, which allow agents to learn the expected return by visiting each state-action pair. The agent can then choose the most valuable action at each time step to maximize the reward. You saw three different ways of estimating the expected return—Monte Carlo, dynamic programming, and temporal-difference methods—but all attempt quantify the value of each state.

Think about the problem again. Why do you want to learn expected values? They allow you to iterate toward an optimal policy. Q-learning finds the optimal policy by repeatedly maximizing the next expected value. But this is an indirect route to a policy. Is it possible to find the optimal policy directly? The answer is yes. Policy-based methods allow the agent to select actions without consulting a value function and learn an optimal policy directly.

Benefits of Learning a Policy Directly

"Optimal Policies" on page 48 defined the policy as the probability of an action given a state. Q-learning delivered that policy by driving actions to produce the optimal policy. This simplification is appropriate for deterministic problems. Take the card game blackjack (also called 21 or pontoon), for example. You play by deciding whether to draw another card to increase the combined sum of the numbers on the cards, or not, by *sticking* with what you have. With a score of 22 or higher you lose the game by going bust. Another player does the same and the highest score wins.

One deterministic policy is to stick when you reach 21, otherwise you will lose every time. Value methods are appropriate for this problem. But what about when your reward is 17 and the other player is looking nervous? In a real game you would make a prediction, based upon the observation of the environment, which is often stochastic in real-life problems. A deterministic policy would choose the same action every time, irrespective of the chance that the person might be bluffing. But a stochastic policy could choose randomly between the two options, using the stochastic observation as evidence toward one or the other.

Using a stochastic policy provides another benefit; it neatly encapsulates the exploration dilemma. The agent can select actions according to arbitrary probabilities, removing the need for forced exploration strategies like ϵ-greedy. And for problems that include function approximation (any algorithm predicting Q-values), the best approximate policy could be stochastic.

A further benefit is that stochastic policy action preferences change smoothly over time. Action-value methods could chatter between two almost equally likely actions, creating unstable transitions. This occurs even when action-value estimates are relatively stable; minor changes in the Q-values are enough to dramatically change the policy. In contrast, stochastic policies provide the capability of probabilistic actions, which may result in more robust policies.

But the key difference is that the policy might be easier to approximate. Industrial problems tend to span a spectrum. Sometimes approximating the action-value function is easier, other times directly obtaining the policy is. Where the policy is easier to approximate, policy-based methods will learn faster.

How to Calculate the Gradient of a Policy

The goal of this section is to establish a method to derive an optimal policy. In general, you cannot use an analytic method; policies are potentially nonlinear and interactions with the environment make the problem nonstationary (which means that the distribution of the data changes). Chapter 4 introduced the idea of using a function to approximate the action-value estimates. This was possible because the agent could store previous interactions with the environment for later use. You can leverage a similar procedure to find an optimal policy, but first you need to define what you are trying to solve.

Recall that the goal of reinforcement learning (RL) is to create an optimal policy, π_*, which maximizes the expected return, G. If you had full observability of all possible trajectories, you could derive the optimal policy directly. But in general the number of permutations is too high (or infinite for continuous states or actions). Instead, you can create a parameterized model of the policy and tinker with the parameters until you find a good policy.

For example, a reasonable long-term index buying strategy could be to hold when the market is increasing and buy when the market is dropping. This way you gain when the market gains and you buy cheap assets when the market drops. Assuming that the index will continue to increase in the long term, this is a safe, low-volatility strategy. The model for such a policy could be a linear coefficient describing the current trend of the index. You could find the optimal policy by testing lots of different values for the linear parameter. But how should you quantify performance?

In the field of optimization, performance is a function, $J(\theta)$, parameterized by a model's parameters, θ. Equation 5-1 is the objective function in this case, which is the expectation of the total reward when following a policy, π.

Equation 5-1. The policy objective function

$$J(\theta) \doteq \mathbb{E}_{\pi}[G \mid s, a]$$

Assuming for a moment that you can calculate the objective function, then the challenge is to nudge the parameters of the policy to maximize the return. One popular method to achieve this is to use the gradient of the objective function, with respect to the parameters, $\nabla_{\theta} J(\theta)$, to direct improvements. This is called *vanilla gradient ascent* and is shown in Equation 5-2 (note that gradient descent is the same as gradient ascent but with the sign changed to move downhill, instead of uphill).

Equation 5-2. Vanilla gradient ascent

$$\theta \leftarrow \theta + \alpha \nabla_{\theta} J(\theta)$$

Policy Gradient Theorem

To restate the previous section, you are trying to calculate the gradient of the total reward, with respect to the policy parameters. This would tell you how to nudge the parameters to increase the reward.

But this depends on calculating the gradient of the objective function (Equation 5-1). This isn't as straightforward as it might seem, because the derivative requires some slightly complicated mathematics. But the main issue is that gradient ascent assumes the distribution of the data is stationary. A policy-based agent is going to be updating the policy at the same time as generating trajectories. This is like trying to pull a rug while standing on it. I will tackle the nonstationary problem later; for now let me carry on with the gradient derivation.

I think it is important that you see how the gradient is derived so I have worked hard to simplify the derivation as much as possible. It is best to read this derivation line by line, referring to the explanation underneath. You can find a formal derivation in the resources found in "Further Reading" on page 143. I have removed the references to θ; in all cases the policy, π_{θ}, is defined by its parameters, θ. Also note that this derivation is for the undiscounted case. The result of this derivation is shown in Equation 5-3.

Equation 5-3. The gradient of a policy

$$\nabla J(\theta) \doteq \nabla \mathbb{E}_\pi \left[G \mid s, a \right] \qquad (1)$$

$$= \nabla \sum_{a \in \mathcal{A}} \left[Q(s, a) \pi(a \mid s) \right] \qquad (2)$$

$$\propto \sum_{a \in \mathcal{A}} \left[Q(s, a) \nabla \pi(a \mid s) \right] \qquad (3)$$

$$\propto \sum_{a \in \mathcal{A}} \left[Q(s, a) \pi(a \mid s) \frac{\nabla \pi(a \mid s)}{\pi(a \mid s)} \right] \qquad (4)$$

$$\propto \sum_{a \in \mathcal{A}} \left[Q(s, a) \pi(a \mid s) \nabla \ln \pi(a \mid s) \right] \qquad (5)$$

$$\propto \mathbb{E}_\pi \left[G \nabla \ln \pi(a \mid s) \right] \qquad (6)$$

The goal is to find the gradient of the objective function (Equation 5-1), which I describe in step (1).

In step (2), I have replaced the expected return with an implementation. You could pick any, but it makes the math a bit easier if you choose the the action-value function. The expected return is equal to the value of each action, Q, multiplied by the probability of visiting that action (as defined by the policy, π).

 Equation 5-1 has a large amount of mathematics between step (2) and (3). It results in a formality that the gradient is dependent on the distribution of states. In other words, the gradient is proportional to the probability of being in a certain state; if it is impossible to land in a state then it doesn't affect the gradient. Therefore, the gradient is only proportional to changes in the policy. I decided to hide these steps and the state distribution because eventually it cancels out due to the return of the expectation. If you are interested in the formal proof, please refer to the resources found in "Further Reading" on page 143.

The gradient is taken with respect to the policy parameters, so I can move the action-value function, Q, outside of the gradient calculation in step (3).

Step (4) uses a cheeky mathematical trick that is only obvious with hindsight. I have multiplied the whole equation by $\pi(a \mid s)/\pi(a \mid s)$, which is equal to one, so it doesn't alter the equation.

Step (5) uses a common mathematical identity, $\nabla \ln x = \nabla x / x$, to replace the fraction with a natural logarithm. This is a common computational trick to prevent the multiplication of small probabilities driving the gradients to zero (this is called the vanishing gradients problem).

Finally in step (6), recall that the sum of the action values multiplied by the action probabilities is precisely what I started with in step (2). So rather than summing over all actions, I can instead tell the agent to follow the policy and return the expectation of that particular action over time.

There you are: the derivation of the policy gradient algorithm. To summarize the result, the gradient of the return, with respect to the policy, is equal to the expected value of the return, multiplied by the gradient of the policy. In other words, the expected return magnifies the gradient of the policy. This makes sense because we prefer to nudge the parameters of the policy more when the expected value is higher.

 The key insight is that the return, G, can be estimated in a wide variety of ways. This is the the only difference between many famous policy gradient algorithms. I return to this in "A Comparison of Basic Policy Gradient Algorithms" on page 135.

Step (6) in Equation 5-3 is a quantity that can be sampled on each time step, whose expectation is equal to the gradient. You can plug this into the gradient ascent algorithm (Equation 5-2) to produce an update rule for an agent, like in Equation 5-4.

Equation 5-4. Policy gradient update rule

$$\theta \leftarrow \theta + \alpha G \nabla \ln \pi(a \mid s, \theta)$$

Policy Functions

Refer back to Equation 5-4. Two key details are missing from the policy gradient algorithm. The first is the definition of G, which I discuss in "Basic Implementations" on page 122.

The second is the gradient of a policy. I need to calculate $\nabla \ln \pi(a \mid s, \theta)$ and to do this I need to specify my policy function.

I must admit that I despair at the need to design another model, but the choice is important. The policy defines how well your agent can plan through all the possible trajectories in your environment. It needs to be complex enough to handle complex trajectories, but simple enough to learn. There has been some focus on attempting to automate this process.[1]

But the major benefit, and one of the major reasons why policy gradient methods are popular, is that you can choose *any* function, as long as it outputs a probability distribution and is differentiable with respect to θ. The world is your oyster, if models are your pearls.

Linear Policies

If you are using a library that performs automatic differentiation, like TensorFlow or PyTorch via back-propagation, then you don't even need to think about the derivative. But I find it helps to think about a simple case to provide the intuition.

Logistic policy

You need a function that predicts an action given a state: $\pi_\theta(a \mid s)$. Recall that the policy has two requirements: it must output probabilities and it must be differentiable. Imagine for a second that you are tackling a problem that has two discrete actions, like the CartPole environment, where you have to decide whether to move the cart to the left or right (see "Example: DQN on the CartPole Environment" on page 94 for a description of the environment). The problem becomes a task of predicting one of two classes, given some inputs; it must output probabilities. The natural choice for this type of problem is the logistic function, commonly used in classification, because it is simple, linear, easy to differentiate, and naturally outputs probability estimates (according to the logistic distribution, which has larger tails when compared to the normal distribution). The logistic function, centered around zero with a maximum value of 1, is shown in Equation 5-5 (also known as the *sigmoid function*).

Equation 5-5. Logistic function

$$f(x) \doteq \frac{1}{1 + e^{-x}}$$

The CartPole environment has four states, so θ is a vector of four weights. To use this policy function, feed in the state and the current estimates for the weights and it will output the probability of selecting an action. In the beginning, the weights are randomly distributed and during training they are nudged toward selecting better actions. These steps will sound familiar if you are used to doing supervised machine learning.

In general you can use multiple logistic functions to model the probability in multiclass problems (this is equivalent to the softmax function that I use in "Softmax policy" on page 121). But since this environment has only two actions, and the output of Equation 5-5 spans from zero to one, you can assign the probability of one class equal to $f(\theta, s)$ and the probability of the other equal to $1 - f(\theta, s)$. This is *dummy encoding*, which is used in data cleaning. A policy that predicts an action, a, given states, s, based upon the logistic function, is shown in Equation 5-6.

Equation 5-6. Logistic policy

$$\pi_\theta(a \mid s) \doteq \begin{pmatrix} \pi_\theta(a = 0 \mid s) \\ \pi_\theta(a = 1 \mid s) \end{pmatrix} = \begin{pmatrix} \dfrac{1}{1 + e^{-\theta_0^T s}} \\ 1 - \dfrac{1}{1 + e^{-\theta_1^T s}} \end{pmatrix}$$

Equation 5-4 provides the equation to improve the weights, but you need the gradient of Equation 5-6 to do that. The result of this is shown in Equation 5-7, but you can see the full calculation in Appendix A.

Equation 5-7. Logistic policy gradient

$$\nabla \ln \pi(a \mid s, \theta) = \begin{pmatrix} s - s\pi(\theta_0^T s) \\ -s\pi(\theta_1^T s) \end{pmatrix}$$

The gradient has an intuitive explanation. Equation 5-7 is the difference between the observed state and the state expected by the policy.

Softmax policy

You can think of the softmax function as a multiclass version of the logistic function. This means you can use this to represent the probability of choosing from multiple actions. A softmax policy is defined in Equation 5-8.

Equation 5-8. Softmax policy

$$\pi_\theta(a \mid s) \doteq \frac{e^{\theta^T s}}{\sum_a e^{\theta_a^T s}}$$

In other words, Equation 5-8 is a logistic-like function normalized over all possible actions to ensure that all actions sum to one. The corresponding gradient is shown in Equation 5-9 and you can see the full derivation in Appendix B.

Equation 5-9. Softmax policy gradient

$$\nabla \ln \pi(a \mid s, \theta) = s - \sum_a s\pi(\theta^T s)$$

Like "Logistic policy" on page 120, the gradient shown in Equation 5-9 works out as the difference between the observed and expected feature vectors.

Arbitrary Policies

Computing the derivatives of policies by hand has allowed me to show you precisely how I can improve a policy via iteration. But in general, this process is both tedious and obfuscating. Instead, you could compute a derivative in the following three ways: finite, automatic, and symbolic.

Finite differences calculate the difference in a policy over a small step in the parameter space, $\nabla f(x) = (f(x + h) - f(x))/2h$. This is simple but prone to numerical error because of the step size, h.

Automatic differentiation tools, like JAX (*https://oreil.ly/lPjjA*) or the backpropagation methods in TensorFlow/PyTorch/MXNet/others, attempt to track the usage of a parameter in an equation to build a directed acyclic graph (DAG). The DAG libraries map each step to the appropriate derivative and combine them through the chain rule.

Symbolic differentiation, using tools like SymPy (*https://www.sympy.org*), is effectively the same as automatic differentiation except it generally works in one direction (forward). Symbolic differentiation tools also place more emphasis on refactoring, which can result in derivatives that are easier to understand, as opposed to automatic methods that can result in chains of chains of chains, and so on.

In other words, if you can leverage a library, I recommend that you don't do the differentiation by hand. Use a library that suits your use case.

Basic Implementations

"Policy Functions" on page 119 showed you how to provide the gradient function required by Equation 5-4. The remaining detail is the use of G. Recall that this is the total reward from a point up until the end of an episode, if episodic, or forever more, if not (see "Discounted Rewards" on page 42).

Chapters 2–4 show three different ways of calculating expected return, from Monte Carlo, full trajectory methods through to approximation, multistep projection methods. These implementation details are the only difference between several basic policy gradient implementations, including the REINFORCE and actor-critic algorithms.

Monte Carlo (REINFORCE)

The first algorithm uses a Monte Carlo approach. It first collects a trajectory, based upon the current policy, for an entire episode. It then updates the policy via Equation 5-4.

Algorithm 5-1 shows the REINFORCE algorithm. In step (6), G refers to the discounted reward from a time t up until the end of the episode, like in Algorithm 2-3. In step (7), I use the value of G to weight the differential of the policy. The differential calculates the direction in which you need to nudge the probability of choosing an action, defined by θ. The collective weighting of $\alpha \gamma^t G$ defines how much you need to nudge it by. I also reintroduce discounting in step (7), which is pulled out of the derivative because it does not depend on θ.

The issue here is that REINFORCE will continue to promote an action in proportion to the calculated return. Even when an agent made the right choice, REINFORCE will continue to push the probability of choosing that action even higher. In the long term, it can overweight the relative importance of an action compared to other actions and this affects learning performance. For example, all actions might have an equal expected return, but REINFORCE will always increase the probability of the last action.

Algorithm 5-1. REINFORCE algorithm

1: **input**: a differentiable parameterized policy $\pi(a \mid s, \theta)$, step size $\alpha > 0$

2: Initialize θ arbitrarily

3: **loop** for each episode:

4:     Generate trajectory following $\pi(\cdot \mid \cdot, \theta)$

5:     **for** each step in episode $t \leftarrow 0, 1, \cdots, T$:

6:         $G \leftarrow \displaystyle\sum_{k=t+1}^{T} \gamma^{k-t-1} r_k$

7:         $\theta \leftarrow \theta + \alpha \gamma^t G \nabla \ln \pi(a \mid s, \theta)$

8:     **endfor**

Example: REINFORCE on the CartPole environment

The beauty of using policy gradients is demonstrated by the low dimensionality of the policy. The CartPole environment has four features. The linear policy has four parameters that weight the importance of each of the features. The result is a probabilistic representation of the best course of action. If the angle of the pole is close to falling over, then the probability of choosing an action to attempt to correct that is very high. The rewards obtained during the training process are shown in Figure 5-1. The policy should look far into the future to obtain good rewards, so I set $\gamma \doteq 0.99$. I chose $\alpha \doteq 0.01$ because at higher values the learning was unstable.

Compare this result to the tabular implementation in "Example: DQN on the Cart-Pole Environment" on page 94. There, I had to use a neural network to approximate the state space. Here, I have a linear mapping using just four parameters. The elegance, the sheer utility, is incredible.

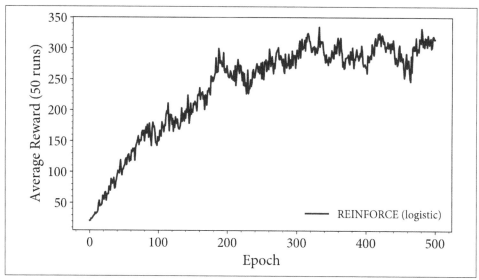

Figure 5-1. The average rewards using a REINFORCE-based policy gradient algorithm on the CartPole environment.

REINFORCE with Baseline

A more common implementation incorporates a baseline expected return, like the advantage function seen in "Dueling Networks" on page 102 (see Equation 4-4). This helps to improve the instability of the gradients due to large changes in the average reward.

Imagine a scenario (like CartPole) that rewards on each time step. This creates high expected returns during early time steps in a trajectory. Large changes in value create large updates to the gradients (as defined by Equation 5-4). But the agent should not concern itself with the machinations of the average return; the goal is to find optimal actions. The agent should instead learn how each action improves the expected return, relative to the average.

Advantage algorithms implement this by maintaining a prediction of the current average return for a given state, which is the same as the state-value function (see Equation 2-8). And as before, you can approximate the state-value function in many different ways: tabular methods or function approximation, for example. Since this is a parameterized Monte Carlo algorithm, it is natural to update a parameterized state-value estimate in a similar way, by calculating the error between predicted and actual values and nudging the parameters according to the update rule, along full episode trajectories.

The net result is an improvement in learning stability. The subtraction of the baseline means each gradient update is less extreme, which leads to lower variance in the gradients. In the long term you should observe that the rewards obtained during learning are more stable. But this depends heavily on the complexity of the state space, whether it is possible to predict the state-value function and the complexity of the actions. In the CartPole example, both are very simple, so you should expect little difference over the standard REINFORCE algorithm.

Algorithm 5-2 describes the REINFORCE algorithm with the baseline. The major difference is the addition of steps (7) and (8). Here, I train a second linear function to approximate the state-value function. Step (7) subtracts the approximation from the reward observed in this trajectory. When applied to the policy weights in step (9), this has the effect of altering the probability of choosing the action according to the difference. If the difference is greater than zero (the reward is higher than the baseline), the probability is increased. If the difference is less than zero, the probability is decreased.

Algorithm 5-2. REINFORCE with baseline algorithm

1: **input**: a differentiable parameterized policy $\pi(a \mid s, \theta)$,
   a differentiable parameterized state-value function $V(s, w)$,
   step sizes $0 < \alpha_w < 0$ and $0 < \alpha_\theta < 1$

2: Initialize θ and w arbitrarily

3: **loop** for each episode:

4:    Generate trajectory following $\pi(\cdot \mid \cdot, \theta)$:

5:    **for** each step in episode $t \leftarrow 0, 1, \cdots, T$:

6:       $G \leftarrow \sum\limits_{k=t+1}^{T} \gamma^{k-t-1} r_k$

7:       $\delta \leftarrow G - V(s, w)$

8:       $w \leftarrow w + \alpha_w \delta \nabla V(s, \alpha_w)$

9:       $\theta \leftarrow \theta + \alpha_\theta \gamma^t \delta \nabla \ln \pi(a \mid s, \theta)$

10:   **endfor**

Example: REINFORCE with baseline on the CartPole environment

There were few changes to the experiment in "Example: REINFORCE on the CartPole environment" on page 123 except for the implementation of Algorithm 5-2. The main architectural decision is the implementation of the state-value estimate, $V(s, w)$. In my experiments I was struggling to find a simple function to fit the data. This was because the underlying state is surprisingly complex.

To keep the experiment as simple as possible, I decided to use a rolling average of the previously observed rewards; in other words, an online implementation of the average reward. Then I retrained the agent and saved the state and discounted rewards. Then I performed principal component analysis on the state to reduce the number of dimensions from four to one, to help simplify the feature space and enable plotting.

 You can read more about dimensionality reduction and principal component analysis in any book on machine learning; some recommendations are in "Further Reading" on page 112.

Figure 5-2 shows the plot of the principal component of the state against the discounted reward. The rewards are forming a triangular shape around the state value of zero. The predicted value is higher if you keep the state values around zero. In other words, if the state values are nonzero then this will, in general, produce a lower total reward, because the pole is falling over. I also find it amusing that the plot looks a lot like the *Eye of Providence* from the back of a dollar bill.

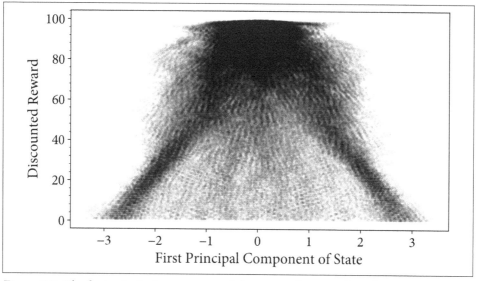

Figure 5-2. The first principal component of the CartPole state plotted against the discounted reward.

Irrespective of the coincidental iconography, you can see that a simple average or linear approximation will not predict the value well. Also, I have shown the first principal component for plotting purposes. The data probably contains complexity in the second, third, and fourth dimensions, too.

For now, I will stick with my choice of using the average and consider a more complicated approximation function in "Example: n-step actor-critic on the CartPole environment" on page 130. But in general, it is important to consider this trade-off. You want to predict the state-value function as well as possible, but you also want the function approximation to be robust (in the sense that an unseen state should not produce a ridiculous result).

The results of my experiment can be seen in Figure 5-3. I had to run the experiment over 50 different runs to obtain results that were statistically significant with the same settings. You can see that the reward initially tracks the standard REINFORCE algorithm, but later diverges. This indicates that the baseline algorithm is slightly more stable. In the REINFORCE algorithm, the large gradient updates accidentally knock the agent back toward worse performance. The baseline agent is able to steadily continue improving performance.

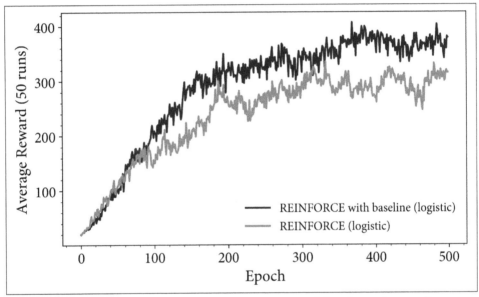

Figure 5-3. The average rewards using a REINFORCE with baseline policy gradient algorithm on the CartPole environment.

Gradient Variance Reduction

In "REINFORCE with Baseline" on page 124 I stated that the baseline method decreases the variance of the gradients. In algorithms like REINFORCE or other basic Monte Carlo methods (see "Monte Carlo Policy Generation" on page 50), the goal is to alter the policy to maximize the reward. Policy gradient methods achieve this by nudging the policy in a certain direction and by a certain amount. They calculate the direction using the derivative of the policy. But the magnitude, for REINFORCE, is the current expected return.

The problem with this is that subsequent samples may experience large differences in the expected return. For example, imagine that a policy is reasonably efficient in the CartPole environment. The pole may, due to chance, accidentally fall over early in the episode. This will cause a large difference in the expected value and a large gradient update. Despite the fact that the policy was a good one, the agent forced a large update.

Another example is in the Pong environment from "Example: Rainbow DQN on Atari Games" on page 103. Early episodes result in rewards close to –21. All actions result in a negative reward. Because all options are bad, the gradient update suppresses all actions. A better solution is to look at the change in the reward. The agent should use the relative difference of the actions compared to the average value.

I captured the gradient updates from a single run of the REINFORCE and REINFORCE with baseline algorithms. You can see the standard deviation of the gradients in Figure 5-4. Notice that after a period of learning, the standard deviation of the baseline algorithm drops dramatically, whereas the REINFORCE algorithm continues to produce large gradients that alter the policy, even after obtaining decent rewards. When the literature talks about "variance reduction," this is what they mean: methods to improve the stability of the gradients without affecting learning performance.

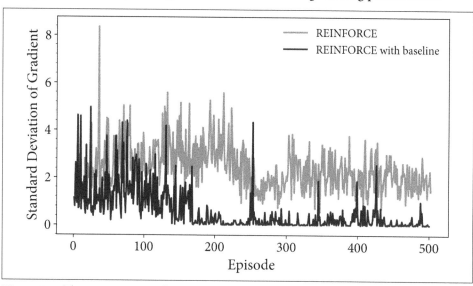

Figure 5-4. The average rewards using a REINFORCE with baseline policy gradient algorithm on the CartPole environment.

n-Step Actor-Critic and Advantage Actor-Critic (A2C)

The next improvement follows the path taken with tabular methods. Monte Carlo agents do not bootstrap, which means they have to wait until the episode is over before they can perform any learning. As in Chapter 3, the solution is to work through temporal-difference methods up to n-step methods. However, policy gradient-based n-step algorithms have an interesting interpretation that you have not seen before.

Before I get there, let me describe the n-step implementation because there is one major change over Algorithm 5-2. In step (5) of Algorithm 5-3, the algorithm performs an update for every time step. This is no longer a Monte Carlo algorithm. Bootstrapping (see "n-Step Algorithms" on page 76) improves learning speed and step (8) implements the bootstrapping, to provide one-step updates $G_{t:t+1} \doteq r + \gamma V(s', w)$, like in Equation 3-3.

Algorithm 5-3. n-step actor-critic

1: **input**: a differentiable parameterized policy $\pi(a \mid s, \theta)$,

 a differentiable parameterized state-value function $V(s, w)$,

 step sizes α_w and $\alpha_\theta > 0$

2: Initialize θ and w

3: **loop** for each episode:

4: Initialize $I \leftarrow 1, t \leftarrow 0,$ and s

5: **while** s is not terminal:

6: Choose a from s using π

7: Take action a, observe s', r

8: $\delta \leftarrow G_{t:t+n} - V(s, w)$

9: $w \leftarrow w + \alpha_w \delta \nabla V(s, w)$

10: $\theta \leftarrow \theta + \alpha_\theta I \delta \nabla \ln \pi(a \mid s, \theta)$

11: $I \leftarrow \gamma I$

12: $s \leftarrow s'$

13: $t \leftarrow t + 1$

Algorithm 5-3 is an incremental improvement over Algorithm 5-2 that includes the temporal-difference return. But this algorithm is more than it seems. You have now derived an algorithm that can learn both a policy and its state-value function on every single step, as opposed to learning a baseline over entire trajectories (the Monte Carlo-inspired baseline algorithm).

This distinction is important. The policy learns and describes the best action to take. In RL parlance, this is known as the *actor*. The n-step baseline prediction criticizes the consequences of the action and is used to update the policy. This is the *critic*. Together they form the basis of *actor-critic* algorithms. Note that Monte Carlo algorithms are not considered to be actor-critic because they are not updated on every step.

This is more commonly called the advantage actor-critic (A2C) algorithm. I presented the algorithm in this way because you are familiar with development from Chapter 3. But another way of formulating the problem is to consider the critic as a measure of the benefit of choosing an action, relative to a baseline. This is the exact definition of the advantage function from Equation 4-4.

In the context of policy gradient algorithms, the only difference is that the agent follows the current optimal policy by definition, so you don't need to calculate the value of each action. You only need the value for the states that the policy is going to visit. An approximation (which is proven in the reference) is presented in Equation 5-10.[2]

Equation 5-10. Advantage function approximation for policy gradient algorithms

$$
\begin{aligned}
A^{\pi}(s, a) &\doteq Q(s, a) - V(s) \\
&= r + Q(s', a') - V(s) \quad\quad\quad\quad \text{(temporal-difference error)} \\
&\approx r + V_{\pi}(s') - V(s) \quad \text{(when the agent is following the optimal policy } \pi\text{)}
\end{aligned}
$$

It is possible to estimate the advantage function or the action-value function directly, but most implementations use the state-value version to reduce the number of models you need to train.

Another common question is the need for I in step (11) of Algorithm 5-3. When including discounting (see "Discounted Rewards" on page 42) in the policy gradient theorem (Equation 5-3), γ is a constant on the outside of the gradient calculation. But the discounting depends on the step number and in an online algorithm like this it makes sense to implement it in this way, although you could simply replace it with a γ^t if you like.

Example: n-step actor-critic on the CartPole environment

The goal of this example is to demonstrate the differences between Monte Carlo (see "REINFORCE with Baseline" on page 124) and temporal-difference policy gradient implementations produced by the use of bootstrapping.

Recall that bootstrapping requires a function that estimates the expected return of a given state. If I used the rolling average of the reward, like I did in "Example: REINFORCE with baseline on the CartPole environment" on page 125, then the estimates for $V(s, w)$ and $V(s', w)$ are the same. This yields $\delta = r + (1 - \gamma)V \approx r$. Using the previous baseline leads to updates that have a magnitude of 1 in the CartPole environment. In other words, the critic has no opinion. Instead, you must design a function that is more capable of predicting the value for a given state. The learning performance of an actor-critic algorithm is dependent on having an accurate value approximation.

You saw in Figure 5-2 that the reward is a complex function of the state. A simple linear combination of the state and some weights is not capable of modeling this complexity. There is a trend to jump straight to a deep learning approach at this point, but I still recommend trying linear approaches first. They are more robust, faster to train, and harder to overfit. In the CartPole environment I can perform feature engineering on the state to obtain features that are learnable via a linear combination of weights.

After some experimentation I chose to use tile coding to convert the last two states (pole angle and angular velocity) into a grid of 10 cells per state with 5 overlaps (you can learn more about common feature engineering techniques in "Converting to discrete states" on page 272). This results in 605 features. I used 605 weights to learn a linear approximation of these features. The settings are the same as before except for the new decay parameter for the weights, $\alpha_w \doteq 0.1$. It is generally recommended that the value estimate should have a learning rate greater than or equal to the learning rate of the policy. In other words, the value estimate should learn at least as fast as the policy.

Figure 5-5 shows the results of intentionally setting the policy learning rate, α_θ, to match the final learning performance of the previous algorithms.

Figure 5-6 shows the results after increasing the policy decay rates (for both actor-critic and baseline algorithms) to $\alpha_\theta \doteq 0.1$. All other settings remain the same. The increase in decay rate means that the updates made to the policy are larger. The policy changes quicker. After removing the training wheels, you can see that the n-step actor-critic algorithm can keep up. It rapidly increases its reward over the first 50 episodes and settles around a reward of 400 (which is dependent on the modeling accuracy of the policy and the state-value function, not the learning rate). The baseline algorithm, however, is unable to learn any faster. The Monte Carlo updates significantly hamper learning performance. They act like a brake; changing the policy learning rate has no effect (and can affect long-term stability).

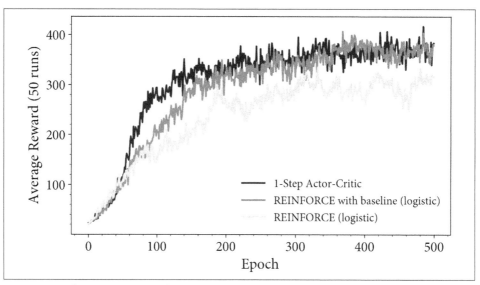

Figure 5-5. The average rewards using a 1-step actor-critic policy gradient algorithm on the `CartPole` *environment.*

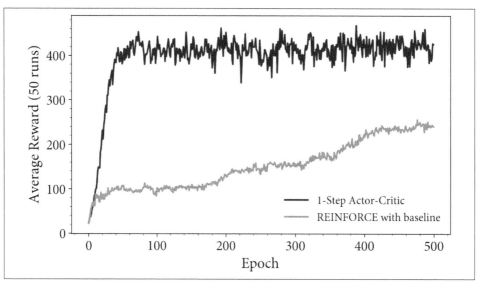

Figure 5-6. The average rewards for the `CartPole` *environment after altering the policy decay rate (α_θ) from* 0.01–0.1 *for both actor-critic and baseline algorithms.*

State-value learning decay rates versus policy decay rates

The decay-rate parameters denoted by α regulate the size of the jump in the update. Since this is a gradient descent algorithm, choose the decay rate to be large enough to learn quickly, but small enough to converge toward the best possible policy. But the n-step policy gradient algorithm uses two decay rates: one for the model that estimates the state value function and another for the policy.

The policy uses the state-value estimate in its update, which introduces a dependency. Setting the state-value estimate α to update slowly will constrain the policy. This is because the temporal-difference error in successive steps will be close to zero and result in a small change to the policy. Setting α to update quickly will cause excessive changes in the temporal-difference error and large changes in the policy. After the policy has changed, the true state value will also change and the state-value estimate will require another large update. The end result is instability and then the agent is unlikely to converge.

The results shown in Figure 5-7 come from an experiment on the `CartPole` environment where I fixed the policy decay rate, $\alpha_\theta \doteq 0.1$, and altered the state-value estimate decay rate, $\alpha_w \doteq \{0.01, 0.1, 0.5\}$. The results show that the optimal decay rate is approximately 0.1, although a value of 0.01 can eke out greater performance in the long run because the smaller step size gets closer to the global optima. A value of 0.5 is too great; it causes unstable updates and prevents convergence.

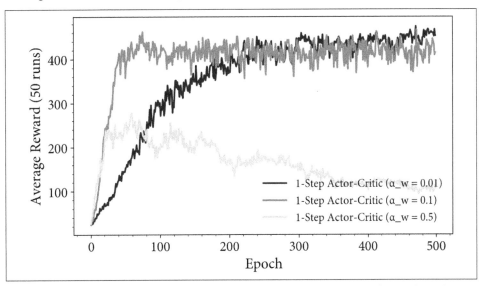

Figure 5-7. The average rewards for the `CartPole` *environment when fixing the policy decay rate and altering the state-value decay rate.*

There is a popular mathematical theorem called "no free lunch," which I excessively summarize as proof that no single algorithm, implementation, or hyperparameters are best for all applications. Similarly, optimal decay rates are entirely dependent on the problem and the algorithm. You must design and tune agents for every new situation.[3]

Eligibility Traces Actor-Critic

Following the developments in "Eligibility Traces" on page 80, Algorithm 5-4 presents an actor-critic algorithm based upon eligibility traces. Like before, it exposes a hyperparameter to allow you to control the level of bootstrapping. The optimal value for the trace-decay hyperparameter is problem dependent. Large values update weights experienced far in the past. Small values only update recent weights. The major difference between Algorithm 5-4 and Algorithm 5-3 is the inclusion of the tracers that track which states to update in steps 9 and 10. These ultimately nudge the value estimate weights, w, and the policy weights, θ, in the direction that the policy visited in the past.

Algorithm 5-4. Actor-critic with eligibility traces

1: **input**: a differentiable parameterized policy $\pi(a \mid s, \theta)$,
   a differentiable parameterized state-value function $V(s, w)$,
   step sizes $0 < \alpha_w, \alpha_\theta < 1$, and trace-decay rates $0 \le \lambda_\theta, \lambda_w \le 1$

2: Initialize θ and w arbitrarily

3: **loop** for each episode:

4:     Initialize $t \leftarrow 0, I \leftarrow 1$ and s,
   $z_w \leftarrow 0$ (same dimensionality as w), and
   $z_\theta \leftarrow 0$ (same dimensionality as θ)

5:     **while** s is not terminal:

6:         Choose a from s using π

7:         Take action a, observe s', r

8:         $\delta \leftarrow r + \gamma V(s', w) - V(s, w)$

9:         $z_w \leftarrow \gamma \lambda_w z_w + \nabla V(s, w)$

10:        $z_\theta \leftarrow \gamma \lambda_\theta z_\theta + I \nabla \ln \pi(a \mid s, \theta)$

11:        $w \leftarrow w + \alpha_w \delta z_w$

12:        $\theta \leftarrow \theta + \alpha_\theta I \delta z_\theta$

13:        $I \leftarrow \gamma I$

14:        $s \leftarrow s'$

15:        $t \leftarrow t + 1$

Example: Eligibility trace actor-critic on the CartPole environment

I made minor modifications to the example in "Example: n-step actor-critic on the CartPole environment" on page 130 to include the decaying eligibility traces. This experiment uses $\alpha_\theta = \alpha_w = \lambda_\theta = \lambda_w \doteq 0.1$; you can observe the results in Figure 5-8.

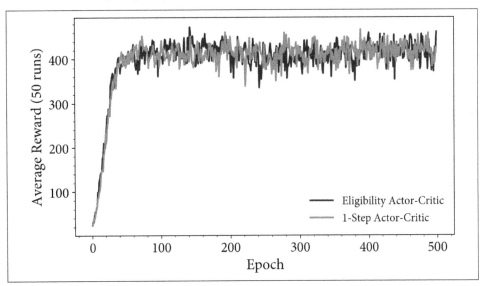

Figure 5-8. The average rewards for the `CartPole` environment for the 1-step actor-critic and eligibility traces algorithm.

The performance is largely unchanged. This demonstrates that a successful agent does not require foresight in the `CartPole` environment. Observing the potential downfall at the next step is adequate.

Changing the value of λ has little effect except for values of 0, where there is no temporal-difference update, and 1, where gradients explode. In my experiments, all values in between led to similar results.

In environments where rewards are infrequent or a significant amount of planning is required, multistep temporal-difference estimates excel.

A Comparison of Basic Policy Gradient Algorithms

This chapter has presented four different implementations of the policy gradient algorithm. All use gradient descent to iteratively improve the policy, but each have different value estimate implementations. A better value estimate reduces unnecessarily large updates; it reduces the variance of the gradients.

You can see the different forms in Equation 5-11. The gradient of the policy is equal to the expectation of the gradient of the parameters multiplied by the return. The only thing that differs between these algorithms is how you quantify the return. I find this high-level interpretation of policy gradient algorithms insightful because it clarifies the subtle changes between distinct implementations.

Equation 5-11. Equivalent implementations of the policy gradient algorithm

$$\nabla_\theta J(\theta) \doteq \mathbb{E}_{\pi_\theta}\!\left[\nabla_\theta \ln \pi_\theta(a \mid s)G\right] \qquad \text{(REINFORCE)}$$

$$\doteq \mathbb{E}_{\pi_\theta}\!\left[\nabla_\theta \ln \pi_\theta(a \mid s)\big(G - V_w(s)\big)\right] \qquad \text{(REINFORCE with Baseline)}$$

$$\doteq \mathbb{E}_{\pi_\theta}\!\left[\nabla_\theta \ln \pi_\theta(a \mid s)Q_w(s, a)\right] \qquad \text{(Actor-Critic)}$$

$$\doteq \mathbb{E}_{\pi_\theta}\!\left[\nabla_\theta \ln \pi_\theta(a \mid s)A_w(s, a)\right] \qquad \text{(Advantage Actor-Critic)}$$

$$\doteq \mathbb{E}_{\pi_\theta}\!\left[\nabla_\theta \ln \pi_\theta(a \mid s)\delta\right] \qquad \text{(Temporal-Difference Actor-Critic)}$$

$$\doteq \mathbb{E}_{\pi_\theta}\!\left[\nabla_\theta \ln \pi_\theta(a \mid s)\delta(\lambda)\right] \qquad \text{(Eligibility Actor-Critic)}$$

Industrial Example: Automatically Purchasing Products for Customers

A recent business model trend is to automatically deliver products to customers and allow them to return those that they are not interested in. Stitch Fix is one of the most famous of the *subscription box model* businesses. After submitting a smorgasbord of initial information about body type and personal preferences, a Stitch Fix customer will be sent a package full of new clothes. The customer is then free to send back any clothes they don't like and they are charged for the items they keep (plus a service fee).

This idea might sound novel, but companies have been doing this for a long time via "no-commitment" subscription models. For example, Hewlett Packard will happily deliver ink for your printer at a prescribed rate. You can subscribe to certain products on Amazon. Hello Fresh will deliver you food. The difference between no-commitment and subscription box models is that if the customer is on the wrong plan (for example, they are receiving too much ink), they are likely to cancel. It is in HP's interest to deliver ink at the right rate to maximize the customer lifetime value.

I want to stress how impressive this challenge is. Here, an agent with no human intervention can automatically send you products and iteratively learn your preferences. You will receive items when you need them without you ordering them. Even better, the agent knows what items you might like, even though you have never thought of buying them yourself. From the perspective of a marketplace, this demonstrates why RL could be so lucrative. Vendors can sell you more stuff and you will be genuinely happy that they have!

The Environment: Gym-Shopping-Cart

This example embodies the subscription box model using publicly available data. I have created an environment (*https://gitlab.com/winderresearch/gym-shopping-cart*) that uses data from Instacart to simulate purchasing behavior.

Instacart open sourced three million orders (*https://oreil.ly/-g1ix*) from its shopping platform. I performed a significant amount of data cleaning that resulted in a state consisting of one-hot encoded day of the week and hour of the day. It also includes the number of days since the last order normalized to a value of 1. The actions are a list of 50,000 one-hot, binary encoded products. To order a product you set the product's column to 1. I keep the reward simple. You will receive a reward of +1 for every product that matches what the customer actually ordered. You will receive a reward – 1 for every incorrectly ordered product. The goal is to order what the customer desires and nothing else. Each order is a step and all orders for a single customer is an epoch.

This is a simplification over what happens in the real world. The actual rewards are unlikely to be as simple as +/– 1. Offering a new product to a customer might cause them to buy more in the future, whereas a mistake could cost a lot if the products are perishable and can't be resold. I am limited by the features offered in the dataset. Other features are likely to be more informative. For example, Stitch Fix has a library of your preferences. You should build a process to gather user preferences about what food they like.

But the greatest issue is that the simulation uses static data. Ideally the agent should explore which products the customer desires. The customer might not even know it yet. But with fixed data, you are optimizing to solve a static solution. In other words, you can use standard machine learning techniques. Actionable exploration is at the heart of RL and in this example there is none. RL is more than just prediction.

One potential solution to this is to model customer purchases. For example, you can build a generative adversarial network to model what customers purchase in a simulated, but dynamic environment. Then you could transfer the learned policy to a live environment (see "Further Reading" on page 143). For the sake of simplicity, I use the static data.

Expectations

The state and actions in this environment are binary, so you could use a tabular technique like Q-learning. But to continue the thread of this chapter I will use the eligibility actor-critic policy gradient algorithm (see "Eligibility Traces Actor-Critic" on page 134). The agent must generate the same number of binary actions as products. I use a linear policy with a logistic function for every action. Note that softmax is not appropriate because that normalizes all actions to have a total value of 1. I also model the value function as a linear function. Both are for the sake of simplicity. You could use more complex models.

Let me stop for a moment to set some expectations. The propensity to buy a product is a function of the customer's profile. You can imagine that if the customer had babies then they might be more likely to buy baby products. If they are vegan then they are unlikely to order meat. If they are young they will probably buy different products compared to someone who is old. All of these are latent features. They are not directly observable from the actions that they take. It is for this reason that it is unlikely that the linear model will perform very well in a real-life test. The linear model will learn how often customers buy products, ignoring *why* they buy them.

 Simplify the problem by reducing the number of latent features. Create explicit features.

In a real application then, it will pay dividends if you invest in building a more sophisticated model that represents the customers, not just the products. Given enough data, you should also look at deep learning to represent these higher-level features.

Another issue is that the linear model has no memory. When I bulk buy washing powder, I rarely buy more in the next shop. The exception is when the kids decide to build a bed-sheet den in the mud. But the linear weights see that I bought lots of washing powder and probably offer more. To learn that people buy products at different rates you have to introduce some memory. One of the simplest ways to achieve this is to include the previous orders in the state. This is how DQN works so well on the Atari environment, for example. The researchers found that four frames worth of pixels were enough to provide a proxy for memory. More advanced solutions include using stateful neural networks like recurrent and long short-term memory neurons (see "Common Neural Network Architectures" on page 89).

Results from the Shopping Cart Environment

Again, for the sake of simplicity, I stick with a linear implementation. To help with the scale of the problem—50,000 actions—I allow the agent to buy only the most popular products.

You can see the first results in Figure 5-9. In this initial experiment I restricted the dataset to a single customer. I chose to keep the 15 most popular products for this customer and trained the agent over 50 epochs. You can also see an agent that randomly orders products, for reference. In this example the customer had 358 purchases of popular products over 71 orders. Hence the highest reward possible is 358.

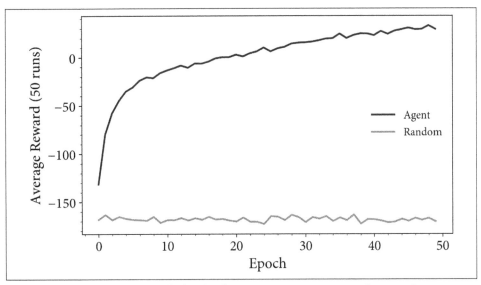

Figure 5-9. The average rewards for the shopping cart environment for a single customer (repeated 50 times) and for the 15 most popular products.

The highest reward for the agent was 57, indicating that the agent was buying products that the customer actually wanted. But this is much lower than the highest possible reward of 358 products. The random agent performs consistently poorly because it repeatedly orders products the customer does not want.

In Figure 5-10 I repeat the same experiment but this time with 50 random customers that have different numbers of orders. In other words, the agent cannot overfit a single customer. It must attempt to generalize to all customers. This time the agent achieves a maximum reward of –1. A little underwhelming compared to the previous experiment. This is saying that the agent is capable of just about breaking even for any given random customer. But you must remember how simple the agent is. The agent has only a handful of linear parameters and it is, to a limited extent, able to capture the complexity of the shopping process. I find this remarkable.

Figure 5-11 shows the performance of the same agent over random customers when altering the number of products that the agent can choose from. In other words, I am altering the number of actions. When the number of products increases the agent receives less reward. However, it does appear that performance is asymptotic. Performance may converge with more training time.

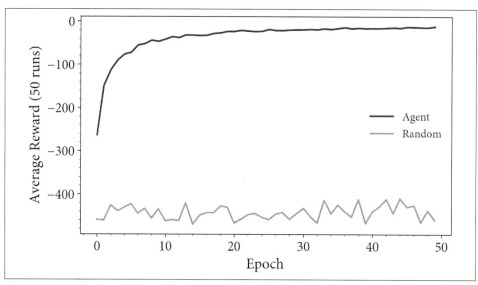

Figure 5-10. The average rewards for the shopping cart environment for 50 random customers (50 epochs) and for the 15 most popular products. The highest reward was –1.

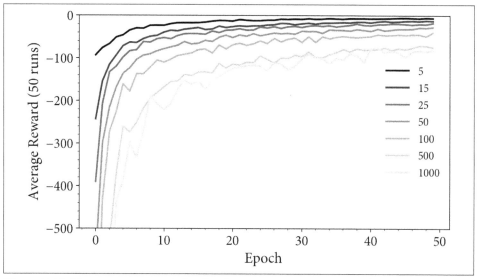

Figure 5-11. The average rewards for the shopping cart environment for 50 random customers (50 epochs) while altering the number of most popular products.

Finally, I want to demonstrate something called *transfer learning*. The goal is to train a model to solve one problem then apply the same model to a different, but related problem. This paradigm works really well with RL because you can potentially learn from offline data or models and fine-tune using online data.

For example, I can use the shopping cart model trained upon random customers (Figure 5-10) then transfer the learned model to a new customer. Figure 5-12 shows the results of such an experiment.

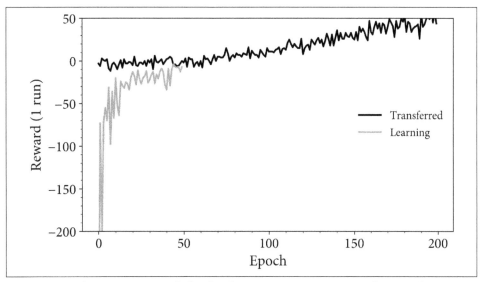

Figure 5-12. The average rewards for the shopping cart environment for a single customer after initially training upon random customer data and transferring the model (15 products, 1 run).

To transfer the model I copied the policy and value estimate weights learned when training on random customers and pasted them into another agent with only a single customer. Also, these results are for a single run. You can imagine a smoother set of results if I were to repeat this 50 times. If you compare this result to Figure 5-9, then you can see there is no initial ramp-up in performance because the pretrained weights are already very good.

Another observation is that it takes a long time (approximately 200 epochs) for the single customer agent to obtain similar performance to the result in Figure 5-9. This is because the agent has learned a policy that works best on average across all customers. When I transfer the policy across to a new agent on the single customer data, it needs to retrain those weights. But the average policy appears to have lowered the probability of exploring the states that are most important to that single customer.

In other words, it seems that in Figure 5-9, the agent has overfit for that particular customer. Typically overfitting is a bad thing, since the model will not generalize to other customers. But in this example, that is exactly the point. I want the agent to fit around the preferences of a single customer.

Here there is a trade-off. You want to start with a reasonable policy, so the customer receives good recommendations quickly. But you don't want to have to wait for 200 orders before they are in positive reward territory. One solution to this problem is to treat the number of pretraining epochs as a hyperparameter and tune it to obtain a satisfactory result.

Summary

Prior to this chapter, I focused on value-based methods, methods that quantify the value of being in a state. The policy is derived as a maximization of the expected value in each state. But another way is to parameterize the policy directly and alter the weights of the parameterization to produce a policy that maximizes the expected return. You can use policy gradient methods to find the updates necessary to optimize a policy.

Policy gradient methods have a range of advantages. They can learn to output probabilities, which negates the need for an explicit exploration algorithm like ϵ-greedy. They can output continuous actions. And sometimes it is easier to model the policy, rather than having to model the state-action value.

On the other hand, policy gradient methods tend to be more sensitive to the choice of model. With value methods, it is fairly easy to alter the complexity of the model to predict the expected value function, whereas the policy model needs to be chosen carefully.

This chapter followed the same derivation as before, from Monte Carlo through to eligibility traces. Even though policy-based methods are optimizing for a slightly different solution, expected value estimates are still incredibly important, as you saw in the actor-critic algorithms.

I presented a simplified industrial example where the goal was to automatically order products for users. You can imagine a large number of improvements to this and the generalization of this idea, recommenders, is an active area of RL research. I know of several organizations that are using RL for recommendation purposes.

Further Reading

- Gradient descent:
  - Ruder, Sebastian. 2017. "An Overview of Gradient Descent Optimization Algorithms." (*https://oreil.ly/iAYEs*) ArXiv:1609.04747, June.
- Policy gradient derivation:
  - A succinct mathematical introduction to on-policy gradients: Kämmerer, Mattis Manfred. 2019. "On Policy Gradients." (*https://oreil.ly/1EAUY*) ArXiv: 1911.04817, November.
  - Sutton, Richard S., and Andrew G. Barto. 2018. *Reinforcement Learning: An Introduction*. MIT Press.
- Building generative models:
  - Foster, David. 2019. *Generative Deep Learning: Teaching Machines to Paint, Write, Compose, and Play*. O'Reilly.

References

[1] Houthooft, Rein, Richard Y. Chen, Phillip Isola, Bradly C. Stadie, Filip Wolski, Jonathan Ho, and Pieter Abbeel. 2018. "Evolved Policy Gradients" (*https://oreil.ly/IQPmY*). ArXiv:1802.04821, April.

[2] Bhatnagar, Shalabh, Mohammad Ghavamzadeh, Mark Lee, and Richard S Sutton. 2008. "Incremental Natural Actor-Critic Algorithms" (*https://oreil.ly/9UYvm*). In *Advances in Neural Information Processing Systems* 20, edited by J. C. Platt, D. Koller, Y. Singer, and S. T. Roweis, 105–112. Curran Associates, Inc.

[3] Wolpert, D. H., and W. G. Macready. 1997. "No Free Lunch Theorems for Optimization" (*https://oreil.ly/lpi8x*). *IEEE Transactions on Evolutionary Computation* 1(1): 67–82.

CHAPTER 6

Beyond Policy Gradients

Policy gradient (PG) algorithms are widely used in reinforcement learning (RL) problems with continuous action spaces. Chapter 5 presented the basic idea: represent the policy by a parametric probability distribution $\pi_\theta \doteq \mathbb{P}[a \mid s; \theta]$, then adjust the policy parameters, θ, in the direction of greater cumulative reward. They are popular because an alternative, like the greedy maximization of the action-value function performed in Q-learning, becomes problematic if actions are continuous because this would involve a global maximization over an infinite number of actions. Nudging the policy parameters in the direction of higher expected return can be simpler and computationally attractive.

Until recently, practical online PG algorithms with convergence guarantees have been restricted to the *on-policy* setting, in which the agent learns from the policy it is executing, the *behavior* policy. In an *off-policy* setting, an agent learns policies different to the behavior policy. This idea presents new research opportunities and applications; for example, learning from an offline log, learning an optimal policy while executing an exploratory policy, learning from demonstration, and learning multiple tasks in parallel from a single environment.

This chapter investigates state-of-the-art off-policy PG algorithms, starting with an in-depth look at some of problems that arise when trying to learn off-policy.

Off-Policy Algorithms

The PG algorithms presented in Chapter 5 were on-policy; you generate new observations by following the current policy—the same policy that you want to improve. You have already seen that this approach, this feedback loop, can lead to overoptimistic expected returns (see "Double Q-Learning" on page 74). Off-policy algorithms decouple exploration and exploitation by using two policies: a target policy and a behavior policy.

All of the RL algorithms presented up to this point have performed a least-squares-like optimization, where estimates of a value approximation are compared to an observed result; if you observe a surprising result, then you update the estimate accordingly. In an off-policy setting, the target policy never has the opportunity to test its estimate, so how can you perform optimization?

Importance Sampling

Before I continue, I want you to understand something called importance sampling, which is the result of some mathematical trickery that allows you to estimate a quantity of interest without directly sampling it.

I've mentioned a few times so far that the expectation of a random variable, X, is the integral of an individual value, x, multiplied by the probability of obtaining that value, $f(x)$, for all possible values of x. In a continuous probability distribution this means $\mathbb{E}_f[x] \doteq \int_x x f(x)$. In the discrete case this is $\mathbb{E}_f[x] \doteq \sum_x x f(x)$. This is called the *population mean*.

But what if you don't know the probabilities? Well, you could still estimate the mean if you were able to sample from that environment. For example, consider a die. You don't know the probability of rolling any particular value, but you know there are six values. You can estimate the expected value by rolling the die and calculating the *sample mean*. In other words, you can estimate the expectation using $\mathbb{E}_f[x] \approx \frac{1}{n}\sum_{i=1}^{n} x_i$.

Now imagine that you had a second instance of a random variable, a second die for example, which resulted in the same values and you know the probability of those values, but you cannot sample from it. Bear with me here—this is not very realistic, but it is the crux of the problem. Say you knew how the second die was weighted, $g(x)$, but you couldn't throw it. Maybe it belongs to a notorious friend that seems to roll far too many sixes. In this case, you can formulate the expectation in the same way: $\mathbb{E}_g[x] = \sum_x x g(x)$. These are shown in steps (1) and (2) in Equation 6-1.

Equation 6-1. Importance sampling

$$\mathbb{E}_f[x] \doteq \sum_x x f(x) \quad (1)$$

$$\mathbb{E}_g[x] \doteq \sum_x x g(x) \quad (2)$$

$$= \sum_x \frac{x g(x)}{f(x)} f(x) \quad (3)$$

$$= \mathbb{E}_f\left[\frac{x g(x)}{f(x)}\right] \quad (4)$$

$$\approx \frac{1}{n} \sum_{i=1}^{n} \frac{x_i g(x_i)}{f(x_i)} \quad (5)$$

Next look at step (3). Here's the trick: I multiply step (2) by $f(x)/f(x) = 1$. Now the sum is with respect to $f(x)$, not $g(x)$, which means I can substitute in step (1) if you imagine that x is now $x g(x)/f(x)$, which results in step (4). In step (5) you can compute this expectation using the sample mean. If you concentrate you can probably follow the logic, but I want you understand what this means at a high level. It means you can calculate an expectation of a second probability function using the experience of the first. This is a crucial element of off-policy learning.

To demonstrate the idea behind Equation 6-1 I simulated rolling two dice: one fair, one biased. I know the probability distributions of the dice, but I can only roll the fair die. I can record the numbers generated by the fair die and plot a histogram. I can also measure the sample mean after each roll. You can see the results in Figure 6-1(a). Given enough rolls the histogram approaches uniformity and the sample mean approaches the population mean of 3.5.

In Figure 6-1(b), you can see the (crucial) known theoretical histogram of the biased die. It is theoretical because I cannot roll it. But, and here is the magic, using Equation 6-1 I can estimate the sample mean and you can see that it tends to 4.3, the correct sample mean for the biased die. Let me restate this again to make it absolutely clear. You cannot just calculate the population mean of the second variable, because you cannot sample from it. Importance sampling allows you to estimate the expected value of a second variable without having to sample from it.

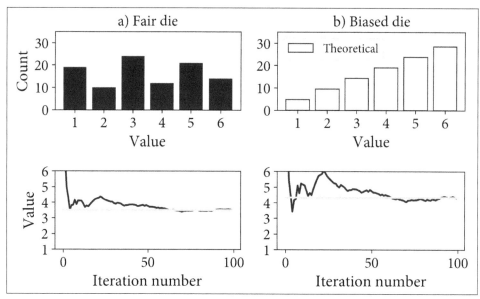

Figure 6-1. Using importance sampling to calculate the expected value of a die that you cannot roll.

Behavior and Target Policies

If you have two policies, one that you can sample, but one that you cannot, you can still obtain an expected value for both. An analogy would be learning to drive by observing someone driving. This calculation opens the door to true off-policy algorithms, where one policy drives the agent through exploration and the other(s) can do something else, like develop a more refined policy.

In RL, the term "off-policy learning" refers to learning an optimal policy, called the *target policy*, using data generated by a *behavior policy*. Freeing the behavior policy from the burden of finding the optimal policy allows for more flexible exploration. I expand upon this idea throughout this chapter.

The target policy is provided with information like my chickens are given food; they don't care where it comes from. The data could come from other agents like previous policies or humans, for example. Or in environments where it is hard or expensive to acquire new data but easy to store old data, like robotics, the data could be from an offline store.

Another interesting avenue of research, which I will return to later, is that you can learn multiple target policies from a single stream of data generated by a single behavior policy. This allows you to learn optimal policies for different subgoals (see "Hierarchical Reinforcement Learning" on page 220).

Off-Policy Q-Learning

One of the keys to off-policy learning is the use of approximations of the action-value function and of the policy. But traditional off-policy methods like Q-learning cannot immediately take advantage of linear approximations because they are unstable; the approximations diverge to infinity for any positive step size. But in 1999, Richard Sutton and his team first showed that stability was possible if you use the right objective function and gradient descent.[1] These methods were the basis for the advanced off-policy algorithms you will see later on.

Gradient Temporal-Difference Learning

In many problems the number of states is too large to approximate, like when there are continuous states. Linear function approximation maps states to feature vectors using a function, $\varphi(s)$. In other words, this function accepts states and outputs an abstract set of values with a different number of dimensions.

You can then approximate the state-value function using linear parameters, θ, by $V_\pi(s) \approx \theta^\mathsf{T} \varphi(s)$ (see "Policy Engineering" on page 268 for more details about policy engineering). Given this definition you can derive a new equation for the TD error like that in Equation 6-2.

Equation 6-2. Parameterized linear TD error

$$\delta \doteq r + \gamma \theta^\mathsf{T} \varphi(s') - \theta^\mathsf{T} \varphi(s)$$

This is the same equation as Equation 3-3 where the linear prediction is explicit. Note that in the literature $\varphi(s)$ is often abbreviated to φ. The steps required to rearrange this equation to solve for θ are involved, but the solution is refreshingly simple: use the TD error as a proxy for how wrong the current parameters are, find the gradient, nudge the parameters toward lower error, and iterate until it converges.

If you are interested in the derivation, then I redirect you to the paper. The resulting algorithm looks like Algorithm 6-1.[2]

Algorithm 6-1. GTD(0) algorithm

1: **input**: a policy that uses the parameterized action-value function, $\pi(a \mid Q(s, a; \theta))$, learning rate parameters, $0 > \alpha > 1$ and $0 > \beta > 1$

2: Initialize θ and u arbitrarily

3: **loop**: for each episode

4:     Initialize s

5:     **while** s is not terminal:

6:         Choose a from s using π, breaking ties randomly

7:         Take action, a, and observe r, s'

8:         $\delta \leftarrow r + \gamma \theta^{\mathsf{T}} \varphi(s') - \theta^{\mathsf{T}} \varphi(s)$

9:         $u \leftarrow u + \beta(\delta \varphi(s) - u)$

10:        $\theta \leftarrow \theta + \alpha(\varphi(s) - \gamma \varphi(s'))\varphi(s)^{\mathsf{T}} u$

11:        $s \leftarrow s'$

The general layout is similar to standard Q-learning. Steps (9) and (10) are the result of calculating the gradient of the TD error and the resulting update rule. If you had the tenacity to work through the mathematics yourself, this would be the result. u is an intermediary calculation to update the parameters, θ.

Of note, this algorithm doesn't use importance sampling, which theoretically provides lower variance updates. In the same paper and a subsequent update (GTD2), Sutton et al. introduce another weighting to correct for biases in the gradient updates.[3]

Greedy-GQ

Greedy-GQ is a similar algorithm that introduces a second linear model for the target policy, as opposed to a single behavior and target policy in GTD. The benefit of fitting a second model for the target policy is that it provides more freedom. The target policy is no longer constrained by a potentially ill-fitting behavior model. Theoretically, this provides a faster learning potential. The implementation is the same as Algorithm 6-1, so I only update the latter stages with the new updates in Algorithm 6-2. w is the weights for the target policy.[4]

Algorithm 6-2. Greedy-GQ algorithm

...

9:         $w \leftarrow w + \beta[\varphi(s') - \varphi(s)^{\mathsf{T}} w]\varphi(s)$

10:        $\theta \leftarrow \theta + \alpha[\delta \varphi(s) - \gamma(w^{\mathsf{T}} \varphi(s))\varphi(s')]$

11:        $s \leftarrow s'$

You can also extend this and other TD-derivative algorithms with eligibility traces.[5]

Off-Policy Actor-Critics

Gradient-temporal-difference (GTD) algorithms are of linear complexity and are convergent, even when using function approximation. But they suffer from three important limitations. First, the target policies are deterministic, which is a problem when there are multimodal or stochastic value functions. Second, using a greedy strategy becomes problematic for large or continuous action spaces. And third, a small change in the action-value estimate can cause large changes in the policy. You can solve these problems using a combination of the techniques discussed previously. But Degris et al. combined GTD with policy gradients to solve these issues in one go.[6]

REINFORCE and the vanilla actor-critic algorithms from Chapter 5 are on-policy. Off-policy actor-critic (Off-PAC) was one of the first algorithms to prove that you can use a parameterized critic. If you recall, you have to compute the gradient of the policy to use policy gradient algorithms. Adding parameterized (or tabular) critics increases the complexity of the derivative. Degris et al. proved that if you approximate policy gradient with a gradient-descent-based optimizer and ignore the critic's gradient, the policy eventually reaches the optimal policy anyway.

The result is an algorithm that is virtually identical to Algorithm 5-3. You can see the update equation in Equation 6-3, where the major addition is importance sampling, $\pi_\theta(a \mid s)/\beta_\theta(a \mid s)$. β represents the behavior policy, π is the target. Think of the importance sampling as a conversion factor. The agent is sampling from the behavior policy, so it needs to convert that experience to use it in the target policy. I have also included specific notation to show that the states are distributed according to the trajectories generated by the behavior policy ($s \sim \rho_\beta$, where ρ is a distribution of states) and the actions are distributed by the choices made by the behavior policy ($a \sim \beta$).

Equation 6-3. Off-policy policy gradient estimate

$$\nabla_\theta J_\beta(\pi_\theta) = \mathbb{E}_{s \sim \rho_\beta, a \sim \beta}\left[\frac{\pi_\theta(a \mid s)}{\beta_\theta(a \mid s)}\nabla_\theta \ln \pi_\theta(a \mid s)Q_\pi(s, a)\right]$$

In summary, Equation 6-3 is calculating the gradient of the target policy, weighted by the action-value estimate and distributed by the behavior policy. This gradient tells you by how much and in what direction to update the target policy. The paper looks more complicated because they use eligibility traces and incorporate the gradient of a parameterized linear function for both policies.

Degris et al. provide a small but important theoretical note about the value of the update rates for each policy. They suggest that the actor update rate should be smaller than and anneal to zero faster than the critic. In other words, it is important that the behavior policy is more stable than the target policy, since that is generating trajectories. A mechanical bull is so difficult to ride because it moves in random directions. Riding a horse is easier because it has consistent trajectories. As an engineer, you need to make it as easy as possible for the target to approximate the action-value function.

Deterministic Policy Gradients

In this section I move back in time to discuss another track of research that revolves around the idea that policies don't have to be stochastic. One major problem in all PG algorithms is that the agent has to sample over both the state space and the action space. Only then can you be certain that the agent has found an optimal policy. Instead, is it possible to derive a deterministic policy—a single, specific action for each state? If so, then that dramatically cuts the number of samples required to estimate such a policy. If the agent was lucky, a single attempt at an action could find the optimal policy. Theoretically, this should lead to faster learning.

Deterministic Policy Gradients

Policy gradient algorithms are widely used in problems with continuous action spaces by representing the policy as a probability distribution that stochastically selects an action in a state. The distribution is parameterized such that an agent can improve the result of the policy via stochastic gradient descent.

Off-policy policy gradient algorithms like Off-PAC (see "Off-Policy Actor-Critics" on page 151) are promising because they free the actor to concentrate on exploration and the critic can be trained offline. But the actor, using the behavior policy, still needs to maximize over all actions to select the best trajectory, which could become computationally problematic. Furthermore, the agent has to sample the action distribution sufficiently to produce a descent estimate of it.

Instead, Silver et al. propose to move the behavior policy in the direction of the greatest action-value estimate, rather than maximizing it directly. In essence, they have used the same trick that policy gradient algorithms used to nudge the target policy toward a higher expected return, but this time they are applying it to the behavior policy. Therefore, the optimal action becomes a simple calculation using the current behavior policy. Given the same parameterization, it is deterministic. They call this algorithm deterministic policy gradients (DPGs).[7]

The researchers prove that DPG is a limited version of standard stochastic PG, so all the usual tools and techniques like function approximation, natural gradients, and actor-critic architectures work in the same way.

However, DPG does not produce action probabilities and therefore has no natural exploration mechanism. Imagine a DPG-based agent that has just succeeded. Subsequent runs will produce the same trajectory because the behavior policy generates the same actions over and over again.

The result is a familiar set of algorithms, but the gradient calculation has changed slightly. For vanilla PG algorithms like REINFORCE or actor-critic, the goal is to find the gradient of the objective function. In the case of DPG, the objective includes a deterministic function, not a stochastic policy.

Equation 6-4 shows the gradients of the objective functions for vanilla and deterministic off-policy actor-critic algorithms. I have used the same terminology as in the DPG paper, so here μ represents the deterministic policy. One major difference is that you don't need to use importance sampling to correct for the bias introduced by the behavior policy, because there is no action distribution. Another difference follows from the determinism: you no longer need to calculate the action-value estimate globally over all actions.

Equation 6-4. Off-policy vanilla and deterministic actor-critic objective function gradients, for comparison

$$\nabla_\theta J_\beta(\pi_\theta) = \mathbb{E}_{s \sim \rho_\beta, a \sim \beta} \left[\frac{\pi_\theta(a \mid s)}{\beta_\theta(a \mid s)} \nabla_\theta \ln \pi_\theta(a \mid s) Q_\pi(s, a) \right] \qquad \text{(Off-Policy AC)}$$

$$\nabla_\theta J_\beta(\mu_\theta) = \mathbb{E}_{s \sim \rho_\beta} \left[\nabla_\theta Q_\mu(s, \mu_\theta(s)) \right]$$

$$= \mathbb{E}_{s \sim \rho_\beta} \left[\nabla_\theta \mu_\theta(s) \nabla_a Q_\mu(s, a) \right] \qquad \text{(Off-Policy Deterministic AC)}$$

The rest of the paper discusses the usual issues of Q-learning divergence using parameterized functions and the gradient of the action-value function not being perfect. They end up with a GTD algorithm in the critic and a PG algorithm in the actor, and the whole thing looks remarkably similar to Off-PAC without the importance sampling and eligibility traces.

The derivatives still depend on the parameterization of the actor and critic. If you want to, you can follow a similar procedure seen in Chapter 5 to calculate them manually. But most applications I see jump straight into using deep learning, partly because they are complex enough to model nonlinearities, but mainly because these frameworks will perform automatic differentiation via back-propagation.

In summary, you don't have to sample every single action to have a good policy, just like Q-learning did in Chapter 3. This is likely to speed up learning. And you can still take advantage of policy gradients to tackle problems with a large action space. But of course, some problems have highly complex action-value functions that benefit from a stochastic policy. In general then, even though stochastic policies are slower to learn they may result in better performance. It all depends on the environment.

Deep Deterministic Policy Gradients

The next logical extension to off-policy DPG algorithms is the introduction of deep learning (DL). Predictably, deep deterministic policy gradients (DDPG) follow the same path set by DQN.

But I don't want to understate the importance of this algorithm. DDPG was and still is one of the most important algorithms in RL. Its popularity arises from the fact that it can handle both complex, high-dimensional state spaces and high-dimensional, continuous action spaces.

Furthermore, the neural networks that represent the actor and the critic in DDPG are a useful abstraction. The previous algorithms complicate the mathematics because the researchers mixed the gradient calculation into the algorithm. DDPG offloads the optimization of the actor/critic to the DL framework. This dramatically simplifies the architecture, algorithm, and resulting implementation. It's flexibility arises from the ability to alter the DL models to better fit the MDP. Often you don't need to touch the RL components to solve a variety of problems.

But of course, using DL presents new problems. You not only need to be an expert in RL, but an expert in DL, too. All of the common DL pitfalls also apply here. The complex DL models add a significant computational burden and many applications spend more time and money on them than they do on the underlying RL algorithm or MDP definition. Despite these issues, I do recommend DDPG given the architectural and operational benefits.

DDPG derivation

In 2015, Lillicrap et al. presented DDPG using the same derivation as DPG. They train a model to predict an action directly, without having to maximize the action-value function. They also work with the off-policy version of DPG from the outset.[8]

The novelty is the use of DL for both the actor and the critic and how they deal with the issues caused by nonlinear approximators. First, they tackle the convergence problem. Like DQN, they introduce a replay buffer to de-correlate state observations. They also use a copy of the actor and critic network weights (see "Double Q-Learning" on page 74) and update them slowly to improve stability.

The second addition was batch normalization, which normalizes each feature using a running average of the mean and variance. You could instead make sure that input features are properly scaled.

The third and final addition was the recommendation of using noise in the action prediction, to stimulate exploration. They state that the probability distribution of the noise is problem dependent, but in practice simple Gaussian noise tends to work well. Also, adding noise to the parameters of the neural network works better than adding noise to the actions (also see "Noisy Nets" on page 102).[9]

DDPG implementation

All RL frameworks have an implementation of DDPG. And as you might have guessed, all of them are different. Don't expect to get the same result with different implementations. The differences range from neural network initialization to default hyperparameters.

Figure 6-2 presents a simplification of the architecture. As usual, the environment feeds an observation of state to the agent. The actor decides upon the next action according to its deterministic policy. The state, action, rewards, and next state tuple is also stored in a replay buffer. Because DDPG is an off-policy algorithm, it samples tuples from the replay buffer to measure the error and update the weights of the critic. Finally, the actor uses the critic's estimates to measure its error and update its weights. Algorithm 6-3 presents the full algorithm, which is slightly different from the algorithm defined in the original paper. This version uses my notation and better matches a typical implementation.

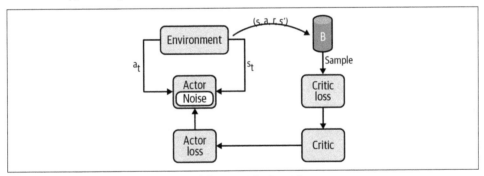

Figure 6-2. A simplified depiction of the DDPG algorithm.

Algorithm 6-3 provides the full DDPG implementation.

> *Algorithm 6-3. DDPG algorithm*
>
> 1: **input**: an actor neural network, $\mu_{\theta_\mu}(s)$, with weights θ_μ,
>
>   a critic neural network, $Q_{\theta_Q}(s, a)$, with weights θ_Q,
>
>   a replay buffer, B,
>
>   the size of a training minibatch, N,
>
>   the network update rate, τ,
>
>   the discount-rate parameter, γ,
>
>   and a noise function for exploration, $\mathcal{N}$
>
> 2: Initialize θ_μ, θ_Q, R,
>
>   and the target weights, $\theta'_\mu \leftarrow \theta_\mu$, $\theta'_Q \leftarrow \theta_Q$
>
> 3: **loop**: for each episode
>
> 4:   Initialize s
>
> 5:   **while** s is not terminal:
>
> 6: $a \leftarrow \mu_{\theta_\mu}(s) + \mathcal{N}$
>
> 7:   Take action, a, and observe r, s'
>
> 8:   Store (s, a, r, s') in B
>
> 9:   Sample a random minibatch of N transitions, (s_i, a_i, r_i, s'_i), from B
>
> 10: $y_i \leftarrow r_i + \gamma Q_{\theta'_Q}\left(s'_i, \mu_{\theta'_\mu}(s'_i)\right)$ (Note the target weights and buffer data)
>
> 11:   Update the critic by minimizing: $\dfrac{1}{N}\sum_i \left(y_i - Q_{\theta_Q}(s_i, a_i)\right)^2$
>
> 12:   Update the actor by minimizing: $\dfrac{1}{N}\sum_i \left(\nabla_{\theta_\mu} Q_{\theta_Q}\left(s_i, \mu_{\theta_\mu}(s_i)\right)\right)^2$
>
> 13: $\theta'_Q \leftarrow \tau\theta_Q + (1 - \tau)\theta'_Q$
>
> 14: $\theta'_\mu \leftarrow \tau\theta_\mu + (1 - \tau)\theta'_\mu$
>
> 15: $s \leftarrow s'$

To use Algorithm 6-3 in your applications you first need to define a neural architecture that matches your problem. You'll need two networks, one for the actor (the policy) and one for the critic (an action-value function approximation). For example, if you were working with raw pixels, then you might use a convolutional neural network in the critic. If you're working with customer information, then you might use a multilayer feed-forward network. For the policy, remember that DDPG is deterministic, so you want to predict a single action for a given state. Therefore, the number of outputs depends on your action space. The hyperparameters of the network are also very important. There should be enough capacity to approximate the complexities of your domain but you don't want to overfit. The learning rate directly impacts the stability of the learning process. If you attempt to learn too quickly, you might find that it does not converge. The remaining inputs in step (1) of Algorithm 6-3 consist of the hyperparameters that control the learning and a noise function that enables exploration.

Steps (2) and (3) initialize the network weights and the replay buffer. The replay buffer must store new tuples and potentially pop off historical tuples when the buffer is full. It also needs to be able to randomly sample from that buffer to train the networks. You can initialize the network weights in different ways and they impact both stability and learning speed.[10] Step (3) initializes copies of both the critic and actor networks, or *target* networks in the literature, to improve stability. In the rest of the algorithm, the copies are denoted by a ' character. This is to save space, but they are easy to miss. If you create your own DDPG implementation, double-check that you are using the right network. Implementations often call the original networks *local*.

Step (6) uses the deterministic policy to predict an action. This is where the original algorithm introduces noise into that decision. But you may want to consider adding noise in different ways (see "Noisy Nets" on page 102, for example).

Step (8) stores the current tuple in the replay buffer and step (9) samples a batch of them ready for training. Many implementations delay the first training of the networks to allow for a more representative sample.

Step (10) marks the beginning of network training process. First it predicts the action value of the next state using the target networks and the current reward. Then step (11) trains the critic to predict that value using the local weights. If you combine steps (10) and (11) together you can see that this is the temporal-difference error.

Step (12) trains the actor network using the local weights by minimizing the gradient of the action-value function when using the actor's policy. This is the equation from Equation 6-4 before applying the chain rule to move the policy gradient out of the action-value function. Implementations use this version because you can get the gradient of the action-value estimate from your DL framework by calling the gradient function. Otherwise you would have to calculate the gradient of the action-value function *and* the gradient of the policy.

Finally, steps (13) and (14) copy the target weights to the local weights. They do this by exponentially weighting the update; you don't want to update the weights too quickly or the agent will never converge.

Twin Delayed DDPG

Twin delayed deep deterministic policy gradients (TD3) are, as the name suggests, an incremental improvement of DDPG. Like the Rainbow algorithm, Fujimoto et al. prove that three new implementation details significantly improve the performance and robustness of DDPG.[11]

Delayed policy updates (DPU)

The first and most interesting proposal is that actor-critic architectures suffer from the implicit feedback loop. For example, value estimates will be poor if the policy generating trajectories is suboptimal. But policies cannot improve if the value estimates are not accurate. In this classic "Which came first, the chicken or the egg?" scenario, Fujimoto et al. suggest that you wait for stable approximations *before* you retrain the networks. Statistical theory states that you need a representative sample before you can estimate a quantity robustly. The same is true here; by delaying updates, you improve performance (also see "Delayed Q-Learning" on page 74).

If you retrain your networks less frequently, performance increases. Training *less*, not more, is better in the long run. Initially this sounds counterintuitive, but I do have an analogy. When I work on complex projects, there are times when something fundamentally affects the work, like funding, for example. In these situations I have learned that knee-jerk reactions are unlikely to be optimal. They are emotionally driven and based upon uncertain, noisy information. Instead, I just listen and gather information. I defer any decisions until a later time. I find that by waiting a few days for the dust to settle, I have a much clearer picture of the situation. Delayed information has a lower variance, so my action predictions become more certain.

This also happens in actor-critic architectures. The implicit feedback loop increases the variance of the updates. When a network changes, the resulting change in actions and trajectories is uncertain. You need to wait a while to see what the effect is. One simple solution is to delay the updates. Retrain your deep learning neural networks after a specified amount of time.

Clipped double Q-learning (CDQ)

The second improvement implements double Q-learning (see "Double Q-Learning" on page 74). If you were to plot the action-value estimate against the true value, you would see that greedy methods tend to overestimate. Double Q-learning solved this by having two action-value estimates. When you retrain those estimates you use the other's weights. But in deep architectures this doesn't work so well, because the estimates are not independent. They use the same replay buffer and are both coupled to the generation policy. One simple solution is to pick the lowest action-value estimate. This prevents overestimation by actively underestimating. Despite the heavy-handed approach, the researchers found that it worked well in practice.

CDQ significantly improves performance in the Ant environment, which suggests that the action-value estimates are likely to be grossly overestimated. I propose that the reason for this is because the reward, which is typically the velocity of the ant, is not solely dependent on that single action. The ant has four legs, so if one of them produces a bad action, the other three can compensate and potentially lead to a good reward. This will mistakenly assign a positive reward to that bad action. CDQ mitigates this issue, by reporting the lowest possible value for any state-action pair, but you could also improve performance with a reward designed to isolate each leg (or joint). I suspect that further performance increases are possible in the Ant environment, or any environment with coupled actions, if you can make the action-reward assignment more independent.

Target policy smoothing (TPS)

The final and least significant improvement is to add noise to the action when predicting the action-value estimate. Because the policy is deterministic, it is very easy to repeatedly sample the same state and action. This leads to peaks in the action-value surface. The researchers suggested one way to smooth out the peak by adding noise to the action before predicting the value. Others have suggested directly smoothing the action-value estimate and adding noise to the network weights directly.

The evidence shows that adding TPS by itself does not improve results significantly. However, removing it from the TD3 algorithm does make a significant difference. I speculate that the reason for this is that it improves exploration. If there are peaks in the action-value estimate, then it would take a lot of visits to neighboring state-action pairs to smooth out that peak, which is unlikely given the large action space. Smoothing makes it easier for the policy to change its mind.

TD3 implementation

The implementation of TD3 is shown in Algorithm 6-4. This is similar to the implementation of DDPG except there is extra logic to handle the double Q-learning and delayed policy updates. The notation is consistent with the rest of the book, which means the algorithm looks slightly different compared to the original paper. You can see that the terminology is beginning to get complicated because of the various copies of data and parameters floating around. This makes it very easy to make an implementation mistake, so be careful.

Algorithm 6-4. TD3 algorithm

1: **input**: an actor neural network, $\mu_{\theta_\mu}(s)$, with weights θ_μ,

two critic neural networks, $Q_{\theta_1}(s,a), Q_{\theta_2}(s,a)$, with weights θ_1, θ_2,

a replay buffer, B,

the size of a training minibatch, N,

the network update rate, τ,

the discount-rate parameter, γ,

a noise clipping threshold, c,

and a noise function for exploration, $\mathcal{N}$

2: Initialize $\theta_\mu, \theta_1, \theta_2$,

and the target weights, $\theta'_\mu \leftarrow \theta_\mu,\ \theta'_1 \leftarrow \theta_1, \theta'_2 \leftarrow \theta_2$

3: **loop**: for each episode

4:     Initialize s

5:     **while** s is not terminal:

6:         $a \leftarrow \mu_{\theta_\mu}(s) + \mathcal{N}$

7:         Take action, a, and observe r, s'

8:         Store (s, a, r, s') in B

9:         Sample a random minibatch of N transitions, (s_i, a_i, r_i, s'_i), from B

10:         $\tilde{a}_i \leftarrow \mu_{\theta'_\mu}(s'_i) + \text{clip}(\mathcal{N}, -c, c)$ (Target policy smoothing)

11:         $y_i \leftarrow r_i + \gamma \min\limits_{j=1,2} Q_{\theta'_j}(s'_i, \tilde{a}_i)$ (Clipped double Q-learning)

12:         Update both critics, $\theta_{j \leftarrow 1,2}$, by minimizing: $\frac{1}{N}\sum_i \left(y_i - Q_{\theta_j}(s_i, a_i)\right)^2$

13:         *if* t mod d *then*:   (Delayed policy update)

14:             Update the actor by minimizing: $\frac{1}{N}\sum_i \left(\nabla_{\theta_\mu} Q_{\theta_1}\left(s_i, \mu_{\theta_\mu}(s_i)\right)\right)^2$

15:             Update both critics, $\theta_{j \leftarrow 1,2}$: $\theta'_j \leftarrow \tau\theta_j + (1-\tau)\theta'_j$

16:         $\theta'_\mu \leftarrow \tau\theta_\mu + (1-\tau)\theta'_\mu$

17:         *end if*

18:         $s \leftarrow s'$

In step (1) you now have to pass in two critic networks, denoted by the parameters θ_1 and θ_2. Most implementations expect you to pass in two independent DL networks and typically these have exactly the same architecture. But don't let this stop you from trying different architectures or possibly a multihead architecture.

The original algorithm clips the action noise to keep the result close to the original action. The intent is to prevent the agent from choosing invalid actions. Most implementations set this value to match the environment's action space. I tentatively suggest that because you control the design of your noise function, clipping is unnecessary. Choose a noise function that matches your action space and smoothing goals, then reuse the standard deterministic action function from DDPG [step (6)].

In step (11) note that the predicted value is the minimum value from both critics from the target networks. In other words, pick the lowest action-value estimate; this is more likely to be correct due to the overestimation bias. Step (12) updates both critics using this prediction of the discounted reward. This helps to restrain the network that is doing the overestimation.

The inner loop after step (13) occurs one every d iterations; this delays the policy update. Line (14) is interesting because it uses the first critic to update the policy, not the critic with the minimum value. I suspect the reasoning here is that because the overestimating network is constrained by step (12), it doesn't make any difference if you pick network one or two, in the long run. Either network is as likely to overestimate. But you might find minor performance gains here by choosing which network to use more intelligently.

All other lines are the same as DDPG.

 Always refer to the original paper and add enough monitoring code to verify your implementation. I find that unfolding loops and calculating by hand is the best way to verify that code is working as I expect.

Case Study: Recommendations Using Reviews

In the era of information overload, users are increasingly reliant on recommendation algorithms to suggest relevant content or products. More recently, services like YouTube and TikTok have begun to leverage interactive recommender systems, which continuously recommend content to individual users based upon their feedback. State-of-the-art non-RL methods attempt to build models that map users to items, leverage locally correlated patterns using convolutional filters, or use attention-based sequential prediction models. Out of these, the sequential models perform the best because they adapt to recurrent feedback. But these methods train offline and must be retrained often to provide up-to-date recommendations. Combined with the complexity of the deep learning models, this adds up to a large training cost.

RL is a natural fit for this type of problem because feedback can be accommodated directly through the reward definition. Wang et al. propose one example in which they make things more interesting by proposing to use text as a feedback mechanism, rather than the usual up- or downvote. They suggest that in the real world sparse voting can severely degrade performance. Instead, they suggest that textual information like reviews and item descriptions contains more information and is less sensitive to sparsity.[12]

Wang et al. formulate the problem using a Markov decision process where the state is the interaction between a user and the recommender system, the action is a number of recommended items, and the reward is determined by the user feedback.

The primary issue, as noted by other recommendation papers, is the high-dimensionality introduced by the sheer numbers of users and items. Wang et al. take the route of using a word embedding to map the item text and user review into a feature vector, then use a clustering method to reduce the feature vector into a manageable number of groups.

Wang et al. then choose DDPG as their algorithm of choice to be able to learn policies in a high-dimensional, continuous action space. They needed the ability to predict continuous actions to work with the continuous user-embedding space. They then combine the set of items with the action to produce an ordered list of items ready to present to the user. Over time the policy learns what actions (i.e., user-item embedding) are preferred given the user and candidate items as a state. As new user feedback or items are added, the policy is able to change to meet the new demands of the users or propose new recommended items.

Unfortunately, Wang et al. only tested this in a simulation. They used a dataset of Amazon products that had reviews. They used the review score to denote a positive or negative review and reward based upon whether the user's well-reviewed item was in the top results. Their method produced results that beat all other state-of-the-art ML implementations.

I like the idea of incorporating textual information as a way to reduce the sparsity of the problem. But I wish that they had tested this in a real environment. Of course, not everyone has access to YouTube or Amazon to be able to test these things out. Only then would we be able to see how well this really performs. My guess is that it should perform at least as well as any highly tuned ML recommender, and probably beat it, with the added benefit of not requiring retraining. And remember that this is without any special tuning or fancy neural networks. The policy was a vanilla multilayer perceptron. I'm also confident that there are improvements to be made, too. Other researchers have looked at tackling the dimensionality problem head on and don't have to perform clustering to create recommendations.[13]

You may also be interested in RecSim (*https://oreil.ly/Dg_xB*), a configurable simulation platform for recommender systems.[14]

Improvements to DPG

You can apply many of the fundamental improvements seen in previous chapters like different exploration strategies, or different ways to represent the expected reward. These can all affect and improve performance. For example, distributed distributional deterministic policy gradients from Barth-Maron et al. not only introduce parallelism (see "Scaling RL" on page 299) but add distributional RL (see "Distributional RL" on page 100) and *n*-step updates (see "n-Step Algorithms" on page 76).[15] Deterministic value-policy gradients by Cai et al. prove that you can use deterministic algorithms for infinite-horizon environments and add *n*-step updates like a cherry on top of a cake.[16]

But there is one fundamental problem that hasn't been fixed, at least not in this context. Despite all their benefits, off-policy algorithms are the same as delta-wing jets like the Eurofighter Typhoon: they are inherently unstable. Without artificial control they will diverge and crash. The Eurofighter achieves this with a complex flight control system. Off-policy algorithms achieve this by slowing down the rate at which parameters update in the neural networks to the point where updates are actively skipped. Surely this is slowing down learning. Is there a better way?

Trust Region Methods

PG algorithms learn to make better choices by following the gradient of a policy toward higher predicted values, weighted by some measure of expected return. The following methods all use the advantage function, $A(s, a)$, but you could plausibly choose any PG interpretation (see "A Comparison of Basic Policy Gradient Algorithms" on page 135).

Delegating Gradient Calculations to a Library

Q-learning and vanilla policy gradient algorithms can solve a significant percentage of problems. But the main reason for developing more advanced RL algorithms is so that agents can tackle more complex tasks, like generating policies for a pick-and-place robot.

A problem that necessitates a more complex RL algorithm also implies that you need more complex approximators. These become harder to encode, manage, and calculate gradients for (in the case of policy gradients) and at some point, which is exceedingly fuzzy, this becomes too difficult. It is increasingly tempting to entrust all of this to a

---

deep learning framework. Yes, neural networks have their problems, but these frameworks make it incredibly easy to create, manage, and update highly complex approximators.

Therefore, in complex policy gradient algorithms, RL practitioners tend to ignore the gradient operator (the ∇) and instead present a loss function (the mathematics inside the ∇). The gradient calculation is outsourced to the reverse-mode auto-differential algorithm provided by TensorFlow, PyTorch, and the like.

Equation 6-5 presents the A2C update in the form of a loss function, where $A_\pi(s, a) \doteq Q_\pi(s, a) - V_\pi(s)$. The advantage function has an intuitive interpretation. Actions with a value estimate greater than zero are better than average. They will result in good performance, on average. Actions lower than zero will, on average, result in poor performance.

Equation 6-5. Advantage actor-critic policy gradient

$$L^{PG}(\theta) \doteq \mathbb{E}_{\pi_\theta}\Big[\ln \pi_\theta(a \mid s) A_w(s, a)\Big]$$

Using the advantage function in combination with the policy gradient forces the policy toward producing more performant actions and away from poorly performing actions. Compare this against using the action-value function instead. For many problems it is likely that all actions have a positive value; if you wander randomly you will eventually stumble across a reward. So if you used that here, like in a vanilla actor-critic, then it will move the policy toward all of these eventualities, but at different rates. This can cause value estimates to increase infinitely and can be unstable when near-optimal, which is why you need to use discounting. The advantage function provides a natural damping. If the policy ever goes too far, like if it makes a massive mistake, the advantage function will kick it back on track. A bad move in policy will manifest in poor results that yield a negative advantage and therefore a negative gradient, which pushes the policy back to better performance.

But you have to be careful not to update the policy too quickly. The advantage function is an approximation (a supervised model), so you must take the result with a pinch of salt. It is noisy and you don't want to ruin your policy with a single bad step. Which leads to a question: how do we quantify the size of a step?

The vanilla advantage actor-critic is promoting the trajectories that yield positive advantages; it is trying to maximize future returns. It achieves this by using an optimization function that moves up the gradient of the policy, which itself depends on the advantages. This gradient is a local linear estimate of a complex nonlinear function. You can't jump directly from where you were to where you want to go, because it is likely that you will end up in the middle of nowhere.

It's like if you go hiking and you set your direction by taking a single compass reading at the start. You will end up miles away from your destination because you can't pick a bearing with enough precision. To solve this problem you take new readings every kilometer or so. You introduce a step size and iteratively take measurements. In this analogy, the step size is a Euclidian distance, the hypotenuse of a triangle, measured in meters. Stochastic gradient ascent/descent uses the same Euclidian distance, but the units are much more complex to interpret. The cost function is in units of policy parameters, which themselves have a complex interaction with states to produce action probabilities.

A related problem is that the data you are using to train your models is nonstationary. For example, consider the common situation where you have sparse rewards (your policy does not observe a reward for a long time). You probably don't want to alter the policy much while it is exploring, so the step size should be small. But when you do find a reward, you want to update the policy significantly, to take advantage of that new knowledge. But by how by much? If you make a mistake and update it too much, then the policy might become so bad that it becomes impossible to find a good reward again.

These problems make it hard to choose a single step size that works in all situations. Practitioners usually treat this as a hyperparameter and scan over a range of values. In other words, brute force.

Trust region methods attempt to solve this problem by attempting to specify a region in parameter space which gradient steps can be trusted. You can use this information to dynamically alter the step size so that the parameters change quickly when gradients are trusted and slowly when they are not. Then you can find ways to quantify that trust, the first of which is based upon using the Kullback–Leibler divergence to measure the difference between two policies.

Kullback–Leibler Divergence

The Kullback–Leibler (KL) divergence is often described as a measure of "surprise" when comparing two distributions. When the distributions are the same, then the KL divergence is zero. When the distributions are dramatically different, the KL divergence is large.

It can also be used to calculate the extra number of bits required to describe a new distribution given another. If the distributions are the same, then you require no extra bits to differentiate the new distribution. If the distributions are different, then you would need many new bits.

For example, if you had a special coin that only ever landed on heads, then you would need zero bits to represent the coin's states. There is only one state—it is always going to be heads—so you need zero bits, just the value zero, to encode that state. If you compared that to a fair coin, you would now have two states, so you would need one full bit to represent those states. In this hypothetical example, the KL divergence between these two distributions is 1 (hypothetical because as one state approaches zero, the division in the KL divergence algorithm will produce a nan).

Equation 6-6 presents the divergence calculation. ∥ represents the divergence operator, which tells you to calculate the divergence between this and that. You can use any base for the logarithm, but most people use a base of 2 (log2), which represents the number of bits.

Equation 6-6. Kullback–Leibler divergence

$$D_{KL}(P \parallel Q) \doteq \sum_{x \in \mathcal{X}} P(x) \log \left(\frac{P(x)}{Q(x)} \right)$$

KL divergence experiments

Consider the following two experiments where I flip coins and roll dice. KL divergence is a measure of how different distributions are, so flipping two fair dice should result in a divergence of zero. Then I simulate a biased coin that is weighted toward landing on tails.

In the second experiment I simulate three six-sided dice. The first is a standard, fair die. The second is a fair die but produces double the value of a standard six-sided die. In other words, the probabilities are similar but the distributions do not align. The third die produces standard values but is biased to produce more sixes than you would expect.

Figure 6-3 shows histograms of these experiments where the KL divergence is shown in brackets. As you would expect, the KL divergence between two fair coins is near zero. However, when comparing with the biased coin, the divergence is nonzero.

Comparing fair and biased dice produces the same nonzero result. But note the result from the comparison between the fair die and the die that produces values that lie outside the range of the fair die. The KL divergence is near zero. This is because where it does overlap, it has the same uniform distribution. This is because KL divergence does not measure the spread between distributions; if you're interested in that, use the total variance divergence instead.

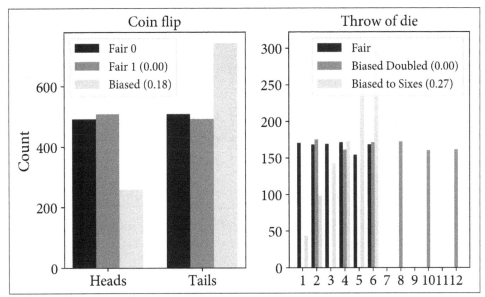

Figure 6-3. Calculating the KL divergence for simulations of coins and dice.

Natural Policy Gradients and Trust Region Policy Optimization

Natural policy gradients (NPG) introduced the idea that you can quantify step size not in terms of policy parameter space, but in terms of a metric based upon the distance between the current policy and the policy after updating by a gradient step.[17]

Figure 6-4 shows an example of the difference between standard policy gradients and natural policy gradients. The contours represent the value of a particular state and the arrows show the direction of the gradient as defined by the type of gradient calculation. It demonstrates that the gradients change direction when you compute the differential with respect to a different feature.

You can estimate the distance between two policies by comparing the distributions of the generated trajectories using one of many statistical measures to compare two distributions. But the trust region policy optimization (TRPO) algorithm uses KL divergence.[18] Recall that optimization algorithms measure step sizes by the Euclidian distance in parameter space; steps have units of $\delta\theta$. TRPO suggests that you can constrain, or limit this step size according to the change in policy. You can tell the optimization algorithm that you don't want the probability distribution to change by a large amount. Remember, this is possible because policies are action-probability distributions.

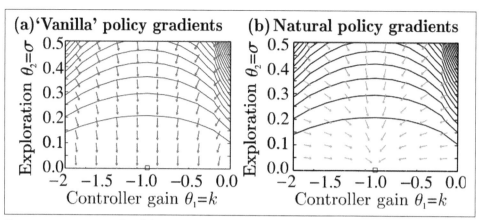

Figure 6-4. An example of the standard (left) and natural (right) policy gradients produced in a simple two-dimensional problem. Image from Peters et al. (2005) with permission.[19]

Equation 6-7 presents a slight reformulation of the A2C policy gradient. If you look at the derivation of the policy gradient theorem in Equation 5-3, at the end I introduced a logarithm to simplify the mathematics. Technically, this gradient is computed using trajectories sampled from an old policy. So if you undo the last step (chain rule), you end up with the same equation, but the use of the old policy parameters is more explicit.

Equation 6-7. Reformulated advantage actor-critic loss function

$$\nabla J(\theta) = \mathbb{E}_{\pi_\theta}\left[\nabla \ln \pi_\theta(a \mid s)A_w(s, a)\right]$$

$$= \mathbb{E}_{\pi_\theta}\left[\frac{\nabla \pi_\theta(a \mid s)}{\pi_{\theta_{old}}(a \mid s)}A_w(s, a)\right]$$

Next, because you can delegate the gradient calculation, you can rewrite Equation 6-7 in terms of the objective, which is to maximize the expected advantages by altering the policy parameters, θ. You can see the result in Equation 6-8.

Equation 6-8. Presenting A2C in terms of maximization of the objective

$$\underset{\theta}{\text{maximize}}\ \ L^{PG}(\theta) = \mathbb{E}_{\pi_\theta}\left[\frac{\pi_\theta(a \mid s)}{\pi_{\theta_{old}}(a \mid s)}A_w(s, a)\right]$$

An alternative interpretation of Equation 6-8 is that this is importance sampling of the advantages (not the gradient, like in "Off-Policy Actor-Critics" on page 151). The expected advantage is equal to the advantage of the trajectories sampled by the old policy, adjusted by importance sampling, to yield the results that would be obtained if you used the new policy.

Equation 6-9 shows the loss function for the NPG algorithm, which as you can see is the same as Equation 6-8, but with a *constraint* (a mathematical tool that limits the value of the equation above it). NPG uses a constraint based upon the KL divergence of the new and old policies. This constraint prevents the divergence from being greater than δ.

Equation 6-9. Natural policy gradients optimization loss function

$$\underset{\theta}{\text{maximize}} \quad L^{TRPO}(\theta) = \mathbb{E}_{\pi_\theta}\left[\frac{\pi_\theta(a \mid s)}{\pi_{\theta_{old}}(a \mid s)} A_w(s, a)\right]$$

$$\text{subject to} \quad \mathbb{E}_{\pi_\theta}\left[\text{KL}\left[\pi_{\theta_{old}}(\cdot \mid s) \,\|\, \pi_\theta(\cdot \mid s)\right]\right] \le \delta$$

This is all well and good, but the major problem is that you can't use stochastic gradient descent to optimize constrained nonlinear loss functions. Instead, you have to use conjugate gradient descent, which is similar to standard gradient descent but you can include a constraint.

TRPO adds a few bells and whistles like an extra linear projection to double-check that the step really does improve the objective.

The major problem, however, is that the implementation involves a complex calculation to find the conjugate gradients, which makes the algorithm hard to understand and computationally complex. There are other issues too, like the fact that you can't use a neural network with a multihead structure, like when you predict action probabilities and a state-value estimate, because the KL divergence doesn't tell you anything about how you should update the state-value prediction. In practice, then, it doesn't work well for problems where good estimates of a complex state-value space are important, like the Atari games.

These issues prevent TRPO from being popular. You can read more about the derivation of NPG and TRPO in the resources suggested in "Further Reading" on page 186. Thankfully, there is a much simpler alternative.

Proximal Policy Optimization

One of the main problems with NPG and TRPO is the use of conjugate gradient descent. Recall that the goal is to prevent large changes in the policy, or in other words, to prevent large changes in the action probability distribution. NPG and

TRPO use a constraint on the optimization to achieve this, but another way is to penalize large steps.

Equation 6-8 is a maximization; it's trying to promote the largest advantage estimates, so you could add a negative term inside the loss function that arbitrarily decreases the advantage value whenever policies change too much. Equation 6-10 shows this in action, where the constraint is moved to a negation and an extra term, β, controls the proportion of penalization applied to the advantages.

The major benefit is that you can use standard gradient ascent optimization algorithms again, which dramatically simplifies the implementation. However, you would struggle to pick a value for β that performs consistently well. How big of a penalization should you apply? And should that change depending on what the agent is doing? These are the same problems presented at the start of this section, which makes this implementation no better than picking a step size for A2C.

Equation 6-10. Penalizing large changes in policy

$$\underset{\theta}{\text{maximize}} \ \mathbb{E}_{\pi_\theta} \left[\frac{\pi_\theta(a \mid s)}{\pi_{\theta_{old}}(a \mid s)} A_w(s, a) - \beta \text{KL}\left[\pi_{\theta_{old}}(\cdot \mid s) \, \| \pi_\theta(\cdot \mid s)\right] \right]$$

But do not despair; Equation 6-10 highlights an important idea. It shows that you can add arbitrary functions to influence the size and direction of the step in an optimization algorithm. This opens a Pandora's box of possibilities, where you could imagine adding things like (simpler) functions to prevent large steps sizes, functions to increase step sizes when you want more exploration, and even changes in direction to attempt to explore different regions in policy space. Proximal policy optimization (PPO) is one such implementation that adds a simpler penalization, an integrated function to allow for multihead networks, and an entropy-based addition to improve exploration.[20]

PPO's clipped objective

Schulman et al. proposed that although TRPO was technically more correct, it wasn't necessary to be so fancy. You can use the importance sampling ratio as an estimate of the size of the change in the policy. Values not close to 1 are indicative that the agent wants to make a big change to the policy. A simple solution is to clip this value, which constrains the policy to change by a small amount. This results in the a new clipped loss function shown in Equation 6-11.

Equation 6-11. Clipping large changes in policy according to the importance sampling ratio

$$L^{CLIP}(\theta) \doteq \mathbb{E}\left[\min\left(r(\theta)A(s, a), \ \text{clip}\left(r(\theta), 1 - \epsilon, 1 + \epsilon\right)\hat{a}(s, a)\right)\right]$$

$r(\theta) \doteq \pi_\theta(a \mid s)/\pi_{\theta_{old}}(a \mid s)$ is the importance sampling ratio. Inside the expectation operator there is a min function. The righthand side of min contains an importance sampling ratio that is clipped whenever the value veers more than ϵ away from 1. The lefthand side of the min function is the normal unclipped objective. The reason for using min is so that the objective results in providing the worst possible loss for these parameters, which is called a *lower bound* or *pessimistic bound*.

At first this sounds counterintuitive. In situations like this I find it useful to imagine what happens when you test the function with different inputs. Remember that the advantage function can have positive and negative values. Figure 6-5 shows the clipped loss when the advantages are positive (left) and negative (right).

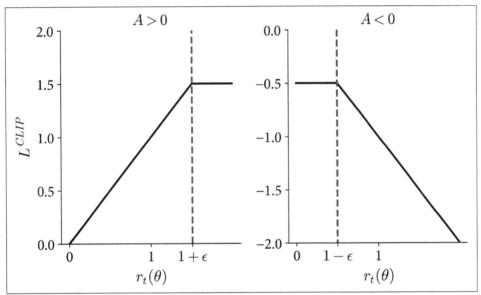

Figure 6-5. A plot of the clipped PPO loss when advantages are positive (left) or negative (right).

A positive advantage (left) indicates that the policy has a better than expected effect on the outcome. Positive loss values will nudge the policy parameters toward these actions. As the importance sampling ratio $[r(\theta)]$ increases, the righthand side of the min function will clip at the $1 + \epsilon$ point and produce the lowest loss. This has the effect of limiting maximum loss value and therefore the maximum change in parameters. You don't want to change parameters too quickly when improving, because a jump too big might push you back into poor performance. Most of the time the ratio will be near 1. The ϵ allows a little room to improve.

A negative advantage suggests that the policy has a worse than expected effect on the outcome. Negative loss values will push the policy parameters away from these actions. At high ratios, the lefthand side of the `min` function will dominate. Large negative advantages will push the agent back toward more promising actions. At low ratios, the righthand side of the `min` function dominates again and is clipped at $1 - \epsilon$. In other words, if the distribution has a low ratio (meaning there is a significant difference in the old and new policies), then the policy parameters will continue to change at the same rate.

But why? Why do this at all? Why not just use the raw advantage? Schulman et al. set out to establish and improve a lower bound on performance, a worst-case scenario. If you can design a loss function that guarantees improvement (they did) then you don't need to care so much about the step size.

Figure 6-6 is a depiction of this problem using notation from TRPO. θ are the parameters of the current policy. Ideally, you want to observe the curve labeled $\eta(\theta)$, which is the true performance using the parameters θ. But you can't because it would take too long to estimate that complex nonlinear curve at every step. A faster method is to calculate the gradient at this point, which is shown as the line labeled $L(\theta)$. This is the gradient of the A2C loss. If you take a large step on this gradient, then you could end up with parameters that over- or undershoot the maximum. The curve labeled $L(\theta) - \beta KL$ is the TRPO lower bound. It is the A2C gradient with the KL divergence subtracted. You can see that no matter what step size you chose, you would still end up somewhere within $\eta(\theta)$; even if the agent makes a really bad step, it is constrained to end up somewhere within that lower bound, which isn't too bad.

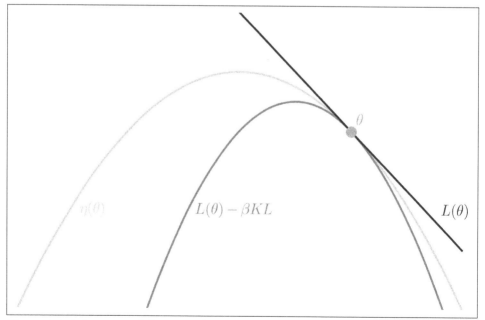

Figure 6-6. A depiction of the TRPO lower bound with gradients.

PPO achieves a similar lower bound by ignoring the importance sampling when the policy is improving (take bigger steps), but includes it and therefore accentuates the loss when the policy is getting worse (provide a lower bound). I like to think of it as a buildup of pressure; PPO is pressuring the advantages to improve.

PPO's value function and exploration objectives

Most techniques for computing the advantages use an approximation to estimate the state-value function. At this point you've probably resigned to using a neural network, so it makes sense to use the same network to predict policy actions and the state-value function. In this scenario PPO includes a squared-loss term in the final objective to allow the DL frameworks to learn the state-value function at the same time as learning the policy: $L^{VF}(\theta) \doteq \left(V_\theta(s) - V^{target}\right)^2$.

PPO also includes a term in the final objective that calculates the entropy of a policy, $\mathcal{H}[\pi_\theta](s)$.[21] This improves exploration by discouraging premature convergence to suboptimal deterministic policies. In other words, it actively discourages deterministic polices and forces the agent to explore. You will learn more about this idea in Chapter 7.

You can see the final PPO objective function in Equation 6-12. C_1 and C_2 are hyperparameters that control the proportion of the loss function attributed to the state-value loss and the entropy loss, respectively.

Equation 6-12. The final objective function for PPO

$$L^{CLIP+VF+S}(\theta) \doteq \mathbb{E}\left[L^{CLIP}(\theta) + C_1 L^{VF}(\theta) + C_2 \mathcal{H}[\pi_\theta](s)\right]$$

Algorithm 6-5 shows the deceptively simple pseudocode from the original paper by Schulman et al.[22] It neglects implementation details like the policy and value function approximation, although it does assume a deep-learning–based implementation to provide the automatic differentiation. Note that the algorithm does have an implicit delayed update in there; it iterates for T time steps before retraining the weights. But it does not concern itself with any other extensions (for example, determinism, replay buffers, separate training networks, distributions of actions/rewards, and so on). Any of these could improve performance for your particular problem.

What is interesting is the use of multiple agents in step (2). I haven't talked much about asynchronous methods, but this is a simple way to improve the learning speed (in wall clock time). Multiple agents can observe different situations and feed that back into a central model. I discuss this idea in more depth in "A Note on Asynchronous Methods" on page 185.

Schulman et al. used values of between 0.1 and 0.3 for the divergence clipping hyper-parameter, ϵ. The hyperparameter C_1 depends on whether you are using the same neural network to predict the policy and the state-value function. Schulman et al. didn't even need to use an entropy bonus in some of their experiments and set $C_2 \doteq 0$. There is no right answer, so use a hyperparameter search to find the optimal values for your problem.

Algorithm 6-5. Asynchronous PPO algorithm

1: **for** iteration $\doteq 0, 1, \cdots$:
2:      **for** agent $\doteq 0, 1, \cdots, N - 1$:
3:          Run policy $\pi_{\theta_{old}}$ in environment for T time steps
4:          Compute advantage estimates $A_0, \cdots, A_{T-1}$
5:          Optimize L with respect to θ, for K epochs and minibatch size $M \leq NT$
6:          $\theta_{old} \leftarrow \theta$

Example: Using Servos for a Real-Life Reacher

You have probably noticed that the majority of RL examples use simulations. This is mostly for practical purposes; it is much easier, cheaper, and faster to train in a simulated environment. But you can easily apply RL to problems that have a direct interface with real life. One of the most common examples of RL in industry is robotic control because RL is especially well suited to deriving efficient policies for complex tasks.

Academia has attempted to standardize robotics platforms to improve reproducibility. The ROBEL platform (*https://oreil.ly/Kki8B*) is one notable example of three simple, standardized robots that are capable of demonstrating a range of complex movements.[23] But even though they are "relatively inexpensive," the $3,500 cost for D'Claw is a large price to justify.

These two challenges, the lack of real-life RL examples and the cost, were the basis for the next experiment. I wanted to re-create a typical RL experiment, but in real life, which lead me back to the classic `CartPole` and `Reacher` problems. Second, the high cost of D'Claw is primarily due to the expensive servo motors. For this experiment I only need a single servo motor and driver, which can be both purchased for less than $20. Full details of the hardware setup can be found on the accompanying website (see "Supplementary Materials" on page xix).

Experiment Setup

This experiment consists of a simulated and a real-life servo motor, which I drive toward a preset goal. Servo motors are like standard DC motors, except they have extra gearing and controls in place to provide accurate control. The servos I used also had positional feedback, which is not found in cheaper servos. Figure 6-7 shows a video of the servo motor while being trained.

Figure 6-7. A video of the PPO agent training the movement of a servo motor.

The state is represented by the current position of the servo and a fixed goal that is changed every episode. There is one action: the position of the servo. States and actions are normalized to fall within the range of –1 to 1. The reward is the negative Euclidian distance to the goal, a classic distance-to-goal metric that is used in many robotics examples. The episode ends when the servo moves within 5% of the goal position. Therefore the goal is to train an agent to derive a policy that moves to the precise position of the goal in the lowest number of moves.

This problem statement is not precisely the same as `CartPole` or `Reacher`. But the idea of training a robot to move to achieve a desired goal is a common requirement. The single servo makes the problem much easier to solve and you could handcode a policy. But the simplicity makes it easy to understand and more complicated variants are just an extension of the same idea.

RL Algorithm Implementation

Always try to solve the next simplest problem. RL is especially difficult to debug because there are so many feedback loops, hyperparameters, and environmental intricacies that fundamentally alter training efficiency. The best mitigation is to take baby steps and verify simpler problems are working before you move onto something more complex.

My first attempt at this problem involved trying to learn to move toward a goal that was completely fixed, for all episodes. I wanted to use PPO for this example. I chose a value of –1 because the random initializations would often accidentally lead to a policy that moved to 0 every step. This means that the agent has to learn an incredibly simple policy: always predict an action of –1. Easy right?

Incredibly, it didn't converge. If I were less tenacious then I would hang up my engineering hat and retire. In general, I find that most problems involve an error between brain and keyboard. So I started debugging by plotting the predicted value function and the policy, the actual actions that were being predicted for a given observation, and I found that after a while the value function was predicting the correct values but the policy was just stuck. It wasn't moving at all. It turned out that the default learning rate (`stable-baselines`, PPO2, $2.5e - 4$) is far too small for such a simple problem. It wasn't that the agent failed to learn, it was just learning too slowly.

After increasing the learning rate massively (0.05)to match the simplicity of the problem, it solved it in only a few updates.

The next problem was when I started tinkering with the number of steps per update and the minibatch size. The number of steps per update represents how many observations are sampled before you retrain the policy and value approximators. The minibatch size is the number of random samples passed to the training.

Remember that PPO, according to the paper implementation, does not have any kind of replay buffer. The number of steps per update represents the size of the minibatch used for training. If you set this too low, then the samples are going to be correlated and the policy will never converge.

You want to set the number of steps parameter to be greater than the minibatch size (so samples are less correlated) and ideally capture multiple episodes to again decorrelate. Another way to think about this is that each episode captured during an update is like having multiple independent workers. More independent workers allow the agent to average over independent observations and therefore break the correlation, with diminishing returns.

The minibatch size impacts the accuracy of the policy and value approximation gradients, so a larger value provides a more accurate gradient for that sample. In machine learning this is considered to be a good thing, but in RL it can cause all sorts of stability issues. The policy and value approximations are valid for that phase of exploration only. For example, on a complex problem with large state spaces, it is unlikely that the first sample is representative of the whole environment. If you use a large minibatch size it will reinforce the current policy behavior, not push the policy toward a better policy. Instead, it is better to use a lower minibatch size to prevent the policy from overfitting to a trajectory. The best minibatch size, however, is problem and algorithm dependent.[24]

For the problem at hand, I set the minibatch size very low, 2 or 4 in most experiments, so that I could retrain often and solve the problem quickly, and the number of steps to 32 or 64. The agent was easily able to solve the environment in this many steps so it was very likely that multiple episodes were present within a single update.

Finally, since the resulting policy was so easy to learn I dramatically reduced the size of the policy and value function networks. This constrained them both and prevented overfitting. The default implementation of a feed-forward multilayer perceptron in stable-baselines does not have any dropout, so I also forced the network to learn a latent representation of the data by using an autoencoder-like fan-in.

Figure 6-8 shows the final policy, which I generated by asking for the predicted action for all position observations for a fixed goal of –1. After only 20 steps of the motor, PPO has learned a policy that produces an action of –1 for all observations.

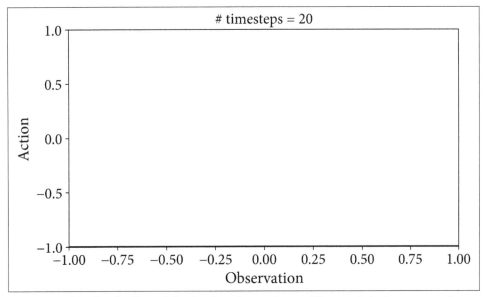

Figure 6-8. The final policy of the fixed goal experiment. The x-axis is the current observation of the position. The y-axis is the resulting action from the policy. There is a straight line at the –1 action, which correctly corresponds to the goal of –1.

Increasing the Complexity of the Algorithm

Now that I have verified that the hardware works and the agent is able to learn a viable policy, it is time to take the next step and tackle a slightly more difficult problem.

I now expand the problem by generating random goals upon every episode. This is more challenging because the agent will need to observe many different episodes and therefore multiple goals to learn that it needs to move to an expected position. The agent won't know that there are different goals until it encounters different goals.

The agent also needs to generalize. The goals are selected uniformly to lie between –1 and 1. This is a continuous variable; the agent will never observe every single goal.

But the goal is still simple, however. The agent has to learn to move to the position suggested by the goal. It is a one-to-one mapping. But this poses a small challenge to RL agents because they don't know that. The agents are equipped to map a very complex function. So similar to before I will need to constrain that exploration to the problem at hand.

From a technical perspective this is an interesting experiment because it highlights the interplay between the environment dynamics and the agent's hyperparameters. Despite this being an easy function to learn (a direct mapping), the agent's exploration and interaction adds a significant amount of noise into the process. You have to be careful to average out that noise. In particular, if the learning rate is too high, then the agent tends to continuously update its value and policy networks, which results in a policy that dances all over the place.

The number of steps is important,too. Previously, it was easy to complete an episode, since there was always a single goal. But now the goal could be anywhere, so an episode can take a lot more time early on in the training. This, coupled with a high learning rate, could lead to samples that are changing rapidly.

I could solve this problem by constraining the agent to use a simpler model, a linear one, for example. Another approach would be to optimize the hyperparameters. I chose the latter option so that I can continue to use the standard multilayer perceptron approach.

I found that a small number of minibatches with a fast update rate learned quickest at the expense of long-term training stability. If you are training to perform a more important task, then you should decrease the learning rate to make training more stable and consistent.

Hyperparameter Tuning in a Simulation

But I didn't do all this tuning with the servos directly. When problems start to get harder, it becomes increasingly difficult to do a hyperparameter search. This is primarily due to the amount of time it takes to execute a step in a real environment, but there are also concerns about safety and wear. In these experiments I successfully managed to damage one servo after only 5 days of development; the positional feedback failed. Figure 6-9 is an image of the dead servo, which is a reminder that in real life excessive movements cause wear and tear.

Figure 6-9. The final resting place of an overworked servo.

Because of this it makes sense to build a simulator to do your initial tuning. It is likely to be far quicker and cheaper to evaluate than the real thing. So I added a basic simulation of the servo and did some hyperparameter tuning.

Here is a list of tips when tuning:

- The learning rate is inversely proportional to the required training time. Smaller, slower learning rates take longer to train.
- Smaller sized minibatches generalize better.
- Try to have multiple episodes in each update, to break the sample correlation.
- Tune the value estimation and policy networks independently.
- Don't update too quickly, or the training will oscillate.
- There is a trade-off between training speed and training stability. If you want more stable training, learn slower.

But to be honest it doesn't matter what hyperparameters you use for this. It can be solved by anything. All we're doing here is attempting to control the stability of the learning and improve the speed. Even so it still takes around 1,000 steps to get a reasonably stable policy. The main factor is the learning rate. You can decrease it and get faster training, but the policy tends to oscillate.

Resulting Policies

Figure 6-10 shows a trained policy over four different stages of training on the simulated environment: 250, 500, 750, and 1,000 environment steps, which correspond to simulated moves of the servo. You can generate a plot like this by asking the policy to predict the action (value denoted by shading) for a given goal (x-axis) and position (y-axis) observation. A perfect policy should look like smooth vertical stripes, smooth because this is a continuous action and vertical because we want an action that maps directly with the requested goal; the position observation is irrelevant.

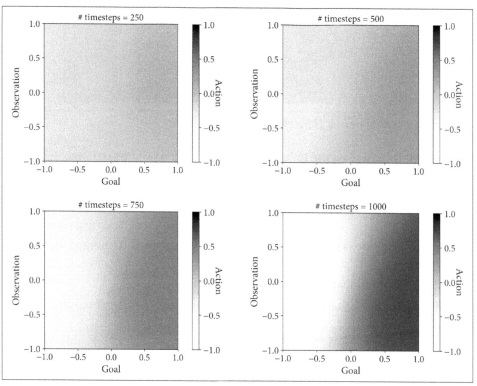

Figure 6-10. A trained policy on the simulated environment at different numbers of environment steps. This image shows the policy predicting the action (shading) for a given goal (x-axis) and observed position (y-axis).

At the start of the training all predictions are zero. Over time the agent is learning to move higher when the goal is higher and lower when the goal is lower. There is a subtle diagonal in the resulting policy because the model has enough freedom to make that choice and the various random samples have conspired to result in this policy over a perfect one. Given more training time and averaging this would eventually be perfect.

Figure 6-11 shows a very similar result when asking the agent to train upon a real servo. The diagonal is more pronounced, but this could just be due to the particular random samples chosen. But the actions aren't quite as pronounced either. The blacks are not as black, and the whites are not as white. It's as if in real-life there is more uncertainty in the correct action, which I account to the fact that the requested movement is not perfect. If I request a position of 0.5, it will actually move to 0.52, for example. I believe this positional error is manifesting as a slightly unsure policy.

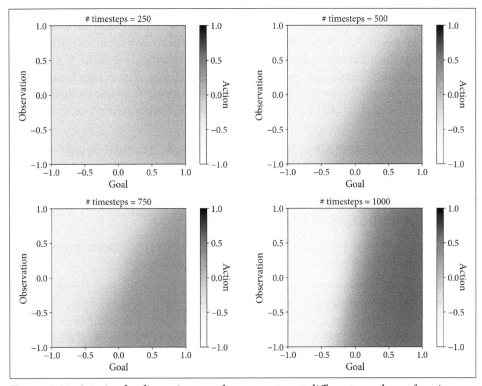

Figure 6-11. A trained policy using a real servo motor at different numbers of environment steps. Axes are the same as Figure 6-10.

Of course, like before, given more training time and averaging it would result in a perfectly viable and useful policy.

Other Policy Gradient Algorithms

Policy gradients, especially off-policy PG algorithms, are an area of enthusiastic research, because of the inherent attractiveness of directly learning a policy from experience. But in some environments, especially environments with complex state spaces, performance lags behind that of value methods. In this section I present introductions to two main streams of research: other ways of stabilizing off-policy updates, which you have already seen in the form of TRPO and PPO, and emphatic methods, which attempt to use the gradient of the Bellman error, rather than advantages.

Retrace(λ)

Retrace(λ) is an early off-policy PG algorithm that uses weighted and clipped importance sampling to help control how much of the off-policy is included in an update.[25]

Munos et al. truncate the importance sampling ratio to a maximum of 1, which is similar to the pessimistic bound in TRPO/PPO, and constrains improvements to the policy. At best the difference is minimal so the update is a standard A2C. At worst the update is negligible because the two policies are so different. The reason for clipping is to prevent variance explosion (repeated high values cause dramatic changes in the policy). The downside is that this adds bias; the result is more stable, but less able to explore.

The returns are also weighted by λ, eligibility traces from "Eligibility Traces" on page 80. This updates the policy based upon previous visitations, which provides a hyperparameter to control the bias–variance trade-off.

Actor-Critic with Experience Replay (ACER)

ACER extends Retrace(λ) by including a combination of experience replay, trust region policy optimization, and a dueling network architecture.[26]

First, Wang et al. reformulate Retrace(λ) to compensate for the bias introduced by truncating the importance sampling. To put it another way, Retrace(λ) prevents large changes in policy, which makes it more stable (more biased), but less able to explore. The compensating factor compensates for this loss of exploration in proportion to the amount of truncation in Retrace(λ).

They also include a more efficient TRPO implementation, which maintains an average policy, predicted by the neural network. If you code the the KL divergence as a penalty, rather than a constraint, then you can use the auto-differentiation of the DL framework.

Finally, they improve sample efficiency using experience replay (see "Experience Replay" on page 92). For continuous action spaces, they include a dueling architecture (see "Dueling Networks" on page 102) to reduce variance. This leads to two separate algorithms: one for discrete actions and one for continuous.

The result is an algorithm that approaches the performance of DQN with prioritized experience replay (see "Prioritized Experience Replay" on page 102), but can also work with continuous action spaces. However, all the corrections lead to a rather complicated algorithm and therefore a complex neural network architecture.

Actor-Critic Using Kronecker-Factored Trust Regions (ACKTR)

In "Natural Policy Gradients and Trust Region Policy Optimization" on page 167 you saw that using the natural policy gradient and constraining by the KL divergence is beneficial because the gradient is independent of the parameterization of the approximating function and the KL constraint improves stability. However, calculating the gradient requires a costly computation to calculate the Fisher information matrix. TRPO's linear projection is another source of inefficiency.

In 2017 Wu et al. proposed using approximations to speed up computation.[27] They use Kronecker-factored approximation (K-FAC), which is an approximation of the Fisher information matrix, to improve computational performance, and a rolling average of this approximation instead of a linear projection, to reduce the number of times the agent has to interact with the environment.

Furthermore, because you can use K-FAC with convolutional neural networks (like PPO), this means that ACKTR can handle discrete, visual state spaces, like the Atari benchmarks.

Since 2017, independent reviews have shown that the performance of ACKTR versus TRPO is highly dependent on environment. For example, in the highly unstable Swimmer-v1 MuJoCo environment, TRPO outperforms most algorithms. But in the HalfCheetah-v1 environment, TRPO performs significantly worse.[28] In the original paper, Henderson et al. present results from Swimmer-v1 that show A2C, TRPO, and ACKTR performing similarly (see "Which Algorithm Should I Use?" on page 185). Anecdotally, practitioners prefer ACKTR over TRPO because the idea and resulting performance is similar but computational efficiency is dramatically improved.

Emphatic Methods

Gradient temporal-difference methods (see "Gradient Temporal-Difference Learning" on page 149) introduced the idea using a function to approximate the state-value function and computing the gradient of the projected Bellman error directly to avoid the approximation from diverging. However, they need two sets of parameters and two learning rates, which make them hard to use in practice. To solve this, Sutton et al. proposed emphatic temporal-difference methods.[29,30]

In its most general form, emphatic temporal-difference learning uses a function to quantify interest in particular states according to the current policy. This is presented alongside importance sampling to compensate for off-policy agents. However, deciding upon a function has proven difficult and performance issues relating to the projection prevent breakout success.[31]

One particularly interesting emphatic proposal called generalized off-policy actor-critic (Geoff-PAC) suggests using the gradient of a counterfactual objective.[32]

Counterfactual reasoning is the process of questioning data that is not observed; for example, asking what the reward of a new policy would be given data collected in the past. Although the details are beyond the scope of this book, the idea is that you can learn an approximation to the emphatic function (using a neural network of course) by predicting the *density ratio*, which is like a continuous version of importance sampling. The results are promising but have not gained widespread popularity.

Extensions to Policy Gradient Algorithms

Throughout this book you have seen a range of enhancements to algorithms that you could, in principle, apply to any algorithm. Every few years researchers release a paper that combines these enhancements to produce state-of-the-art results in benchmark environments and gains media attention. But from a practitioner's point of view, it is the accompanying ablation study that tends to be more interesting, because it shows you which tweaks might be best for your problem. To demonstrate this approach, here is an example of how you can add distributional RL to PG algorithms.

Quantile Regression in Policy Gradient Algorithms

Richter et al. demonstrate how you can incorporate distributional RL into policy gradient algorithms in much the same way "Improving Rewards" on page 109 did for value methods.[33] They use a neural network to predict the quantiles for each action. Like before, this is useful because the mapping from actions to rewards is often stochastic and many environments have distributions that are multimodal. The key difference in this paper is the adaption to policy gradient algorithms. They begin with the standard A2C loss function (Equation 6-8) and instead of learning the advantage function, they replace it with quantile estimates. Next they make a series of approximations to factor out the quantile estimate, which leads to a version that iteratively updates the quantile estimates according to a temperature hyperparameter. They implemented an on-policy version of this algorithm, which beat TRPO in some of the benchmarks (they didn't compare it against PPO) and suggest that it should be possible to use this off-policy in a similar way.

Summary

In this rather extensive chapter you have seen a variety of state-of-the-art policy gradient algorithms, with a focus on off-policy actor-critic methods. Chapter 5 introduced the idea of abstracting policy evaluation and policy improvement into actor-critic architectures. The aim of this chapter was to explain and demonstrate the power of learning off-policy.

The promise of off-policy learning is great, whereby an agent learns a multitude of policies that are different from the behavior policy. Learning off-policy frees the agent from the tyranny of the exploration–exploitation trade-off, allowing the behavior policy to freely explore. Since the optimal policy is separate, you can use offline logs of data or learn from human demonstration. But the primary advantage is that you retrain your approximation functions as much as you like, because there is no environmental cost. This leads to algorithms that are far more sample-efficient, albeit at the expense of computational complexity, especially if you involve neural networks.

Which Algorithm Should I Use?

Your confusion over which algorithm is best is not lost on researchers. There have been a number of studies that have attempted to provide an answer, but to paraphrase one summary, it is very tempting for researchers to present opportunistic results that might not be entirely robust.[34] To give one specific example, the original ACKTR paper presents results for a number of environments that others have struggled to reproduce. Of course, this is probably due to an implementation detail or a lucky set of hyperparameters. But it does highlight the issue. However, I can make some general recommendations:

- Prefer TD3 over DDPG
- Prefer a trust region method in environments that have unstable dynamics, which is the situation where a slight move in policy can have disastrous consequences
- Prefer deterministic methods in environments that have stable dynamics
- Consider simpler algorithms and smaller neural networks if performance or robustness is a concern, like PPO or TD3

A Note on Asynchronous Methods

Another important feature of off-policy algorithms is that it frees you from using a single critic. I haven't mentioned it yet (see "Scaling RL" on page 299) but because the critics are learning from a replay buffer, there is no reason why you can't have many duplicate critics all learning separate policies. In these *asynchronous methods*, you need to recombine that knowledge back into the behavior policy at some point, but this can dramatically improve the wall-clock performance of algorithms. I haven't discussed it yet because I believe this is an implementation detail and depends on having a problem that needs to learn faster to justify the extra expense. For industrial problems, I would first suggest that you consider simplifying the problem or the domain to remove the need for such methods, because it adds a significant amount of operational complexity and cost.

Further Reading

- Natural policy gradients and TRPO (papers in references):
  - Brief, but nice lectures from John Schulman (*https://oreil.ly/eOhYM*)
  - Slides from CMU 10703 (*https://oreil.ly/-Ys4X*)
  - Lecture from Sergey Levine (*https://oreil.ly/604zI*)
  - Explanation video from Xander Steenbrugge (*https://oreil.ly/AzF9z*)
- Numerical optimization:
  - Nocedal, Jorge, and S. Wright. 2006. *Numerical Optimization* (*https://doi.org/10.1007/978-0-387-40065-5*). 2nd ed. Springer Series in Operations Research and Financial Engineering. New York: Springer-Verlag.

References

[1] Sutton, Richard S., Hamid R. Maei, and Csaba Szepesvári. 2009. "A Convergent O(n) Temporal-Difference Algorithm for Off-Policy Learning with Linear Function Approximation" (*https://oreil.ly/iq9Pg*). In *Advances in Neural Information Processing Systems* 21, edited by D. Koller, D. Schuurmans, Y. Bengio, and L. Bottou, 1609–1616. Curran Associates, Inc.

[2] Sutton, Richard S., Hamid Reza Maei, Doina Precup, Shalabh Bhatnagar, David Silver, Csaba Szepesvári, and Eric Wiewiora. 2009. "Fast Gradient-Descent Methods for Temporal-Difference Learning with Linear Function Approximation" (*https://oreil.ly/aprqz*). In *Proceedings of the 26th Annual International Conference on Machine Learning*, 993–1000. ICML 09. Montreal, Quebec, Canada: Association for Computing Machinery.

[3] Sutton, Richard S., Hamid Reza Maei, Doina Precup, Shalabh Bhatnagar, David Silver, Csaba Szepesvári, and Eric Wiewiora. 2009. "Fast Gradient-Descent Methods for Temporal-Difference Learning with Linear Function Approximation" (*https://oreil.ly/qpk-g*). In *Proceedings of the 26th Annual International Conference on Machine Learning*, 993–1000. ICML 09. Montreal, Quebec, Canada: Association for Computing Machinery.

[4] Maei, Hamid Reza, Csaba Szepesvári, Shalabh Bhatnagar, and Richard S. Sutton. 2010. "Toward Off-Policy Learning Control with Function Approximation." In *Proceedings of the 27th International Conference on International Conference on Machine Learning*, 719–726. ICML'10. Haifa, Israel: Omnipress.

[5] White, Adam, and Richard S. Sutton. 2017. GQ(λ) "Quick Reference and Implementation Guide" (*https://oreil.ly/pj7Wc*). ArXiv:1705.03967, May.

[6] Degris, Thomas, Martha White, and Richard S. Sutton. 2013. "Off-Policy Actor-Critic" (*https://oreil.ly/zcR5K*). ArXiv:1205.4839, June.

[7] Silver, David, Guy Lever, Nicolas Heess, Thomas Degris, Daan Wierstra, and Martin Riedmiller. 2014. "Deterministic Policy Gradient Algorithms" (*https://oreil.ly/PU2hT*). In *International Conference on Machine Learning*, 387–95.

[8] Lillicrap, Timothy P., Jonathan J. Hunt, Alexander Pritzel, Nicolas Heess, Tom Erez, Yuval Tassa, David Silver, and Daan Wierstra. 2019. "Continuous Control with Deep Reinforcement Learning" (*https://oreil.ly/D_Zjm*). ArXiv:1509.02971, July.

[9] Plappert, Matthias, Rein Houthooft, Prafulla Dhariwal, Szymon Sidor, Richard Y. Chen, Xi Chen, Tamim Asfour, Pieter Abbeel, and Marcin Andrychowicz. 2018. "Parameter Space Noise for Exploration" (*https://oreil.ly/klLak*). ArXiv:1706.01905, January.

[10] Salimans, Tim, and Durk P. Kingma. 2016. "Weight Normalization: A Simple Reparameterization to Accelerate Training of Deep Neural Networks" (*https://oreil.ly/LFWvR*). In *Advances in Neural Information Processing Systems* 29, edited by D. D. Lee, M. Sugiyama, U. V. Luxburg, I. Guyon, and R. Garnett, 901–909. Curran Associates, Inc.

[11] Fujimoto, Scott, Herke van Hoof, and David Meger. 2018. "Addressing Function Approximation Error in Actor-Critic Methods" (*https://oreil.ly/r0qaN*). ArXiv: 1802.09477, October.

[12] Wang, Chaoyang, Zhiqiang Guo, Jianjun Li, Peng Pan, and Guohui Li. 2020. "A Text-Based Deep Reinforcement Learning Framework for Interactive Recommendation" (*https://oreil.ly/32vIS*). ArXiv:2004.06651, July.

[13] Ie, Eugene, Vihan Jain, Jing Wang, Sanmit Narvekar, Ritesh Agarwal, Rui Wu, Heng-Tze Cheng, et al. 2019. "Reinforcement Learning for Slate-Based Recommender Systems: A Tractable Decomposition and Practical Methodology" (*https://oreil.ly/lPePY*). ArXiv:1905.12767, May.

[14] Ie, Eugene, Chih-wei Hsu, Martin Mladenov, Vihan Jain, Sanmit Narvekar, Jing Wang, Rui Wu, and Craig Boutilier. 2019. "RecSim: A Configurable Simulation Platform for Recommender Systems" (*https://oreil.ly/ZnQs6*). ArXiv:1909.04847, September.

[15] Barth-Maron, Gabriel, Matthew W. Hoffman, David Budden, Will Dabney, Dan Horgan, Dhruva TB, Alistair Muldal, Nicolas Heess, and Timothy Lillicrap. 2018. "Distributed Distributional Deterministic Policy Gradients" (*https://oreil.ly/Uz0S5*). ArXiv:1804.08617, April.

[16] Cai, Qingpeng, Ling Pan, and Pingzhong Tang. 2019. "Deterministic Value-Policy Gradients" (*https://oreil.ly/AXfzI*). ArXiv:1909.03939, November.

[17] Kakade, Sham M. 2002. "A Natural Policy Gradient" (*https://oreil.ly/yQkbV*). In *Advances in Neural Information Processing Systems* 14, edited by T. G. Dietterich, S. Becker, and Z. Ghahramani, 1531–1538. MIT Press.

[18] Schulman, John, Sergey Levine, Philipp Moritz, Michael I. Jordan, and Pieter Abbeel. 2017. "Trust Region Policy Optimization" (*https://oreil.ly/d4qxR*). ArXiv: 1502.05477, April.

[19] Peters, Jan, Sethu Vijayakumar, and Stefan Schaal. 2005. "Natural Actor-Critic" (*https://oreil.ly/Ks5mV*). In *Machine Learning: ECML 2005*, edited by João Gama, Rui Camacho, Pavel B. Brazdil, Alípio Mário Jorge, and Luís Torgo, 280–91. Lecture Notes in Computer Science. Berlin, Heidelberg: Springer.

[20] Schulman, John, Filip Wolski, Prafulla Dhariwal, Alec Radford, and Oleg Klimov. 2017. "Proximal Policy Optimization Algorithms" (*https://oreil.ly/HDdBG*). ArXiv:1707.06347, August.

[21] Mnih, Volodymyr, Adrià Puigdomènech Badia, Mehdi Mirza, Alex Graves, Timothy P. Lillicrap, Tim Harley, David Silver, and Koray Kavukcuoglu. 2016. "Asynchronous Methods for Deep Reinforcement Learning" (*https://oreil.ly/x84W3*). ArXiv:1602.01783, June.

[22] Schulman, John, Filip Wolski, Prafulla Dhariwal, Alec Radford, and Oleg Klimov. 2017. "Proximal Policy Optimization Algorithms" (*https://oreil.ly/-QFNj*). ArXiv:1707.06347, August.

[23] Ahn, Michael, Henry Zhu, Kristian Hartikainen, Hugo Ponte, Abhishek Gupta, Sergey Levine, and Vikash Kumar. 2019. "ROBEL: Robotics Benchmarks for Learning with Low-Cost Robots" (*https://oreil.ly/yJsP2*). ArXiv:1909.11639, December.

[24] Song, Xingyou, Yilun Du, and Jacob Jackson. 2019. "An Empirical Study on Hyperparameters and Their Interdependence for RL Generalization" (*https://oreil.ly/LDusn*). ArXiv:1906.00431, June.

[25] Munos, Rémi, Tom Stepleton, Anna Harutyunyan, and Marc G. Bellemare. 2016. "Safe and Efficient Off-Policy Reinforcement Learning" (*https://oreil.ly/29RAJ*). ArXiv:1606.02647, November.

[26] Wang, Ziyu, Victor Bapst, Nicolas Heess, Volodymyr Mnih, Remi Munos, Koray Kavukcuoglu, and Nando de Freitas. 2017. "Sample Efficient Actor-Critic with Experience Replay" (*https://oreil.ly/4dMmv*). ArXiv:1611.01224, July.

[27] Wu, Yuhuai, Elman Mansimov, Shun Liao, Roger Grosse, and Jimmy Ba. 2017. "Scalable Trust-Region Method for Deep Reinforcement Learning Using Kronecker-Factored Approximation" (*http://arxiv.org/abs/1708.05144*). ArXiv:1708.05144, August.

[28] Henderson, Peter, Riashat Islam, Philip Bachman, Joelle Pineau, Doina Precup, and David Meger. 2019. "Deep Reinforcement Learning That Matters" (*https://oreil.ly/zgyQ4*). ArXiv:1709.06560, January.

[29] Sutton, Richard S., A. Rupam Mahmood, and Martha White. 2015. "An Emphatic Approach to the Problem of Off-Policy Temporal-Difference Learning" (*https://oreil.ly/95_Z3*). ArXiv:1503.04269, April.

[30] Zhang, Shangtong, Wendelin Boehmer, and Shimon Whiteson. 2019. "Generalized Off-Policy Actor-Critic" (*https://oreil.ly/tHEt8*). ArXiv:1903.11329, October.

[31] Gelada, Carles, and Marc G. Bellemare. 2019. "Off-Policy Deep Reinforcement Learning by Bootstrapping the Covariate Shift" (*https://oreil.ly/1TKVs*). ArXiv: 1901.09455, January.

[32] Zhang, Shangtong, Wendelin Boehmer, and Shimon Whiteson. 2019. "Generalized Off-Policy Actor-Critic" (*https://oreil.ly/NCo2a*). ArXiv:1903.11329, October.

[33] Richter, Oliver, and Roger Wattenhofer. 2019. "Learning Policies through Quantile Regression" (*https://oreil.ly/6I-C9*). ArXiv:1906.11941, September.

[34] Henderson, Peter, Riashat Islam, Philip Bachman, Joelle Pineau, Doina Precup, and David Meger. 2019. "Deep Reinforcement Learning That Matters" (*https://oreil.ly/F9Xvc*). ArXiv:1709.06560, January.

CHAPTER 7

Learning All Possible Policies with Entropy Methods

Deep reinforcement learning (RL) is a standard tool due to its ability to process and approximate complex observations, which result in elaborate behaviors. However, many deep RL methods optimize for a deterministic policy, since if you had full observability, there is only one best policy. But it is often desirable to learn a stochastic policy or probabilistic behaviors to improve robustness and deal with stochastic environments.

What Is Entropy?

Shannon entropy (abbreviated to *entropy* from now on) is a measure of the amount of information contained within a stochastic variable, where information is calculated as the number of bits required to encode all possible states. Equation 7-1 shows this as an equation where $X \doteq \{x_0, x_1, \cdots, x_{n-1}\}$ is a stochastic variable, $\mathcal{H}$ is the entropy, I is the information content, and b is the base of the logarithm used (commonly bits for $b \doteq 2$, bans for $b \doteq 10$, and nats for $b \doteq e$). Bits are the most common base.

Equation 7-1. The information content of a random variable

$$\mathcal{H}(X) \doteq \mathbb{E}[I(X)] = -\sum_{x \in X} p(x) \log_b p(x)$$

For example, a coin has two states, assuming it doesn't land on its edge. These two states can be encoded by a zero and a one, therefore the amount of information contained within a coin, measured by entropy in bits, is one. A die has six possible states, so you would need three bits to describe all of those states (the real value is 2.5849...).

A probabilistic solution to optimal control is a stochastic policy. To have an accurate representation of the action-probability distribution, you must sample enough states and actions. You could measure the number of states and actions you have visited, like in UCB (see "Improving the ϵ-greedy Algorithm" on page 33). But this isn't directly coupled to a policy; UCB is an exploration strategy, not part of the policy. Instead, you can use a proxy measure of how well distributed a policy is, like entropy, and include that as a penalty term in the objective function.

Maximum Entropy Reinforcement Learning

Maximizing the entropy of a policy forces the agent to visit all states and actions. Rather than aiming to find a deterministic behavior that maximizes the reward, the policy can learn *all* behaviors. In other words, instead of learning the best way of performing a task, the entropy term forces the agent to learn *all* the ways to solve a task. This leads to policies that can intuitively explore and provide more robust behavior in the face of adversarial attacks—pelting a robot with bricks, for example. See the videos on the PPO blog post (*https://oreil.ly/ckDQo*) for some fun. I talk more about this in Chapter 10.

Equation 7-2 shows the objective function for maximum entropy RL, where α is a hyperparameter (called the *temperature*, which links back to the thermodynamic definition of entropy) that determines the relative importance of the entropy term against the reward and controls the stochasticity of the optimal policy.

Equation 7-2. Maximum entropy objective function

$$\pi^* \doteq \underset{\pi}{\operatorname{argmax}} \sum_{s \in \mathcal{S}, a \in \mathcal{A}} \mathbb{E}\left[r + \alpha \mathcal{H}\left(\pi(a \mid s)\right)\right]$$

Equation 7-2 states that the optimal policy is defined as the policy that maximizes the return regularized by the entropy of the policy. This is similar to the standard definition of an optimal policy except that it is augmented with a bonus to promote nondeterministic policies, the exact opposite of deterministic policy gradients.

How well this works depends on the problem. If you have a discretized problem that only has one optimal trajectory, and you never expect that the agent will veer off that trajectory, then a deterministic policy is a good choice. But in continuous problems, where it is likely that the agent will veer away from the optimal policy, then this might be a better option.

The α hyperparameter allows you to control how much of a bonus is included. Values close to zero become deterministic and larger values promote nondeterminate actions and therefore more exploration.

Soft Actor-Critic

The soft actor-critic (SAC) algorithm is an off-policy policy gradient approximation of the maximum entropy objective function.[1] The term "soft" is used to emphasize the nondeterministic elements within the algorithm; the standard Bellman equation with no entropy term could be considered "hard," so Q-learning and DDPG are corresponding "hard" algorithms.

Haarnoja et al. begin by defining the critic as a soft approximation of the action-value function presented in an earlier paper.[2] Recall that the goal is to generate a policy that maximizes the entropy, which means the agent should value high entropy states more than others. Following Equation 7-2, Equation 7-3 shows that the value of a state is the action value plus a bonus for the entropy of that new state. I have simplified the notation to match the rest of this book; Equation 7-3 assumes that you are following a policy, but I hide that information to make the mathematics easier to understand. V and Q represent state-value and action-value functions, respectively.

Equation 7-3. Maximum entropy state-value function

$$V(s) = \mathbb{E}\big[Q(s, a) + \alpha \mathcal{H}\big(\pi(a \mid s)\big)\big]$$
$$= \mathbb{E}\big[Q(s, a) - \alpha \log \pi(a \mid s)\big]$$

Using Equation 7-3, Equation 7-4 shows the corresponding action-value function from dynamic programming.

Equation 7-4. Maximum entropy action-value function

$$Q(s, a) \doteq \mathbb{E}\big[r + \gamma \mathbb{E}\big[V(s')\big]\big]$$

To handle complex state spaces you can train a function to approximate Equation 7-4, for which you need an objective function (Equation 7-5).

Equation 7-5. Maximum entropy action-value objective function

$$J_Q(\theta) = \mathbb{E}\Big[\frac{1}{2}\big(Q_\theta(s, a) - Q(s, a)\big)^2\Big]$$
$$= \mathbb{E}\Big[\frac{1}{2}\big(Q_\theta(s, a) - \big(r + \gamma \mathbb{E}\big[V_\theta(s')\big]\big)\big)^2\Big]$$

You can derive the gradient of Equation 7-4 (you will see this shortly), but SAC implementations typically leverage the automatic differential frameworks included with your deep learning library. Next, you need a policy for the actor and a similar objective function. It is possible to derive a soft policy gradient analytically.[3] But Haarnoja et al. chose to minimize the Kullback–Leibler (KL) divergence instead (see

"Kullback–Leibler Divergence" on page 165). The reason for this was because Liu and Wang developed an approach called *Stein variational gradient descent*, which is an analytical solution to the gradient of the KL divergence, the derivation of which is beyond the scope of the book.[4] Haarnoja et al. applied this technique to the soft policy, which results in the policy objective shown in Equation 7-6, which you can solve using auto-differentiation.

Equation 7-6. SAC policy objective function

$$J_\pi(\varphi) = \mathbb{E}\left[\alpha \log\left(\pi_\varphi(a \mid s)\right) - Q_\theta(s, a)\right]$$

SAC Implementation Details and Discrete Action Spaces

There are details within the derivation that impact the implementation. First, performance is highly sensitive to the choice of temperature parameter. You need to perform a hyperparameter scan to establish the best temperature for each problem. Second, because of the sensitivity to the temperature hyperparameter, this also means that it is sensitive to the scale of the rewards. For example, large rewards would overwhelm small temperature values. Rescale your rewards to mitigate. These two issues are fixed in the next algorithm.

Finally, Haarnoja et al. assume Gaussian actions, which makes the problem tractable (called the *reparameterization trick*) and allows it to work with continuous action spaces.[5] SAC does not work with discrete action spaces out of the box.

This capability is added in the SAC algorithm suggested by Christodoulou, which reformulates the maximum entropy problem with discrete actions—the differences are minimal.[6] You might ask why use a policy gradient algorithm over something like DQN. The major benefit of using SAC with discrete action spaces is that it can compete with value methods in terms of learning performance but with zero hyperparameter tuning. SAC implements this via a subsequent algorithm that automatically adjusts the temperature.

Automatically Adjusting Temperature

A follow-up paper from Haarnoja et al. presented a way to automatically adjust the SAC temperature parameter by converting the problem into a constraint, rather than a penalty. They constrain the current policy to have a higher entropy than an expected minimum entropy of the solution. Then they find that they can iteratively update a model of the temperature parameter to minimize the difference between the entropy of the current policy and expected entropy, as shown in Equation 7-7, where α is the temperature parameter and $\overline{\mathcal{H}} \doteq -\dim(\mathcal{A})$ is the expected entropy, which is the same as the negative of the number of actions.[7]

Equation 7-7. SAC temperature parameter objective function

$$J_\alpha = \mathbb{E}\left[-\alpha \log\left(\pi(a \mid s)\right) - \alpha\overline{\mathcal{H}} \right]$$

Haarnoja et al. add this line to the original SAC algorithm to turn it into a hyperparameter-free off-policy policy gradient algorithm. This is an enticing feature, because it mitigates against developer bias and speeds up development, with state-of-the-art performance. Of course, you still have tuning to do: neural network structure, state engineering, action class, and so on. But this is a step in the right direction.

Case Study: Automated Traffic Management to Reduce Queuing

There is nothing more universal than the synchronized groan from passengers when approaching a traffic jam. Bottlenecks generated by work zones and incidents are one of the most important contributors to nonrecurrent congestion and secondary accidents. "Smart" highways aim to improve average speed in a high-density flow by suggesting when users should merge into open lanes. Recent developments in automated driving like adaptive cruise control, which matches your speed with the vehicles in front of you, allow vehicles to drive at high speed while maintaining a small gap. But this doesn't take advantage of knowledge of vehicles in other lanes or behind. In the future, vehicles will be able to access greater amounts of local information, which will potentially allow vehicles to collaborate. If vehicles can collaborate, then you can use RL to derive a global optimal policy to increase speed and density to reduce congestion and the number of secondary incidents.

Ren, Xie, and Jiang have developed an RL approach to solving this problem. They first split the road into zones, one of which is a merging zone where vehicles are forced to merge into an open lane. A previous zone allows for the vehicle to speed up or slow down so that they can align with traffic in an open lane.[8]

The state of the MDP is a velocity and acceleration matrix within this zone, and local information about the vehicle under control. This is fed into quite a complicated neural network that includes convolutional, fully connected, and recurrent elements.

The action is control over a single vehicle's speed, in order to position it within a safe gap. They iterate over all vehicles currently within the control zone.

The reward is complex, but aims to promote successful merges (no crashes and with a safe distance) and increased speed.

They choose SAC as the algorithm of choice, because of the continuous actions, its off-policy sample efficiency, and its stability during exploration.

They simulate this formulation in a traffic simulation tool called VISSIM (*https://oreil.ly/48EpL*) and compare the RL implementation to common road-sign–based merge strategies, which either tell vehicles to merge into the open lane early or late.

The RL solution significantly improves mobility over the basic algorithms, reducing delays by an order of magnitude. It is also much safer, with stable, low-valued densities throughout the queue, whereas the basic algorithms promoted a dangerous backward-forming shockwave.

Despite impressive results, there is quite a lot of room for improvement. First, this is a simulation. It would have been great to have some real-life results, although I know from experience that it is incredibly difficult to develop against potentially dangerous environments such as this. I also would like to see more realistic observations. For example, vehicle position and local information can be inferred from video cameras. There is no need to assume that the vehicles or the oracle have perfect knowledge of the vehicles around them. Finally, I am concerned about the complexity of the policy model for what is quite a simple state space. I don't believe that this much complexity is required, and that the state representation should be delegated. I'm confident the policy itself, for selecting the right speed to fit into a gap, is actually quite simple to learn.

Extensions to Maximum Entropy Methods

SAC provides you with a simple and performant off-policy algorithm out of the box but like other algorithms, researchers continue to offer improvements in the search for maximum performance. As usual, these improvements do not guarantee better performance for your specific problem; you have to test them.

Other Measures of Entropy (and Ensembles)

Shannon entropy is only one way of measuring entropy. There are other forms that alter the way SAC penalizes the policy to prefer or ignore unpromising actions. Chen and Peng try Tsallis and Rényi entropy and find that these improve performance on baseline algorithms.[9] They also demonstrate the use of an ensemble of policies, whereby you train multiple policies at the same time. Upon each new episode, the agent uses a random policy from this ensemble to choose actions. This approach comes from bootstrapped DQN to improve exploration (see "Improving Exploration" on page 108).

Optimistic Exploration Using the Upper Bound of Double Q-Learning

Similar to how double Q-learning formulates a lower bound on the action-value estimate (see "Double Q-Learning" on page 74) Ciosek et al. propose using the pessimistic bound as the target policy (with an entropy term that makes it look similar to standard SAC), but the *upper bound*, the action value that overestimates the reward, for the behavior policy.[10] They suggest that this helps prevent *pessimistic under-exploration* caused by relying on the lower bound. Empirically, the results on the standard MuJoCo environments are better, but not dramatically. You might want to consider this approach if you are working in an environment where agents are struggling to explore fully.

Tinkering with Experience Replay

As described in "Prioritized Experience Replay" on page 102, which experiences you choose to learn from have an impact on learning performance. Wang and Ross demonstrate that adding prioritized experience replay can improve SAC on some environments, but oversampling more recent experience improves results consistently across all environments.[11] This is a simple addition and worth a try, but watch out for *catastrophic forgetting* (see "Experience Replay" on page 92), whereby the agent forgets previous experiences. A large replay buffer mitigates against this effect.

Soft Policy Gradient

Rather than penalizing by an entropy measure, why not derive an entropy-inspired soft policy gradient instead? Shi, Song, and Wu introduced the soft policy gradient method that is reportedly more principled and stable than SAC.[12]

Shi et al. start by taking the maximum entropy definition of RL and differentiate the policy to result in an gradient calculation that is surprisingly simple, as shown in Equation 7-8. This is more effective than using the automatic differential frameworks because you can then observe and operate directly on the gradients, so they chose to clip the gradients directly rather than apply trust-region optimization, to prevent catastrophic updates. This results in a simpler implementation and better stability. I would not be surprised if this becomes the "default" maximum entropy interpretation in the future.

Equation 7-8. Deep soft policy gradient

$$\nabla J_\pi(\varphi) = \mathbb{E}\left[\left(Q_\theta(s, a) - \log \pi(a \mid s) - 1\right)\nabla_\varphi \log \pi(a \mid s)\right]$$

Soft Q-Learning (and Derivatives)

You can also apply maximum entropy RL to Q-learning. Haarnoja et al. first showed that you can derive entropy-based value and action estimates.[13] Others have applied the same idea to calculate the advantage function and found it to work well on complex, potentially continuous environments that have discrete action spaces.[14] I can imagine that integrating these estimates into other algorithms, like PPO, may bring positive results.

Path Consistency Learning

Path consistency learning (PCL) from Nachum et al. is related to SAC, because it appreciates that entropy encourages exploration and derives the same soft state and action value functions as soft Q-learning. However, PCL investigates using rollouts, in the style of *n*-step algorithms, and leads to an *n*-step off-policy algorithm that does not need any correction (importance sampling, for example).[15] A subsequent paper implemented a KL-divergence–based trust method (Trust-PCL) that beats TRPO.[16] This highlights that even with deep learning and off-policy sampling techniques, you can still incorporate improvements to the underlying temporal-difference algorithms. Despite this, SAC tends to dramatically outperform PCL methods.

Performance Comparison: SAC Versus PPO

There is an elephant in the room and it runs amok throughout RL: which algorithm is better for continuous control tasks, PPO or SAC? It is generally accepted that SAC and its derivatives perform better than PPO. But it's not as clear as it should be. As I mentioned before, researchers measure performance in different ways and implementation details severely alter performance.[17] The main issue for this section was that researchers mostly don't publish the raw values for learning curves. And often they don't even report values in tables, just in plots. This makes it incredibly hard to compare results between papers.

Table 7-1 shows a sample of results from papers and implementations. All results were taken at 1 million steps, except for (†) at 1.5 million steps. (*) only published images of results, so I estimated performance from the images.

Table 7-1. Performance results from continuous control benchmarks for SAC and PPO

Environment	SAC[a]	SAC[b]	SAC†[c]	SAC-auto*[d]	PPO[e]	PPO†[f]	SAC-auto[g]	PPO[h]
MuJoCo Walker	3475	3941	3868	4800	3425	3292		
MuJoCo Hopper	2101	3020	2922	3200	2316	2513		
MuJoCo Half-cheetah	8896	6095	10994	11000	1669			
MuJoCo Humanoid	4831		5723	5000	4900	806		
MuJoCo Ant	3250	2989	3856	4100				
MuJoCo Swimmer			42		111			
AntBulletEnv-v0							3485	2170
BipedalWalker-v2							307	266
BipedalWalkerHardcore-v2							101	166
HalfCheetahBulletEnv-v0							3331	3195
HopperBulletEnv-v0							2438	1945
HumanoidBulletEnv-v0							2048	1286

Environment	SAC[a]	SAC[b]	SAC†[c]	SAC-auto*[d]	PPO[e]	PPO†[f]	SAC-auto[g]	PPO[h]
InvertedDoublePendulumBulletEnv-v0							9357	7703
InvertedPendulumSwingupBulletEnv-v0							892	867
LunarLanderContinuous-v2							270	128
MountainCarContinuous-v0							90	92
Pendulum-v0							-160	-168
ReacherBulletEnv-v0							18	18
Walker2DBulletEnv-v0							2053	2080

[a] Haarnoja, Tuomas, Aurick Zhou, Pieter Abbeel, and Sergey Levine. 2018. "Soft Actor-Critic: Off-Policy Maximum Entropy Deep Reinforcement Learning with a Stochastic Actor" (*https://oreil.ly/JjjwB*). ArXiv:1801.01290, August.

[b] Wang, Tingwu, Xuchan Bao, Ignasi Clavera, Jerrick Hoang, Yeming Wen, Eric Langlois, Shunshi Zhang, Guodong Zhang, Pieter Abbeel, and Jimmy Ba. 2019. "Benchmarking Model-Based Reinforcement Learning" (*https://oreil.ly/9ZBoU*). ArXiv: 1907.02057, July.

[c] Wang, Che, and Keith Ross. 2019. "Boosting Soft Actor-Critic: Emphasizing Recent Experience without Forgetting the Past" (*https://oreil.ly/eigQt*). ArXiv:1906.04009, June.

[d] Haarnoja, Tuomas, Aurick Zhou, Kristian Hartikainen, George Tucker, Sehoon Ha, Jie Tan, Vikash Kumar, et al. 2019. "Soft Actor-Critic Algorithms and Applications" (*https://oreil.ly/s3apP*). ArXiv:1812.05905, January.

[e] Dhariwal, Prafulla, Christopher Hesse, Oleg Klimov, Alex Nichol, Matthias Plappert, Alec Radford, John Schulman, Szymon Sidor, Yuhuai Wu, and Peter Zhokhov. 2017. OpenAI Baselines (*https://oreil.ly/9642Z*). GitHub Repository.

[f] Logan Engstrom et al. 2020. "Implementation Matters in Deep Policy Gradients: A Case Study on PPO and TRPO" (*https://oreil.ly/pOPdK*). ArXiv:2005.12729, May.

[g] Raffin, Antonin. (2018) 2020. Araffin/Rl-Baselines-Zoo. Python. *https://oreil.ly/H3Nc2*

[h] Raffin, Antonin. (2018) 2020. Araffin/Rl-Baselines-Zoo. Python. *https://oreil.ly/H3Nc2*

The first thing you will notice is the variance of the results. Some SAC implementations and experiments perform far worse than others. In these it is likely that worse hyperparameter tuning caused worse performance. This is why the automatic temperature variant of SAC is so important. This achieves good results without tuning. If you scan across all the numbers, then SAC mostly outperforms PPO in the MuJoCo environments. Looking at the open source PyBullet results also suggests that automatic temperature SAC is better on the whole, but there are many environments where performance is similar.

These numbers also don't tell the whole story, though. They don't tell you whether performance will continue to increase if you left them training. They also represent average performance; this doesn't tell you how stable training runs were. As I have recommended several times already, always retest algorithms and implementations yourself for your specific problems. Your results might not match published baselines.

How Does Entropy Encourage Exploration?

Maximum entropy reinforcement learning encourages application, but how? Equation 7-2 added a bonus proportional to the entropy of the actions in a state, which means that the agent observes an artificial reward higher than the actual reward. The amount of extra reward is defined by the temperature value and the entropy of the actions.

Imagine a child in a candy store. You could measure candy anticipation using entropy; more choices mean more enjoyment. In the middle of the shop, the child could move in hundreds of different directions and get a new candy. But at the door, right at the edge, there's only a few to choose from. Entropy suggests that the child would have more choices if they move toward the center of the shop.

By combining the reward with an entropy bonus you are promoting actions that are not strictly optimal. This helps to ensure that all states are adequately sampled.

To demonstrate, I created a simple grid environment with the goal in the top right-hand corner and the starting point in the middle. The agent is allowed to move in any direction (including diagonals) and there is a sparse reward of one when the agent reaches the goal. The episode ends with zero reward if agents do not reach the goal within 100 steps.

I used an ϵ-greedy Q-learning agent as a baseline. Figure 7-1 shows the result of running the agent with action values plotted as pixels; white colors represent high action values, black low. The arrow denotes the optimal trajectory (no exploration) for the policy. You can see that it has found a path to the goal, but it is suboptimal in terms of the number of steps (remember, I am not penalizing for steps and the exploration is dependent on the random seed) and the agent hasn't explored other regions of the state. If you changed the starting location of the agent, it would not be able to find its way to the goal. This is not a robust policy.

One simple enhancement that accounts for much of SAC's performance is the use of the action values as a distribution, rather than relying on the random sampling of ϵ-greedy for exploration. When this crude probabilistic approach is applied to the Q-learning algorithm by using a softmax function to convert the action values to probabilities, exploration improves dramatically, as you can see in Figure 7-2. I also plot the most probable action as arrows for each state, of which the direction and magnitude is based upon the weighted combination of action values. Note how the direction arrows are all pointing toward the optimal trajectory, so no matter where the agent starts, it will always reach the goal. This policy is far more robust and has explored more of the state space than the previous agent.

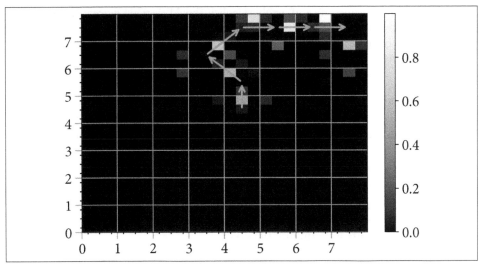

Figure 7-1. The results of using an ε-greedy Q-learning agent on a grid environment. Pixels represent action values and the grid represents the state. The arrows are the optimal trajectory according to the current policy.

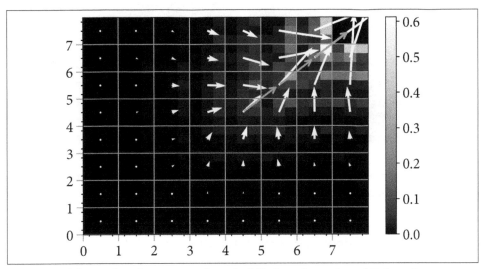

Figure 7-2. The results of using a crude probabilistic, softmax-based Q-learning agent on a grid environment. Decorations are the same as Figure 7-1 except state arrows represent the most probable action with a direction and magnitude that is weighted by the action values.

The performance of a robust policy should degrade gracefully in the presence of adversity. Policies that have uncharted regions near the optimal trajectory are not robust because the tiniest of deviations could lead to states with an undefined policy.

Next I implemented soft Q-learning (see "Soft Q-Learning (and Derivatives)" on page 197) and set the temperature parameter to 0.05. You can see the results in Figure 7-3. The optimal policies are unremarkable, even though they generally point in the right direction. But if you look closely, you can see that the action values and the direction arrows are smaller or nonexistent on the Q-learning side of the plot. Soft Q-learning has visited states other than the optimal trajectory. You can also see that the white colors representing larger action values are shifted toward the center of the images for soft Q-learning. The reason is explained by the candy store example; entropy promotes states with the greatest amount of choice.

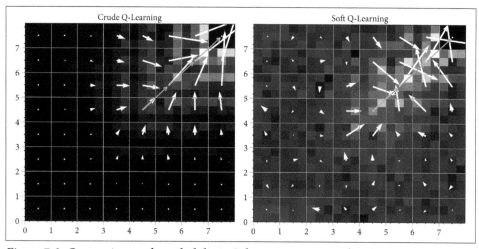

Figure 7-3. Comparing crude probabilistic Q-learning against soft Q-learning with the same setup as Figure 7-2.

The lack of exploration in the Q-learning agent is even more pronounced if you keep track of the number of times each agent visits each action, as I did in Figure 7-4. You can see that the soft Q-learning agent has sampled states more uniformly. This is why entropy helps exploration in more complex state spaces.

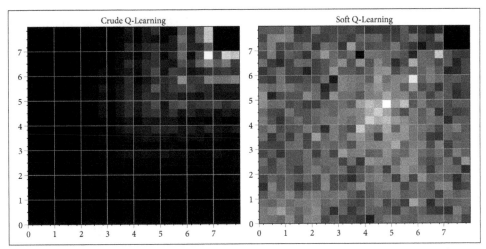

Figure 7-4. Number of action-value interactions for both agents. Colors represent the number of times the agent has visited each action.

How Does the Temperature Parameter Alter Exploration?

The soft Q-learning (SQL) or SAC algorithm is very dependent on the temperature parameter. It controls the amount of exploration, and if you weight entropy too highly then the agent receives higher rewards for exploration than it does for achieving the goal!

There are two solutions to this problem. The simplest is *annealing*. By reducing the temperature parameter over time, this forces the agent to explore early on, but become deterministic later. A second approach is to automatically learn the temperature parameter, which is used in most SAC implementations.

In the experiment in Figure 7-5 I increase the temperature value to promote more exploration. As you can see from the magnitudes of the action values, the entropy term is now so large that it overpowers the reward (with a value of 1). So the optimal policy is to move toward the states with the highest entropy, which are the states in the middle, like in the candy store.

To combat this problem, you can reduce the temperature over time to guide the child, I mean agent, toward the goal. In the experiment shown in Figure 7-6 I anneal the temperature parameter from 0.5 to 0.005. Note that the original SAC paper used annealing.

This experiment demonstrates how annealing helps the agent explore in early episodes. This is extremely useful in complex environments that require large amounts of exploration. The change in temperature causes the agent to become more Q-learning-like and homes in on the optimal policy.

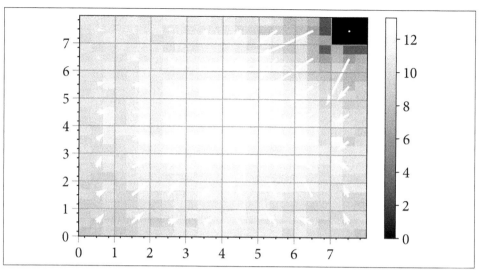

Figure 7-5. Setting the temperature parameter to 1 in the soft Q-learning agent. To emphasize the effect, I increased the number of episodes to 500. All other settings are as in Figure 7-3.

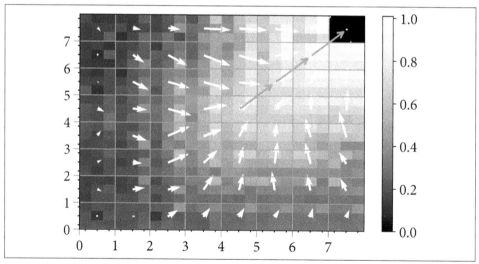

Figure 7-6. Annealing the temperature parameter to from 0.5 to 0.005 in the soft Q-learning agent. All other settings are as in Figure 7-5.

However, the starting, stopping, and annealing rate parameters are important. You need to choose these carefully according to your environment and trade off robustness against optimality.

Industrial Example: Learning to Drive with a Remote Control Car

`Donkey Car` began life as an open source Raspberry Pi–based radio control car and made the bold move to include a *single* sensor; a wide-angle video camera. All of the control is derived from a single image, which poses a significant challenge and opportunity for RL. The name Donkey was chosen to set low expectations. But don't let the name fool you; this straightforward piece of hardware is brought to life through advanced machine learning. Take a look at some of the impressive results and learn more on the Donkey Car website (*https://www.donkeycar.com*).

Tawn Kramer, a Donkey Car enthusiast, developed a simulation environment based upon the Unity framework.[18] You can use this as a rapid development platform to develop new self-driving algorithms. And after I was inspired by Antonin Raffin, one of the core contributors to the `Stable Baselines` range of libraries, I decided to have a go myself.[19] In this example I demonstrate that a SAC-based RL approach generates a viable policy.

Description of the Problem

The state is represented by an observation through a video camera. The video has a resolution of 160×120 with 8-bit RGB color channels. The action space is deceptively simple, allowing a throttle amount and a steering angle as input. The environment rewards the agent for speed and staying in the center of a lane/track on every time step. If the car is too far outside its lane it receives a negative reward. The goal is to reach the end of the course in the fastest time possible.

There are several tracks. The simplest is a desert road with clearly defined and consistent lanes. The hardest is an urban race simulation, where the agent has to navigate obstacles and a track without clear boundaries.

The Unity simulation is delivered as a binary (*https://oreil.ly/2B3Nl*). The `Gym` environment connects to the simulation over a websocket and supports multiple connections to allow for RL-driven competitive races.

Minimizing Training Time

Whenever you work with data that is based upon pixels, the majority of your training time will be taken up by feature extraction. The key to rapid development of a project like this is to split the problem; the more you can break it down, the faster and easier it is to improve individual components. Yes, it is possible to learn a viable policy directly from pixels, but it slows down development iterations and is costly. Your wallet will thank you.

One obvious place to start is to separate the vision part of the process. The RL agent doesn't care if the state is a flattened image or a set of high-level features. But performance is impacted by how informative the features are; more informative features lead to faster training and more robust policies.

One computer vision approach could be to attempt to segment the image or detect the boundaries of the track. Using a perspective transformation could compensate for the forward view of the road. A segmentation algorithm or a trained segmentation model could help you pick out the road. You could use a Hough or Radon transform to find the lines in the image and use physical assumptions to find the nearest lanes. You can probably imagine more. The goal, remember, is to make the observation data more informative.

Another (or symbiotic) approach is to train an autoencoder (see "Common Neural Network Architectures" on page 89) to constrain the number of features to those that are the most informative. This consists of using a convolutional neural network that is shaped like an hourglass to decompose and reconstruct images from a dataset until the small number of neurons in the middle reliably encode all necessary information about the image. This is an offline process, independent of the RL. The pretrained low-dimensional representation is then used as the observation for RL.

Figures 7-7 and 7-8 show the original observation and reconstruction, respectively, after training a variational autoencoder for 1,000 training steps. Note how there are blurry similarities at this stage.

Figure 7-7. Raw observation of the DonkeyCar environment at 1,000 training steps.

Figure 7-8. Reconstruction of the DonkeyCar environment at 1,000 training steps by the variational autoencoder.

Figures 7-9 and 7-10 show another observation and reconstruction after 10,000 training steps. Note how much detail is now in the reconstruction, which indicates that the hidden neural network embedding has learned good latent features.

Figure 7-9. Raw observation of the DonkeyCar environment at 10,000 training steps.

Figure 7-10. Reconstruction of the DonkeyCar environment at 10,000 training steps by the VAE.

Figure 7-11 compares videos of the observation from the RGB camera on the Donkey Car against a reconstruction of the low-dimensional observation, which is the input to the SAC algorithm.

Figure 7-11. A reconstruction of the DonkeyCar simulation through the eyes of a variational autoencoder. The video on the left shows the raw video feed from the simulation. On the right is the reconstructed video from a low-dimensional state. This reconstructed video has been cropped to remove the sky region, which is unnecessary for this problem.

Reducing the state space, the input to the reinforcement learning algorithm, will reliably cut down RL training time to a matter of minutes, rather than days. I talk more about this in "Transformation (dimensionality reduction, autoencoders, and world models)" on page 267.

Dramatic Actions

In some environments it is possible to apply actions that dramatically alter the environment. In the case of DonkeyCar, large values for the steering action cause the car to spin, skid, and otherwise veer off the optimal trajectory. But of course, the car needs to steer and sometimes it needs to navigate around sharp corners.

But these actions and the subsequent negative rewards can cause training to get stuck, because it constantly skids and never manages to capture enough good observations. In the DonkeyCar environment, this effect becomes worse when large jumps in actions are allowed. For example, when you ride a bike, you know it is technically possible to turn the steering sharply at speed, but I doubt that you have ever tried it. You've probably tried something much less vigorous and had a bad experience, so you will never try anything like turning the steering by 90 degrees. Figure 7-12 shows some example training footage with the original action space.

Figure 7-12. A video of DonkeyCar training when the action space is left unaltered.

You can influence the training of the agent by including this prior information in your RL model. You could alter the reward signal to promote (or demote) certain states. Or, as in this case, you can filter the action of the agent to make it behave in a safer way.

If you try training the agent using the full range of steering angles (try it!) then you will see that after a long time it learns to steer away from the edges, but it does it so forcefully it sends the car into a three-wheel drift. Despite this looking cool, it doesn't help finish the course. You need to smooth out the steering.

One of the simplest ways of constraining how an agent behaves is to alter the action space. Like in machine learning, constraining the problem makes it easier to solve. In the training shown in Figure 7-13 I have limited the throttle to a maximum of 0.15 (originally 5.0) and steering angle to an absolute maximum of 0.5 (originally 1.0).

The slow speed prevents the car from going into a skid and the smaller steering angle helps to mitigate against the jerky steering. Note that training performance is greatly impacted by these parameters. Try altering them yourself.

Figure 7-13. A video of DonkeyCar training after simplifying the action space.

Hyperparameter Search

The maximum throttle and steering settings are hyperparameters of the problem; they are not directly tuned. Changes to the problem definition tend to impact performance the most, but there are a host of other hyperparameters from the SAC algorithm, like the architecture of the policy model. The objective is to find what combination of parameters leads to the best rewards. To do this you would perform a hyperparameter search, by writing some code that iterates through all permutations and reruns the training. You can read more about hyperparameter tuning in "Hyperparameter tuning" on page 324.

I ran an optimized grid search using the optuna library to tune the hyperparameters of the SAC algorithm and viewed all the results in TensorBoard. I found that I could increase the learning rates by an order of magnitude to speed up learning slightly. Tweaking the entropy coefficient also helped; by default the stable-baselines implementation starts with a value of 1.0 and learns the optimal value. But in this example the agent trains a small number of steps, so it doesn't have time to learn the optimal coefficient. Starting from 0.1 and learning the optimal coefficient worked better. But overall I was underwhelmed by how much the hyperparameters affected performance (which is a good thing!). Altering the hyperparameters of the variational autoencoder and the changing the action space impacted performance much more.

Final Policy

After all the engineering work, all the code, and searching for hyperparameters, I now have a viable policy that has been trained for between 5,000 and 50,000 environment steps, depending on the environment and how perfect you want to the policy to be. This took about 10–30 minutes on my old 2014 Macbook Pro. Figures 7-14 and 7-15 show example policies for the `donkey-generated-track-v0` and `donkey-generated-road-v0` environments, respectively.

Figure 7-14. A video of the final DonkeyCar policy for the `donkey-generated-track-v0` environment.

Figure 7-15. A video of the final DonkeyCar policy for the `donkey-generated-road-v0` environment.

But note throughout this I barely touched upon the RL algorithm. All the hard work went into feature engineering, hyperparameter searches, and constraining the problem to make it simpler. These are precisely the tasks that take all the time in industrial ML projects. Also like ML, RL algorithms will become standardized over time, which will lead to the situation where you won't need to touch the RL algorithms at all.

Further Improvements

You could make a multitude of improvements to this policy. By the time you read these words, other engineers will have crushed my feeble effort. You could spend your time improving the autoencoding or trying any of the other ideas suggested in "Minimizing Training Time" on page 205. You could alter the action space further, like increasing the maximum actions until it breaks. One thing I wanted to try was annealing the action space limit, whereby the action space starts small and increases up to the maximum values over training time. You could try altering the rewards, too;

maybe speed shouldn't be rewarded so highly. Attempting to penalize jerkiness makes sense, too.

You can probably imagine many more, but if you are working on an industrial problem then you will need to take more care: take baby steps, make sure you are evaluating correctly, make sure what you are doing is safe, split the problem up, constrain the problem, and test more. You can read more about this in Chapter 9.

Summary

RL aims to find a policy that maximizes the expected return from sampled states, actions, and rewards. This definition implies maximization of the expected return irrespective of the consequences. Research has shown that bounding or constraining the policy updates leads to more stable learning and better rounded policies.

Chapter 6 approached this problem by constraining updates so they don't dramatically alter the policy. But this can still lead to brittle, overly sparse policies where most actions have zero value except for the optimal trajectory. This chapter introduced entropy-based algorithms, which modify the original definition of MDP returns to rescale or *regularize* the returns. This lead to proposals that other definitions of entropy might perform better, because Shannon entropy is not sparse enough. I would argue that it is possible to tweak the temperature parameter to produce a policy that suits your own problem. But it is reasonably likely that another entropy measure will perform better for your specific problem.

The logical conclusion of this argument is to use an arbitrary function. This was proposed by Li, Yang, and Zhang in *regularized MDPs* and mandates several theoretical rules that the function has to follow, like that it should be strictly positive, differentiable, concave, and fall to zero outside of the range of zero to one. They suggest that other exponential-based functions and trigonometric functions are interesting proposals.[20]

Irrespective of the implementation, augmenting the value function with an exploration bonus is a good thing for production implementations. You want your agent to be robust to change. Be careful not to overfit to your environment.

Equivalence Between Policy Gradients and Soft Q-Learning

To round this chapter off I wanted to come back to a comparison of value methods to policy methods. Simplistically, Q-learning and policy gradient methods both attempt to reinforce behavior that leads to better rewards. Q-learning increases the value of an action whereas policy gradients increase the probability of selecting an action.

When you add entropy-based policy gradients to the mix (or equivalent) you boost the probability of an action proportional to some function of the action value (refer to Equation 7-2). Or more succinctly, the policy is proportional to a function of the Q-values. Hence, policy gradient methods solve the same problem as Q-learning.[21]

Even empirically, comparisons of Q-learning and policy gradient approaches conclude that performance is similar (look at Figure 4 in the ACER paper, where policy gradient and Q-learning approaches are almost the same).[22] Many of the differences can be accounted for when considering external improvements to things like sample efficiency or parallelism. Schulman and Abbeel went so far as to normalize Q-learning and policy gradient–based algorithms to be equivalent and prove they produce the same results.[23]

What Does This Mean For the Future?

The conclusion you can draw from this is that given time there will be little difference between value methods and policy gradient methods. The two disciplines will merge (which they have already done to some extent with the actor-critic paradigm) since both policy improvement and value estimation are inextricably linked.

What Does This Mean Now?

But for now it is clear that no one single implementation is good for all problems, the classic interpretation of the *no free lunch* theorem. You have to consider several implementations to be sure that you have optimized the performance. But make sure you pick the simplest solution that solves your problem, especially if you are running this in production. The cumulative industrial knowledge and experience of these algorithms also helps. For example, you wouldn't pick some esoteric algorithm over SAC by default, because people, platforms, and companies have more experience with SAC.

References

[1] Haarnoja, Tuomas, Aurick Zhou, Pieter Abbeel, and Sergey Levine. 2018. "Soft Actor-Critic: Off-Policy Maximum Entropy Deep Reinforcement Learning with a Stochastic Actor" (*https://oreil.ly/7sUno*). ArXiv:1801.01290, August.

[2] Haarnoja, Tuomas, Haoran Tang, Pieter Abbeel, and Sergey Levine. 2017. "Reinforcement Learning with Deep Energy-Based Policies" (*https://oreil.ly/zBwzW*). ArXiv:1702.08165, July.

[3] Shi, Wenjie, Shiji Song, and Cheng Wu. 2019. "Soft Policy Gradient Method for Maximum Entropy Deep Reinforcement Learning" (*https://oreil.ly/j-5Pg*). ArXiv: 1909.03198, September.

[4] Liu, Qiang, and Dilin Wang. 2019. "Stein Variational Gradient Descent: A General Purpose Bayesian Inference Algorithm" (*https://oreil.ly/_PHaF*). ArXiv:1608.04471, September.

[5] Haarnoja, Tuomas, Aurick Zhou, Pieter Abbeel, and Sergey Levine. 2018. "Soft Actor-Critic: Off-Policy Maximum Entropy Deep Reinforcement Learning with a Stochastic Actor" (*https://oreil.ly/PE_dM*). ArXiv:1801.01290, August.

[6] Christodoulou, Petros. 2019. "Soft Actor-Critic for Discrete Action Settings" (*https://oreil.ly/6sVHP*). ArXiv:1910.07207, October.

[7] Haarnoja, Tuomas, Aurick Zhou, Kristian Hartikainen, George Tucker, Sehoon Ha, Jie Tan, Vikash Kumar, et al. 2019. "Soft Actor-Critic Algorithms and Applications" (*https://oreil.ly/8GIoC*). ArXiv:1812.05905, January.

[8] Ren, Tianzhu, Yuanchang Xie, and Liming Jiang. 2020. "Cooperative Highway Work Zone Merge Control Based on Reinforcement Learning in A Connected and Automated Environment" (*https://oreil.ly/p6kSZ*). ArXiv:2001.08581, January.

[9] Chen, Gang, and Yiming Peng. 2019. "Off-Policy Actor-Critic in an Ensemble: Achieving Maximum General Entropy and Effective Environment Exploration in Deep Reinforcement Learning" (*https://oreil.ly/M7mW-*). ArXiv:1902.05551, February.

[10] Ciosek, Kamil, Quan Vuong, Robert Loftin, and Katja Hofmann. 2019. "Better Exploration with Optimistic Actor-Critic" (*https://oreil.ly/2m-c-*). ArXiv:1910.12807, October.

[11] Wang, Che, and Keith Ross. 2019. "Boosting Soft Actor-Critic: Emphasizing Recent Experience without Forgetting the Past" (*https://oreil.ly/1f1sl*). ArXiv: 1906.04009, June.

[12] Shi, Wenjie, Shiji Song, and Cheng Wu. 2019. "Soft Policy Gradient Method for Maximum Entropy Deep Reinforcement Learning" (*https://oreil.ly/AcQXD*). ArXiv: 1909.03198, September.

[13] Haarnoja, Tuomas, Haoran Tang, Pieter Abbeel, and Sergey Levine. 2017. "Reinforcement Learning with Deep Energy-Based Policies" (*https://oreil.ly/8Kn1_*). ArXiv: 1702.08165, July.

[14] "End to End Learning in Autonomous Driving Systems" (*https://oreil.ly/gi7ZM*). EECS at UC Berkeley. n.d. Accessed 5 May 2020.

[15] Nachum, Ofir, Mohammad Norouzi, Kelvin Xu, and Dale Schuurmans. 2017. "Bridging the Gap Between Value and Policy Based Reinforcement Learning" (*https://oreil.ly/2lhFk*). ArXiv:1702.08892, November.

[16] Nachum, Ofir, Mohammad Norouzi, Kelvin Xu, and Dale Schuurmans. 2018. "Trust-PCL: An Off-Policy Trust Region Method for Continuous Control" (*https://oreil.ly/dplSx*). ArXiv:1707.01891, February.

[17] Engstrom, Logan, Andrew Ilyas, Shibani Santurkar, Dimitris Tsipras, Firdaus Janoos, Larry Rudolph, and Aleksander Madry. 2020. "Implementation Matters in Deep Policy Gradients: A Case Study on PPO and TRPO" (*https://oreil.ly/mznN4*). ArXiv:2005.12729 Cs, Stat, May.

[18] Kramer, Tawn. 2018. Tawnkramer/Gym-Donkeycar (*https://oreil.ly/64YPf*). Python.

[19] Raffin, Antonin and Sokolkov, Roma. 2019. *Learning to Drive Smoothly in Minutes* (*https://oreil.ly/XvPVj*). GitHub.

[20] Li, Xiang, Wenhao Yang, and Zhihua Zhang. 2019. "A Regularized Approach to Sparse Optimal Policy in Reinforcement Learning" (*https://oreil.ly/iXHx4*). ArXiv: 1903.00725, October.

[21] Schulman, John, Xi Chen, and Pieter Abbeel. 2018. "Equivalence Between Policy Gradients and Soft Q-Learning" (*https://oreil.ly/ZjQ67*). ArXiv:1704.06440, October.

[22] Mnih, Volodymyr, Adrià Puigdomènech Badia, Mehdi Mirza, Alex Graves, Timothy P. Lillicrap, Tim Harley, David Silver, and Koray Kavukcuoglu. 2016. "Asynchronous Methods for Deep Reinforcement Learning" (*https://oreil.ly/QeJ1M*). ArXiv:1602.01783, June.

[23] Schulman, John, Xi Chen, and Pieter Abbeel. 2018. "Equivalence Between Policy Gradients and Soft Q-Learning" (*https://oreil.ly/gw2Nd*). ArXiv:1704.06440, October.

CHAPTER 8

Improving How an Agent Learns

Complex industrial problems can often be decomposed into *directed acyclic graphs* (DAGs). This helps development productivity, by splitting one long project into many smaller projects that are easier to solve. It helps reinforcement learning (RL) because smaller components are often easier and quicker to train and can be more robust. "Hierarchical Reinforcement Learning" on page 220 shows one common formalism, which is to derive a hierarchy of policies, where low-level policies are responsible for fine-grained "skills" and high-level policies do long-term planning.

So far in this book I have only considered single-agent problems. Some problems need teams of agents, or at least there may be multiple agents operating within the same environment. "Multi-Agent Reinforcement Learning" on page 225 shows you how agents can cooperate or compete to solve multi-agent problems with global or local rewards.

Another rapidly evolving area of RL is redefining how you should think about rewards. Traditionally, it is the sole responsibility of the agent to use the reward signal to learn a policy. But you can augment this process by providing extra, potentially external information in the form of expert guidance. "Expert Guidance" on page 235 discusses how to incorporate expertise into policies that ultimately help to speed up learning by improving exploration. It's even possible to *learn* the optimal reward, which aims to negate the need for reward engineering.

But first, RL is inextricably linked to Markov decision processes (MDPs) by the Bellman equation, and all RL algorithms rely on theoretical guarantees of optimality when making sequential decisions (you might want to review "Markov Decision Processes" on page 35). But a variety of real-life scenarios break the underlying assumptions of an MDP, which often leads to the silent failure of the assumptions made by the Bellman equation and manifest as policies that won't converge, no matter how much hyperparameter tinkering you do. The next section investigates variations on the basic MDP to accommodate these scenarios.

 This chapter summarizes the state-of-the-art. I think that the four most important themes are how you define the MDP, hierarchical RL, multi-agent RL, and providing expert guidance. But all of these can be considered as "advanced" and if discussed in full would take another book. However, I do think it is useful to present an overview so that you know it is there and can dig deeper if you want to. As usual, the citations and recommendations in "Further Reading" on page 242 can provide a wealth of extra information.

Rethinking the MDP

RL algorithms that leverage the MDP framework and the resulting guarantees from the Bellman equation assume that the underlying environment is Markovian. Although there may be a great deal of uncertainty about the effects of an agent's actions, the perception of the state of the environment must be perfect. The agent then uses this omnipotent knowledge to choose the next action according to the current policy, or $\pi(a \mid s)$.

But what if the state representation is not perfect? What if when you tell the servo to move to a position, it moves to a position that is randomly distributed about that position? Or what if there are latent, hidden features that represent how likely a person is to click a recommendation? In these situations the state is not fully observable and the Markovian assumptions are broken.

Partially Observable Markov Decision Process

One solution to this *partial observability* is to split the representation of the state. A partially observable Markov decision process (POMDP) includes extra parameters over the MDP to include a finite set of observations that the agent can experience, Ω, and an *observation function*, O, that maps a state and action to a probability distribution over actions. You can then convert the problem back into an MDP by approximating the inverse of the observation function and using it to convert observations back into states.

Figure 8-1 shows that a POMDP is an extension of the MDP, in which the agent is unable to directly observe the current state of the environment. Instead it uses an observation and information about the previous action and state to generate a prediction of the current state, $\hat{s}$. The prediction of the state is often called the *belief state*, b, which you can describe as "this is the state that I believe the environment is in."

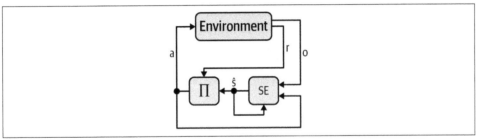

Figure 8-1. You can decompose a POMDP into an MDP (with states, actions, rewards, and a policy) and a state estimator (SE) that predicts states from observations (o).

Predicting the belief state

So what is the belief state and how can you predict it? Consider an example where you were trying to direct a robot through a simple maze. The agent doesn't know the layout of the maze, but it might be intelligent enough to be able to detect that there is a "T-junction" ahead and it needs to make a choice on which direction to take. A naive policy would overfit the training environments and converge to a point where it suggests a single decision every time.

A simple solution to this problem, as indicated by the recurrence in Figure 8-1, is that the best action can be based upon past experience. I don't mean past experience in the training sense, not a replay buffer, but past experience of the current episode and environment. For example, if you know that the robot has already tried left and that led to a dead end, then the hidden state of the maze (the best route) is probably the option to the right.

Many sophisticated examples leverage this simple idea by including past actions and observations in the state representation. For example, the Atari benchmarks always stack four frames of pixel observations in order to retain some "history" of the environment. This allows the agent to predict trajectories of Pong balls or the movement of enemies. And many robotics examples include previous actions and states to help account for inaccuracies in positioning and smooth out movement.

Although this idea helps in many cases, it is not sufficient in general. In order to act optimally, the agent needs to actively consider how uncertain it is about the current situation. A more sophisticated solution is to model the state estimator using an approximator that is capable of learning time-dependent features.

There are multiple options for solving this problem. You can attempt to track the belief state; a simple version could utilize a Kalman filter although more recent approaches attempt to build neural networks to derive the optimal Bayes filter.[1] You could incorporate an approximation of the belief model directly into the policy model using memory-enabled predictors or belief trackers.[2,3]

But the simplest (the previous reference had 24 authors!) and most common approach is to slap on a recurrent neural network (RNN) at the end of the state representation function. Depending on the problem, the RNNs don't need to be complicated and they allow the agent to make reasoned decisions based upon past observations. This allows you to train the RNN using standard techniques and tooling.

As a conceptual example, consider the experiment from "Industrial Example: Learning to Drive with a Remote Control Car" on page 205, where I used a variational autoencoder to represent the state. I could add an RNN to the output of the state representation and train it by predicting future observations. Eventually it would be able to provide predictions of what would happen given certain actions and therefore break the partial observability problem. The policy would have full observability of all possible future observations so you can optimize the MDP using standard RL methods.

Case Study: Using POMDPs in Autonomous Vehicles

You might suggest that the previous example is too contrived to apply to real life. But a surprising number of real-life scenarios fit perfectly into the previous model. One such example is that of autonomous vehicles.

A common autonomous task is to decide when it is safe for the vehicle to move; for example, traversing an intersection with stop signs or a roundabout is a common driving situation. Upon arrival, an agent has to time its actions to perfection to avoid hitting other vehicles. Yet if the vehicle waits too long, valuable time is lost and the efficiency of the intersection decreases.

The vehicle has a limited view of the road. The onboard sensors, such as a camera or a LIDAR module, are line of site and cannot see around obstacles. This makes the problem only partially observable, because the agent cannot sense important features outside of this space, like a speeding vehicle hurtling toward the intersection.

Traditional algorithms attempt to quantify the time to collision, but estimating the time accurately and dealing with unexpected situations is hard and not reliable enough for autonomous operation.

By modeling the problem as a POMDP, you can lean an optimal policy using RL. Qiao et al. demonstrate (in a simulation) that an agent with an LSTM-enabled policy is capable of learning when to set off from a four-way intersection to turn left, right, or move straight ahead.[4] The LSTM policy is able to learn which partially observed situations lead to a collision, via an appropriately engineered reward, and avoid them. You can see the results of this experiment on YouTube (*https://oreil.ly/ivbfj*).

Qiao et al. went on to add hierarchical RL to the previous model to better model the high-level actions (or low-level subtasks, depending on how you think of it) of go, stop, follow vehicle in front, and so on.[5] You read more about hierarchical RL in "Hierarchical Reinforcement Learning" on page 220.

Contextual Markov Decision Processes

There are many problems in which the underlying MDP is the same, but the contextual situation is different. For example, imagine you were training an agent to administer a drug to a diabetes patient based upon their sugar levels. The underlying MDP is the same for every patient, sugar levels are the observation, and administering the drug is the action. But the observation is affected by external variables, like the gender or age of the patient.[6]

This sounds like a situation similar to POMDPs, but there is a crucial difference. These contextual variables do not change with each measurement. By modeling the context as a set of fixed parameters you constrain the space the agent has to search, which can lead to more robust models and quicker learning.[7]

This extension is crucial when presented with a problem that has a small number of steps in an episode (short Markov chains) but massive numbers of independent episodes. This is precisely the situation that recommendation algorithms find themselves in, which is why most of the contextual MDP (CMDP) research is driven by recommendation or ranking applications.[8]

MDPs with Changing Actions

Some applications have changing action sets and the research has followed two paths that lead to similar results. The first set of research concentrates on situations when actions are not always available. For example, in path planning applications like vehicle or packet routing, paths may be closed due to damage or maintenance, or in advertising, ad selection may change depending on the time of day.[9]

The premise is a stochastic action set (SAS), which includes a set of actions available at a certain time, modeled as a random variable. A common solution to this problem is to learn a policy derived from only the actions observed in that particular state. Boutilier et al. showed that you can then utilize standard Q-learning variants.[10] Chandak et al. extended the idea to incorporate policy gradient methods.[11]

A second, but more general strand of research focuses more on lifelong learning, or continuous learning. Here, action sets change because problems and priorities change. For example, you might want to add a new capability to your robotic arm or introduce a new set of ads without having to retrain your model and lose that useful experience. The major problem here is the curse of dimensionality, with ever-growing potential action sets and a lack of data to sample those actions. In theory, adding more actions is as simple as adding them to the MDP. But creating an architecture that can handle such a change is challenging.

Chandak et al. demonstrated that this was possible by splitting the policy in two. The first is responsible for making decisions based upon the state, but the output of this is in a meta-space, not the action space. The second component then maps this meta-space to the action space. Together they form a complete policy.[12]

The benefit is that you can alter the meta-action model parameters to account for new actions without touching the state-representation part. Then you can use standard supervised learning on a replay buffer to train the new meta-action model. This limits the amount of retraining required from the live environment to only the parts of the model that impact the new action.

Regularized MDPs

It is worth mentioning again that the class of algorithms that include regularizers are also a reformulation of the MDP. If you recall (see "Summary" on page 211), SAC and other similar algorithms attempt to find an optimal policy that maximizes the discounted return, like any algorithm based upon an MDP, but they also include a regularization term. The idea here is that you can use this term to enforce robustness, similar to how regularizers impact linear regression. But the addition fundamentally alters the the Bellman equality, which means there is an impact on the underlying MDP. Thankfully, Li et al. proved that it doesn't matter what regularization you apply, the algorithm will still converge, so long as you follow some rules defining the regularizing function.[13]

Hierarchical Reinforcement Learning

A range of problems utilize low-level behaviors that are atomic and repetitive; they involve mastering a "simple" skill like picking up an object or recommending a single product. Problems that involve multilevel reasoning or combine several skills together are much more complex.

In engineering, splitting challenges into smaller components can help to simplify a complex problem. *Hierarchical reinforcement learning* (HRL) uses this idea by decomposing a problem into subtasks, where solving each subtask is easier or better than solving it in entirety. This can lead to computational improvements, greater robustness, more flexibility, and sometimes better performance. It is also one way to mitigate the "curse of dimensionality," by reducing the search space. For example, when learning to walk, there's little point searching the action space that includes walking on your hands, unless you're a gymnast.

With a hierarchy of policies, where only the low-level policies interact with the environment, you can train high-level policies to plan or make strategic decisions over a longer timescale. Another appealing idea is that of encapsulating policies to perform one task well, which you can reuse in other problems; a library of policies.

However, there are a range of challenges that you must consider. How do you define and produce well-encapsulated, low-level policies? How to you train higher-level policies and how do you design the hierarchy? And how do you train all of this in a reasonable amount of time?

Naive HRL

You should consider designing hierarchies manually because in many problems there is a clear separation of concerns. For example, teaching a complex robot to move is clearly distinct from teaching it to make coffee, a rewarding conversation is dependent on the words and utterances used in the conversation, and successful completion of an educational course depends on the content within it.[14,15] Optimizing these high-level goals through low-level, bespoke skills leads to policies that are flexible, robust, and performant.

In simpler situations it may be preferable to design the abstractions, and therefore the hierarchy, manually. You can then design a bespoke RL implementation that takes advantage of this hand-designed, problem-specific model. Figure 8-2 shows an example of decomposing a notional coffee-making task into a hierarchy of behaviors.

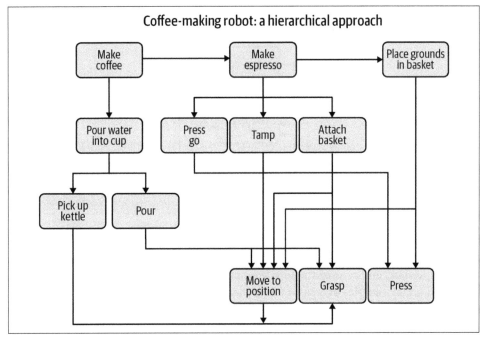

Figure 8-2. You can manually decompose complex tasks into a hierarchy of atomic behaviors and treat each challenge separately. This is an example of decomposing a notional coffee-making task into dependent subskills. Follow the arrows to find the "base" skill.

The major benefit of this approach is that it is likely to be more robust and simpler than a more sophisticated, general approach. It's a bit like asking a neural network to predict the price of a car from a photo; you will be far more successful building sub-networks that are capable of classifying the make and model, locating the number plate for automated number plate recognition, and so on, and feeding those into a high-level model that predicts price. From a practical standpoint, it also helps you focus on neat, pint-sized problems, rather than one big make-or-break unicorn.

But this approach can only take you so far. In many problems the demarcation of boundaries in the hierarchy is a challenge in itself and an arbitrary line is likely to be suboptimal. When riding a bike, for example, is "pedal" a base skill, or should it be "push down on right foot"? You need a way to automatically find these skills.

High-Low Hierarchies with Intrinsic Rewards (HIRO)

The first step toward an automated HRL solution is to split the policy. A low-level policy is responsible for interacting with the environment through states and actions, as usual, but it does not receive the reward. A high-level policy suggests a high-level action and rewards the low-level policy with a reward that is intrinsic to the requested goal. When the environment produces a reward, it is given the high-level policy. Figure 8-3 presents this idea and is explained in full by Nachum et al.[16]

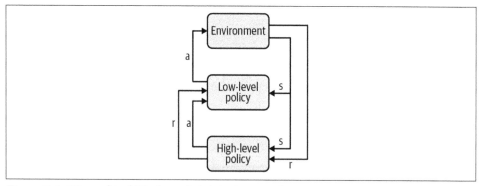

Figure 8-3. Hierarchical RL through intrinsic rewards.

For example, the high-level policy would tell the low-level policy to attempt to move to a specific state, and reward the low-level policy according to how close it gets. The high-level policy samples at a slower rate than the low-level policy to provide a temporal abstraction.

You can parameterize the low-level reward function in any way you like. But researchers propose that a distance-to-state reward helps speed up learning.

The next challenge is that although you can use on-policy algorithms like PPO out of the box, you'd likely want to use a replay buffer to improve sample efficiency. The problem is that the high-level replay buffer will contain observations from previous low-level policies, like right at the start when the low-level policy is random. This means the replay buffer isn't representative and will lead to convergence issues. A simple solution could be to weight the random sample to prefer more recent observations, a form of prioritized experience replay.

But Nachum et al. chose to dynamically *relabel* the high-level action/goals to match the actions that occurred. For example, imagine the coffee example again and the agent has a replay buffer full of the skill "grasp coffee," but the current goal being trained is "push button." In their implementation, the high-level agent sampling from this replay buffer will dynamically change the goal to suit the requested skill. In this example it would alter the goal to be "grasp coffee," to match what is in the buffer.

This might feel like you are fudging the results after the fact to make the current high-level policy look better. But the reward from the environment tends to counteract some of the bias added by the relabeling. In the worst case it is like duplicating observations that are already in the replay buffer. Ideally you want a large selection of uncorrelated, randomly distributed transitions. But if you don't, random sampling helps to make it appear more random.

The results show (*https://oreil.ly/x7FIC*) that a complex legged simulated robot is capable of both learning to walk and learning high-level tasks such as block pushing, hidden goal finding, and resource gathering.

Learning Skills and Unsupervised RL

A major problem with the previous interpretation of HRL is that this is still a closed-loop system that optimizes for the specific problem at hand. There is no generalization. You couldn't use this in any other situation. It is overfitting the environment.

But you know that a robot arm, for example, moves in a similar way for every task. A command of "move to position x" is specific to the robot and the way it is built, not the environment. All this time I have been describing an agent as if it is implicit to the problem, but actually it is an independent entity. So how can you teach policies, or *skills*, that relate to the agent, not the environment?

Researchers propose that agents should be trained to perform a wide variety of skills, even those that don't produce positive rewards. Another higher-level policy can then choose which skills to use to solve a problem. Training an unmanned aerial vehicle (UAV) to do a flip might not be a good thing for a stable communication network, but it might be useful at a Metallica concert (*https://oreil.ly/HZyeo*).

Diversity is all you need (DIAYN) is a novel idea that promotes the unsupervised discovery of low-level policies. Eysenbach et al. propose that skills should be distinguishable, so they should aim to produce policies that visit different states, and the resulting skills should be as diverse as possible. To encourage randomness you can maximize an entropy measure conditioned on states, actions, or both. Figure 8-4 shows a simplified depiction of this process.[17]

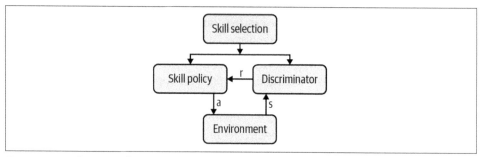

Figure 8-4. Schematic diagram of unsupervised skill learning framework (DIAYN). A skill is chosen at random and a policy acts upon the environment. A discriminator calculates the entropy of the policy, states, and actions that is used as a reward. Over time the policy leans distinct skills.

The result is a collection of diverse policies (*https://oreil.ly/m68lG*) that may or may not be useful for a problem. But the diversity acts like a stepping stone to help solve more complicated problems. I particularly like the results from the HalfCheetah environment that show running, crawling, and sitting (*https://oreil.ly/wVVYT*).

Using Skills in HRL

Given a library of skills, how can you train an HRL algorithm to solve a specific problem? I can imagine that pretrained skills could help nearly all RL algorithms by allowing them to concentrate on environment exploration rather than exploring how to explore. This is especially true in environments where there is a significant amount of complexity in the agent itself.

HRL with advantage-based rewards (HAAR) is one algorithm that takes advantage of pretrained skills to dramatically improve initial exploration and therefore speed up learning. Li et al. also introduce the idea of using advantages as the reward signal, rather than a Euclidean distance to state like in HIRO. The reason for this is that the state space isn't necessarily mapped to the real distance to goal. For example, if you are using a video camera, pixel distance isn't the same as physical distance. So instead they propose using the advantage estimate from the high-level policy to retrain and reward the low-level skills. This way, skills that produce a positive advantage, the ones that do well in the high-level task, are promoted over those that don't.[18]

Another interesting idea is to anneal the amount of time that each skill is repeated to further encourage long-range exploration.

HRL Conclusions

Building a hierarchy of policies is useful when your problem is sufficiently complex to benefit from splitting. From an engineering point of view, if you can imagine that splitting your policy will help simplify the problem or build more robust abstractions, then HRL might be a good fit. The potential for hierarchical policies is hard to spot. Look for situations where agents have to manipulate complex domains. Robotics is an obvious example, but other domains are just as complex, like agents that deal with text.[19] Conversely, in many real-life problems it is the environment that is complex, not the agent, so HRL may not be beneficial.

In the extreme, HRL is akin to a graph problem, where connections between mini-subpolicies form a large graph. Recent research attempts to treat state as a graph and use topological features with graph convolutional neural networks to help solve grid-based problems.[20]

Even if you do not work with complex agents, I think that HRL shows that unsupervised learning has an important role to play in RL. And yet it is only just gaining attention from researchers.[21] Take the time to consider if your problem could benefit from an initial library of skills or pretraining; it could significantly improve learning speed.

Another interesting question is how much influence do you need over your policies? The skills generated by HRL are not determined by an expert, so they may produce action sequences that are unfamiliar, unexpected, or even unwanted. Of course they are directed by the definition of the unsupervised or supervised reward, so you can influence the skills that way. But an open question, which is probably problem specific, is whether you should interfere to produce human "imagineered" policies or allow the agent to discover its own. I suspect that in most real-life problems it is some combination of both. You don't want to be overly prescriptive, because that is the whole point of RL—you can't handcode an optimal policy in complex problems. But you also need to constrain the problem and restrain the agent so that it doesn't overfit and become brittle.

Multi-Agent Reinforcement Learning

Throughout this text I have considered lone agents. But many problems involve more than one player/agent and it is likely that you can improve performance if you systematically model the problem with multiple agents in mind.

Multi-agent reinforcement learning (MARL) addresses the sequential decision-making problem of multiple autonomous agents that operate in a common environment. Each agent attempts to optimize the long-term return by interacting with the environment and other agents.

MARL applications into fall into three main groups: cooperative, competitive, or a mixture of both. In the cooperative setting, agents attempt to collaborate to optimize a common long-term goal. For example, a cooperative MARL can simulate and optimize a taxation policy.[22] In competitive settings, the global reward often sums to zero, since agents can only improve their policy at another agent's expense. This situation is common in domains that include price bidding, like trading and advertising. Finally, the environment may contain both of the previous two situations. For example, an advertisement marketplace wants to maximize both global revenue and long-term user engagement, which means that a cooperative model would be optimal, but advertisers want to pay the least amount of money for the highest impact, which adds a competition into the environment.

The literature generally discusses MARL in the context of games, often traditional games like chess or poker, and increasingly computer games. Like in standard RL, the reason for using games is that they are easy to simulate and verify. Real-life or industrial examples are less common, but are emerging. For example, applications include using MARL to formally define governmental policies, low-level TCP packet congestion mitigation, and multi-robot human-assistance collaboration.[23,24,25]

MARL Frameworks

The literature tends to model MARL problems in one of two ways, which you can see in Figure 8-5.

Looking at Figure 8-5(a), first recall that an MDP is modeled as an agent that acts upon an environment, which in return produces a new state and a reward. If the environment is episodic then the environment also produces a termination signal.

Figure 8-5(b) illustrates how the first MARL framework is an extension of an MDP called a *Markov game* (MG), where multiple agents operate in parallel. Agents submit unique actions and receive unique rewards, but the state of the environment is global. This is the most obvious extension to an MDP, in the context of RL.

Figure 8-5(c) presents the second and more common model, an *extensive-form game* (EFG), where chance, state, and actions are represented as a tree, much like the rollout of an MDP. An EFG still alters the state of an environment through actions, even though it is not explicitly shown. For example, if you choose to bet in a poker game then your opponent is forced to match or fold. Your action is impacting the state of the game. But you can see that sequential actions between agents are far more explicit. In Figure 8-5(c), it is clear that agent 2 cannot have a turn until agent 1 has completed theirs. This scenario is not possible with an MG. Note that EFGs are always considered from the point of view of one of the agents.

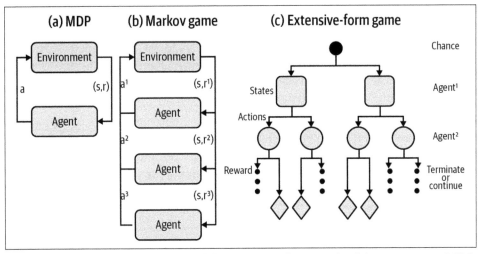

Figure 8-5. Schematic diagrams for different MARL frameworks. (a) represents an MDP, where agents act upon environments that produce states and rewards. (b) is a Markov game where multiple agents have independent actions and rewards. (c) is an extensive-form game, where dots represent chance, squares and circles represent two agents, and diamonds represent terminal states.

Simultaneous actions (like an MG) or imperfect information (like a POMDP) can be represented by *information sets*, which are groups of nodes belonging to a single agent that does not know which node has been reached. These are usually represented by a dotted line or an enclosing circle. You can see an example in Figure 8-6.

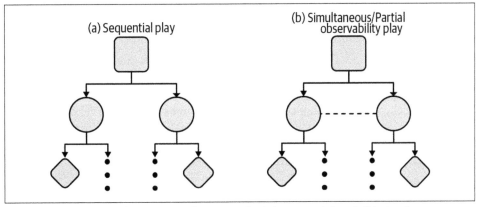

Figure 8-6. Extensive-form game schematics for (a) sequential and (b) simultaneous or imperfect/partially observable games. The only difference is whether other agents know what state they are going to land in.

As an example, consider a game of Rock, Paper, Scissors. This is a classic simultaneous game where two people reveal one of these three actions at the same time to receive the reward. To map this into an EFG you could ask the people to write the actions on a piece of paper, then reveal the choices simultaneously. The agents acted at different times and the second agent could not observe the action of the first player. This means, from the perspective of agent 2, the game is in one of three potential states, but it doesn't know which one.

EFGs are more general and are preferred by theorists. But intuitively, I still like to use MGs as my mental model because the vast majority of industrial situations can be designed to use simultaneous actions and I find the simplicity of a recursive diagram less burdensome than a rolled-out tree. Many researchers agree and use MGs in their applications.

Centralized or Decentralized

Other than the cooperative/competitive distinction, the most important decision to make is whether your problem would benefit from centralized or decentralized learning. Figure 8-7 depicts four scenarios with differing amounts of agent independence.

In centralized learning, or more typically centralized learning and distributed execution, experiences are fed back to a single learner and policies are returned for local execution. The primary benefit of this method is that you can create policies from the experience of multiple actors. For example, if a child could learn centrally, through the experiences of others, they would benefit from the large number of experiences and their diversity. Similarly, using the experience of a disparate set of agents allows them to search the state-action space much more quickly. In essence, independent experiences help exploration and centralized learning ensures all agents have similar, viable policies.

In a decentralized model (often called a *DEC-MDP*), both the execution *and* the learning happens locally. This is more scalable because it doesn't matter how many agents you introduce. For example, imagine if everyone "drove" an autonomous vehicle. A single centralized learning process is unlikely to be optimal for all driving conditions. Local learning allows agents to adapt to their local perception of the environment. For example, a policy for driving on the left side of the road is likely to be subtly different than a policy for driving on the right.

Another problem is that agents may have different capabilities. For example, the experience of a cyclist is just as valid as the experience of a car, but combining these experiences in a centralized way is difficult. Robots may have different configurations. Decentralized learning allows agents to learn to use the actions at their disposal.

A further benefit is that the decentralized model potentially allows you to use standard single-agent RL algorithms, because you can treat each agent independently.

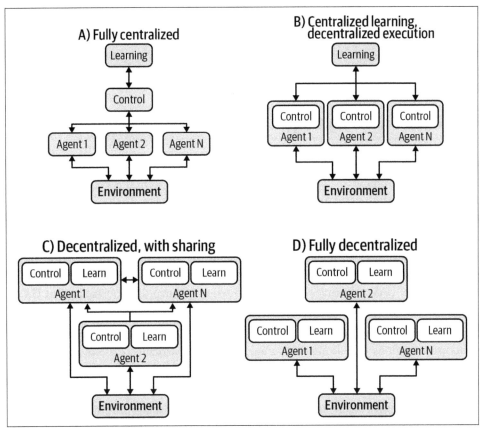

Figure 8-7. Different forms of control and learning in MARL. (a) In fully centralized settings, agents have no control over execution or learning. (b) In centralized learning, agents have full execution control but policies are distributed by a central source. (c) In a decentralized setting, if communication is possible, then agents can share experience and policies. (d) In a fully decentralized model, agents are independent.

Single-Agent Algorithms

The first and most obvious route to solving MARL problems is to assume each agent is independent and apply any of the single-agent RL approaches discussed in this book. Unfortunately, traditional RL algorithms such as Q-learning or policy gradient are poorly suited to multi-agent environments. The primary concern is that during training other agents are interacting and altering the environment state. This makes the environment nonstationary from the perspective of any single agent. When the environment is constantly changing, this impedes the agent's ability to create a stable policy. This also means that common RL add-ons, like basic experience replay, do not help. This does not mean that they fail completely, however. The agent can learn stable policies in simple environments, but they are usually suboptimal and tend not to converge when environments increase in complexity.

It is technically possible to use model-based policy gradient algorithms, because the model provides you with a perfect description of the dynamics of the environment, but for many problems a model is not available.

Case Study: Using Single-Agent Decentralized Learning in UAVs

Using UAVs, often called drones, is becoming increasingly common in applications where geospatial coverage is important but hard to achieve. UAVs can fly into an unknown environment to monitor wildfires, perform search and rescue, and establish communication networks.[26,27,28] Their popularity is due to the low operational cost, the array of sensors, and their flexibility of application.

It is impractical to attempt to handcode controllers to perform tasks due to the lack of an accurate model. RL provides a natural model-free solution that is capable of navigating through difficult environments. There are a variety of examples of using RL to learn low-level UAV primitives like flying, moving, and avoiding obstacles. But UAVs shine when they are used in collaboration to solve a problem.

Cui, Liu, and Nallanathan use a simulated fleet of UAVs to provide wireless infrastructure to regions with limited coverage. UAVs are particularly useful in this situation because it is typically easy to establish line of sight. The researchers use MARL to solve a complex optimization problem that maximizes network performance.

Their work assumed agent independence and leveraged a simple single-agent solution. They used Q-learning to learn the optimal choice of user to connect to, subchannel, and power level. Note that positions are fixed in this work. They develop a reward function based upon quality metrics and solve in a simulation of three UAVs. Note that there is no correction for the nonstationarity of the environment and agents must compete for reward.

So there is a lot of room for improvement. A better decentralized technique could account for the instability of the environment. Or since they have a network, a centralized technique would make development easier. And a more sophisticated agent could handle a much more complex state space, like spatial positioning, which would help the solution scale. With these fixes it should be feasible to run this in real life. The problem with the way that research is celebrated today is that it only promotes success, not failure. It's likely that Cui, Liu, and Nallanathan tried some of these ideas but ran out of time.

Despite this I am optimistic and can imagine a more stable set of algorithms that are able to learn more complex behaviors (like optimal multi-agent positioning).

Centralized Learning, Decentralized Execution

Recent successes have arisen by combining improvements in RL with the sample efficiency of centralized learning. One such algorithm that gained notoriety combines DDPG ("Deep Deterministic Policy Gradients" on page 154) with a centralized learning, decentralized execution approach called *multi-agent DDPG* (MADDPG).[29]

DDPG (or TD3/PPO/others) provides the backbone that allows agents to learn policies without a model of the environment. Policy gradient algorithms provide a theoretical basis for combining the gradients of multiple agents, as opposed to value methods in which the global action-value function is not representative of local situations. Using a centralized learning approach during training time improves sample efficiency and speeds up learning. During evaluation, agents use independent policies and local observations.

The primary motivation for this approach is that if you know the actions of all agents, then it is possible to predict or track the changes to the environment. Like in quantum mechanics, if you know the state and actions of all atoms in the universe, then life is stationary, and you can predict the future (or past).

To calculate the value of a policy for an individual agent, you need to know the outcome of the agent's policy and the value predicted in the environment. But the environment is affected by all other agents, so you need to provide information about the actions of all other agents. Looking back at the different policy gradient implementations (Equation 5-11) it is clear that the actor-critic paradigm naturally considers the actions of an agent, so all you need to do is extend it to consider the actions of *all* agents, which is shown from the perspective of a single agent in Equation 8-1, with N other agents in the environment.

Equation 8-1. Multi-agent actor-critic

$$\nabla_\theta J(\theta) = \mathbb{E}_{\pi_\theta}\left[\nabla_\theta \ln \pi_\theta(a \mid s) Q_w(s, a)\right] \qquad \text{(Actor-Critic)}$$

$$= \mathbb{E}_{\pi_\theta}\left[\nabla_\theta \ln \pi_\theta(a \mid s) Q_w(s, a_1, a_2, \cdots, a_N)\right] \text{ (Multi-Agent Actor-Critic)}$$

This leads to the idea that we can have a local, independent actor but a centralized critic. Interestingly, because there is an actor and critic learned for every agent, agents can have different policies and rewards, which means that this works in both cooperative and competitive settings. Next, and I leave this as a homework exercise, you can apply the various improvements to vanilla policy gradient algorithms to end up with multi-agent versions of standard actor-critic RL algorithms.

Most actor-critic algorithms need the policy to generate the next action for the training of the action-value function. See any of the actor-critic algorithms, for example. One simple solution is to ask every agent to pass the policy, or all of the next actions (depending on the algorithm), back to the centralized critic. This causes synchronization and latency issues, which hampers efficiency, but is quite simple.

The approach that MADDPG took was to *learn* the policies of the other agents, while they themselves are learning. This is an obvious source of nonstationarity. To limit the effects of nonstationarity, MADDPG slows down the learning rate by updating a limited subset of random policies. Not ideal, but it works. See the paper for more details.

Decentralized Learning

If you can't use a centralized model, then you need ways in which to stabilize decentralized learning. Temporal-difference hysteresis is a technique that uses two different learning rates depending on the size of the temporal-difference error.[30] If the temporal-difference error is below a threshold usually set at zero, which means that the agent obtained less reward than expected, a slower (smaller) update rate is applied. It assumes that the bad return was because the agent was exploring—you wouldn't want your child to copy you if you do something stupid. When the error is positive, the agent uses the normal learning rate. In essence it is biasing the algorithm to be more optimistic, which itself can lead to issues, but that can often be controlled by the learning rate hyperparameters. The key, however, is that it helps with the non-stationarity of the environment; the agent doesn't revert a potentially good policy just because of a few lousy updates that were due to a changing environment.

The second challenge in decentralized learning is partial observability. The classic and simplest solution is to include a recurrent layer to record histories, although other approaches are available. I anticipate that more formal approaches are just around the corner.

The final challenge is the inability to use standard replay buffers. The problem is that experiences are local and nonstationary when sampled independently, despite agents learning concurrently. The local view at that point in time is unlikely to represent the environment at a future point in time. A related issue is that randomly sampling from different parts of the replay buffer may have entirely different environmental states, which in the worst case could cause two agents with exactly the same local conditions resulting in completely different policies. There are many potential ways to improve upon this, but Omidshafiei et al. implemented a replay buffer that was synchronized over all agents. Concurrent experience replay tends to lead to local correlations, which is typically a bad thing and resolved by random sampling, but in this situation helps because it forces all agents to focus on the current replay, which should all have the same environmental conditions. For example, if two agents had similar local conditions, then sampling from the buffer at the same point should yield similar experiences and therefore lead to similar policies. In this particular instance the experiences are trajectories in order to train the recurrent neural networks. This combination of DQN, hysteresis, and synchronized replay buffer is called Dec-HDRQN.[31]

Note that this is just one of many potential ways to solve the problem of nonstationarity during updates, different local optima during experience replay, and partial observability. You could swap out any of the previous components with other implementations, although they will have their own idiosyncrasies.

Other Combinations

The centralized and decentralized paradigms can be mixed together in a huge variety of ways to suit the application. For example, you could use a centralized critic, with a centralized policy that is shared with agents for remote execution. Or you could use agents with decentralized critics and policies that are shared with their immediate neighbors. Many permutations have been investigated and there is likely to be an algorithm that suits your use case. A detailed investigation of this varied field is outside of the scope of this book, but there are some great resources in "Further Reading" on page 242.

For me, MARL highlights the importance of the problem design. The sheer number of permutations, combined with the number of RL algorithms, combined with the number of neural network possibilities, means that it is computationally difficult to automate or perform a large-scale hyperparameter scan. You have to choose a small subset of algorithms and architectures to make the feedback cycle small enough to produce anything in a reasonable amount of time. This means that it is vitally important to have a correct and robust problem definition; otherwise, if you make a small change to the problem, this can have huge impacts on the implementation. In the worst case you might have to throw away all your work and all your research and start again.

The Difficulties of Making RL Work in Real Life

Imagine you had a problem where you decided that centralized training was possible. You spent many weeks doing your research, building simulators and testing lots of algorithms. Your initial tests were performing well and you told your stakeholders that you are ready to move to the next step. Then you start testing in the real world on a much greater number of agents. You leave for the day happy and sleep well.

In the morning you turn on your laptop, excited to see what new policies have been found. But you realize that (a) all policies are no better than random and (b) there have only been four training steps. After denial, anger, "quick fixes," and depression, you realize that most of the time the agents weren't able to communicate with the server and your code waits until every agent has checked in before it runs a training step. It quickly dawns on you that in real life agents do not have reliable

---

communication and even if they did, you will eventually have too many agents, which will slow down the whole system. You need a decentralized model.

The only option is to report a failure to your stakeholders and go back to the start. I wouldn't call it a complete waste of time, because this experience allowed you to learn a lot of transferable knowledge and skills, but in my experience, stakeholders generally don't like moving backward on a product roadmap.

This pattern of failure, an incorrect problem definition, is common in data science, too. But in RL there tends to be a much higher barrier to experimentation because of the agent–environment interaction, so the amount of time wasted can be much greater.

One mitigation, among others discussed throughout this book, is to take your time when defining the problem and subsequent modeling. Your model needs to be simple enough to solve and reason about, but it must also be representative of the real problem. It's like software: the best code is simple and obvious, yet seems to handle the majority of situations. But don't think that simple means easy; simplicity arises out of effort, trial, and many errors.

Challenges of MARL

Despite significant progress and a daunting amount of research, MARL is hard. This doesn't mean that it is impossible and I don't want to dissuade you from going down this path; the research shows that solutions are entirely doable. But I want to make you aware of the challenges to watch out for, which include:

Diversity of problems
    You need to accurately model your environment, making decisions about cooperative or competitive, sharing policies or not, sequential or simultaneous, and you also need to consider all of the normal MDP questions like value or policy or fully observable or partial. Once you have a solid model, then you need to dig to find an appropriate algorithm that works within the assumptions of your model. MARL is a much more complex problem, so there are far more potential solutions.

Multidimensional and multimodal goals
    The goal of one agent may be significantly different than another, due to the local conditions of the environment. This can make it challenging to share policies.

Scalability
    In many tasks it is important to synchronize information, whether that be external, like the current state of an agent, or internal, like the current policy, which leads to communication efficiency issues in larger deployments.

Instability

Since agents are actively altering the environment, from the perspective of another agent, the environment is nonstationary. This breaks or invalidates some of the basic assumptions provided by the MDP and leads to lack of stability.

Optimality

It's hard to precisely define optimality for all but the simplest of examples, which means there are no convergence guarantees for nontrivial environments.

These challenges are unique to MARL, but they sit on top of all the standard challenges in RL like partial observability and sample efficiency. It is likely that given time these challenges will reduce in severity as researchers find different ways of tackling RL.

MARL Conclusions

MARL is an exciting and rapidly developing extension of RL. I anticipate that significant improvements are just around the corner. In the month of June 2020, for example, there were more than 50 new MARL research papers on arXiv. But even now it is possible to leverage MARL to solve a variety of commercially viable use cases, some of which you can see on the accompanying website (*https://rl-book.com/applications*).

In this brief overview of MARL I have ignored most of the game-related literature. It is still very important from a research and theoretical perspective, but out of the scope of this book.

Expert Guidance

In many of the examples or situations presented throughout this book I have talked about teaching an agent a policy from scratch. But humans possess domain knowledge that can direct, encourage, and improve how agents learn. For example, the age at which children start school varies by country. In the US and United Kingdom, kids start around the age of four or five, but in many countries like Serbia, Singapore, South Africa, and Sweden, children don't start until they are seven. The argument for starting later is that children are given more time to randomly explore, to fine-tune low-level emotional and motor skills before they are forced to learn arbitrary high-level abstractions. Whereas the counterargument is that children waste time with random exploration and that it's better to subtly guide them using a curriculum. The same is true in RL; expert guidance is likely to provide valuable information, but the agent also needs to explore by itself. There isn't a correct amount of either.

But I am certain when saying that problems can benefit from some amount of expert tutelage. This section introduces how to incorporate this expertise into your policy.

Behavior Cloning

A traditional approach to incorporating expert policies is to use supervised learning to maximize the likelihood of an agent choosing actions that are the same as the expert for encountered states. This is called *behavior cloning* but isn't popular because it overfits the expert demonstrations. If an agent were to find itself in a state that wasn't demonstrated, then the agent wouldn't know what to do. This situation, because of high-dimensionality in complex problems, is very likely to happen, which makes it important to use algorithms that continue to learn from their actions, even if they aren't demonstrated.[32]

Imitation RL

In 2017, Hester et al. proposed that in many real-life situations an accurate simulation is not available or feasible; the only possibility is to train the agent in situ. But there are external sources that already use viable policies, like a previous controller or human guidance. Developing solutions to transfer knowledge from these experts to agents enables a range of solutions for problems where demonstrations are common but accurate simulators are not.[33]

First, an expert (human or machine) generates trajectories in the environment. Then a supervised loss is incorporated into the Bellman update that measures the difference between the actions of the expert and the agent. Over time the agent learns to generate trajectories similar to the expert.

The problem with this method is that you don't want the agent to mimic the expert, since the expert's policy is likely to be suboptimal. *Deep Q-learning from demonstrations (DQfD)* accounts for this by attempting to prevent overfitting to the expert trajectory through a series of regularizations. *Generative adversarial imitation learning* (GAIL) suggests a similar approach that adversarially perturbs action distributions toward an expert. But this doesn't answer or have an intuitive knob to tweak that controls *how* much expert advice to use.[34]

Soft Q imitation learning (SQIL) provides one idea and at the same time simplifies DQfD and GAIL by changing the way standard algorithms use experience replay. Reddy et al. found that (a) carefully controlling the trajectories that reside in the replay buffer, (b) reconstructing the reward signal for those trajectories, and (c) using a loss function that allows exploration but stays close to expert trajectories allows the agent to learn from experience even when there is no extrinsic reward signal. The resulting algorithm is broadly similar to behavior cloning, except that it allows for deviations into states that were not demonstrated. It penalizes those states through regularization and nudges the agent back toward expert behavior. You could even control the amount of expert advice to use by weighting the regularization. So I can imagine an annealing version that initially uses expert demonstrations and tends toward pure RL over time. But the main selling point is the simplicity, and this can be adapted to any off-policy algorithm, discrete or continuous.[35]

Inverse RL

The problem with imitation RL is that there is no guarantee that the expert is demonstrating an optimal policy. For example, imagine you were training your car to "drive well" and to help your algorithm you recorded your driving and submitted that as an expert demonstration. Are you really an expert driver? Even if you are, should the agent be learning from your biased view of driving?

Another approach is ignoring the trajectories and concentrating on the goal. Producing a reward for "driving well," however, is hard to quantify. You could suggest that you want to get to your destination in the shortest time possible and use total elapsed time as a reward, but this ignores getting there safely. You could iteratively establish all of the main concerns but then how do you weight them? In general, it is difficult to design rewards for complex domains so instead, why not learn the reward?

Inverse RL (IRL) attempts to predict what a reward would look like, given demonstrations from an environment.[36] The general aim is to find an arbitrary reward function, based upon demonstrated trajectories, that explain expert behavior. Designing reward functions is a major challenge in RL, and IRL promises to replace the manual specification with demonstrations, which are arguably less biased and easier to specify. It is also argued that learning from demonstrations is more robust because they don't make any assumptions about the underlying environment.

Most IRL methods fit the following pattern:

1. Assume the expert's demonstrations as a solution to an MDP
2. Use a parameterized model as the reward function
3. Solve the MDP with the current reward function
4. Update the reward function to minimize the difference between the expert's trajectory and the learned trajectory (or policies if those are available)
5. Repeat until stable

Figure 8-8 depicts this process for a simple 3×3 discrete grid. An RL agent is trained to solve MDP with a parameterized reward function. Each time the MDP has learned an optimal policy it is compared to the expert trajectories. If the learned policy visits a state that is also visited by the expert, the reward for that state is increased (or equivalent reward parameters are changed). Over time the reward function tends toward the expert trajectory.

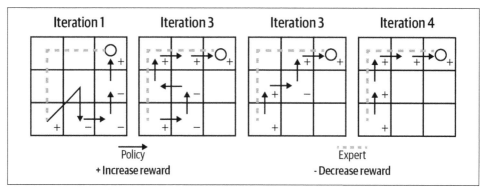

Figure 8-8. Example iterations of a notional IRL problem. The environment is a 3×3 grid. A single expert trajectory is provided (dashed lines). The policy (solid lines) uses a parameterized reward function in the MDP. Over time the reward function is altered to be more likely to produce expert trajectories. Eventually you end up with a reward function that mimics expert behavior.

Most of the problems with IRL stem from the fact that the expert trajectories are likely to be noisy and suboptimal. Researchers have developed a wide range of algorithms that adapt this basic process to improve robustness against noise (see the entropy-based or probabilistic IRL algorithms) or to loosely direct learning toward optimality, rather than matching the expert trajectory, which tends to be more problem specific.

Another major problem is that these methods expect you to repeatedly retrain RL algorithms, which as you know can take a long time. This means IRL doesn't scale to anything but the simplest of state spaces. All is not lost, though; you can use a dimensionality reduction technique like autoencoding or hashing to reduce the high-dimensional state into something that IRL can handle.[37,38]

One final remark I want to make is that when researchers talk about expert guidance in their papers, they tend to assume that the experts are successful at what they do. Failure is far more common than success, and there is no reason why you can't include disastrous trajectories in IRL; just demote the rewards for these trajectories instead. Shiarlis et al. suggest that generating failed demonstrations is even easier than generating good ones.[39]

Curriculum Learning

When you learn science, sailing, or snowboarding, there is a well-defined series of steps or tests that you have to achieve before you can move onto something more advanced. In snowboarding you first train your leg muscles how to control the edge, then you train your core to shift your weight to turn, and finally you learn how to twist in order to carve and spin. In science you first learn about atoms before fusion,

Newton's laws of motion before fluid dynamics, and cell structures before DNA. These are curricula, high-level meta-learning guides that show you common strategies to learning advanced policies.

Curricula can be used in RL to help reduce the amount of exploration an agent needs to perform. You can specify a series of simpler subgoals that lead to learning the main goal. This sounds very similar to "Imitation RL" on page 236 and several techniques under the curriculum banner use imitation techniques to derive curriculum subtasks.

Markov games (or other MARL frameworks) are important use cases for curriculum learning. You can often alter the formulation of a problem to play agents against each other in *self-play*. The most obvious form of self-play is in the highly publicized board game examples, but researchers have applied the same idea to slightly more realistic environments like mazes or robotic movement.[40,41] There are many options for how to design the interaction in self-play but one common form is to use one instantiation of an agent as a teacher and another as a student. The teacher suggests "tasks" by performing them in the environment (and therefore generating a trajectory) and the student solves that task by trying to perform the same "task." I say "task" because in practice they are just moves to a particular state, which may or may not translate to something humans would consider a task. Rewards are shaped to encourage the student to tackle more complex tasks over time by increasing the path length of the teacher. Another common form is to incorporate imitation-like techniques to automatically classify skills and repeatedly ask the agent being trained to practice skills.[42]

Another interesting idea that is similar to both imitation and curriculum learning is the combination of policies. *Residual RL* defines a way of combining two policies to solve a single task. It's not presented as hierarchical RL but could also be considered as such. The idea is that if you have an accurate model for part of the task, which is common in robotics, for example, then you can combine that policy with another to achieve tasks that are much harder to model like grasping or touching. This is introduced through the addition of policies. I like this idea because it is so simple. You have seen many examples of altering the reward function or the loss function by arbitrarily adding bonuses or penalties, but this is the first example of combining actions. Intuitively, I think there is more to this than first meets the eye. I can imagine a more general action-altering framework that is applicable to other areas of RL (safe-RL, for example).[43]

Curriculum learning is another hot topic because it is one avenue that could potentially help RL and ML to scale to really complex problems. The idea that you can engineer your problem so that there is an unsupervised solution to learn a range of important skills or possibly even solutions is enticing. For more information see the recent reviews in "Further Reading" on page 242.

Other Paradigms

Researchers like to coin a term. This can lead to a deluge of other paradigms that can be hard to interpret. Often some of them will break out into popular parlance, like Q-learning, whereas others could be big in the future but might not be, like meta-learning. I introduce this here along with transfer learning because they didn't quite fit anywhere else. They are big topics in their own right, but I consider them to be quite advanced and therefore a detailed discussion is out of the scope of this book.

Meta-Learning

Meta-learning, or learning-to-learn, aims to develop a general framework that optimizes the performance of learning. In other words, if you knew the best way to learn, you derive an algorithm that is optimal for your task.

One of the most important applications of meta-learning is quantifying or improving learning performance when there are few observations or rare events. Humans are capable of learning patterns and policies from small numbers of observations by transferring knowledge from past experience or other domains.

The problem with *meta-RL* is that it is so abstract there are many ways in which you could imagine improving learning performance. For example, some implementations implement artificial curiosity and boredom.[44] Others use genetic, evolutionary, or adversarial approaches.[45] Some even combine imitation and inverse RL to the mix.[46]

All this noise makes it hard to define precisely what meta-RL is or where it is heading. If the previous research is anything to go by, then meta-RL will continue to be a mash-up of RL and ML techniques with the goal of solving problems with less data, faster.

Transfer Learning

Transferring the experience of one agent to another is of obvious interest. If you can train a robot in simulation and then optimally transfer that knowledge to the real world, you can artificially increase the sample efficiency of your RL algorithm. Historically, transfer learning was considered separately, but today it tends to be absorbed into meta-learning. It is still important for industrial applications, however.

A common problem when converting research-oriented RL algorithms to industrial applications is that nearly all research papers train from scratch. But most of the time similar problems have already been solved, as demonstrated in the literature or by your previous work. It makes no sense to throw away all that experience and the resulting policy.

Like meta-RL, however, there are many ways in which you can reincorporate past experience into new models. You could reuse raw experiences via replay buffers, copy/paste autoencoders, use previous policies to help guide the new one via curriculum learning or concoct some kind of cooperative MARL solution. The possibilities are endless and there is no right way.

Fundamentally there are three types of transfer. The first, and most common, is to attempt to transfer policies that are used for the same task in the same domain. Pretraining with a simulation is an example of this. The second is transferring a policy in the same domain to achieve a slightly different task. This is the goal of curriculum learning and common in applications where a single agent is capable of solving multiple tasks, like robotics. The third is transferring policies across domain boundaries, where there may be different states and actions. This happens often accidentally due to partial observability, but a classic example would be attempting to train an RL algorithm to play the Atari game *Pong*, then get the same policy to play *Breakout*.

I think this is still an important subject for industrial applications, because it allows you to build solutions and train algorithms in a more sample-efficient way, which is often the bottleneck in real applications. But it is beyond the scope of this book, so if you are interested, I provide some starting points in "Further Reading" on page 242.

Summary

The purpose of RL is to learn optimal strategies, so it makes perfect sense to include as much extra information as you can to help solve your problem better and quicker. The first step on this journey is to ensure that your basic assumptions are valid and to check if your problem definition can be improved. This often starts by questioning the validity of the MDP and leads down new avenues of potential solutions. The classic example is that many real-life domains are partially observable, but are rarely modeled as such. Accepting the partial observability can lead you to solutions that happily handle uncertainty.

Hierarchical RL (HRL), especially skill-aware RL, has the potential to significantly scale industrial solutions. If original equipment manufacturers or vendors can derive and reuse "skills," this might help them provide more solutions using the same processes, hardware, and software. This will help open up new use cases and help diversify revenue streams. For these reasons I believe that HRL has a very important part to play in industry.

Multi-agent RL (MARL) is a very popular research topic because it presents a good way to solve distributed problems. For example, bush fires are increasing in both quantity and intensity, so having intelligent solutions for geospatial problems like this can help in that fight.[47] On a technical level, too, it makes sense to tackle the exploration problem by using the experience of multiple agents in the same environment, perhaps cooperatively. And competitive scenarios arise in a number of domains, especially in those that involve money.

Utilizing expert advice to guide strategies is another pattern that doesn't need explaining. One of the main issues in complex industrial problems is constraining the problem definition and therefore the exploration space. Industry expects and demands more performance and improved efficiencies and one of the best ways to get there is to bootstrap, just like *n*-step methods did way back in Chapter 3. On a strategic level, bootstrapping is essentially a process of copying successful strategies, whether that be from expert guidance or another model. Once you have extracted that expertise then you can work on fine-tuning it with standard RL techniques.

And finally, RL is a rapidly expanding topic and as abstractions become higher and higher they tend to veer off in weird and wonderful directions. Some of these will become the next big thing, others will sit quietly in a corner. I think that the use of meta-learning in RL, for example, will become more important as engineers gain more practical experience with RL. I think we're in the *what* phase now and soon engineers will be asking *why*. With adoption that will turn toward *how* and meta-RL presents a set of ideas to answer that question. But as the name suggests, the topic is very philosophical and can be hard to qualify. I'm sure that will improve with time, if indeed that is the right direction to head in.

Further Reading

- Hierarchical reinforcement learning:
  - Great overview video of the technical difficulties by Doina Precup. (*https://oreil.ly/v9qm3*)
- Multi-agent reinforcement learning:
  - Schwartz, H. M. 2014. *Multi-Agent Machine Learning: A Reinforcement Approach.* John Wiley & Sons.
  - A great RL-focused recent review from Oroojlooy and Hajinezhad.[48]
  - Another review that spans games and EFGs from Zhang et al.[49]
    - Decentralized MARL:
      - A great introduction to decentralized MARL from Christopher Amato (*https://oreil.ly/z7WOr*), and accompanying book by Oliehoek and Amato.[50]
  - Expert guidance:
    - A recent survey of inverse RL.[51]
  - Curriculum learning:
    - Two recent surveys.[52,53]
    - Lillian Weng's blog (*https://oreil.ly/IstUv*) is always a great resource and has a nice overview on curriculum learning.

— Meta-RL:

    — Huimin Peng has bravely created a good review on meta-RL.[54]

— Transfer learning:

    — There's a great chapter by Alessandro Lazaric that develops transfer learning at a high level.[55]

    — An interesting recent review of transfer learning in general (not RL-specific).[56]

References

[1] Karl, Maximilian, Maximilian Soelch, Justin Bayer, and Patrick van der Smagt. 2017. "Deep Variational Bayes Filters: Unsupervised Learning of State Space Models from Raw Data" (*https://oreil.ly/ixzns*). ArXiv:1605.06432, March.

[2] Hefny, Ahmed, Zita Marinho, Wen Sun, Siddhartha Srinivasa, and Geoffrey Gordon. 2018. "Recurrent Predictive State Policy Networks" (*https://oreil.ly/ThHPZ*). ArXiv:1803.01489, March.

[3] Wayne, Greg, Chia-Chun Hung, David Amos, Mehdi Mirza, Arun Ahuja, Agnieszka Grabska-Barwinska, Jack Rae, et al. 2018. "Unsupervised Predictive Memory in a Goal-Directed Agent" (*https://oreil.ly/778pX*). ArXiv:1803.10760, March.

[4] Qiao, Zhiqian, Katharina Muelling, John Dolan, Praveen Palanisamy, and Priyantha Mudalige. 2018. "POMDP and Hierarchical Options MDP with Continuous Actions for Autonomous Driving at Intersections" (*https://oreil.ly/w3rv8*). 2018 21st International Conference on Intelligent Transportation Systems (ITSC), 2377–82.

[5] Qiao, Zhiqian, Zachariah Tyree, Priyantha Mudalige, Jeff Schneider, and John M. Dolan. 2019. "Hierarchical Reinforcement Learning Method for Autonomous Vehicle Behavior Planning" (*https://oreil.ly/VmupK*). ArXiv:1911.03799, November.

[6] Hochberg, Irit, Guy Feraru, Mark Kozdoba, Shie Mannor, Moshe Tennenholtz, and Elad Yom-Tov. 2017. "A Reinforcement Learning System to Encourage Physical Activity in Diabetes Patients" (*https://oreil.ly/g0jLx*). *Journal of Medical Internet Research* 19 (10): e338.

[7] Hallak, Assaf, Dotan Di Castro, and Shie Mannor. 2015. "Contextual Markov Decision Processes" (*https://oreil.ly/jiudo*). ArXiv:1502.02259, February.

[8] Ie, Eugene, Chih-wei Hsu, Martin Mladenov, Vihan Jain, Sanmit Narvekar, Jing Wang, Rui Wu, and Craig Boutilier. 2019. "RecSim: A Configurable Simulation Platform for Recommender Systems" (*https://oreil.ly/GjSoP*). ArXiv:1909.04847, September.

[9] Chandak, Yash, Georgios Theocharous, Blossom Metevier, and Philip S. Thomas. 2020. "Reinforcement Learning When All Actions Are Not Always Available" (*https://oreil.ly/gGau0*). ArXiv:1906.01772, January.

[10] Boutilier, Craig, Alon Cohen, Amit Daniely, Avinatan Hassidim, Yishay Mansour, Ofer Meshi, Martin Mladenov, and Dale Schuurmans. 2018. "Planning and Learning with Stochastic Action Sets" (*https://oreil.ly/Y6Any*). ArXiv:1805.02363, May.

[11] Chandak, Yash, Georgios Theocharous, Blossom Metevier, and Philip S. Thomas. 2020. "Reinforcement Learning When All Actions Are Not Always Available" (*https://oreil.ly/JnQgq*). ArXiv:1906.01772, January.

[12] Chandak, Yash, Georgios Theocharous, Chris Nota, and Philip S. Thomas. 2020. "Lifelong Learning with a Changing Action Set" (*https://oreil.ly/sYCBs*). ArXiv: 1906.01770, May.

[13] Li, Xiang, Wenhao Yang, and Zhihua Zhang. 2019. "A Regularized Approach to Sparse Optimal Policy in Reinforcement Learning" (*https://oreil.ly/Ha65T*). ArXiv: 1903.00725, October.

[14] Saleh, Abdelrhman, Natasha Jaques, Asma Ghandeharioun, Judy Hanwen Shen, and Rosalind Picard. 2019. "Hierarchical Reinforcement Learning for Open-Domain Dialog" (*https://oreil.ly/fY01Z*). ArXiv:1909.07547, December.

[15] Zhou, Guojing, Hamoon Azizsoltani, Markel Sanz Ausin, Tiffany Barnes, and Min Chi. 2019. "Hierarchical Reinforcement Learning for Pedagogical Policy Induction" (*https://oreil.ly/rrzsW*). *Artificial Intelligence in Education*, edited by Seiji Isotani, Eva Millán, Amy Ogan, Peter Hastings, Bruce McLaren, and Rose Luckin, 544–56. Lecture Notes in Computer Science. Cham: Springer International Publishing.

[16] Nachum, Ofir, Shixiang Gu, Honglak Lee, and Sergey Levine. 2018. "Data-Efficient Hierarchical Reinforcement Learning" (*https://oreil.ly/prP31*). ArXiv: 1805.08296, October.

[17] Eysenbach, Benjamin, Abhishek Gupta, Julian Ibarz, and Sergey Levine. 2018. "Diversity Is All You Need: Learning Skills without a Reward Function" (*https://oreil.ly/HSs_I*). ArXiv:1802.06070, October.

[18] Li, Siyuan, Rui Wang, Minxue Tang, and Chongjie Zhang. 2019. "Hierarchical Reinforcement Learning with Advantage-Based Auxiliary Rewards" (*https://oreil.ly/r0zu7*). ArXiv:1910.04450, October.

[19] Saleh, Abdelrhman, Natasha Jaques, Asma Ghandeharioun, Judy Hanwen Shen, and Rosalind Picard. 2019. "Hierarchical Reinforcement Learning for Open-Domain Dialog" (*https://oreil.ly/_nkHe*). ArXiv:1909.07547, December.

[20] Waradpande, Vikram, Daniel Kudenko, and Megha Khosla. 2020. "Deep Reinforcement Learning with Graph-Based State Representations" (*https://oreil.ly/PX_BB*). ArXiv:2004.13965, April.

[21] Sharma, Archit, Shixiang Gu, Sergey Levine, Vikash Kumar, and Karol Hausman. 2020. "Dynamics-Aware Unsupervised Discovery of Skills" (*https://oreil.ly/BRM9C*). ArXiv:1907.01657, February.

[22] Zheng, Stephan, Alexander Trott, Sunil Srinivasa, Nikhil Naik, Melvin Gruesbeck, David C. Parkes, and Richard Socher. 2020. "The AI Economist: Improving Equality and Productivity with AI-Driven Tax Policies" (*https://oreil.ly/230sL*). ArXiv: 2004.13332, April.

[23] Cox, Tony. 2019. "Muddling-Through and Deep Learning for Managing Large-Scale Uncertain Risks" (*https://oreil.ly/ms1Yu*). *Journal of Benefit-Cost Analysis* 10(2): 226–50.

[24] Xiao, Kefan, Shiwen Mao, and Jitendra K. Tugnait. 2019. "TCP-Drinc: Smart Congestion Control Based on Deep Reinforcement Learning" (*https://oreil.ly/w4-pt*). *IEEE Access* 7:(11) 892–904.

[25] Xiao, Yuchen, Joshua Hoffman, Tian Xia, and Christopher Amato. 2020. "Learning Multi-Robot Decentralized Macro-Action-Based Policies via a Centralized Q-Net" (*https://oreil.ly/RgXHj*). ArXiv:1909.08776, March.

[26] Pham, Huy X., Hung M. La, David Feil-Seifer, and Matthew Deans. 2017. "A Distributed Control Framework for a Team of Unmanned Aerial Vehicles for Dynamic Wildfire Tracking" (*https://oreil.ly/CtE3Q*). ArXiv:1704.02630, April.

[27] Tomic, Teodor, Korbinian Schmid, Philipp Lutz, Andreas Domel, Michael Kassecker, Elmar Mair, Iris Lynne Grixa, Felix Ruess, Michael Suppa, and Darius Burschka. 2012. "Toward a Fully Autonomous UAV: Research Platform for Indoor and Outdoor Urban Search and Rescue" (*https://oreil.ly/L34Rn*). IEEE Robotics Automation Magazine 19(3): 46–56.

[28] Cui, Jingjing, Yuanwei Liu, and Arumugam Nallanathan. 2018. "Multi-Agent Reinforcement Learning Based Resource Allocation for UAV Networks" (*https://oreil.ly/7in8V*). ArXiv:1810.10408, October.

[29] Lowe, Ryan, Yi Wu, Aviv Tamar, Jean Harb, Pieter Abbeel, and Igor Mordatch. 2020. "Multi-Agent Actor-Critic for Mixed Cooperative-Competitive Environments" (*https://oreil.ly/yTYdm*). ArXiv:1706.02275, March.

[30] Matignon, Laetitia, Guillaume J. Laurent, and Nadine Le Fort-Piat. 2007. "Hysteretic Q-Learning: An Algorithm for Decentralized Reinforcement Learning in Cooperative Multi-Agent Teams" (*https://oreil.ly/ZSWmT*). *2007 IEEE/RSJ International Conference on Intelligent Robots and Systems*, 64–69.

[31] Omidshafiei, Shayegan, Jason Pazis, Christopher Amato, Jonathan P. How, and John Vian. 2017. "Deep Decentralized Multi-Task Multi-Agent Reinforcement Learning under Partial Observability" (*https://oreil.ly/2I9aX*). ArXiv:1703.06182, July.

[32] Ross, Stephane, Geoffrey J. Gordon, and J. Andrew Bagnell. 2011. "A Reduction of Imitation Learning and Structured Prediction to No-Regret Online Learning" (*https://oreil.ly/md4Pd*). ArXiv:1011.0686, March.

[33] Hester, Todd, Matej Vecerik, Olivier Pietquin, Marc Lanctot, Tom Schaul, Bilal Piot, Dan Horgan, et al. 2017. "Deep Q-Learning from Demonstrations" (*https://oreil.ly/ENvFp*). ArXiv:1704.03732, November.

[34] Ho, Jonathan, and Stefano Ermon. 2016. "Generative Adversarial Imitation Learning" (*https://oreil.ly/N0pWb*). ArXiv:1606.03476, June.

[35] Reddy, Siddharth, Anca D. Dragan, and Sergey Levine. 2019. "SQIL: Imitation Learning via Reinforcement Learning with Sparse Rewards" (*https://oreil.ly/6s1Oy*). ArXiv:1905.11108, September.

[36] Ng, Andrew Y., and Stuart J. Russell. 2000. "Algorithms for Inverse Reinforcement Learning." *Proceedings of the Seventeenth International Conference on Machine Learning*, 663–670. ICML 2000. San Francisco, CA: Morgan Kaufmann Publishers Inc.

[37] Tucker, Aaron, Adam Gleave, and Stuart Russell. 2018. "Inverse Reinforcement Learning for Video Games" (*https://oreil.ly/yssiM*). ArXiv:1810.10593, October.

[38] Cai, Xin-Qiang, Yao-Xiang Ding, Yuan Jiang, and Zhi-Hua Zhou. 2020. "Imitation Learning from Pixel-Level Demonstrations by HashReward" (*https://oreil.ly/06bk4*). ArXiv:1909.03773, June.

[39] Shiarlis, Kyriacos, Joao Messias, and Shimon Whiteson. 2016. "Inverse Reinforcement Learning from Failure." *Proceedings of the 2016 International Conference on Autonomous Agents & Multiagent Systems*, 1060–1068. AAMAS 2016. Singapore: International Foundation for Autonomous Agents and Multiagent Systems.

[40] Sukhbaatar, Sainbayar, Zeming Lin, Ilya Kostrikov, Gabriel Synnaeve, Arthur Szlam, and Rob Fergus. 2018. "Intrinsic Motivation and Automatic Curricula via Asymmetric Self-Play" (*https://oreil.ly/Y7oEa*). ArXiv:1703.05407, April.

[41] Laux, Melvin, Oleg Arenz, Jan Peters, and Joni Pajarinen. 2020. "Deep Adversarial Reinforcement Learning for Object Disentangling" (*https://oreil.ly/wA_3s*). ArXiv:2003.03779, March.

[42] Jabri, Allan, Kyle Hsu, Ben Eysenbach, Abhishek Gupta, Sergey Levine, and Chelsea Finn. 2019. "Unsupervised Curricula for Visual Meta-Reinforcement Learning" (*https://oreil.ly/O_A7w*). ArXiv:1912.04226, December.

[43] Johannink, Tobias, Shikhar Bahl, Ashvin Nair, Jianlan Luo, Avinash Kumar, Matthias Loskyll, Juan Aparicio Ojea, Eugen Solowjow, and Sergey Levine. 2018. "Residual Reinforcement Learning for Robot Control" (*https://oreil.ly/m1l7m*). ArXiv: 1812.03201, December.

[44] Alet, Ferran, Martin F. Schneider, Tomas Lozano-Perez, and Leslie Pack Kaelbling. 2020. "Meta-Learning Curiosity Algorithms" (*https://oreil.ly/azstP*). ArXiv: 2003.05325, March.

[45] Wang, Rui, Joel Lehman, Jeff Clune, and Kenneth O. Stanley. 2019. "Paired Open-Ended Trailblazer (POET): Endlessly Generating Increasingly Complex and Diverse Learning Environments and Their Solutions" (*https://oreil.ly/rGJoo*). ArXiv: 1901.01753, February.

[46] Paine, Tom Le, Sergio Gómez Colmenarejo, Ziyu Wang, Scott Reed, Yusuf Aytar, Tobias Pfaff, Matt W. Hoffman, et al. 2018. "One-Shot High-Fidelity Imitation: Training Large-Scale Deep Nets with RL" (*https://oreil.ly/Q-u9W*). ArXiv:1810.05017, October.

[47] Pham, Huy X., Hung M. La, David Feil-Seifer, and Matthew Deans. 2017. "A Distributed Control Framework for a Team of Unmanned Aerial Vehicles for Dynamic Wildfire Tracking" (*https://oreil.ly/1YSSS*). ArXiv:1704.02630, April.

[48] OroojlooyJadid, Afshin, and Davood Hajinezhad. 2020. "A Review of Cooperative Multi-Agent Deep Reinforcement Learning" (*https://oreil.ly/p98r_*). ArXiv: 1908.03963, June.

[49] Zhang, Kaiqing, Zhuoran Yang, and Tamer Başar. 2019. "Multi-Agent Reinforcement Learning: A Selective Overview of Theories and Algorithms" (*https://oreil.ly/rnl2q*). ArXiv:1911.10635, November.

[50] Oliehoek, Frans A., and Christopher Amato. 2016. *A Concise Introduction to Decentralized POMDPs*. 1st ed. Springer Publishing Company.

[51] Arora, Saurabh, and Prashant Doshi. 2019. "A Survey of Inverse Reinforcement Learning: Challenges, Methods and Progress" (*https://oreil.ly/ZolV1*). ArXiv: 1806.06877, August.

[52] Narvekar, Sanmit, Bei Peng, Matteo Leonetti, Jivko Sinapov, Matthew E. Taylor, and Peter Stone. 2020. "Curriculum Learning for Reinforcement Learning Domains: A Framework and Survey" (*https://oreil.ly/_uqkd*). ArXiv:2003.04960, March.

[53] Portelas, Rémy, Cédric Colas, Lilian Weng, Katja Hofmann, and Pierre-Yves Oudeyer. 2020. "Automatic Curriculum Learning For Deep RL: A Short Survey" (*https://oreil.ly/Rq2uZ*). ArXiv:2003.04664, May.

[54] Peng, Huimin. 2020. "A Comprehensive Overview and Survey of Recent Advances in Meta-Learning" (*https://oreil.ly/0lt2U*). ArXiv:2004.11149, June.

[55] Lazaric, Alessandro. 2012. "Transfer in Reinforcement Learning: A Framework and a Survey" (*https://oreil.ly/qFqhC*). *Reinforcement Learning: State-of-the-Art*, edited by Marco Wiering and Martijn van Otterlo, 143–73. Adaptation, Learning, and Optimization. Berlin, Heidelberg: Springer.

[56] Zhuang, Fuzhen, Zhiyuan Qi, Keyu Duan, Dongbo Xi, Yongchun Zhu, Hengshu Zhu, Hui Xiong, and Qing He. 2020. "A Comprehensive Survey on Transfer Learning" (*https://oreil.ly/xaQxM*). ArXiv:1911.02685, June.

CHAPTER 9

Practical Reinforcement Learning

Reinforcement learning (RL) is an old subject; it's decades old. Only recently has it gained enough prominence to raise its head outside of academia. I think that this is partly because there isn't enough disseminated industrial knowledge yet. The vast majority of the literature talks about algorithms and contrived simulations, until now.

Researchers and industrialists are beginning to realize the potential of RL. This brings a wealth of experience that wasn't available in 2015. Frameworks and libraries are following suit, which is increasing awareness and lowering the barrier to entry.

In this chapter I want to talk less about the gory algorithmic details and more about the process. I want to answer the question, "What does a real RL project involve?" First I will go over what an RL project looks like and propose a new model for building industrial RL products. Along the way I will teach you how to spot an RL problem and how to map it to a learning paradigm. Finally, I'll describe how to design, architect, and develop an RL project from simple beginnings, pointing out all of the areas that you need to watch out for.

The RL Project Life Cycle

Typical RL projects are designed to be solved by RL from the outset, typically because of prior work, but sometimes because designers appreciate the sequential nature of the problem. RL projects can also emerge from a machine learning (ML) project where engineers are looking for better ways to model the problem or improve performance. Either way, the life cycle of an RL project is quite different from ML and very different to software engineering. Software engineering is to RL what bricklaying is to bridge building.

RL development tends to follow a series of feelings that are probably familiar to you. This rollercoaster is what makes engineering such a fulfilling career. It goes something like this:

1. *Optimism*: "RL is incredible, it can control robots so surely it can solve this?"

2. *Stress and depression*: "Why doesn't this work? It can control robots so why can't it do this? Is it me?"

3. *Realization*: "Oh right. This problem is much harder than controlling robots. But I'm using deep learning so it will work eventually (?). I'm going to pay for more GPUs to speed it up."

4. *Fear*: "Why is this still not working? This is impossible!"

5. *Simplification*: "What happens if I remove/replace/alter/augment the real data?"

6. *Surprise*: "Wow. It converged in only 5 minutes on my laptop. Note to self, don't waste money on GPUs again…"

7. *Happiness*: "Great, now that's working I'll tell my project manager that I'm getting close, but I need another sprint…"

8. *GOTO 1*

In a more general form, this is true for any project that I've worked on. I've found one simple trick that helps to manage stress levels and improve project velocity. And if you only take one idea away from this book, then make it this:

Start Simple

That's it. Starting simple forces you to think about the most important aspects of the problem, the MDP. It helps you create really big abstractions; you can fill in the details later. Abstractions help because they free up mental resources that would otherwise be ruminating on the details; they allow you to communicate concepts to other people without the gory technicalities.

I know nothing about neuroscience or psychology, but I find that stress during development, which I think is different than normal stress, is proportional to the amount of mental effort expended on a problem and inversely proportional to the probability of success. If I had a long day of intense concentration, which was required because the darn thing wasn't working properly, I'm much more stressed and grumpy when I see my family. Having an easier problem, which leads to more successes, seems to help reduce my stress levels.

Project velocity is the speed at which development is progressing. It is a fictional measure made up by process coaches. When comparing you or your team's velocity over a period of time (not between teams or people) then it becomes easier for an outsider to spot temporary issues. On a personal level, velocity is important for the reasons in the previous paragraph. If you get stuck, you have to force yourself to work harder on the problem and without successes you get stuck in a spiral of despair.

One problem with the typical points-based velocity measures is that it doesn't take task complexity or risk into consideration. One week you can be doing some boiler-plate software and burn through a load of single-point tasks (5×1 points, for example), the next you can be working on a model and banging your head against the wall (1×5 points). They might have exactly the same number of estimated points, but the second week is far more stressful.

To alleviate this problem, here is my second tip:

Keep Development Cycles as Small as Possible

I think of a development cycle as the time between my first keystrokes and the point at which things work as I intended. One representational metric is the time between git commits, if you use commits to represent working code. The longer these cycles get, the greater the chance of nonworking code and more stress. Furthermore, long cycles mean that you have to wait a long time for feedback. This is especially trouble-some when training big models on lots of data. If you have to wait for two days to find out whether your code works, you're doing it wrong. Your time is far too valua-ble to sit doing nothing for that length of time. And undoubtedly you will find a mis-take and have to cancel it anyway. Reduce the amount of time between cycles or runs to improve your efficiency and if you have to, run those long training sessions over-night; new models fresh out of the oven in the morning is like a being a kid at Christmas.

Neither of these ideas is new, but I find they are incredibly important when doing RL —for my own sanity, at least. It is so easy to get sucked into solving a problem in one attempt, a whirlpool of intent. The likely result is failure due to a mismatch between problem and MDP or model and data, all of which are due to too much complexity and not enough understanding. Follow the two preceding tips and you have a fight-ing chance.

Life Cycle Definition

Other than the proceeds of the MDP paradigm, many of the tools and techniques used in machine learning are directly transferable to RL. Even the process is similar.

Data science life cycle

Figure 9-1 presents a diagram of the four main phases of a data science project that I see when working with my colleagues at Winder Research. It largely follows the classic cross-industry standard process for data mining from the '90s, but I have simplified it and accentuated the iterative nature.

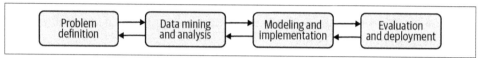

Figure 9-1. A diagram of the four main phases of a data science project, a simplified version of the CRISP-DM model.

All projects start with a problem definition and it is often wrong. When the definition changes it can massively impact engineering work, so you must make sure that it both solves a business challenge and is technically viable. This is one of the most common reasons for perceived failure—*perceived* because technically projects can work as intended, but they don't solve real business challenges. Often it takes several iterations to refine the definition.

Next is data mining and analysis. Around two-thirds of the time of a data scientist is spent in this phase, where they attempt to discover and expose new information that might help solve the problem and then analyze and clean the data ready for modeling.

In the modeling and implementation phase, you build and train models that attempt to solve your problem.

Finally, you evaluate how well you are solving the problem using quantitative and qualitative measures of performance and deploy your solution to production.

At any one of these phases you may find it necessary to go back a step to reengineer. For example, you may develop a proof of concept in a Jupyter notebook to quickly prove that there is a viable technical solution, but then go back to build production-ready software. Or you might find that during initial evaluation you don't have enough of the right data to solve the problem to a satisfactory standard. Even worse, you have a solution and report back to the stakeholders only to find that you solved the wrong problem.

Reinforcement learning life cycle

Figure 9-2 shows a depiction of a typical process for an RL project. The first thing you will notice is how similar the phases are. The goals are the same (to solve a business challenge using data) so it is reasonable to expect the process to be similar, too. But the similarities exist only on the surface. When you dig into each phase the tasks are quite different.

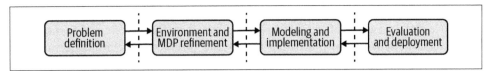

Figure 9-2. A diagram of the four main phases of an RL project.

In an ML project, it is unlikely that you have the ability to dramatically alter the problem definition. You can probably tinker with the performance specification, for example, but fundamentally the problem you are trying to solve is defined by the business. Then you would search for and locate any data that already exists within the business, get permission to use it, and put the technology in place to access it. If you don't have any data, then you can try to gather new data or use an external source. Once you have the data at your disposal you would spend time analyzing, understanding, cleaning, and augmenting to help solve the problem. This represents the first two boxes of the data science process.

In RL the situation is quite different, even perverse at times. First you are given a business challenge. The problem is strategic, at a higher level of abstraction compared to "normal" data science problems, and it has a real-life definition of success like profit, number of subscribers, or clicks. Then you, yes you, take that definition of success and carefully engineer the problem to fit into an MDP and design the reward function. Until there is an inverse RL (see "Inverse RL" on page 237) algorithm that works in every situation, you will need to design the reward yourself. This is a big burden to place on your shoulders. You have the power to decide how to quantify performance, in real terms. In one sense this is great, because it directly exposes how the project affects the business in human-readable terms like lives saved (not accuracy or F1-score, for example). But this also places more burden on the engineer. Imagine a strategic-level agent that chooses the direction of the business and it leads to a bad result. Historically, this risk is carried by the executives in your company—hence the girth of the paycheck—but in the future it will be delegated to algorithms like RL, which are designed by engineers. I haven't seen any evidence of how this is going to affect the hierarchical control structures present in so many companies but I anticipate that there will be a shakeup. Shareholders pay for productivity and when productivity is driven by the engineers that design the algorithms, does that also mean they run the company?

The next phase in the process is to decide how best to learn. In machine learning you only need to iterate on the data you have. But in RL, because it relies on interaction and sequential decisions, you will never have all the data you need to generate realistic rollouts. In the vast majority of cases it makes sense to build simulations to speed up the development feedback cycle, rather than use a live environment. Once you have a viable solution then you can roll out to real life.

Notice the difference here. Either you are generating artificial observations or you don't have real data until you actively use your algorithm. If someone said to me that I had to deploy my fancy deep learning model into production before collecting *any* data, I'd probably cry a little inside.

But this is precisely the situation in RL and what makes state, action, and reward engineering so important. You can't hope to build a robust solution unless you fully understand your state and actions and how they affect the reward. Trying to throw deep learning at a problem you don't understand is like buying a $1,000 golf club and expecting to become a golf pro.

There's more, too, which I discuss throughout this chapter. But I want to emphasize that although there are similarities and transferable skills, RL is a totally different beast. The first two boxes in Figure 9-2, problem definition and environment/MDP refinement, I discuss in this chapter. I will leave the final two boxes until the next chapter.

Problem Definition: What Is an RL Project?

I think by now you have a fairly good idea about the definition of RL, but I want to spend this section talking about applying RL to everyday challenges. To recap, you should base your model on a Markov decision process (MDP, see Chapter 2 and "Rethinking the MDP" on page 216). The problem should have unique states, which may be discrete or continuous—I find that it often helps to think of discrete states, even if it is continuous. In each state there should be some probability of transitioning to another state (or itself). And an action should alter the state of the environment.

Although this definition captures nearly everything, I find it intuitively difficult to think in terms of states and transition probabilities. So instead I will try to paint a different picture.

RL Problems Are Sequential

RL problems are sequential; an RL agent optimizes trajectories over several steps. This alone separates RL from ML; the paradigm of choice for single-step decision making. ML cannot optimize decisions for a long-term reward. This is crucial in many business challenges. I don't think any CEO with an inkling of humanity would squeeze a prospect for every penny *right now*. Instead, they know that managing the relationship and managing how and when the sales that are made to optimize for the long-term support of the customer is the best route toward a sustainable business.

This philosophy maps directly to how you would solve industrial, customer-centric problems. You shouldn't be using ML models to optimize your ad placement or recommend which product to buy because they optimize for the wrong thing. Like a voracious toddler, they can't see the bigger picture. ML models are trained to make the best possible decision at the time, irrespective of the future consequences. For example, ML models are very capable of optimizing product recommendations, but they might include the product equivalent of click-bait: products which get lots of clicks but are ultimately disappointing. Over time, a myopic view will likely annoy users and could ultimately hurt profit, retention, or other important business metrics.

RL algorithms are perfectly suited to situations where you can see that there are multiple decisions to be made, or where the environment doesn't reset once you've made a decision. This opens up a massive range of possibilities, some of which you saw in "RL Applications" on page 7. These may be new problems or problems that already have a partial solution with ML. In a sense, a problem that has already been partially solved is a better one than a new project, because it's likely that engineers are already very familiar with the domain and the data. But be cognizant that initial RL results may produce worse results in the short term while algorithms are improved. Visit the accompanying website (*https://rl-book.com/applications/?utm_source=oreilly&utm_medium=book&utm_campaign=rl*) to get more application insipration.

RL Problems Are Strategic

I like to think of software engineering as a way of automating processes and machine learning can automate decisions. RL can automate strategies.

Figure 9-3 hammers this idea home. Modern businesses are made of three core functions. Businesses have a plethora of processes, from performance reviews to how to use the printer. Enacting of any one of these processes is rarely valuable, but they tend to occur often. Because of the frequency and the fact it takes time and therefore money for a human to perform this process, it makes sense to automate the process in software.

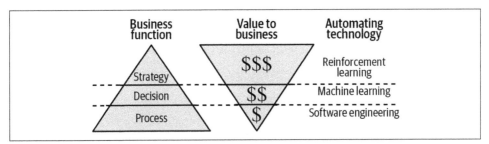

Figure 9-3. A depiction of the different functions of a modern business, the value of each action in that function, and the technology that maps to the function.

Business decisions are rarer than business processes, but they still happen fairly often. Making the decision to perform CPR, phone a warm prospect, or block a suspicious looking transaction can save lives/be profitable/prevent fraud. All of these challenges can be solved using machine learning. These actions are quantifiably valuable, but like I said previously, they have a limited life span. They intentionally focus on the single transitive event. Decisions need processes in place to make them possible.

Business strategies form the heart of the company. They happen rarely, primarily because there are limited numbers of people (or one) designing and implementing the strategy. They are closely held secrets and direct a multitude of future people, decisions, and processes. They have wide-reaching consequences, like the healthcare for a nation or the annual profits of the company. This is why optimal strategies are so valuable and why RL is so important.

Imagine being able to entrust the running of your company/healthcare/country to RL. How does that sound? What do you think?

You might suggest that this is a pipe dream, but I assure you it is not. Taxation is being tackled with MARL.[1] Healthcare use cases are obvious and there are thousands of references.[2] And companies must automate to become more competitive, which is nothing new—companies have been automating for over a century now.

The future, therefore, is in the hands of the engineers, the people who know how to build, adapt, and constrain algorithms to be robust, useful, and above all, safe.

Low-Level RL Indicators

The previous two suggestions, that RL problems are sequential and strategic, are high level. On a lower level you should be looking for individual components of the problem.

An entity

Look for entities, which are concrete things or people, that interact with the environment. Depending on the problem, the entity could sit on both sides of the environment interface. For example, a person viewing a recommendation is an entity but they are part of the environment. Other times people are simulated agents, like in the taxation example.

An environment

The environment should be, in the language of domain-driven design, a bounded context. It should be an interface that encapsulates all of the complexities of the situation. You should not care whether behind the interface there is a simulation or real life; the data at the interface should be the same. Beware of making an environment too big or too complex, because this impacts the solvability of the problem. Splitting or simplifying the environment makes it easier to work with.

A state

The easiest way to spot state is to observe or imagine what happens when the state changes. You might not think of it as a change, but look carefully. The price of a stock changes because the underlying state of all investors changes. The state of a robot changes because it has moved from position A to position B. After showing a recommendation your target's state may have changed from "ignore recommendation" to "click on the recommendation."

What can you observe about the environment (which may include entities)? What are the most pertinent and informative features? Like in ML, you want to be careful to only include clean, informative, uncorrelated features. You can add, remove, or augment these features as you wish but tend toward minimizing the number of features if possible, to reduce the exploration space, improve computational efficiency, and improve robustness. Don't forget that you can merge contextual information from other sources, like the time of day or the weather.

The domain of the state can vary dramatically depending on the application. For example, it could be images, matrices representing geospatial grids, scalars representing sensor readings, snippets of text, items in a shopping cart, browser history, and more. Bear in mind that from the perspective of an agent, the state may be uncertain or hidden. Remind yourself often that the agent is not seeing what you can see, because you have the benefit of an oracle's view of the problem.

An action

What happens to the environment when you apply an action? The internal state of an environment should have the potential to change (it may not, because the action was to stay put or it was a bad one) when you apply an action. Ideally you want to observe that state change and if you don't, consider looking for observations that expose this information. Again, try to limit the number of actions to reduce the exploration space.

Quantify success or failure

In this environment, how would you define success or failure? Can you think of a way to quantify that? The value should map to the problem definition and use units that are understandable to both you and your stakeholders. If you are working to improve profits, then quantify in terms of monetary value. If you are trying to improve the click rate of something, go back and try to find a cash amount for that click. Think about the real reason why your client/boss/stakeholder is interested in you doing this project. How can you quantify the results in terminology they understand and appreciate?

Types of Learning

The goal of an agent is to learn an optimal policy. The rest of this book investigates *how* an agent learns, through a variety of value-based and policy gradient–based algorithms. But what about *when* it learns?

Online learning

The overwhelming majority of examples, literature, blog posts, and frameworks all assume that your agent is learning *online*. This is where your agent interacts with a real or simulated environment and learns at the same time. So far in this book I have only considered this regime. One of the major problems with this approach is the sample efficiency, the number of interactions with an environment required to learn an optimal policy. In the previous couple of decades researchers have been chasing sample efficiency by improving exploration and learning guarantees. But fundamentally there is always going to be an overhead for exploration, sampling delays due to stochastic approximation, and the all important stability issues. Only recently have they begun to consider learning from logs.

Offline or batch learning

Until quite recently, it was thought that all learning had to be performed online because of the inherent coupling between the action of an agent and the reaction of an environment.[3] But researchers found that it was possible to learn from a *batch* of stored data, like data in a replay buffer. Because this data has no further interaction with the environment it is also known as learning *offline* or in *batches*. Figure 9-4 presents the idea. First, data is generated online using a policy (possibly random) and saved in a buffer. Offline, a new policy is trained upon the data in the buffer. The new policy is then deployed for use.

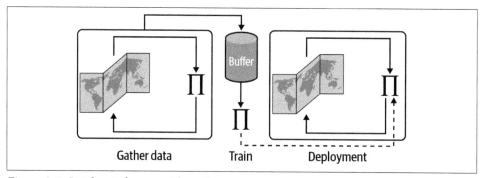

Figure 9-4. Batch reinforcement learning.

The primary benefit of learning offline is the increase in sample efficiency. You can capture or log a set of data and use it to train models as many times as you like with zero impact on the environment. This is an incredibly important feature in many domains where collecting new samples is expensive or unsafe.

But hang on. If I collect and train upon a static snapshot of data, then isn't this pure supervised learning? The answer is yes, kind of. It is supervised in the sense that you have a batch of data with labeled transitions and rewards. But this doesn't mean you can use any old regression or classification algorithm. The data is (assumed to be) generated by an MDP and therefore the algorithms designed to find optimal policies for MDPs are still useful. The major difference is that they can no longer explore.

If an agent can't explore, then it can't attempt to improve the policy by "filling in the gaps," which was the primary reason for rapid advances in RL over the past decade. A similar argument is that it prevents the agent from asking counterfactual questions about the action. Again, this is a theoretical method to provide more robust policies by allowing them to ask "what if" questions. Fundamentally, the distribution of the training data (for state, actions, and rewards) is different than that observed at deployment. Imagine how that affects a typical supervised learning algorithm.

In principle, *any* off-policy RL algorithm could be used as an offline RL algorithm, by removing the exploration part from the algorithm. However, this is problematic in practice for a number of reasons. Value methods struggle because they rely on accurate value estimates. But many of the states or actions will not be present in the buffer and therefore estimates will be inaccurate at best. Policy gradient methods struggle because of the distribution shift, which at best produces gradients that point in the wrong direction and at worst blow up. These problems get worse when you use overly specified models like deep learning.[4]

At the time of this writing, researchers are working hard to solve these problems to open up the next large gains in sample efficiency. One avenue of research is to further refine the stability guarantees of basic RL algorithms so that they don't misbehave when encountering unstable distributions or undersampled states or actions. Better theoretical guarantees when using deep learning is an obvious avenue that would dramatically improve the situation. Other approaches are attempting to use techniques like imitation learning to lean policies that generate positive rewards.[5] An even simpler approach is to train an autoencoder upon the buffer to create a simulated environment that agents *can* explore in.[6] In practice these techniques are already being applied and are showing impressive results, especially in robotics (*https://oreil.ly/cXXDc*).[7] From a practical perspective, then, you might find the Deep-Mind RL Unplugged benchmark (*https://oreil.ly/hdtXK*) a useful tool to find or prototype ideas.[8]

Concurrent learning

The literature contains a mix of learning techniques that fall somewhere between multi-agent RL (MARL) and multiprocess frameworks, but are interesting enough to mention here.

The length of your feedback cycles are dictated by the complexity of the problem; the harder the challenge, the longer it takes to solve. This is partially caused by increasing model complexities, but primarily it is an exploration problem. Large state and action spaces need more exploration to "fill in the gaps."

Many researchers have concentrated on improving exploration in the single-agent case, which has worked wonders. But that only scales to a point. Ultimately an agent still needs to visit all of the state-action space. One option is to run multiple agents at the same time (see "Scaling RL" on page 299), but if they are using the same exploration algorithm then they can tend to explore the same space, again negating the efficiency as the state-action space is scaled up.

Instead, why not explore *concurrently*, where teams of agents have the *joint* task of exploring the state-action space. Beware that this term is overloaded, though; researchers have used the word *concurrent* to mean anything from cooperative MARL to concurrent programming for RL.[9,10] I use the term to denote the goal of performing coordinated exploration of the same environment, first suggested in 2013.[11]

The implementation of this idea is somewhat domain dependent. As one example, many companies are interacting with thousands or millions of customers in parallel and are trying to maximize a reward local to that customer, like lifetime value or loyalty. But these customers reside within the confines of the same environment; a company only has a limited set of in-stock products and you have roughly the same demographic information for each customer. The learnings from one customer should be transferred to others, so this implies either centralized learning or at least parameter sharing.

I don't think there is one right answer because there are many small challenges that need unique adaptations. Like what would happen if you introduced the ability to retarget customers with emails or ads? This would improve the performance metrics but the rewards may be delayed. So you would have to build in the capacity to "skip" actions and deal with the partial observability.

Dimakopoulou and Van Roy formalized this idea in 2018 and proved that coordinated exploration could both increase learning speed and scale to large numbers of agents.[12] Their solution is surprisingly simple: make sure each agent has a random seed that maximizes exploration. The benefit of this approach is you can use standard RL algorithms and each agent is independently committed to seeking out optimal performance. It also adapts well to new data because starting conditions are repeatedly randomized. The challenge, however, is that the optimal seed sampling technique is different for every problem.

In concurrent learning then, agents are independent and do not interact. Agents may have different views of the environment, like different customers have different views of your products. Despite the different name, this is very similar to MARL with centralized learning. So if you are working on a problem that fits this description, then make sure you research MARL as well as concurrent RL.

Reset-free learning

Included in the vast majority of examples and algorithms is the implicit use of "episodes," which imply that environments can be "reset." This makes sense for some environments where the starting position is known, fixed, or easily identifiable. But real life doesn't allow "do-overs," even though sometimes I wish it would, and would require omnipotent oversight. To avoid an Orwellian version of the film *Groundhog Day*, many applications need some way of not specifying a reset.

Early solutions suggested that agents could learn how to reset.[13] Agents are in control of their actions so you can store previous actions in a buffer. To get back to the starting point you can "undo" those actions. This works in many domains because action spaces have a natural opposite. But action uncertainties and unnatural "undos" prevent this approach being generally applicable.

Another idea is to predict when terminations or resets or unsafe behavior is going to occur and stop it before it happens.[14] But again this requires oversight, so another suggestion is to learn a function to predict when resets will occur as part of the learning itself.[15] As you can see from the vocabulary this has hints of meta-learning. But none of these approaches is truly reset free; why not eliminate resets entirely?

You could, technically, never reset and use a discounting factor of less than one to prevent value estimates tending toward infinity. But the reset is more important than you realize. It allows agents to have a fresh start, like when you quit your boring job and start an exciting career in engineering. It is very easy for exploring agents to get stuck and spend significant time in similar states. The only way to get out of a rut is for someone or something to give it a kick. A reset is a perfect solution to this problem because it gives the agent another chance to try a different path.

A related problem is when an agent is able to reach a goal or a global optimum, then the best next action is to stay put, gorging on the goal. Again, you need a reset or a kick to explore more of the suboptimal state to make the policy more robust.

So rather than learning how to reset, maybe it is better to learn how to encourage the agent away from the goal and away from regions it can get stuck. Or provide a simple controller to shuffle the environment like Zhu et al., which results in robust robotic policies (*https://oreil.ly/VLwJb*) with no resets.[16]

To conclude, reset-free learning is possible in some simple applications but it's quite likely that your agents will get stuck. At some point you will need to consider whether you are able to manipulate your environment to move the agent to a different state. You might also be able to get the agent to move itself to a different state. Again, different problem domains will have different solutions.

RL Engineering and Refinement

RL problems, like any engineering problem, have high-level and low-level aspects. Changing the high-level design impacts the low-level implementation. For lack of a better term, I denote the high-level analysis and design as *architectural* concerns. These include refining the model of the Markov decision process, defining the interfaces, defining interactions between components, and how the agent will learn. These decisions impact the implementation, or *engineering* details.

I've talked a lot already about high-level architectural aspects, so in this section I want to discuss the implementation details. I endeavor to cover as many of the main concerns as possible, but many implementation details are domain and problem specific. In general, I recommend that you search the literature to find relevant examples and then scour the implementation details for interesting tidbits. These details, often glossed over in the researcher's account, offer vital insight into what works and what doesn't.

Process

Before I dive into the details I think it is worth explaining how I perform this engineering work in general terms. I find that most tasks in engineering, irrespective of the abstraction level, tend to follow some variant of the the observe, orient, decide, act (OODA) loop. What is ostensibly the scientific method, the OODA loop is a simple, four-step approach to tackling any problem, popularized by the American military. The idea is that you can iterate on that loop to utilize context and make a quick decision, while appreciating that decisions may change as more information becomes available. Figure 9-5 shows this loop in engineering terms, where I suggest the words *analysis*, *design*, *implementation*, and *evaluation* are more appropriate, but they amount to the same thing.

The most important aspect is that this is a never-ending process. On each iteration of the loop you evaluate where you are and if that is not good enough, you analyze where improvements could be made. You then pick the next best improvement and implement that.

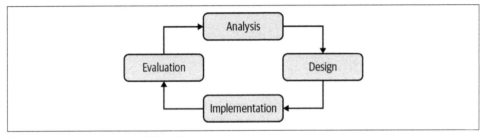

Figure 9-5. The process of RL refinement.

No one single improvement will ever be enough and there is always one more improvement that you could make. You have to be careful not to get stuck in this loop, and you can do that by remembering the Pareto distribution (*https://oreil.ly/iAWCX*): 80% of the solution will take 20% of the time and vice versa. Consider if implementing that last 20% is really worth it, given all the other value you could be providing with that time.

Environment Engineering

I find that the most productive first step of an RL project is to create an *environment*. Throughout this book I use this term to denote an abstraction of the world that the agent operates within. It is the interface between what actually happens and what the agent wants (see "Reinforcement Learning" on page 4).

But now I am specifically talking about the implementation of this interface. Whether you are working in real life submitting real trades or you are creating a simulation of a wind turbine, you need an implementation of the environment interface.

The benefit of concentrating on this first is that you will become intimately acquainted with the data. This maps to the "data understanding" step in the CRISP-DM model. Understanding your environment is crucial for efficiently solving industrial challenges. If you don't, what tends to happen is what I call the "improvement shotgun." By throwing a bunch of different ideas at the problem you will probably find one that hits the target, but most will miss. This type of work is not productive, efficient, or intelligent.

Instead, understand the environment fully, pose scientifically and engineeringly—yes, apparently that is a word—robust questions, and implement functionality that answers those questions. Over time you will gain insight into the problem and you will be able to explain *why* improvements are important, not just state that they are.

Implementation

OpenAI's Gym has organically become the de facto environment interface in the RL community.[17] In fact, it's one of the most cited RL papers of all time. You've probably come across it before, but just in case you haven't, a Gym is a Python framework for expressing environments. It exposes useful primitives like definitions for action and state space representation and enforces a simple set of functionality via an interface that should suit most applications. It also comes with a big set of example environments that are used throughout the internet as toy examples.

From an industrial perspective, the interface is a great way to model your problem and help refine your MDP. And because it is so popular, it is likely that you can rapidly test different algorithms because the majority expect the Gym interface.

 I'm not going to go through a detailed example of an implementation, because it is out of the scope of this book, but you can find many great examples from a quick search or visiting the Gym GitHub website (*https://oreil.ly/Geupc*).

Simulation

A simulation is supposed to capture the most important aspects of a real-life problem. Simulations are not intended to be perfect representations, although many people, researchers, and businesses invest vast amounts of time making simulations more realistic. The benefit of having a simulation is that it is easier, cheaper, and quicker to operate within the confines of a simulation than it is in real life. This reduces the length of the developmental feedback cycles and increases productivity. But the precise benefits depend on the problem; sometimes learning in real life is easier and simpler than building a simulation.

You should first search to see if someone has already attempted to build a simulation. Understanding the fundamental aspects of the problem, the physics, biology, or chemistry, is often more difficult than solving the problem, although building a simulation will certainly improve your knowledge about the subject, so it might be worthwhile for that reason alone. Many commercial simulators like MuJoCo or Unity are available, but come with a commercial price tag. You will have to decide whether the cost is worth the money for your problem. In general I recommend evaluating whether the simulation is a competitive differentiator for your business or product. If it is, it may be worth investing in development; if not, save yourself a lot of time and buy off-the-shelf. And I have found that these vendors are immensely helpful and professional, so ask them for help. It is in their interest for your idea or business to succeed, because that means future revenue for them.

If you do decide to implement the simulator yourself then you will need to build models to simulate the problem and decide which aspects to expose. This is where

MDP design plays a crucial role. In general, you should try to expose the same aspects of the problem that can be observed in real life. Otherwise, when you try to transfer your learnings to real life you will find that your agent doesn't behave as you expect.

Similarly, many researchers attempt to take models trained in simulation and apply them to real-life tasks. This is certainly possible, but is entirely defined by how representative the simulation is. If this is your intention, then you should implicitly couple the implementations of the simulation and real life. The vast majority of algorithms and models don't like it when you change the underlying state or action space.

Simulations are perfect for proof-of-concept projects, to validate that an idea is technically viable. But be careful to not place too much hope on the simulation because there is no guarantee that the policy your agent has derived is possible in real life. It is eminently possible that real-life projects can fail spectacularly even though simulations work perfectly. More often than not the simulation misses some crucial aspect or information.

Interacting with real life

If your experience with the simulation is encouraging, or you have decided that it is easier to skip the simulation, then the next step is to build another (Gym) interface to interact with real life. The development of such an implementation is often much easier, because you don't need to understand and implement the underlying mechanics; nature does that for you. But adapting your algorithms to suit the problem is utterly dependent on understanding and controlling the data.

The primary concerns of the real-life implementation consist of the operational aspects, things like scaling, monitoring, availability, and so on. But architecture and design still plays an important part. For example, in real life there are obvious safety concerns that are not present in a simulation. In some domains a significant amount of time must be invested in ensuring safe and reliable operation. Other common problems include partial observability, which doesn't exist in an omnipotent simulation, and excessive amounts of stochasticity; you would have thought that motors move to the position you tell them to, but often this is not the case.

I don't think this small section sufficiently expresses the amount of engineering time that can go into real-world implementations. Of course, implementations are wildly domain specific, but the main problem is that this work is pretty much pure research. It is hard to accurately estimate how long the work will take, because neither you nor anyone else in the world has tackled this exact problem before. You are a digital explorer. Remember to remind your project managers of this fact. And remember the process from the start of this chapter. *Start simple.* Life is hard enough without you making it harder.

State Engineering or State Representation Learning

In data science, *feature engineering* is the art/act of improving raw data to make it more informative and representative of the task at hand. In general, more informative features make the problem easier to solve. A significant amount of time after a proof of concept is spent cleaning, removing, and adding features to improve performance and make the solution more robust.

I like to use similar terminology to refer to the engineering of the state, although I haven't seen it used much elsewhere. *State engineering*, often called *state representation learning*, is a collection of techniques that aim to improve how the observations represent the state. In other words, the goal is to engineer better state representations. There is no right way of doing this, however, so you are primarily guided by metrics like performance and robustness.

Although there are parallels, this isn't feature engineering. The goal is not to solve the problem by providing simpler, more informative features. The goal is to create the best representation of the state of the environment as you can, then let the policy solve the problem. The reason for this is that in most industrial challenges, it is very unlikely that you are capable of crafting features that can compete with an optimal multistep policy. Of course, if you can, then you should consider using standard supervised learning techniques instead.

Like in feature engineering, domain expertise is important. The addition of a seemingly simple feature can dramatically improve performance, far more than trying different algorithms. For example, Kalashnikov et al. found that in their robotics experiments that used images as the state representation, adding a simple "height of gripper" measurement improved the robot's ability to pick up unseen objects by a whopping 12%.[19] This goes to show that even though researchers are always trying to learn from pixels, simple, reliable measurements of the ground truth are far better state representations.

Note that many papers and articles on the internet bundle both the state engineering and policy/action engineering into the same bucket. But I do consider them separate tasks because the goal of state engineering is to concentrate on better representations of the state, not improve how the policy generates actions.

Learning forward models

In some cases it may be possible to access ground truth temporarily, in a highly instrumented laboratory experiment, for example, but not in general. You can build a supervised model to predict the state from the observations and ship that out to the in-field agents. This is also called learning a *forward model*.

Constraints

Constraining the state space helps to limit the amount of exploration required by the agent. In general, policies improve when states have repeated visits, so limiting the number of states speeds up learning.

Apply constraints by using *priors*, information that is known to be true, formally defined by a probability distribution. For example, if you know that features should be strictly positive, then ensure your policy knows that and doesn't attempt to reach those states.

Transformation (dimensionality reduction, autoencoders, and world models)

Dimensionality reduction is a task in data science where you try to reduce the number of features without removing information. Traditional techniques are useful in RL too. Using principal component analysis, for example, reduces the state space and therefore reduces learning time.[20]

But the crown jewels of state engineering are the various incarnations of autoencoders to reconstruct the observation. The idea is simple: given a set of observations, train a neural network to form an internal representation and regenerate the input. Then you tap into that internal representation and use it as your new state.

Typically, implementations attempt to reduce the dimensionality of the input by using a neural architecture that progressively compresses the state space. This constraint tends to force the network to learn higher-level abstractions and hopefully, an important state representation. However, there are suggestions that *increasing* the dimensionality can improve performance.[21] I remain somewhat skeptical of this claim as it actively encourages overfitting.

Learning representations of individual observations is one thing, but MDPs are sequential, therefore there are important temporal features locked away. A new class of MDP-inspired autoencoders is beginning to treat this more like a prediction problem. Given an ordered set of observations, these autoencoders attempt to predict what happens in the future. This forces the autoencoder to learn temporal features as well as stateful features. The particular implementation differs between domains, but the idea remains the same.[22,23]

The term *world models*, after the paper with the same name, refers to the goal of attempting to build a model of an environment from offline data, so that the agent can interact as if it was online. This idea is obviously important for practical implementations where it is hard to learn on live data and so the term has become popular to describe any method that attempts to model an environment.[24] Ha and Schmidhuber deserve extra kudos because of their excellent interactive version (*https:// oreil.ly/wHT_w*) of their paper. I consider this work to be a specific implementation of state engineering, which may or may not be useful depending on your situation, but it is a very useful tool to help segment the RL process.

These techniques can be complicated by MDP issues like partial observability, but in general autoencoder research can be directly applied to RL problems. If this is important for your application then I recommend you dig into these papers. Frameworks are also beginning to see the value in state representation, like SRL-zoo (*https:// oreil.ly/Gfr5r*), a collection of representation learning methods targeting PyTorch, which you might find useful.

Policy Engineering

An RL policy is responsible for mapping a representation of the state to an action. Although this sounds simple, in practice you need to make careful decisions about the function that implements this mapping. Like in machine learning, the choice of function defines the limits of performance and the robustness of the policy. It also impacts learning performance, too; using nonlinear policies can cause divergence and generally take much longer to train.

I generalize this work under the banner of *policy engineering*, where the goal is to design a policy that best solves a problem given a set of constraints. The vast majority of the RL literature is dedicated to finding improved ways of defining policies or improving their theoretical guarantees.

The policy is fundamentally limited by the Bellman update, so unless there is a major theoretical shift, all policies have a similar aim. Researchers introduce novelty by affixing new ways to represent state, improve exploration, or penalize some other constraint. Underneath, all RL algorithms are value-based or policy-based.

Given this similarity between all algorithms I visualize a policy as having three distinct tasks, like in Figure 9-6. First it has to convert the representation of state into a format that can be used by an internal model. The internal model is the decision engine, learning whatever it needs to learn to be able to convert state to possible actions. A policy has to explore and you have a lot of control over that process. Finally, the policy has to convert the hidden representation into an action that is suitable for the environment.

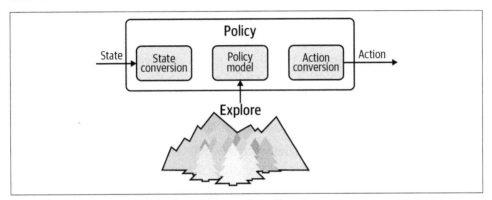

Figure 9-6. A depiction of the three phases of a policy.

The engineering challenge is to design functions to perform these three phases in an efficient and robust way. The definition of the policy model has been the subject of most of this book. In the following subsections I describe how to use discrete or continuous states and actions.

Discrete states

A *discrete* feature is permitted to only take certain values, but can have an infinite range. The vast majority of data is received in a form quantized by analog-to-digital converters, so you can consider most data to be discrete. But in practice when people say "discrete space" they typically mean an integer-based state space, where state can take only integer values. Most of the time quantized data is converted to a float and is considered continuous.

Discrete state inputs are useful because of their simplicity. There are fewer states that an agent has to explore and therefore training performance and time can be reduced, even predicted. Problems with smaller state spaces will converge faster than larger ones.

A discrete state space is any GridWorld-like environment. Geospatial problems are a good example. Even though positions could be encoded by continuous measures like latitude and longitude, it is often computationally and intuitively simpler to convert a map into a grid, like Chaudhari et al. did when optimizing ride-share routing policies in the city of New York.[25]

Problems with discrete state spaces are considered to be easier to solve, mainly because it is so easy to debug and visualize. Discrete domains are often easy to reason about, which makes it possible to make accurate theoretical priors and baselines. You can directly compare policies to these assumptions, which makes it easy to monitor training progress and fix problems as they arise. Another benefit is that value functions can be stored in a dictionary or lookup table, so you can leverage industrially robust technology like databases.

But the most important benefit is that discrete spaces are fixed; there is no chance of any "in-between" state, so there is no need for any approximation of any kind. This means you can use basic Q-learning. Using a simpler, more theoretically robust algorithm like Q-learning leads to simpler and more robust implementations, a very important factor when using these models in production.

The problem, however, is that naturally occurring discrete states are uncommon. In most implementations the engineer has forced the discrete state upon the problem to obtain the aforementioned benefits. This arbitrary discretization is likely to be suboptimal at best and causes a loss of information detail. Even though the arguments for discrete state spaces are enticing, it is unlikely that they yield the best performance. In the previous example, for instance, the diameter of each cell in New York's grid was about 2 miles. Even after optimizing the positioning of ride-share vehicles, they could end up being 2 miles from their customer.

Continuous states

A *continuous* feature is an infinite set of real values. They may be bounded, but there is no "step" between neighboring values. An example could be the speed of an autonomous vehicle or the temperature of a forge. Continuous state spaces are considered to be slightly more difficult to work with than discrete spaces because this leads to an infinite number of potential states, which makes it impossible to use a simple lookup table, for example.

Policies of continuous states have to be able to predict the best next action or value for a given state, which means that the policies must approximate, rather than expect known states. You can provide an approximation using any standard machine learning technique, but functional approximators are most common. Neural networks are increasingly popular due to the unified approach and tooling.

The main worry about continuous state spaces is that they are only provably convergent when using linear approximators. As of 2020, no convergence proofs exist for nonlinear approximators, which means that any "deep" algorithm isn't guaranteed to converge, even if it is a good model, although empirical evidence suggests they do. Linear approximations can model a significant amount of complexity via domain transformations. Simplicity, stability, and configurable amounts of complexity mean that like in machine learning, linear methods are very useful. In general, there are three ways to provide an approximation:

Linear approximations

Learning a set of linear weights directly based upon the input features is possibly one of the simplest approaches to deal with continuous states. This is effectively the same as linear regression. You can also improve the quality of the regression through any standard linear regression extension, like those that reduce the influence of outliers, for example. A linear policy is provably convergent.

Nonparametric approximations

You can use a classification-like model to predict values, if that makes sense. For example, nearest neighbor and tree-based algorithms are capable of providing robust, scalable predictions. Again, their simplicity and popularity has led to a wide range of off-the-shelf, robust industrial implementations, which you can leverage to make your implementation more scalable and robust. There is no guarantee that nonparametric policies will converge.

Nonlinear approximation

Nonlinear approximations provide a flexible amount of complexity in a uniform package: neural networks. You can control the amount of complexity through the architecture of the network. Neural networks have produced state-of-the-art results in many domains so it would be wise to evaluate them in your problem. There is no guarantee that nonlinear policies will converge.

The provable convergence guarantees are a strong feature of linear approximations. And you can obtain a surprising amount of model complexity by transforming the data before passing to the linear approximation. The following below is a selection of popular techniques to increase model complexity while maintaining the simplicity and guarantees of linear methods:

Polynomial basis

A polynomial expansion is the generation of all possible combinations of features up to a specified power. Polynomials represent curves in value space, which enables slightly more complexity over linear methods.

Fourier basis

Fourier expansions generate oscillations in value space. These oscillations can be combined in arbitrary ways to generate complex shapes, similar to how sounds are comprised of tonal overlays. Fourier bases are complete, in the sense that they can approximate any (well-behaved) function for a given level of complexity, controlled by the order of the basis function. They work well in a range of domains.[26] The Fourier basis struggles in environments with discontinuities, like the Cliffworld environment, however.

Radial basis

Radial basis functions are often Gaussian-shaped transformations (other radial bases exist) that measure the distance between the state and the center of the basis, relative to the basis's width. In other words, these are parameterized Gaussian-like shapes that can be moved and resized to approximate the value function. The main problem with radial basis functions (and other tiling schemes) is that you have to choose the width of the basis, which effectively fixes the amount of "smoothing." Optimal trajectories tend to produce "spikes" in the value function so you end up having to use quite narrow widths, which can lead to problematic local optima. Despite this radial basis functions are useful because the width hyperparameter provides a simple and effective way to control the "amount of complexity."

Other transforms

Signal processing provides a wide range of other transformations that could be applied to generate different feature characteristics, like the Hilbert or Wavelet transforms, for example. But they are not so popular, typically because most RL researchers have a mathematical or machine learning background. Those with an electronics background, for example, would be more than happy to use these "traditional" techniques.

For more details about linear transformations, see the extra resources in "Further Reading" on page 288.

Converting to discrete states

You may want to consider discretizing your domain. Converting continuous states is especially common where there are natural grid-like representations of a domain, like on a map. The main benefit of discretizing is that it might remove the need for a function approximator, because of the fixed size of the state space. This means that simple, fast, and robust Q-learning-based algorithms can be used. Even if you do still need a function approximator, discretization decreases the apparent resolution of the data, making it much easier for agents to explore and easier for models to fit. This has proven to result in an increase in raw performance for difficult continuous problems like in the Humanoid environment.[27] The following list presents an overview of discretization possibilities (more information can be found in "Further Reading" on page 288):

Binning

Fix the range of a feature and quantize it into bins, like a histogram. This is simple and easy to comprehend but you lose accuracy. You can place bin boundaries in a range of nonuniform ways, like constant width, constant frequency, or logarithmically, for example.

Tile coding

Map overlapping tiles to a continuous space and set a tile to 1 if the observation is present in that tile's range. This is similar to binning, but provides increased accuracy due to the overlapping tiles. Tiles are often square, but can be any shape and nonuniformly positioned.

Hashing

When features are unbounded, like IP or email addresses, you can forcibly constrain the features into a limited set of bins without loss of information by hashing (there will still be a loss in accuracy due to binning).

Supervised methods

In some domains you may have labeled data that is important to the RL problem. You might want to consider building a classification model and pass the result into the RL algorithm. There are a wide variety of algorithms suitable for this purpose.[28]

Unsupervised methods

If you don't have labels you could use unsupervised machine learning methods, like k-means, to position bins in better locations.[29]

Mixed state spaces

If you have a mixed state space then you have three options:

1. Unify the state space through conversion

2. Cast the discrete space to a continuous one and continue using continuous techniques

3. Split the state space into separate problems

Options 1 and 2 are self explanatory. The majority of functional approximators will happily work with discretized values, even though it may not be optimal or efficient.

Option 3, however, is interesting. If you can split the state into different components that match bounded contexts in the problem domain, that might indicate that it is more efficient to use submodels or subpolicies. For example, a crude approach could be to separate the continuous and discrete states, feed them into two separate RL algorithms, then combine them into an ensemble.[30] As you can see this is touching upon hierarchical RL, so be sure to leverage ideas from there.

Mapping Policies to Action Spaces

Before you attempt to define how a policy specifies actions, take a step back and consider what type of actions would be most suitable for your problem. Ask yourself the following questions:

- *What value types can your actions take?* Are they binary? Are they discrete? Are they bounded or unbounded? Are they continuous? Are they mixed?

- *Are simultaneous actions possible?* Is it possible to select multiple actions at the same time? Can you iterate faster and interleave single actions to approach selecting multiple actions?

- *When do actions need to be made?* Is there a temporal element to action selection?

- *Are there any meta-actions?* Can you think of any high-level actions that might help learning or handle the temporal elements?

- *Can you split the actions into subproblems?* Are there obvious bounded contexts in your actions? Can these be split into separate problems? Is this a hierarchical problem?

- *Can you view your actions in another way?* For example, rather than moving to a continuous-valued position, could you consider a "move forward" action? Or vice versa?

All of these decisions have grave impacts on your work, so be careful when making them. For example, switching an action from continuous to discrete might force you to change algorithms. Or realizing that your agent requires simultaneous actions might make your problem much harder to solve.

Binary actions

Binary actions are possibly the simplest to work with, because they are easy to optimize, visualize, debug, and implement. Policies are expected to output a binary value mapping to the action that they want to choose. In problems where only a single action is allowed, picking the maximum expected return (for value methods) or the action with the highest probability (for policy gradient methods) is a simple implementation.

As seen in "How Does the Temperature Parameter Alter Exploration?" on page 203, you can encourage broad exploration by making the policy output probabilities, or values that can be interpreted as probabilities. The agent can then randomly sample from this action space according to the assigned probabilities. For value methods, you can assign the highest probabilities to the highest expected values. I would recommend using advantages, rather than values directly, to avoid bias. An exponential softmax function is recommended to convert values to probabilities. In policy gradient methods you can train the models to predict probabilities directly.

Continuous actions

Continuous actions are very common, like determining the position of a servo or specifying the amount to bid on an ad. In these cases it is most natural to use some kind of approximation function to output a continuous prediction for a given state (just like regression); deterministic policy gradients do this. But researchers have found that modeling the output as a random variable can help exploration. So rather than directly predicting the output value, they predict the mean of a distribution, like a Gaussian. Then a value is sampled from distribution. Other parameters of the distribution, like the standard deviation for the Gaussian, can also be predicted. Then you can set the initial standard deviation at the beginning high, to encourage exploration, and allow the algorithm to shrink it as it learns. I like to think of this as a crude attempt to incorporate probabilistic modeling. Of course this assumes that your actions are normally distributed, which may not be accurate, so think carefully about what distribution you should choose for your actions.

An alternative is to leverage newer methods that are based upon Q-learning, but have been adapted to approximate continuous functions: continuous action Q-learning.[31] This is by no means as common as using policy gradient methods but claims to be more efficient.

One final trick that I want to mention, which is helpful in simple examples, is called the *dimension scaling trick*. When using linear approximators that need to predict multiple outputs, like the mean and standard deviation, you can have distinct parameters for each action and update the parameters for the chosen action individually. This is effectively a dictionary of parameters, where the key is the action and the values are the parameters for the continuous mapping, like the mean and standard deviation.

Hybrid action spaces

Spaces with both discrete and continuous actions are relatively common, like deciding to buy and how much to spend, and can be tricky to deal with. First consider if you can split the problem. If it's a hierarchical problem, go down that route first. Next consider if you can get away with only continuous or only discrete. You'll probably lose a little bit of granularity, but it might make it easier to get something up and running.

New algorithms are emerging that learn when to select either a continuous algorithm or a discrete one, depending on the required action space. Parameterized DQN is one such example, but the idea could be applied to any algorithm.[32] Another approach called *action branching* simply creates more heads with different activations and training goals on a neural network, which seems like a nice engineering solution to the problem.[33] This multihead architecture also enables simultaneous actions. In a sense this just a handcrafted form of hierarchical RL.

When to perform actions

Here's a curveball: what about when you want to output no action? That's actually a lot harder than it sounds, because everything from the Bellman equation to neural network training is set up to expect an action on every step. The Atari games implement frame skipping without really considering how many frames to skip; 4 are just taken as given. But researchers have found that you can optimize the the size of number of skipped frames to improve performance.[34]

A more generalized approach is to use the *options* framework, which include a termination condition. These methods learn not only *how* to act optimally, but also when.[35,36] A potentially simpler solution is instead to add an action that causes the agent to repeat previous actions; I have seen this used in robotics to reduce wear and tear on motors. It is also possible to learn to skip as many actions as possible, to reduce costs associated with an action.[37]

As usual, the best solution is problem dependent. Generally I would recommend staying within the realms of "normal" RL as much as possible, to simplify development.

Massive action spaces

When state spaces become too large you can use state engineering to bring them back down to a reasonable size. But what about when you have massive action spaces, like if you are recommending one of millions of products to a customer? YouTube has 10^8 items in its corpus, for example.[38]

Value-based methods like Q-learning struggle because you have to maximize of a set of possible action on every step. The obvious challenge is that when you have continuous actions, the number of actions to maximize over is infinite. But even in discrete settings there can be so many actions that it might take an infeasibly long time to perform that maximization. Policy gradient methods overcome this problem because they sample from a distribution; there is no maximization.

Solutions to this problem include using embeddings to reduce the total number of actions to a space of actions.[39] This has instinctive appeal due to the successes of embeddings in other ML challenges, like in natural language processing. If you have action spaces that are similar to problems where embeddings have been successful, then this might be a good approach. Another approach is to treat the maximization as an optimization problem and learn to predict maximal actions.[40]

A related issue is where you need to select a fixed number of items from within the action space. This presents a combinatorial explosion and is a common enough issue to have attracted research time. There are a wide range approximate solutions like hierarchical models and autoencoders.[41,42] A more general solution is to move the complexity in the action space into the state space by inserting fictitious dummy states and using group actions predicted over multiple steps to produce a selection of recommendations.[43] A simpler and more robust solution is to assume that users can select a single action. Then you only need to rank and select the top-k actions, rather than attempting to decide on what combination of actions is best. This solution has been shown to increase user engagement on YouTube.[44]

 Consider this result in the context that Google (which owns YouTube) has access to one of the most advanced pools of data scientists in the world. This algorithm is competitive with its highly tuned recommendations model that (probably) took teams of highly experienced data scientists many years to perfect. Incredible.

Exploration

Children provide personal and professional inspiration in a range of sometimes surprising ways, like when I'm working on a presentation or a new abstraction I routinely try to explain this to my kids. If I can't explain it in a way that sounds at least coherent to them, then that's a signal to me that I need to work harder at improving my message. The book *The Illustrated Children's Guide to Kubernetes* (*https://oreil.ly/bz90V*) is a cute testament to this idea.

Children also provide direction for improvements in exploration. This is necessary because I have spent most of this book explaining that most problems are an exploration problem: complex states, large action spaces, convergence, optima, and so on. All these problems can be improved with better exploration. Recent research has shown that children have an innate ability, at a very early age, to actively explore environments for the sake of knowledge. They can perform simple experiments and test hypotheses. They can weave together multiple sources of information to provide a rich mental model of the world and project this knowledge into novel situations.[45]

RL algorithms, on the other hand, are primarily driven by error, and learning is almost random. Without a goal, agents would stumble around an environment like an annoying fly that is seemingly incapable of flying back through the open window it came through.

It seems that children tend to operate using an algorithm that approaches *depth-first search*. They like to follow through with their actions until there is a perceived state that blocks the current path, like a dead end in a maze. Incredibly, this works without any goal, which means they are transferring knowledge about the states from previous experience. When the same children are then presented with a goal, they are able to use the mental map produced by their exploration to dramatically improve the initial search for a goal. Contrast this with current RL algorithms that generally rely on finding a goal by accident.

To this end, there is a large body of work that investigates how to improve exploration, especially in problems that have sparse rewards. But first consider whether you can provide expert guidance in the form of improved algorithms (like replacing ϵ-greedy methods with something else) or intermediary rewards (like distance-to-goal measures), or using something like imitation RL to actively guide your agent. Also consider altering your problem definition to make the rewards more frequent. All of these will improve learning speed and/or exploration without resorting to the following methods.

Is intrinsic motivation exploration?

Researchers are trying to solve the problem of exploration by developing human-inspired alternatives to random movement, which leads to a glut of proposals with anthropomorphic names like surprise, curiosity, or empowerment. Despite the cutesy names, exploration methods in humans are far too complex to encode in a simple RL algorithm, so researchers attempt to generate similar behavior through mathematical alterations to the optimization function.

This highlights the problem with all of these methods; there is no right answer. I'm sure you can imagine several mathematical solutions to encourage exploration, like the entropy bonus in the soft actor-critic, but they will never come close to true human-like exploration without prior experience. This is why I think that this field is still young and why words like "curiosity" or "intrinsic motivation" are bad monikers, because they imply that exploration is all about trying new actions. It's not. Exploration *is* RL. You use prior knowledge to explore new states, based upon the anticipation of future rewards.

Imagine a classic RL game where your agent is looking at a wall. If it knows anything about walls, it should never explore the states close to the wall, because there is no benefit from doing so. All RL algorithms neglect the simple physical rule that you can't walk through walls, so they waste time literally banging their head against the wall. But it's also interesting to note that these assumptions can prevent us from finding unexpected states, like those annoying invisible blocks in the Super Mario series.

So if you want to perform optimal exploration then you need prior experience. I think that transferring knowledge between problems is the key to this problem and unsupervised RL has a potential solution. And counterfactual reasoning will become more important as algorithms begin to start using "libraries" of prior knowledge.

Intrinsic motivation and the methods discussed next are not really about exploration at all. They attempt to improve the *cold start* problem. When you have zero knowledge with sparse rewards, how can you encourage deep exploration?

Visitation counts (sampling)

One of the simplest ways to improve the efficiency of exploration is to make sure that the agent doesn't visit a state too many times. Or conversely, encourage the agent to visit infrequently visited states more often. Upper-confidence-bound methods attempt to prevent the agent from visiting states too often (see "Improving the ϵ-greedy Algorithm" on page 33). Thompson sampling is an optimal sampling technique for this kind of problem and probabilistic random sampling, based upon the value function or policy predictions, can serve as a useful proxy.

Information gain (surprise)

Information gain is used throuhout machine learning as a measure of the reduction in entropy. For example, tree-based algorithms use information gain to find splits in feature space that reduce the amount of entropy between classes; a good split makes pure or clean classes, so the information gain is high.[46]

Many researchers have attempted to use information gain to direct the agent toward regions of greater "surprise." The major benefit over raw sampling techniques is that they can incorporate internal representations of the policy, rather than relying on external observations of the movement of an agent.

One example of this is *variational information maximizing exploration* (VIME), which uses the divergence (see "Kullback–Leibler Divergence" on page 165) between observed trajectories and those expected by a parameterized model as an addition to the reward function.[47] Note the similarity between this idea and thtose discussed in "Trust Region Methods" on page 163. This results in exploration that appears to "sweep" through the state space.

State prediction (curiosity or self-reflection)

Curiosity is a human trait that rewards seeking out and finding information that surprises. The previous approach focused upon encouraging surprising trajectories, but you might not want this, because interesting paths are quite likely to lead to a result that is not very surprising at all. Consider if this is important in your problem. For example, you might be searching for new ways of achieving the same result, in which case this would be very useful. In many problems, however, it is the result that is important, not how you got there.

So rather than encouraging different paths, like different routes to school, another solution is to encourage new situations, like going to a different school. One example of this is to create a model that attempts to predict the next state based upon the current state and action, then rewarding according to how wrong the prediction is.[48] The problem with this method is that predicting future states is notoriously difficult due to the stochastic and dynamic nature of the environment. If it was that easy, you could use machine learning to solve your problem. So they attempt to model only the parts of the state that affect the agent. They do this by training a neural network that predicts an action from two consecutive states, which creates an internal representation of the policy, and then rewarding based upon the difference between a model that predicts what the internal representation *should be* and what it actually is after visiting that state. A simpler, similar approach would be to use a delayed autoencoder that compares the hidden representation against that which is observed.

Curious challenges

In the real world, novel states are encountered all the time. Like the previous method suggests, we build long-term models to predict what is novel. That implies that we have also learned how to ignore the noise. Think of when you are driving a car. You have somehow learned how to automatically ignore 99% of the irrelevant information around you and concentrate on the hazards. But put a TV screen or a mobile phone in view and your eyes will be drawn toward it. This promise of seeing something new, at the expense of spotting hazards, is what makes driving with phones or tablets so dangerous.

Researchers have found that a similar problem exists in RL. Figure 9-7 shows a hilarious scenario where a TV was placed upon a wall.[49] The state-curiosity-driven agent is perpetually rewarded because it cannot predict what is going to be shown next on TV. Obviously this result is a little contrived; the whole point of these models is to filter out such noise, which should be fairly easy to do if you understand the domain. But in general, researchers need to focus more on improving global exploration, not local.

Figure 9-7. Using observations as a source of surprise can encourage agents to get stuck in noisy states. Adapted from a video by © Deepak Pathak, used under CC BY 2.0 license.

Random embeddings (random distillation networks)

One idea to overcome the "noisy-TV" problem, where agents become fixated with stochastic states, is to use random embeddings. *Random distillation networks* are a pair of neural networks, one of which is randomly initialized and never touched again. The random network is used to generate random embeddings. A second network is trained to predict the random embeddings. In the work of Burda et al., the error between the random and predicted embedding is used as a "novelty" measure; a greater error means that this type of observation is not well represented in the buffer and therefore should be visited again in the future. This error value is appended to the reward to promote visiting new states.[50]

The major benefit of this approach is that it is not predicting the next observation; it is just comparing the next observation to its current model of the environment. This means that the stationary view of a stochastic states, like a single image on the TV, can be modeled quite well and therefore the agent is not rewarded for being a "couch potato."

I find the idea of using a randomly initialized neural network as an embedding hard to fathom. But imagine if your vision was afflicted by some random transformation. Given time your brain would learn to compensate for this and would develop new abstractions; survivors of a stroke have to go through this ordeal. Another benefit is that this architecture is simpler, in the sense that there is only a single network to train. But the exploration is still purely local; it does not promote exploration in depth. Another problem is that it is crucial to have an architecture that produces an effective embedding in the domain. Convolutional neural networks clearly work well in image-based domains, but what about others? These cases need your domain and modeling expertise.[51]

Distance to novelty (episodic curiosity)

One interesting avenue of research to promote global exploration is to use distance between states as a better measure of novelty. Savinov et al. propose using an experience buffer to record novel states, which are encoded by an embedding. The buffer is cleared at the start of every episode. When an agent happens upon a new state, the distance between the states in the buffer and the current state is estimated. If the new state is within a few environment steps of those in the buffer, it is not novel and is punished. If the new state is further than a few steps away then the agent is rewarded for finding novel states. This encourages agents to seek out new states on an episodic basis.[52]

Figure 9-8 is a representation of the trajectory followed during one episode. It shows the sign of the reward and when embedded observations were placed in the buffer. You can see that the algorithm has the effect of forcing the agent to keep moving, which promotes depth-first exploration and prevents the agent from becoming a "couch-potato."

The implementation is quite complex. First, images are converted to hidden embeddings by a convolutional neural network using one-half of a *siamese* network, which is a neural network architecture used in image matching tasks.[53] I don't like this name but that's what the literature calls it. Next, the current embedding is compared to all of the embeddings in the buffer, creating a measure of distance to all other observations. Finally, an aggregation is performed to find the distance to next closest state, which represents the novelty of this observation, and is used to calculate the reward.

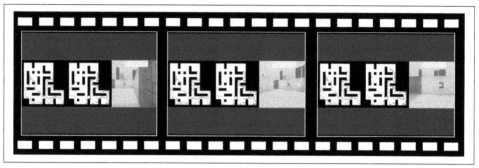

Figure 9-8. Trajectories from an episode of the DMLab environment with episodic curiosity. The lefthand box shows how the agent was rewarded for that state (green means positive reward, red means negative). The middle box represents when "memories" were added to the episodic buffer. The right box is the first-person view of the agent. Video adapted from Savinov et al.

Exploration conclusions

We know that people explore in depth, using prior knowledge. Transferring that idea to RL is incredibly difficult, because there is no obvious way to direct exploration without breaking the assumptions of an MDP. It feels like there is a gap, one that an MDP cannot fill, where part of the problem is purely supervised, like revising for an exam, but another is entirely opportunistic, like spending time in a different culture.

This is an important problem to solve, because sparse states occur often in RL, due to the nature of goal-driven engineering. Sparse rewards are difficult to work with because they are hard to find. Creating an alternative, pseudoreward that encourages an arbitrary exploration strategy is one solution, but in many problems it is relatively straightforward to manually design rewards to suit your problem (see "Reward Engineering" on page 283), or alter the problem definition to make it easier.

Current attempts to automate exploration take a local, episodic view and do not consider global or long-term exploration goals. In fact, researchers have observed that promoting novelty actively encourages dangerous states, like walking along the edge of the cliff, because they are difficult to get close to and are rarely represented in the agent's past experience.[54]

All efforts encourage exploration by augmenting the reward function, rather than by guiding action selection. There are clear parallels between this, curriculum learning, and inverse RL that could improve this situation. To be sure, the future of exploration research will be directed toward either altering the fundamental definition of the

MDP, by allowing some high-level coordination (thus breaking the Markovian assumption), or incorporating the work of other fields in RL to encourage long-time horizon planning.

Reward Engineering

Designing a reward to solve your problem is arguably the most important task in RL. This is where, as an engineer, it is your job to convert the problem definition into a metric that guides the agent toward a solution. This is incredibly important. Your definition dictates the solution and it is easy to accidentally cause the agent to solve the wrong problem. Figure 9-9 is a great visual example of this happening. An agent in the Unity framework is encouraged to reach a goal and it can use a box to jump over a wall. Instead, because of the slight edge around the environment, the agent has learned to sneak around the side. Despite having a reasonable reward, the agent has learned to exploit the environment in ways that you cannot imagine.

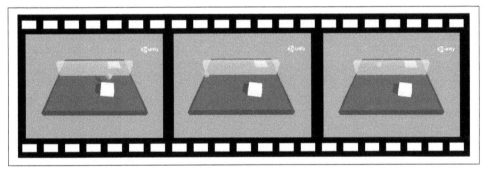

Figure 9-9. In this example from Unity, the goal was to train an agent to use a box to jump over a wall by encouraging the agent to get closer to the goal. Instead, it learned to cheat and sneak around the edge. Adapted from a presentation by Danny Lange, © Unity Technologies, with permission.

In machine learning, you directly define the algorithm to solve a problem. So as long as you have a reasonable grasp of the problem, which is a problem in itself, it is easy to observe when projects go awry. But in RL, you have to wait until training is complete to see how an agent solves a problem. This dramatically increases the length of the feedback loop and demonstrates why understanding the resultant policy is so important.

To make matters worse, the reward also defines the ultimate performance of an algorithm and how fast it gets there. Rewards should help guide the agent, and the more guidance you provide the faster it should learn. However, many problems are sparse, in the sense that there is only a reward when a task is complete. Researchers have proposed many ways in which to mitigate the sparsity, but the simplest thing you can do is design a reward that is a proxy of the task you want to complete. But remember, there is no optimal policy without a reward and your reward changes the optimal policy.

Reward engineering guidelines

Each domain has its own specific problems, which makes it difficult to create hard and fast rules about how to specify a reward. But in this section I want to outline a few high-level objectives that apply to any situation. A reward should do the following:

Be fast
Reward functions should be fast to compute, because they are called millions of times in complex environments.

Correlate with the "true" reward
Proxy rewards should correlate with true rewards, otherwise you run the risk of solving the wrong problem. This means they should equate or approximate the terminology used in the problem domain; for example, monetary value, numbers of customers, lives saved.

De-noise
Proxy rewards can be noisy, which means that they don't perfectly correlate to the true reward. Consider combining different proxy rewards to reduce reward variance.

Encode nonfunctional requirements
Consider adding reward proxies that map to nonfunctional requirements like safety, efficiency, or speed.

Consider time
The discounting factor forces the agent to become more or less *myopic*; it controls how much emphasis is placed on optimizing short- or long-term rewards. Consider this when shaping rewards.

Prevent plateaus
Your reward should provide strong discrimination between states and the difference should be greater than the noise of the Q-values. If states have very similar rewards, agents tend to go around in circles.

Smooth
To produce "smooth" behavior, policies need to learn from smooth rewards. Discontinuities in the reward space can manifest as "sharp," "jolting" actions in the policy.

Be simple

Like everything else in RL, complexity makes it much harder to understand. If you have a simple reward, the policy is easy to understand. If it is complex, you will see unexpected policies.

Reward shaping

This may be an obvious statement to make, but it is still worth saying. Policies are affected by the magnitude of the reward, since agents set out to maximize the total reward. Since you are designing the reward, you also have to specify the size of the reward when the goal is achieved. When there are subgoals, multiple goals, or situations that must be avoided, balancing the rewards of each type can be excruciating. In circumstances such as these you might want to attempt to split the problem or look at hierarchical RL.

In general, you can arbitrarily alter the *shape* of the reward to encourage certain behavior or improve learning speed, for example. When designing a reward you should:

Normalize rewards

Be vary careful with the scale of the reward. In general, all algorithms benefit from normalized rewards because they reduce the variance of the gradients in the policy or value function optimization.

Clip rewards

Clipping rewards is a common form of normalization but the truncation can throw away information. For example, DQN recommends clipping rewards to +/−1, but in the game *Pac-Man* this treats both dots and fruit as having the same reward, which is not true; fruit produces a much higher score (this proxy reward does not correlate to the true reward). If you instead normalize the rewards in *Pac-Man*, the DQN agent becomes a hunter-gatherer and learns to actively hunt ghosts and search for fruit, not just collect dots.[55]

Transform rewards

Altering the gradient of the reward can help smooth policies and provide greater encouragement when the agent is far away from the goal. For example, a linear reward provides the same amount of urgency irrespective of where the agent currently resides in the state space. You could pass your reward through a function where rewards change rapidly when the agent is far away from the goal. This is a slippery slope, because transformations in the reward can have unexpected manifestations in the policy.

Model rewards

Many domains have environments where some modeling is possible, at least locally, so it might be possible to derive a proxy reward that effectively encodes domain knowledge. For example, in a robotics problem you might be able to include some prior knowledge, like the fact that a robot has to stand up before it can run; you could include a sensor that measures how far off the ground the robot is. In general, including ground truth such as this improves performance.

Common rewards

Check to see if there are any published problems that are similar to yours. Common domains tend to stick to tried and tested reward definitions. Following is a list of common types of reward:

Sparse
> Many tasks are only considered complete when a particular state is reached, sometimes multiple states in a specific order. It is common to see a big reward when this task is complete, but they are hard to solve because rewards don't guide the agent toward the goal.

Distance to goal
> Distance-to-goal metrics are very strong reward proxies because they not only correlate strongly to the true reward, but they also guide the agent toward the goal, no matter where the agent is in the state space. This improves exploration and speeds up learning time.

Punishing steps
> Punishing an agent for every action it takes encourages it to take as few steps as possible.

Punishing damaging or dangerous behaviors
> A strong negative reward for destructive behaviors is often used, but be careful that this doesn't adversely impact optimal reward paths, like veering a mile away from a cliff when 10 meters would be fine.

Image-based rewards
> Rewards are usually based upon a low-dimensional state. But increasingly researchers are using high-dimensional observations like images to define the goal state. For example, Zhu et al. use a set of images as a definition of a goal state, and use both random network distillation and a latent model produced by an autoencoder. This is incredibly powerful in many real-world applications, because you only need to collect a batch of images representing your goal state and then leave RL to do the rest.[56]

Reward conclusions

Specifying a reward that solves the problem definition, promotes swift learning, and results in optimal policies is a tremendously difficult thing to achieve. I would suggest that in many applications this list of issues is also in priority order, to the point where so long as the problem definition is correct, engineers tend not to worry about optimality or speedy learning, because you can use other techniques to address these problems. But if you can find a balance, then the result will be simpler, more efficient algorithms.

Again, you might have noticed that some of the suggestions are linked to other topics. Indeed, automated reward generation is the whole goal of intrinsic motivation, unsupervised RL, and even meta-learning. You must take a holistic view of these techniques and choose to use them at the right times, to solve the right problems. Otherwise you might be overcomplicating the problem, which often leads to wasted time or even complete failure.

There is more research that attempts to combine some of these ideas into a unified algorithm. For example, one interesting idea suggests that reward shaping can lead to local optima that can be hard to get out of. Trott et al. use two independent counterfactual rollouts to check if there is another optima greater than the current one.[57]

Summary

Despite RL being decades old, it has only recently gained prominence as an industrially viable and practical tool. I believe the reason for this delay is not a technical one. I think the main problem is that abstracting the technicalities in a way that makes it understandable is difficult. It's hard enough to define what a "strategy" is, or how it can help a business, without sounding all "robots will rule the world." The idea is powerful, but as an engineer, it is your responsibility to translate the potential (and the caveats) in a way that resonates with your stakeholders.

In this chapter I focused less on the gory details and more on the process. But remember that this is a new field, with new opportunities. I have presented what I think is reasonable, but you might have better ideas. Don't be afraid to customize your approach to suit your problem. This also means that these best practices will continue over time. When you do use RL in an industrial project, I would love to hear about your experiences!

Hopefully you now have enough knowledge to at least start an RL project. If you don't, get in touch (see About the Author for contact details) and I'll do my best to help out. Now you know what the process looks like and what to look for in an RL project. You also know about the amount engineering effort that goes into making a project viable and then optimal. There's also a wealth of research freely available on the internet that may map directly to your problem and I also include some important materials in "Further Reading" on page 288 that I found useful during my research.

Further Reading

- Offline reinforcement learning:
  - Slightly old, but still relevant chapter.[58]
  - Recent review of challenges.[59]
- Reset-free learning:
  - A nice review of lifelong learning focusing on robotics.[60]
- State engineering:
  - A good review on state representation.[61]
- Policy engineering:
  - There is a concise but robust section on linear approximation and transformation in the book by Sutton and Barto. Also good for details on continuous action parameterization.[62]
  - An old but relevant review of discretization techniques in ML.[63]
  - I found this video about Gaussian policies (*https://oreil.ly/VWfLm*) very helpful.
- Exploration:
  - Interesting comparison of psychological intrinsic motivation against computational approaches.[64]
  - Comprehensive tutorial on Thompson sampling.[65]

References

[1] Zheng, Stephan, Alexander Trott, Sunil Srinivasa, Nikhil Naik, Melvin Gruesbeck, David C. Parkes, and Richard Socher. 2020. "The AI Economist: Improving Equality and Productivity with AI-Driven Tax Policies" (*https://oreil.ly/hXqcT*). ArXiv: 2004.13332, April.

[2] Håkansson, Samuel, Viktor Lindblom, Omer Gottesman, and Fredrik D. Johansson. 2020. "Learning to Search Efficiently for Causally Near-Optimal Treatments" (*https://oreil.ly/hX-GL*). ArXiv:2007.00973, July.

[3] Lange, Sascha, Thomas Gabel, and Martin Riedmiller. 2012. "Batch Reinforcement Learning" (*https://oreil.ly/yAHBp*). *Reinforcement Learning: State-of-the-Art*, edited by Marco Wiering and Martijn van Otterlo, 45–73. Adaptation, Learning, and Optimization. Berlin, Heidelberg: Springer.

[4] Levine, Sergey, Aviral Kumar, George Tucker, and Justin Fu. 2020. "Offline Reinforcement Learning: Tutorial, Review, and Perspectives on Open Problems" (*https://oreil.ly/R_vjH*). ArXiv:2005.01643, May.

[5] Chen, Xinyue, Zijian Zhou, Zheng Wang, Che Wang, Yanqiu Wu, and Keith Ross. 2020. "BAIL: Best-Action Imitation Learning for Batch Deep Reinforcement Learning" (*https://oreil.ly/tYOKM*). ArXiv:1910.12179, February.

[6] Dargazany, Aras. 2020. "Model-Based Actor-Critic: GAN + DRL (Actor-Critic) ⇒ AGI" (*https://oreil.ly/UC65B*). ArXiv:2004.04574, April.

[7] Mandlekar, Ajay, Fabio Ramos, Byron Boots, Silvio Savarese, Li Fei-Fei, Animesh Garg, and Dieter Fox. 2020. "IRIS: Implicit Reinforcement without Interaction at Scale for Learning Control from Offline Robot Manipulation Data" (*https://oreil.ly/RP5Q5*). ArXiv:1911.05321, February.

[8] Gulcehre, Caglar, Ziyu Wang, Alexander Novikov, Tom Le Paine, Sergio Gomez Colmenarejo, Konrad Zolna, Rishabh Agarwal, et al. 2020. "RL Unplugged: Benchmarks for Offline Reinforcement Learning" (*https://oreil.ly/Lxpf0*). ArXiv:2006.13888, July.

[9] Banerjee, Bikramjit, Sandip Sen, and Jing Peng. 2004. "On-Policy Concurrent Reinforcement Learning" (*https://oreil.ly/5caMf*). *Journal of Experimental & Theoretical Artificial Intelligence* 16(4): 245–60.

[10] Marthi, Bhaskara, Stuart Russell, David Latham, and Carlos Guestrin. 2005. "Concurrent Hierarchical Reinforcement Learning." *Proceedings of the 19th International Joint Conference on Artificial Intelligence*, 779–785. IJCAI '05. Edinburgh, Scotland: Morgan Kaufmann Publishers Inc.

[11] Silver, David, Leonard Newnham, David Barker, Suzanne Weller, and Jason McFall. 2013. "Concurrent Reinforcement Learning from Customer Interactions" (*https://oreil.ly/BD4R-*). *International Conference on Machine Learning*, 924–32.

[12] Dimakopoulou, Maria, and Benjamin Van Roy. 2018. "Coordinated Exploration in Concurrent Reinforcement Learning" (*https://oreil.ly/Cd72Q*). ArXiv:1802.01282, February.

[13] Han, Weiqiao, Sergey Levine, and Pieter Abbeel. 2015. "Learning Compound Multi-Step Controllers under Unknown Dynamics" (*https://oreil.ly/z2S9L*). *2015 IEEE/RSJ International Conference on Intelligent Robots and Systems (IROS)*, 6435–6442.

[14] Richter, Charles, and Nicholas Roy. 2017. "Safe Visual Navigation via Deep Learning and Novelty Detection" (*https://oreil.ly/C6Bi_*). MIT Web Domain, July.

[15] Eysenbach, Benjamin, Shixiang Gu, Julian Ibarz, and Sergey Levine. 2017. "Leave No Trace: Learning to Reset for Safe and Autonomous Reinforcement Learning" (*https://oreil.ly/p2nwJ*). ArXiv:1711.06782, November.

[16] Zhu, Henry, Justin Yu, Abhishek Gupta, Dhruv Shah, Kristian Hartikainen, Avi Singh, Vikash Kumar, and Sergey Levine. 2020. "The Ingredients of Real-World Robotic Reinforcement Learning" (*https://oreil.ly/kaodL*). ArXiv:2004.12570, April.

[17] Brockman, Greg, Vicki Cheung, Ludwig Pettersson, Jonas Schneider, John Schulman, Jie Tang, and Wojciech Zaremba. 2016. "OpenAI Gym" (*https://oreil.ly/tnnqe*). ArXiv:1606.01540, June.

[18] Ruiz, Nataniel, Samuel Schulter, and Manmohan Chandraker. 2019. "Learning to Simulate" (*https://oreil.ly/jwxX0*). ArXiv:1810.02513, May.

[19] Kalashnikov, Dmitry, Alex Irpan, Peter Pastor, Julian Ibarz, Alexander Herzog, Eric Jang, Deirdre Quillen, et al. 2018. "QT-Opt: Scalable Deep Reinforcement Learning for Vision-Based Robotic Manipulation" (*https://oreil.ly/Mchmp*). ArXiv: 1806.10293, November.

[20] Karakovskiy, Sergey, and Julian Togelius. 2012. "The Mario AI Benchmark and Competitions" (*https://oreil.ly/6KKCf*). *IEEE Transactions on Computational Intelligence and AI in Games* 4(1): 55–67.

[21] Ota, Kei, Tomoaki Oiki, Devesh K. Jha, Toshisada Mariyama, and Daniel Nikovski. 2020. "Can Increasing Input Dimensionality Improve Deep Reinforcement Learning?" (*https://oreil.ly/_JNf9*). ArXiv:2003.01629, June.

[22] Hafner, Danijar, Timothy Lillicrap, Jimmy Ba, and Mohammad Norouzi. 2020. "Dream to Control: Learning Behaviors by Latent Imagination" (*https://oreil.ly/2T1oB*). ArXiv:1912.01603, March.

[23] Hafner, Danijar, Timothy Lillicrap, Ian Fischer, Ruben Villegas, David Ha, Honglak Lee, and James Davidson. 2019. "Learning Latent Dynamics for Planning from Pixels" (*https://oreil.ly/fRp2X*). ArXiv:1811.04551, June.

[24] Ha, David, and Jürgen Schmidhuber. 2018. "World Models" (*https://oreil.ly/rrPrn*). ArXiv:1803.10122, March.

[25] Chaudhari, Harshal A., John W. Byers, and Evimaria Terzi. 2020. "Learn to Earn: Enabling Coordination within a Ride Hailing Fleet" (*https://oreil.ly/L57Kf*). ArXiv: 2006.10904, July.

[26] "Value Function Approximation in Reinforcement Learning Using the Fourier Basis" (*https://oreil.ly/FmeN3*). *Proceedings of the Twenty-Fifth AAAI Conference on Artificial Intelligence*. n.d. Accessed 18 July 2020.

[27] Tang, Yunhao, and Shipra Agrawal. 2020. "Discretizing Continuous Action Space for On-Policy Optimization" (*https://oreil.ly/cukso*). ArXiv:1901.10500, March.

[28] Gonzalez-Abril, L., F. J. Cuberos, F. Velasco, and J. A. Ortega. 2009. "Ameva: An Autonomous Discretization Algorithm" (*https://oreil.ly/eb7oY*). Expert Systems with Applications: An International Journal 36 (3): 5327–5332.

[29] Dougherty, James, Ron Kohavi, and Mehran Sahami. 1995. "Supervised and Unsupervised Discretization of Continuous Features." *Proceedings of the Twelfth International Conference on International Conference on Machine Learning*, 194–202. ICML'95. Tahoe City, California, USA: Morgan Kaufmann Publishers Inc.

[30] Seijen, Harm van, Bram Bakker, and L. J. H. M. Kester. 2017. "Switching between Different State Representations in Reinforcement Learning" (*https://oreil.ly/eJ1go*). November.

[31] Ryu, Moonkyung, Yinlam Chow, Ross Anderson, Christian Tjandraatmadja, and Craig Boutilier. 2020. "CAQL: Continuous Action Q-Learning" (*https://oreil.ly/G_AOF*). ArXiv:1909.12397, February.

[32] Xiong, Jiechao, Qing Wang, Zhuoran Yang, Peng Sun, Lei Han, Yang Zheng, Haobo Fu, Tong Zhang, Ji Liu, and Han Liu. 2018. "Parametrized Deep Q-Networks Learning: Reinforcement Learning with Discrete-Continuous Hybrid Action Space" (*https://oreil.ly/z2kSN*). ArXiv:1810.06394, October.

[33] Tavakoli, Arash, Fabio Pardo, and Petar Kormushev. 2019. "Action Branching Architectures for Deep Reinforcement Learning" (*https://oreil.ly/iLcmj*). ArXiv: 1711.08946, January.

[34] Khan, Adil, Jiang Feng, Shaohui Liu, Muhammad Zubair Asghar, and Ling-Ling Li. 2019. "Optimal Skipping Rates: Training Agents with Fine-Grained Control Using Deep Reinforcement Learning" (*https://oreil.ly/GfKDp*). *Journal of Robotics 2019* (January).

[35] Sutton, Richard S., Doina Precup, and Satinder Singh. 1999. "Between MDPs and Semi-MDPs: A Framework for Temporal Abstraction in Reinforcement Learning" (*https://oreil.ly/1iEJc*). *Artificial Intelligence* 112(1): 181–211.

[36] Khetarpal, Khimya, Martin Klissarov, Maxime Chevalier-Boisvert, Pierre-Luc Bacon, and Doina Precup. 2020. "Options of Interest: Temporal Abstraction with Interest Functions" (*https://oreil.ly/KDyb9*). ArXiv:2001.00271, January.

[37] Biedenkapp, A., R. Rajan, F. Hutter, and M. Lindauer. 2020. "Towards TempoRL: Learning When to Act." In *Workshop on Inductive Biases, Invariances and Generalization in RL* (BIG@ICML '20).

[38] Ie, Eugene, Vihan Jain, Jing Wang, Sanmit Narvekar, Ritesh Agarwal, Rui Wu, Heng-Tze Cheng, et al. 2019. "Reinforcement Learning for Slate-Based Recommender Systems: A Tractable Decomposition and Practical Methodology" (*https://oreil.ly/y7Fpd*). ArXiv:1905.12767, May.

[39] Dulac-Arnold, Gabriel, Richard Evans, Hado van Hasselt, Peter Sunehag, Timothy Lillicrap, Jonathan Hunt, Timothy Mann, Theophane Weber, Thomas Degris, and Ben Coppin. 2016. "Deep Reinforcement Learning in Large Discrete Action Spaces" (*https://oreil.ly/BeS1T*). ArXiv:1512.07679, April.

[40] Van de Wiele, Tom, David Warde-Farley, Andriy Mnih, and Volodymyr Mnih. 2020. "Q-Learning in Enormous Action Spaces via Amortized Approximate Maximization" (*https://oreil.ly/Rjmv9*). ArXiv:2001.08116, January.

[41] Mehrotra, Rishabh, Mounia Lalmas, Doug Kenney, Thomas Lim-Meng, and Golli Hashemian. 2019. "Jointly Leveraging Intent and Interaction Signals to Predict User Satisfaction with Slate Recommendations" (*https://oreil.ly/py0m8*). *The World Wide Web Conference*, 1256–1267. WWW 2019. San Francisco, CA, USA: Association for Computing Machinery.

[42] Jiang, Ray, Sven Gowal, Timothy A. Mann, and Danilo J. Rezende. 2019. "Beyond Greedy Ranking: Slate Optimization via List-CVAE" (*https://oreil.ly/aOeNP*). ArXiv: 1803.01682, February.

[43] Metz, Luke, Julian Ibarz, Navdeep Jaitly, and James Davidson. 2019. "Discrete Sequential Prediction of Continuous Actions for Deep RL" (*https://oreil.ly/i7OAG*). ArXiv:1705.05035, June.

[44] Ie, Eugene, Vihan Jain, Jing Wang, Sanmit Narvekar, Ritesh Agarwal, Rui Wu, Heng-Tze Cheng, et al. 2019. "Reinforcement Learning for Slate-Based Recommender Systems: A Tractable Decomposition and Practical Methodology" (*https://oreil.ly/o-qVT*). ArXiv:1905.12767, May.

[45] Kosoy, Eliza, Jasmine Collins, David M. Chan, Sandy Huang, Deepak Pathak, Pulkit Agrawal, John Canny, Alison Gopnik, and Jessica B. Hamrick. 2020. "Exploring Exploration: Comparing Children with RL Agents in Unified Environments" (*https://oreil.ly/dqM6q*). ArXiv:2005.02880, July.

[46] Murphy, Kevin P. 2012. *Machine Learning: A Probabilistic Perspective*. The MIT Press.

[47] Houthooft, Rein, Xi Chen, Yan Duan, John Schulman, Filip De Turck, and Pieter Abbeel. 2017. "VIME: Variational Information Maximizing Exploration" (*https://oreil.ly/fHafR*). ArXiv:1605.09674, January.

[48] Pathak, Deepak, Pulkit Agrawal, Alexei A. Efros, and Trevor Darrell. 2017. "Curiosity-Driven Exploration by Self-Supervised Prediction" (*https://oreil.ly/3a5RL*). ArXiv:1705.05363, May.

[49] Burday, Yuri, Harry Edwards, Deepak Pathak, Amos Storkey, Trevor Darrell, Alexei A. Efros. "Large-Scale Study of Curiosity-Driven Learning" (*https://oreil.ly/9zP22*). n.d. Accessed 22 July 2020.

[50] Burda, Yuri, Harrison Edwards, Amos Storkey, and Oleg Klimov. 2018. "Exploration by Random Network Distillation" (*https://oreil.ly/w3UVl*). ArXiv:1810.12894, October.

[51] Saxe, Andrew M., Pang Wei Koh, Zhenghao Chen, Maneesh Bhand, Bipin Suresh, and Andrew Y. Ng. 2011. "On Random Weights and Unsupervised Feature Learning." *Proceedings of the 28th International Conference on International Conference on Machine Learning*, 1089–1096. ICML '11. Bellevue, Washington, USA: Omnipress.

[52] Savinov, Nikolay, Anton Raichuk, Raphaël Marinier, Damien Vincent, Marc Pollefeys, Timothy Lillicrap, and Sylvain Gelly. 2019. "Episodic Curiosity through Reachability" (*https://oreil.ly/GGuyL*). ArXiv:1810.02274, August.

[53] Zagoruyko, Sergey, and Nikos Komodakis. 2015. "Learning to Compare Image Patches via Convolutional Neural Networks" (*https://oreil.ly/UpYiy*). ArXiv: 1504.03641, April.

[54] Burda, Yuri, Harrison Edwards, Amos Storkey, and Oleg Klimov. 2018. "Exploration by Random Network Distillation" (*https://oreil.ly/w3UVl*). ArXiv:1810.12894, October.

[55] Hasselt, Hado van, Arthur Guez, Matteo Hessel, Volodymyr Mnih, and David Silver. 2016. "Learning Values across Many Orders of Magnitude" (*https://oreil.ly/mTaNn*). ArXiv:1602.07714, August.

[56] Zhu, Henry, Justin Yu, Abhishek Gupta, Dhruv Shah, Kristian Hartikainen, Avi Singh, Vikash Kumar, and Sergey Levine. 2020. "The Ingredients of Real-World Robotic Reinforcement Learning" (*https://oreil.ly/ArO_j*). ArXiv:2004.12570, April.

[57] Trott, Alexander, Stephan Zheng, Caiming Xiong, and Richard Socher. 2019. "Keeping Your Distance: Solving Sparse Reward Tasks Using Self-Balancing Shaped Rewards" (*https://oreil.ly/tNsJD*). ArXiv:1911.01417, November.

[58] Lange, Sascha, Thomas Gabel, and Martin Riedmiller. 2012. "Batch Reinforcement Learning" (*https://oreil.ly/QSSBK*). *Reinforcement Learning: State-of-the-Art*, edited by Marco Wiering and Martijn van Otterlo, 45–73. Adaptation, Learning, and Optimization. Berlin, Heidelberg: Springer.

[59] Levine, Sergey, Aviral Kumar, George Tucker, and Justin Fu. 2020. "Offline Reinforcement Learning: Tutorial, Review, and Perspectives on Open Problems" (*https://oreil.ly/BZxIP*). ArXiv:2005.01643, May.

[60] Wong, Jay M. 2016. "Towards Lifelong Self-Supervision: A Deep Learning Direction for Robotics" (*https://oreil.ly/iIJ-H*). ArXiv:1611.00201, November.

[61] Lesort, Timothée, Natalia Díaz-Rodríguez, Jean-François Goudou, and David Filliat. 2018. "State Representation Learning for Control: An Overview" (*https://oreil.ly/B7LML*). *Neural Networks* 108 (December): 379–92.

[62] Sutton, Richard S., and Andrew G. Barto. 2018. *Reinforcement Learning: An Introduction*. MIT Press.

[63] Dougherty, James, Ron Kohavi, and Mehran Sahami. 1995. "Supervised and Unsupervised Discretization of Continuous Features." *Proceedings of the Twelfth International Conference on International Conference on Machine Learning*, 194–202. ICML'95. Tahoe City, California, USA: Morgan Kaufmann Publishers Inc.

[64] Oudeyer, Pierre-Yves, and Frederic Kaplan. 2007. "What Is Intrinsic Motivation? A Typology of Computational Approaches" (*https://oreil.ly/Hi5yn*). *Frontiers in Neurorobotics*. 1 November.

[65] Russo, Daniel, Benjamin Van Roy, Abbas Kazerouni, Ian Osband, and Zheng Wen. 2020. "A Tutorial on Thompson Sampling" (*https://oreil.ly/t4DUY*). ArXiv: 1707.02038, July.

CHAPTER 10

Operational Reinforcement Learning

The closer you get to deployment, the closer you are to the edge. They call it the cutting edge for good reason. It's hard enough getting your reinforcement learning (RL) project to this point, but production implementations and operational deployment add a whole new set of challenges.

To the best of my knowledge, this is the first time a book has attempted to collate operational RL knowledge in one place. You can find this information scattered throughout the amazing work of the researchers and books from many of the industry's brightest minds, but never in one place.

In this chapter I will walk you through the process of taking your proof of concept into production, by detailing the implementation and deployment phases of an RL project. By the end I hope that these ideas will resonate and you will have a broad enough knowledge to at least get started, and understand what you need to dig in further. With this chapter, and of course the whole book, my goal is to bring RL to industry and demonstrate that production-grade industrial RL is not only possible, but lucrative.

In the first half I review the implementation phase of an RL project, looking deeper into the available frameworks, the abstractions, and how to scale. How to evaluate agents is also prominent here, because it is not acceptable to rely on ad hoc or statistically unsound measures of performance.

The second half is about operational RL and deploying your agent into production. I talk about robust architectures and the necessary tooling you will need to build robust agents. And finally, but possibly most importantly, there is a section about making RL safe, secure, and ethical; make sure you read this.

Implementation

Personally, I find the implementation phase of a machine learning/artificial intelligence/big data/{insert buzzword here} project one of the most fascinating and interesting parts of the whole life cycle. This is the phase where you need to take care in the code that you write because this code might survive for decades, maybe more. GitHub has just created an archive in the Arctic that has stored all active projects on microfilm and is predicted to last at least 1,000 years.[1] Some people are privileged enough to talk about a legacy, but for the vast majority of engineers around the world this is about as good as it gets. If you have ever committed to a reasonably popular GitHub repo, congratulations, people in the year 3000 might read your code.

As humbling as this sounds, the primary reason for quality code is to reduce the maintenance burden. Every line of code adds another source of potential error. You can mitigate the probability of error via simplicity, testing, and more eyes on the code. Another reason for quality code is that it makes it easier to use. Projects can increase in scope quite rapidly, so following fundamental software quality guidelines can help make that transition easier.

The previous topics are not specific to RL; there are a host of excellent software engineering books that I recommend every engineer reads, some of which I suggest in "Further Reading" on page 332. This section concentrates on the aspects that are specific to RL.

Frameworks

One of the fastest ways to develop quality RL applications is to use a framework. Engineers have invested significant amounts of time to make it easier for you to develop your project.

RL frameworks

Open source RL frameworks benefit from the number of people using them. Greater popularity means more testing and more impetus to help refine the project. The ability to inspect the public source code is immensely valuable, especially when you come up against a tricky bug.

The problem with popularity is that it tends to be proportional to the size of the marketing budget and the perceived expertise. For example, any repository that has some relationship with Google (look for the staple "not an official Google product," which generally means it was developed during work time, but is not officially supported) tends to be immensely popular, even when there are few actual users. A similar thing can be suggested for OpenAI, too.

Consider whether the aims of an open source framework align with your goals. For example, many of the frameworks out there are strongly biased toward research, since they were developed by individuals or organizations that are paid to perform research. They are not designed to be used in products or operationally. OpenAI's baselines project (*https://oreil.ly/Zkbbp*) is a classic example of this, which remains one of the most popular RL codebases available, but the open source project Stable Baselines (*https://oreil.ly/4hDLC*), which is far less visible from a marketing perspective, is much easier to use and more robust, in my experience.[2,3]

So what should you look for? This depends on what you are trying to do. If you are looking to rapidly test different algorithms on your problem then you would have different requirements over someone who needs to run a framework in production. You should prioritize and weight factors according to your circumstances and needs, but the following list presents some of the things that I look for:

Abstractions
> Does the framework have good abstractions that make it easier to swap out RL components? Like policy models, exploration techniques, replay buffer types, and so on. How easily can you develop new ones that suit your problem? This tends to be the most difficult to evaluate, because you really don't know until you try it.

Simplicity
> Is the codebase simple enough to navigate around? Does it make sense and is it intuitive? Or is it so large or have so many abstractions that you need weeks just to figure out how to install it?

Observability
> Does it include logging and monitoring? If not, is it easy to add when you need it?

Scalability
> Can it scale when you need it to?

Minimal dependencies
> How dependent is it on other software? Is it locked into a particular framework, like a specific deep learning library? If so, do you approve of the underlying libraries?

Documentation and examples
> Is the project well documented? Not just API documentation: are there examples? Are they up-to-date and tested? Is there architecture documentation? Use case documentation? Algorithm documentation?

Included algorithms
> Does it come with algorithm implementations baked in? Are these well covered by tests and examples? How easy is it to switch out algorithms?

Ancillary algorithms

Does it come with code for a wide variety of other situations, like inverse RL, hierarchical learning, different replay buffer implementations, or exploration algorithms, and so on?

Support

Is there support? Is there a community? Is it well represented on crowd-sourced self-help websites? Is the support pleasant or aggressive?

Commercial offerings

Is it backed by a company (not necessarily a good thing, but at least you should be able to talk to someone)? Is there an opportunity to receive commercial support?

There are a variety of RL frameworks available, all placing emphasis on different elements in this list. Software evolves quickly and any comments about specific frameworks would be quickly out of date. Instead, please visit the accompanying website (*https://rl-book.com/rl-frameworks*) to find an up-to-date review of many RL frameworks.

Other frameworks

Alone, an RL framework is not enough. You will need a variety of other frameworks to build a solution. Many parts of an RL algorithm have been abstracted away, like the various deep learning frameworks used in policy models and value approximations. PyTorch (*https://pytorch.org*) and TensorFlow (*https://oreil.ly/01Uno*) tend to be the most common, of which I tend to prefer PyTorch because of its simpler and intuitive API, but the Keras (*https://keras.io*) API can help overcome that. Most deep learning frameworks are mature and have similar feature sets, but their APIs are quite different. It is a significant source of lock-in, so choose carefully.

There are also an increasing number of libraries that abstract other common components of RL. For example, experience replay is important for many algorithms. Reverb (*https://oreil.ly/CxJAZ*) is a queuing library that was specifically designed to handle implementations like prioritized experience replay.[4] Apache Bookkeeper (*https://oreil.ly/1RM4z*) (a distributed ledger) is an example of a production-grade tool that could be leveraged as part of an operational architecture as a log.

I do want to stress that you need to think carefully about an operational architecture and evaluate what tools are available to help solve that problem (see "Architecture" on page 319). You can find more up-to-date information about tooling on the website (*https://rl-book.com*) that accompanies this book.

Scaling RL

Complex domains are harder to solve so they need more complex models and sophisticated exploration. This translates to increased computational complexity, to the point where it becomes infeasible to train an agent on a single machine.

During development, the feedback cycle time is the most important metric to monitor, because all the time you are waiting for a result is time not spent improving the agent. You can run experiments in parallel but this has a limited impact at this point (see "Experiment tracking" on page 323). In the early phases of RL research the largest improvements come from rapid, repeated improvement cycles. So I recommend that you initially constrain the scope of your work by oversimplifying the problem, using simulations, and massively reducing the complexity of your models. When you have working code, you can scale up.

But how do you scale up? Unlike other machine learning techniques, providing more horsepower doesn't necessarily improve training speed or performance. The following is a list of reasons why you need dedicated algorithms to scale RL:

Sequential
An agent's actions have to be ordered, which makes it difficult to scale an individual agent across machines.

Combining experience
If you use multiple agents, then they need synchronizing, otherwise you'd end up with many independent copies that aren't capable of sharing experience. *When* you synchronize can have a big impact on training speed and aggregate performance. Network bandwidth and latency can also become a problem.

Independence
Agent independence means that some agents may get stuck or never end, which can cause blocking if the synchronization is waiting for agents to finish.

Environment complexity
Some environments are so complex, like 3D simulators, that they themselves need acceleration, which can cause GPU contention if not intelligently orchestrated.

Cost efficiency
Scaling can be expensive, so you want to be sure you fully utilize the hardware. Creating architectures and algorithms that better leverage the benefits of both GPU and CPU computation is necessary.

The last item, cost, is a big problem in machine learning in general. For example, OpenAI's recent GPT-3 language model (*https://oreil.ly/KtNHP*) would cost in the range of $10 million to train from scratch at the current cloud vendor's list prices. And that's assuming a single run. Imagine the horror when you find a bug!

This is obviously an extreme example. A recent paper by Espeholt et al. measured the cost of running 1 billion frames in the DeepMind Lab and Google Research Football environments. Both environments provide 3D simulation for a range of tasks. They tested two algorithms called IMPALA and SEED (discussed shortly) and found that the total cost for a single run (one billion frames) was $236 and $54 for DeepMind Lab and $899 and $369 for Google Research Football, respectively. These aren't astronomical figures, in the context of an enterprise IT project, but they are worth considering.[5]

Distributed training (Gorila)

Early attempts at scaling RL concentrated on creating parallel actors to better leverage multicore machines or multimachine clusters. One of the earliest was the *general reinforcement learning architecture* (Gorila), which was demonstrated with a distributed version of deep Q-networks (DQN), based upon a distributed system for training neural networks called *DistBelief*.[6,7] DistBelief consists of two main components: a centralized parameter server and model replicas. The centralized parameter server maintains and serves a master copy of the model and is responsible for updating the model (with new gradients) from the replicas. The replicas, spread out across cores or machines, are responsible for calculating the gradients for a given batch of data, sending them to the parameter server, and periodically obtaining a new model. To use this architecture in an RL setting, Gorila makes the following changes. The centralized parameter server maintains and serves the model parameters (which are dependent on the chosen RL algorithm). Actor processes obtain the current model and generate rollouts in the environment. Their experience is stored in a centralized replay buffer (if appropriate for the algorithm). Learner processes use the sampled trajectories to learn new gradients and hand them back to the parameter server. The benefit of this architecture is that it provides the flexibility to scale the parts of the learning process that pose a bottleneck. For example, if you have an environment that is computationally expensive, then you can scale the number of actor processes. Or if you have a large model and training is the bottleneck, then you can scale the number of learners. Figure 10-1 depicts these two architectures in a component diagram.

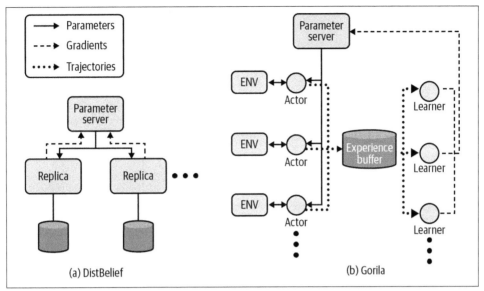

Parameters

Gradients

Trajectories

Parameter server

Replica   Replica   • • •

(a) DistBelief

Parameter server

ENV   Actor

ENV   Actor   Experience buffer   Learner

ENV   Actor   Learner

Learner

(b) Gorila

Figure 10-1. A component diagram summarizing the architecture for (a) DistBelief and (b) Gorila. Gorila enables scaling by separating the tasks of acting and learning and then replicating.

Single-machine training (A3C, PAAC)

Using Gorila in the Atari environments led to superior performance over 20 times faster (wall-clock time) than DQN alone, but researchers found that a distributed architecture, although flexible, required fast networks; transferring trajectories and synchronizing parameters started to become a bottleneck. To limit the communication cost and simplify the architecture, researchers demonstrated that parallelizing using a single multicore machine is a viable alternative in an algorithm called *asynchronous advantage actor-critic* (A3C).[8] This is a parallel version of the advantage actor-critic algorithm (A2C). Since updates reside within the same machine, the learners can share memory, which greatly reduces the communication overhead due to speedy RAM read/writes. Interestingly, they don't use a lock when writing to shared memory across threads, which is typically an incredibly dangerous thing to do, using a technique called *Hogwild*.[9] They find that the updates are sparse and stochastic, so overwrites and contention isn't a problem. Figure 10-2 shows the differences between A2C and A3C algorithms, which both run on a single machine.

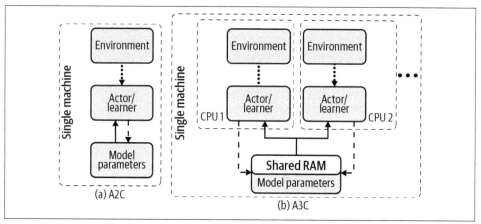

Figure 10-2. A component diagram summarizing the architecture for (a) A2C and (b) A3C. Both algorithms run on a single machine, but A3C uses multiple threads with replicated agents that write to a shared memory.

Surprisingly, using a single machine with 16 CPU cores with no GPU, A3C obtained comparable results to Gorila in one-eighth of the time (1 day) and better results in about half the time (4 days). This clearly demonstrates that synchronization and communication overheads are a big problem.

The simplicity of not using GPUs holds A3C back. It is very likely that a GPU will speed up training of anything "deep," for greater cost, of course. The *parallel advantage actor critic* (PAAC) implementation, which isn't a great name because you can use this architecture with any RL algorithm, brings back the ability to use a GPU. It uses a single learner thread, which is able to use a single attached GPU, and many actors in as many environments. In a sense, this is an intentionally less scalable version of both Gorila and A3C, but it produces comparable results to A3C in one-eighth of the time (again!) creating efficient policies for many Atari games in about 12 hours, depending on the neural network architecture. This implementation shows that increasing exploration through independent environments is a very good way of decreasing the wall-clock training time; training time is proportional to the amount of the state-action space you can explore. Similar to A3C, this implementation demonstrates that data transfer and synchronization is a bottleneck and if your problem allows, you will benefit from keeping the components as close to each other as possible, preferably inside the same physical machine. This is simple, too, in the sense that there are no orchestration or networking concerns. But obviously this architecture might not fit all problems. Figure 10-3 presents this architecture.[10]

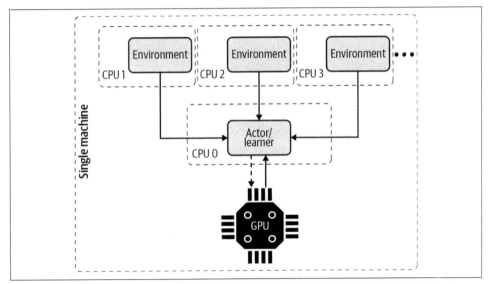

Figure 10-3. A component diagram summarizing the architecture for PAAC. A single machine with a GPU and many CPUs is used to scale the number of environments.

Distributed replay (Ape-X)

Using other types of replay buffer in a distributed setting is as simple as augmenting Gorila's (or other's) architecture. *Ape-X* is one such example, in which greater exploration via distributed actors with environments led to better results, because more diverse experiences were collected. Performance measures on Atari environments were approximately three times greater than AC3 and four times greater than Gorila. But these scores were trained on 16 times the number of CPUs (256 versus 16 for A3C), which led to two orders of magnitude more interaction with the environment. It is unclear whether there was a difference in performance when using the same number of environments/CPUs.[11]

Synchronous distribution (DD-PPO)

Attempting to use a single machine with many CPUs for training an RL algorithm, like in PAAC or AC3, is enticing due to the simplicity of the architecture. But the lack of GPUs becomes a limiting factor when your problem uses 3D simulators that need GPUs for performance reasons. Similarly, a single parameter server with a single GPU, like in Gorila or PAAC/AC3, becomes a limiting factor when you attempt to train massive deep learning architectures, like *ResNet50*, for example. These factors call for a distributed architecture that is capable of leveraging multiple GPUs.

The goal of *decentralized distributed proximal policy optimization* (DD-PPO) is to decentralize learning, much like decentralized, cooperative multi-agent RL. This architecture alternates between collecting experience and optimizing the model and then synchronously communicating with other workers to distribute updates to the model (the gradients). The workers use a distributed parallel gradient update from PyTorch and combine the gradients through a simple aggregation of all other workers. The results show that DD-PPO is able to scale GPU performance by increasing the number of workers almost linearly, tested up to 256 workers/GPUs. The primary issue with this implementation is that the update cannot occur until all agents have collected their batch. To alleviate this blocking, Wijmans et al. implemented a preemptive cutoff, which forces a proportion of stragglers to quit early. Figure 10-4 summarizes this architecture and Wijmans et al. suggest that it is feasible to implement any RL algorithm.[12] Other researchers have suggested a similar architecture.[13]

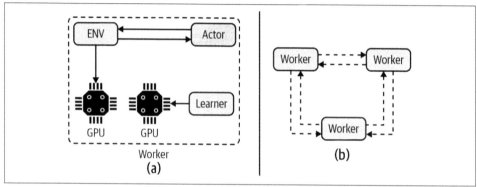

Figure 10-4. A component diagram summarizing the architecture for DD-PPO. A worker (a) comprises an environment, actor, and learner that are able to leverage GPUs. (b) After the agent collects a batch of data each worker performs a distributed update to share weights.

Improving utilization (IMPALA, SEED)

Importance weighted actor-learner architecture (IMPALA) is like a combination of Gorila and DD-PPO. The key advancement is that it uses a queue to remove the need for synchronizing updates. The actor repeatedly rolls out experience and pushes the data into a queue. A separate machine (or cluster of machines) reads off the queue and retrains the model. This means that the update is off-policy; the learner is using data from the past. So IMPALA uses a modified version of the retrace algorithm (see "Retrace(λ)" on page 182) to compensate for the lag in policy updates. This also enables the use of a replay buffer, which improves performance.

Espeholt et al. demonstrate that the basic off-policy actor-critic (see "Off-Policy Actor-Critics" on page 151) works almost as well, which implies that more sophisticated versions like TD3 might work better. Indeed, OpenAI used an IMPALA-inspired framework with PPO for its Dota 2 video game competition.[14]

Single learners with multiple actors typically run on a single machine. You can duplicate the architecture to increase the number of learners and use distributed training like DD-PPO. This architecture, depicted in Figure 10-5, improves training speed by an order of magnitude compared to A3C, but is proportional to the amount of hardware in the cluster (they used 8 GPUs in their experiments). Espeholt et al. also claim that this architecture can be scaled to thousands of machines.[15]

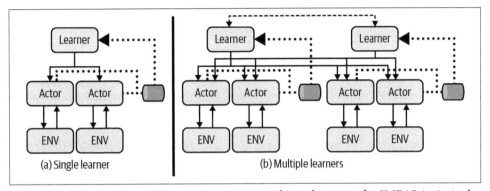

Figure 10-5. A component diagram summarizing the architecture for IMPALA. A single learner (a) has multiple actors (typically on the same machine). Actors fill a queue and training is performed independently of the actors. When using multiple learners (b) gradients are distributed and trained synchronously (like DD-PPO).

Although IMPALA is efficient and is capable of state-of-the-art results, there are still parts of the architecture that can be optimized. One problem is the communicating of the neural network parameters. In large networks these are represented by up to billions of floats, which is a large amount of data to transfer. Observations, on the other hand, are typically much smaller, so it might be more efficient to communicate observations and actions. Also, environments and actors have different requirements, so it could be inefficient to colocate them on the same CPU or GPU. For example, the actor might need a GPU for quick prediction, but the environment only needs a CPU (or vice versa). This means that for much of the time the GPU won't be utilized.

Scalable and efficient deep RL with accelerated central inference (SEED) aims for an architecture where environments are distributed, but request actions from a central, distributed model. This keeps the model parameters close to the model and allows you to choose hardware that maps directly to either environment simulation or model training and prediction. This leads to increased utilization and slightly faster training times (approximately half the time under similar conditions). Figure 10-6 depicts a simplified version of the architecture.[16]

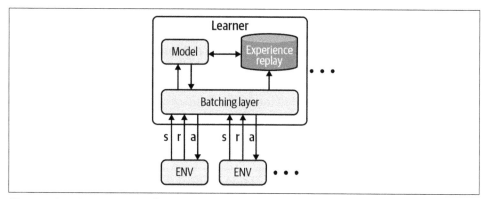

Figure 10-6. A component diagram summarizing the architecture for SEED RL. Hardware is allocated according to the need of the model or environment.

One interesting aspect of the SEED paper is that it highlights how coupled the architecture is to performance. In order to generate their results the researchers had to treat the number of environments per CPU *and* the number of CPUs as hyperparameters. In general more replicas produced higher scores in less time, but precise configurations are probably environment dependent and therefore hard to pinpoint. Another point to make is that SEED goes to great lengths to optimize on a software level, too, using a binary communication protocol (gRPC) and compiled C++.

Both IMPALA and SEED are capable of running on a single machine, like A3C and PAAC, and are generally more performant due to higher utilization.

Scaling conclusions

The previous algorithms achieve state-of-the-art results in a short period of time. But these comparisons are made on toy environments—the Atari environment, mostly, but sometimes more continuous environments like `Google Research Football`. You can extrapolate results from these environments to real-life scenarios, but the reality is you are going to have to do your own testing to be sure.

Researchers have a lot of experience with these environments, so they don't have to waste too much time tuning them and they already know the pitfalls to look out for. But they also aim for headline results, like state-of-the-art performance or speed. There is a hyper-focus on utilization and uber-scale and that sometimes comes at a cost. For example, having a fully distributed deployment like DD-PPO might actually be better for operational use because it would be easy to make it self-healing (just form a cluster of some number of distributed components), which increases robustness and high-availability. This might not be of interest for your application, but my point is that fastest isn't always best. There are other important aspects, too.

Similarly, you can start to see diminishing returns, too. Early improvements yielded a reduction of an order of magnitude in training speed. The difference between IMPALA and SEED was about half. Researchers are having to go into increasing depth to extract more performance, like statically compiling code and using binary protocols. Again, this may not be appropriate for your problem. If you had to write code in C++ rather than Python, for example, the cost of your time or the opportunity loss may be greater than the gains obtained through code-level optimization.

Finally, some of these architectures tend to blur the abstractions that have emerged in the frameworks. It is common to have abstractions for agents, environments, replay buffers, and the like, but these architectures enforce locations for these abstractions, which might not be ideal from a design perspective. For example, bundling the model, the training, the replay buffer, and some custom batching logic into the learner in the SEED architecture could get messy. It would have been great if they were physically distinct components, like distributed queues and ledgers. Obviously there is nothing stopping you from implementing something like that, but it is generally not a priority for this kind of performance-driven research.

Evaluation

To add value to a product, service, or strategy, you and your stakeholders need to carefully consider what you are trying to achieve. This sounds abstract and high level, but it is too easy to work hard on a problem only to find that the thing that you are optimizing for doesn't fit the goal. The reason is that engineers can forget, or even ignore, to connect their work back to the objective.

Psychologists and neurologists have studied multitasking at great depth. They found that humans have a limited amount of mental energy to spend on tasks and that switching between several severely impacts performance. But when working on engineering problems, switching between abstraction levels is just as difficult. Your brain has to unload the current stack of thought, save it to short-term memory, load up a new mental model for a different abstraction level, and start the thought process. This switching, along with the effort of maintaining your short-term memory, is mentally taxing. This is one reason why it is easier to ignore high-level objectives when working on low-level day-to-day challenges.

Another reason, even after the dawn of DevOps, is that engineering is deemed to be successful when forward progress is made: new products, new features, better performance, and so on. Moving backward is viewed as a lack of progress; I want to make it clear that it is not. "Going back to the drawing board" is not a sign of failure, it is a sign that you have learned important lessons that you are now exploiting to design a better solution.

Even though it can be hard, try to take time to move around the development process, and up and down through abstraction layers to make sure they are all aligned toward the goal you are trying to achieve.

 Here's one trick that I use to force myself to switch abstractions or contexts: ask the question "Why?" to move up an abstraction layer and ask the question "How?" to move down.

Coming back to the task at hand, when evaluating your work, you should initially ask *why* you want to measure performance. Is this to explain results to your stakeholders? Or is it to make it more efficient? Answers to this question will help direct *how* you want to implement.

Policy performance measures

The efficacy of an RL agent can be described by two abstract metrics: *policy performance* and *learning performance*. Policy performance is a measure of how well the policy solves your problem. Ideally, you should use units that map to the problem domain. Learning performance measures how fast you can train an agent to yield an optimal policy.

In a problem with a *finite horizon*, which means there is a terminating state, the policy performance is most naturally represented by the sum of the reward. This is the classic description of an optimal policy. In *infinite-horizon* problems you can include discounting to prevent rewards tending to infinity. Discounting is often used in finite problems, too, which might lead to a subtly different policy, so you should consider removing it when you compute the final performance measure. For example, your stakeholders are probably not interested in discounted profit; they want to talk about profit.

Another option is the maximization and measurement of average rewards. In the *average-reward* model, you have to be careful to ensure that the mean is a suitable summary statistic for your distribution of rewards. For example, if your reward is sparse, then an average reward is a poor summary statistic. Instead, you could choose other summary statistics that are more stable, like the median or some percentile. If your rewards conform to a specific distribution, then you might want to use parameters of that distribution.

Measuring how fast an agent can learn an optimal policy is also an important metric. It defines your feedback cycle time, so if you use an algorithm that can learn quicker you can iterate and improve faster. In problems where agents learn online, for example if you are fine-tuning policies for specific individuals, learning quickly is important to mitigate the cost of missing an opportunity due to suboptimal policies.

The simplest measure of training performance is the amount of time it takes for the agent to reach optimality. Optimality is usually an asymptotic result, however, so the *speed of convergence to near-optimality* is a better description. You can arbitrarily define what constitutes "near" for your problem, but you should set it according to the amount of noise in your reward score; you may need to perform averaging to reduce the noise.

You can define time in a few different ways, depending on what is important to your problem. For simulations, using the number of steps in the environment is a good temporal measure because it is independent of confounders and environment interactions tend to be expensive. Wall-clock time could be used if you are concerned about feedback cycle time and can limit the number of environment interactions. The number of model training steps is an interesting temporal dimension to analyze model training performance. And computational time can be important if you want to improve the efficiency of an algorithm.

Your choice of temporal dimension depends on what you are trying to achieve. For example, you might initially use environment steps to improve the sample efficiency. Then you might start looking at wall-clock time when you are ready to speed up training. Finally, you might squeeze out any remaining performance by looking at process time. Typically you would use all of these dimensions to gather a broad picture of performance.

Regret is used in online machine learning to measure of the total difference between the reward if an agent was behaving optimally in hindsight and the actual reward obtained over all time. It is a positive value that represents the area between the optimal episodic reward and the actual, as shown in Figure 10-7. Imagine you run a solar power plant. The total amount of power you generate in an episode, which might be one day, has a fixed maximum that is dependent on the amount of sun and the conversion efficiency of the solar panels. But you are training a policy to alter the pitch of the panels to maximize power output. The regret, in this case, would be the difference between the theoretical maximum power output and the result of the actions of your policy summed over a period of time.

Regret has been used by researchers as a mathematical tool during the formulation of policy algorithms, where the policy optimizes to limit the regret. This often takes the form of a regularization term or some adaptation of the rewards to promote statistically efficient exploration (see "Delayed Q-Learning" on page 74, for example). Regret is important conceptually, too, since humans reuse experience to infer causation and question the utility of long-term decisions.[17]

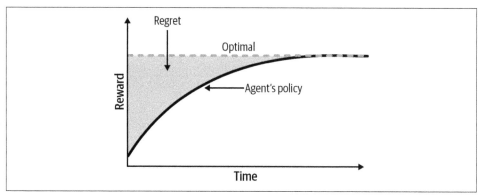

Figure 10-7. A depiction of how to calculate regret while training a policy over time. Regret is the shaded area.

You can use regret as a measurement of performance, too, but how you decide what the optimal policy is, even in hindsight, is dependent on the training circumstances. You might not be able to obtain a theoretically optimal policy or it may not be stationary, for example. If the policies are operating in a nonstationary environment, then approaches include attempting to calculate the regret within a small interval. In simpler problems you might be able to, in hindsight, establish what the best action was and use that as the optimal reward. In more complex problems you should be able to use another algorithm as a baseline and make all comparisons to that. If possible, you could use self-play to record the opponent's positions and then after the game has finished see if there were better actions you could have played. There isn't yet a simple unified method of calculating regret for any problem.

Statistical policy comparisons

Whenever you are making comparisons I always recommend that you visualize first. Statistics is full of caveats and assumptions and it's very easy to think that you are doing the right thing, only to have someone more mathematically inclined say that what you did only makes sense in a very specific circumstances. Visualizing performance is much easier because it is intuitive. You can leverage visual approximations and models that you have learned throughout your life. For example, fitting a linear regression model by eye, even with noise and outliers, is much easier for humans than the mathematics suggest. Similarly, comparing the performance of two algorithms is as simple as plotting two metrics against each other and deciding which is consistently better than the other.

However, there are times when you do need statistical evidence that one algorithm is better than another. If you want to automate the search for a better model, for example, then you don't want to have to look at thousands of plots. Or if you want a yes/no answer (given caveats!). Here is a list of possible statistical tests with brief notes of their assumptions when comparing two distributions:

Student's t-test
> Assumes normal distributions and equal variances.

Welch's t-test
> Same as Student's but relaxes equal variance assumption.

Wilcoxon Mann-Whitney rank sum test
> Compares medians, is nonparametric, therefore no assumption on distribution shapes. But does assume they are continuous and have the same shape and spread.

Ranked t-test
> Compares medians, are ranked and then fed into t-test. Results are essentially the same as the Wilcoxon Mann-Whitney rank sum test.

Bootstrap confidence interval test
> Randomly samples from distributions, measures difference in percentiles, and repeats many times. Requires very large sample size, approximately greater than 10^3. No other assumptions.

Permutation test
> Randomly samples from distributions, randomly assigns them to hypotheses, and measures the difference in percentiles, and repeats many times. Similar to the bootstrap confidence interval test but instead tests to see if they are the same, to some confidence level. Requires very large sample sizes again.

You can see that there are a lot of varied assumptions, which make it really easy to accidentally use the wrong test. And when you do, they fail silently. The results won't show you that you have done something wrong. So it's really important to have strong expectations when performing these tests. If the results don't make sense, you've probably made a mistake.

What are the problems with these statistical assumptions?

- RL often produces results that are not normal. For example, an agent can get stuck in a maze 1 in 100 times and produce an outlier.

- Rewards may be truncated. For example, there may be a hard maximum reward that results in discontinuity in the distribution of results.

- The standard deviations of the runs are not equal between algorithms and may not even be stationary. For example, different algorithms might use different exploration techniques that lead to different variations in results. And within the evaluation of a single algorithm, there may be some fluke occurrence like a bird flying into a robotic arm.

Colas et al. wrote an excellent paper on statistical testing specifically for comparing RL algorithms. They compare the performance of TD3 and SAC on the Half-Cheetah-v2 environment and find that they need to rerun each training at least 15 times to get statistically significant evidence that SAC is better than TD3 (on that environment). They suggest that for this environment, rewards tend to be somewhat normal so Welch's t-test tends to be the most robust for small numbers of samples. The nonparametric tests have the least assumptions but require large sample sizes to approach the power of assuming a distribution.[18] They also have a useful repository (*https://oreil.ly/b_ZeC*) that you can leverage in your experiments.

You might be asking, "What does he mean by rerun?" That's a good question. If you read through enough papers on RL algorithms you will eventually see a common evaluation theme. Researchers repeat an experiment 5 or 10 times then plot the learning curves, where one experiment represents a full retrain of the algorithm on a single environment. Upon each repeat they alter the *random seed* of the various random number generators.

This sounds simple but I've found it to be quite tricky in practice. If you use the same seed on the same algorithm it should, in theory, produce the same results. But often it doesn't. Usually I find that there is yet another random generator somewhere buried within the codebase that I haven't set. If you train an algorithm using a typical set of RL libraries then you have to set the seed on the random number generators for Python, Numpy, Gym, your deep learning framework (potentially in several places), in the RL framework, and in any other framework you might be using, like a replay buffer. So first check that you can get exactly the same result on two runs. Then you can repeat the training multiple times with different values for the random seed. This produces a range of performance curves that are (hopefully) normally distributed.

The problem is that researchers tend to use a small, fixed number of repeats because training is expensive. If there is a large separation between the two distributions then a small sample, just enough to be confident of the mean and standard deviation, is adequate. But when the difference in performance is much smaller, you need a much larger sample size to be confident that performance is different. Another paper by Colas et al. suggests that you should run a pilot study to estimate the standard deviation of an algorithm, then use that to estimate the final number of trials required to prove that it outperforms the other algorithm, to a specified significance level.[19]

Finally, statistical performance measures are one way of quantifying how robust a policy is. The standard deviation of an obtained reward is a good indication of whether your policy will survive the natural drift of observations that occur so often in real life. But I would recommend taking this a step further, actively perturbing states, models, and actions to see how robust the policy really is. Adversarial techniques are useful here, because if you can't break your model, this makes it less likely that real life will break your model, too—life breaks everything eventually.[20]

Algorithm performance measures

I would suggest that in most industrial problems you have a single or a small number of problems to target and therefore a small number of environments. However, if you are more involved in pure research or you are trying to adapt your implementation to generalize over different problems, then you should consider more abstract performance measures that explain how well it performs at RL-specific challenges.

One of the most useful solutions so far is the *behavior suite* (*https://oreil.ly/HLb_0*) by Osband et al. They describe seven fundamental RL challenges: credit assignment, basic (a competency test, like bandit problems), scalability, noise, memory, generalization, and exploration. An agent is tested against a handpicked set of environments that correspond to the challenge. The agent then receives a final aggregated score for each challenge that can be represented in a radar plot, like in Figure 10-8.[21]

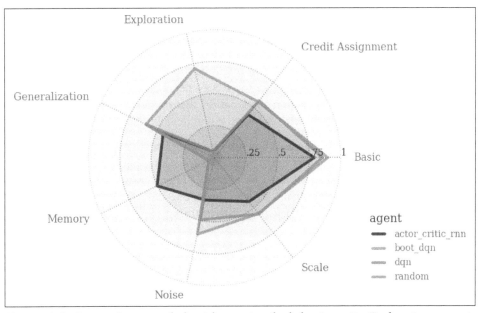

Figure 10-8. Comparing several algorithms using the behavior suite. Each axis represents a different RL challenge. Note how the random agent performs poorly on all challenges and standard DQN performs well on many except for exploration and memory. Used under license, Apache 2.0.

Problem-specific performance measures

There are also a range of benchmarks available for domain-specific tasks, or for tasks that have a particularly tricky problem. For example, there are benchmarks for offline RL (*https://oreil.ly/i6csS*), robotics (*https://oreil.ly/N27IC*), and safety (*https://oreil.ly/008IE*).[22,23,24] Many more excellent benchmarks exist.

These can be useful when you know you also have the same generic problem in your domain and can be confident that improvements in the benchmarks translate to better performance in the real world.

Explainability

An emerging phase in the data science process is *explainability*, often abbreviated to *explainable artificial intelligence* (XAI), where you would use techniques to attempt to describe how and why a model made a decision. Some algorithms, like tree-based models, have an inherent ability to provide an explanation whereas others, like standard neural networks, must rely on *black-box* approaches, where you would probe with known inputs and observe what happens at the output.

Explainability is important for several reasons. One is trust; you shouldn't put anything into production that you don't trust. In software engineering this trust is established through tests, but the complexity of models and RL means that the "coverage" is always going to be low. Another reason might be that there is a regulatory or commercial reason to explain decisions like the EU General Data Protection Regulation or Facebook's post recommendation explanation feature. Being able to explain an action or decision can also help with debugging and development.

Explainability is harder in RL than in machine learning because agents select sequential actions whose effects interact and compound over long periods. Some RL algorithms have an intrinsic capability to explain. Hierarchical RL, for example, decomposes policies into subpolicies, which combine to describe high-level behavior. But most research focuses on black-box, post-training explainability, because it is more generally applicable.

The black-box techniques tend to operate on either a global or local level. Global methods attempt to derive and describe the behavior at all states, whereas local methods can only explain particular decisions.

Global methods tend to consist of training other, simpler models that are inherently explainable, like tree or linear models. For example, the *linear model U-trees* model uses a tree structure to represent a value function, with linear approximators at the leaf of each tree to improve generalization. From this model you can extract feature importance and indicative actions for all of the state space.[25]

Local methods comprise two main ideas. The word "local" is usually meant to denote a global method evaluated in a small region of the state space. For example, Yoon et al. use RL to guide the process that trains the local approximation.[26] Other ideas expand upon the predictive nature of global methods by considering the *counterfactual*, the opposite action or what could have happened. Madumal et al. achieve this by training a model to represent a causal graph that approximates the environment transition dynamics. This sounds promising but only works with discrete states.[27]

Similar to explaining decisions, it can also be useful to indicate what parts of the state influence a decision. For problems with visual observations, or states that have some notion of position or adjacency, you can use *saliency maps* to highlight regions that are important to action selection.[28]

Evaluation conclusions

Evaluation is an inherent part of life, from karate belts to food critics. In industrial applications, evaluating your work helps you decide when you are finished. In software engineering, this is usually when acceptance tests have passed. In machine learning acceptable performance is often defined by an evaluation metric. But in RL, because of the strategic nature of the decisions being made, it is very hard to state when enough is enough. You can always make more profit, you can always save more lives.

In general, the performance of an agent is defined by the reward obtained by the policy and how fast it got there. But there are a range of other measures that you should also consider if you want to train and utilize a stable, robust policy in a production situation. This also includes the ability to explain the decisions of a policy, which could be vitally important in high-impact applications.

Deployment

By *deployment*, I refer to the phase where you are productionizing or operationalizing your application. Projects come to a point where everyone agrees that they are both viable and valuable, but to continue being viable and valuable they need to be reliable. This section is about how to take your budding RL proof of concept into the big league so that you can serve real users.

The tricky part is that there isn't much prior work on running RL (RL) applications operationally. So much of this has to be extrapolated from running software and machine learning applications, my experience running Winder Research, and the many luminaries who have penned their own experiences.

Goals

Before I dig into the details of deployment, I think it is important to consider the goals of this phase of the process. This will help you focus on your situation and help you decide what is important to you, because no one idea or architecture is going to suit all situations.

Goals during different phases of development

First, consider how the deployment priorities change depending on what phase of development you are in. There are three phases where you need to be able to deploy an agent: during development, hardening, and production.

During development it is important to have an architecture that allows you to rapidly test new ideas; flexibility and speed trumps all other needs. This is because during early phases of a project it is important to prove the potential viability and value. It is not important to be infinitely scalable or exactly repeatable; that comes later. The largest gains come from rapid and diverse experimentation, so the largest cost at this point in time is the length of that feedback loop.

Once a project has proven to be viable and valuable, then it goes through a phase of hardening. This involves improving the robustness of the processes involved in maintaining a policy. For example, offline policies or ancillary models must be trained, which may require large amounts of computational resource, and the provenance (the origin of) of a codebase or model is vital to ensure you know what will be running in production.

Finally, policies and models are deployed to production and used by real people or processes. Because RL optimizes sequences of actions, it is highly unlikely that you will be able to retrain your policy by batching data once every so often, which is the predominant technique used in production machine learning systems, so care must be taken to preserve the state of the policy. This phase encourages the development and adoption of sophisticated monitoring and feedback mechanisms, because it is so easy for the policy to diverge (or at least not converge).

When deploying an RL solution into a product or service, the value of performing a task changes. Early on, the quickest way to extract value is through rapid experimentation and research; later on reliability, performance, and robustness become more important. This leads to a range of best practices that are important at different times.

Best practices

Machine learning operations (MLOps) is an emerging description of the best practices and appropriate tooling that is required to run production-quality models. The need for this has arisen because machine learning models have different operational requirements compared to traditional software projects, but fundamentally the core needs are exactly the same. I like to summarize these needs into three topics: reliability, scalability, and flexibility.

Reliability lies at the core of modern software engineering. Thousands of books have been written on the topic and these ideas are directly applicable to machine learning and RL, ideas like testing, continuous integration and delivery, architecture, and design. Moving toward machine learning, ideas such as building data pipelines, provenance, and repeatability all aim to solidify and further guarantee that models will continue to work into the future. RL poses its own challenges and over time I expect new best practices to emerge.

For example, I caught up with an old colleague recently and I was asking about some previous projects that we collaborated on. I had developed some algorithms to perform traffic and congestion monitoring around 2012 and these had been deployed to some major roads in the UK on dedicated hardware. I learned that the hardware had failed twice but my algorithms (in Java!) were still going strong, nearly 10 years later. This fact isn't due to my algorithms, it is due to my colleagues' software engineering expertise and a commitment to reliable software.

Scalability is particularly important to both machine learning and RL, arguably more so than typical software, because they need so much horsepower to do their job. If you consider all software ever written, the vast majority of those applications will probably run on the resources provided by a standard laptop. Only rarely do you need to build something that is as scalable as a global messaging or banking system. But in machine learning and RL, nearly every single product ever produced needs far more than what a laptop can provide. I posit that the average computational requirement for an RL product is several orders of magnitude greater than a software product. I am being intentionally vague, because I don't have any hard facts to support this. But I think my hypothesis is sound and this is why scalability is an important factor when deploying RL.

I think *flexibility* is one of the most underrated best practices. In industry, reliable software was the theme of the first decade in the 21st century, with software architecture, test-driven development, and continuous integration being hot topics at conferences around the world. In the second decade, scalability was the golden child and resulted in important changes like cloud adoption and the subsequent need for orchestration. I think the third decade (I'm ignoring specific themes like artificial intelligence and RL and machine learning) will focus on flexibility, purely because I see industry trending toward hyper-responsibility, where the most valuable engineers are defined by their ability to fulfill all of the roles expected in an enterprise environment, from business development through to operations. The field of DevOps can only ever expand; it can never shrink back to two separate roles.

A similar argument can be made about the pace of change today. Engineers are continuously creating new technologies and it's hard to predict which will withstand the test of time. But I find that when tools attempt to enforce a fixed, inflexible, or proprietary way of working, they quickly become cumbersome to work with and are quickly outdated. No, flexibility is the only way to future-proof systems, processes, and solutions.

Hierarchy of needs

Maslow's hierarchy of needs was an early psychological model suggesting human necessities depicted as a hierarchical model; in order to have safety you need access to air and water, in order to have friendship you need to be safe, and so on. RL has a similar hierarchy of needs.

To have a viable RL problem then you need an environment in which you can observe, act, and receive a reward. You need the computational ability to be able to decide upon actions given an observation. These things are required and if you don't have them, then you can't do RL.

Above that comes things that are valuable, but not strictly necessary. For example, pipelines to transform data in a unified, reliable way will prevent data errors. Being able to specify exactly what is running in production—provenance—is operationally useful.

The layer above this represents an optimal state, one that is probably more conceptual than practical in many cases, because tackling other problems or developing new features might be more valuable in the short term. Here you might consider fully automating the end-to-end process of whatever it is you are doing, or incorporating a sophisticated feedback mechanism to allow your product to automatically improve itself.

Table 10-1 presents some example implementation and deployment challenges that you might face. I want to stress that these have a range of solutions with variations in the amount of automation. But the value of each level of automation depends on your or your stakeholder's assessment of other pressing needs. Just because there is a more sophisticated solution that doesn't mean what you have isn't good enough already. Get the basics right first.

Table 10-1. Example hierarchy of needs for different implementation challenges: the bottom row represents basic requirements, the middle row represents some amount of automation, the top row represents the state-of-the-art

	Infrastructure	State representation	Environment	Learning	Algorithm improvement
Optimal	Self-healing	Continuously learning	Combination	Meta	Automated
Valuable	Automated deployment	Model-driven dimensionality reduction	Real life	Offline	Brute-force selection
Required	Manual deployment	Fixed mapping	Simulation	Online	Manual

Architecture

There hasn't been a huge amount of research into generic RL architectures and I can think of a few reasons to explain this. The first is that RL still isn't universally accepted as a useful tool for industrial problems, yet. Hopefully this book will start to change that. This means that there isn't enough combined experience of designing these kinds of systems and therefore it has not been disseminated to a wider audience. Secondly, researchers, especially academic researchers, tend to be more focused on groundbreaking research, so you will find few papers on the subject. Third, I don't think there is a one-size-fits-all approach. Compare the differences between single-agent and multi-agent RL, for example. And finally, the deployment architecture is mostly a software engineering concern. Of course there are RL-specific needs, but I think that typical software architecture best practices fit well.

With that said, there is some literature available from the domain of contextual bandits. It's not generally applicable, but because industry has been quicker to adopt this technique, many lessons have already been learned. Two of the biggest problems that lead to architectural impacts are the fact that agents can only observe partial feedback and that rewards are often delayed or at worst, sparse:[29]

- Machine learning is considered to be simpler, because feedback, or ground truth, is complete. The label represents the single correct answer (or answers if multiple are correct). RL only observes the result of a single action; nothing is learned from the unexplored actions (which are possibly infinite).
- Rewards observed by the agent are often delayed, where the delay ranges from millisecond scales in bidding contests to days when people are involved. Even then, the reward may be sparse because the sequence of actions doesn't lead to a real reward for some time, like a purchase.

Some problems have a relationship with prior work in machine learning, but are accentuated by RL. For example, online learning, or continuous learning, is important in some machine learning disciplines, but RL takes this to a whole new level, since decisions have wide reaching consequences and policies are nonstationary. Even if you are incorporating batch RL, it is important to have a low-latency learning loop. Reproducibility becomes a big problem, too, since both the policy and the environment are constantly shifting.

All of these facets lead to the following range of architectural abstractions that might be useful in your problem:

Serving interface
> Like a personalized shopping assistant, one abstraction should contain the ability to serve action suggestions and embed exploration. This should implement the

Markov decision process interface and communicate with the wider system or environment. This is the both the entry and exit point of the system and presents a great location to decouple RL from wider deployments.

Log

Like in a message bus queue, it is vitally important to be able to retain state, for several reasons. First is for disaster recovery; you may need to replay interactions to update a policy to the last known state. The second is that it can be used as part of a wider batch or transfer learning effort to improve models. And third, it acts as a queue to buffer potentially slow online updates.

Parameter server

A place for storing the parameters of a model, like a database, crops up in multi-agent RL, but it is useful for situations where you need to replicate single-agent policies, too, to handle a larger load.

Policy servers

Since RL algorithms tend to be customized for a particular problem it makes sense to have an abstraction that encapsulates the implementation. In simpler, more static problems you might be able to bake the parameters of the model into the encapsulation, otherwise you can leverage a parameter server. You can replicate the policy servers to increase capacity.

Replay buffers

Many algorithms leverage replay buffers to increase sample efficiency. This might be an augmentation of the log or a dedicated database.

Actors and critics

You might want to consider splitting the policy server into smaller components.

Learning

Ideally you should use the same policy code to learn or train as you do to serve. This guarantees that there is no divergence between training and serving.

Data augmentation

You might have parts of your algorithm that rely on augmented data; a state representation algorithm, for example. These should exist as traditionally served ML models with their associated continuous integration and learning pipelines.

All or none of these abstractions might appear in your architecture design. Unfortunately they are very domain and application specific, so it doesn't make sense to enforce these abstractions. Also, more abstractions generally increase the maintenance burden; it's easier to work from a single codebase, after all. Instead, provide the tools and technologies to enable these architectural capabilities on a per-application basis.

Ancillary Tooling

I'm hesitant to talk about tooling in detail, because of the fast-pace change in the industry; a component I describe here could be obsolete by the time this book goes to print. Instead, I will talk abstractly about the functionality of groups of tooling and provide a few (historical) examples. Refer back to "RL frameworks" on page 296 for a discussion specific to RL tooling.

Build versus buy

I think the traditional build versus buy recommendations are true in RL, too. If the tool of interest represents a core competency or value proposition then you should build, so that you retain the intellectual property, have much greater depth, and have full control over the customization. Another way of thinking about this is to ask yourself: what are your customers paying you to do?

But if this particular tool does not represent your core competency or if it does not provide a competitive differentiation, then you should consider buying or using off-the-shelf components. A middle ground also exists, where you can leverage an open source project to get you to 80% complete and adapt it or bolt on components to get you the rest of the way.

Monitoring

When your product reaches production, you should invest in monitoring. This, single-handedly, gives you advance warning of issues that affect trust in an algorithm. And trust is important, because unlike traditional software that simply stops working, machine learning and RL are scrutinized like a racing driver critiques the way their car handles. If users receive an odd or unexpected result, this can knock their confidence. Sometimes it's better to simulate a broken product than it is to serve a bad prediction or recommendation.

I was speaking to a technical lead for a games company once and he said that users react negatively if they play against an automated agent that doesn't conform to their social norms. For example, if the agent were to take advantage of an opportunity in the game that left the user weak, the user would consider that bad sportsmanship and stop playing the game. And often they had to de-tune their agents to intentionally make bad choices to make the user feel like they had a fighting chance. RL can help in this regard, to optimize for what is important, like user retention, rather than raw performance.

"Evaluation" on page 307 talked about a range of RL-specific performance measures that you could implement in a monitoring solution. This is in addition to all the standard machine learning statistics you might monitor and low-level statistical indicators of the underlying data. Of course, software-level monitoring is vitally important.

This forms a hierarchy of metrics that you should consider implementing to gain operational insight and spot issues before your users do.

Logging and tracing

A log is an important debugging tool. It tends to be most important during development, to help you tune and debug your agents, and after a failure, to perform a post-mortem analysis. Bugs in traditional software appear when the state of the program changes in a way that is unexpected. So logging these state changes is a good way of tracking down issues when they do occur. But in RL, every interaction with an agent is a state change, so this can quickly become an overwhelming amount of information. This is why I recommend having a dedicated log for Markov state changes, to free your software of this burden.

One of the most common bugs in RL is due to differences in the runtime and expected shape of data. It is a good idea to log these shapes, maybe in a low-level debug log, so you can quickly find where the discrepencies are when they happen. Some people go to the extent of making these assertions to halt the code as soon as an exception is found. The next most common arise from the data, but I wouldn't save data directly to a text-based log. It's too much data. Summarize it and save it as a metric in the monitoring or dump it to a dedicated directory of offline inspection.

Tracing decisions through a log can be quite tricky because of the potential length of trajectories. A bad recommendation might not have been caused by the previous action. An action a long time ago could have led to this bad state. This problem is very much like the tracing systems used in microservice deployments to track activity across service boundaries. These systems use a correlation identifier (a unique key) that is passed around all calls; this key is used to link activity. A similar approach could be used to associate trajectories.

There can be other sources of state change, too: changes in the policy, user feedback, or changes in the infrastructure, for example. Try to capture all of these to be able to paint a picture when things go wrong. If you do have failures and you don't know why, be sure to add appropriate logging.

Continuous integration and continuous delivery

Continuous integration is a standard software engineering practice of building automated pipelines to deploy your solutions. The pipelines perform tests to maintain the quality of your product. *Continuous delivery* is the idea that if you have enough confidence in your quality gates, then you can release a new version of your software upon every commit.

CI/CD is an important and necessary tool for production deployments, but it only operates on offline, static artifacts like software bundles. It can't provide any guarantees that the data flowing into, through, or out of your agent is valid.

You can tackle the internal part with testing. You can monitor and alert upon the data flowing out. But even though you could monitor the data flowing in, it might still cause a catastrophic failure.

To handle problems with incoming data you need to test it. I call this "unit testing for data." The idea is that you specify what you expect incoming data to look like in the form of a schema and test that it conforms. If it doesn't you can either correct it or inform the user there was something wrong with their data. You have to make an architectural decision about where to perform this testing. The simplest place is in the serving agent, but this could bloat the code. You could have a centralized sentry that manages this process, too.

Experiment tracking

During development you will be performing a large number of experiments. Even after this phase, you need to keep track and monitor the performance of your agent or model as you gather new observations. The only way to do this consistently is to track performance metrics.

The underlying goals are similar to monitoring: to maintain quality and improve performance. But monitoring only provides information about the current instantiation of the agent. Experiment tracking intends to provide a longer-term holistic view, with an eye on potential improvements.

The idea is that for every run of an agent, you should log and track the performance. Over time you will begin to see trends in the performance of agents as the data evolves. And you can compare and contrast that to other experiments.

But the main reason why it is important is that training can sometimes take days, so to maintain efficiency you have to run experiments in parallel. For example, imagine you had designed a recommendations agent and had a hypothesis that it was easier to learn policies for older people, because they knew what they wanted. So you segmented the training data by age and started training upon several different datasets. Instead of waiting for each one to finish, you should run all experiments in parallel, and track their results. Yes, your efficiency is down because of the time it takes to get feedback on your hypothesis, but at least you'll get all the results at the same time. For this reason, you should track these experiments with an external system so that you can spend the time effectively elsewhere—or take the day off, it's your call.

In effect, you want to track the metrics, the things you are monitoring, and store them in a database. TensorBoard is one common solution and works well for simple experimentation, but it doesn't scale very well. Even for individuals it can get hard to organize different experiments. It gets even worse when multiple individuals use the same instance. Proprietary systems are available, but many of them are catered toward traditional machine learning, not RL, and because they are proprietary they are hard to improve or augment.

Hyperparameter tuning

The premise of hyperparameter tuning is quite simple: pick values for the hyperparameters, train and evaluate your agent, then repeat for different hyperparameter values. Once again the main problem is the amount of time it takes to do this by brute force, where you exhaustively test each permutation, because of the time it takes to perform a single run.

It is likely that the insight you can provide into your problem will lead to a carefully selected subset of parameters for which brute force might be enough. But there are newer approaches that attempt to build a model of performance versus the hyperparameter values to iterate toward an optimal model faster. They can also cut training runs short if they see that the final performance is going to be suboptimal. I've used Optuna (*https://optuna.org*) for this purpose and it works well when your hyperparameters are continuous and the performance measure is robust. You can run into problems like when hyperparameters slow down learning and the framework thinks the result is suboptimal, but it might lead to better performance in the long run.

Having a good infrastructure setup that autoscales is important to reduce the amount of time it takes to perform hyperparameter experiments.

Deploying multiple agents

The microservice architectural pattern suits machine learning and RL well. Running multiple agents in production is easier than it was because of advancements in tooling that allow you to create advanced deployments. Here is a list of possible deployment strategies:

Canary
> Route a certain proportion of users to a new agent, altered over time. Make sure you have the ability to provide *stickiness* so that the user's trajectory is dictated by the same agent. This is usually implemented using the same ideas as tracing.

Shadowing
> Running other agents hidden in the background, on real data, but not serving the results to users. This can be tricky to validate, because the hidden agent is not allowed to explore.

A/B testing and RL
> Yes, you can use bandits or RL to optimally pick your RL agents. Again, ensure *stickiness*.[30]

Ensembles
> This is more likely to fall under the banner of algorithmic development, but it is possible to use an ensemble of RL agents to make a decision.[31] The theory suggests that the resulting action should be more robust, if agents are diverse.

Deploying policies

There is significant risk involved in deploying a new policy, because it is hard to guarantee that it will not become suboptimal or diverge when learning online. Monitoring and alerting helps, but another way of viewing this problem is in terms of *deployment efficiency*.

In a way that is similar to measuring sample efficiency, you can count how many times the policy needs to be updated to become optimal, during training. Policies that need to be updated less often are likely to be more robust in production. Matsushima et al. investigate this in their work and propose that policies update only when the divergence between the trajectories of the current and prospective policies become large. This limits the frequency of policy updates and therefore mitigates some of the deployment risk.[32]

Considering when you want to update your policy is an interesting exercise. You will find that your agent sits somewhere on a continuum that ranges from continuous learning (updating on every interaction) through to batch learning (updating on a schedule) and ending at never updating, as shown in Figure 10-9. There is no right answer, as it depends on your problem. But I recommend that you stay as close to never updating your policy as possible, since this limits the frequency at which you have to monitor your deployment for errors or divergence.[33]

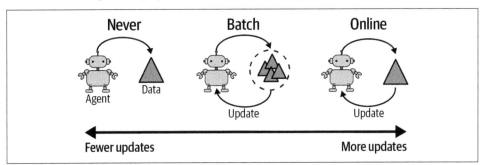

Figure 10-9. How often you update your production policy affects your deployment strategy. It falls on a continuum between never updating (manual deployment) and fully online.

I recommend that you try to make the deployments stateless and immutable, if possible. If you update the parameters of the model this is called a *side effect* of calling a function. These are considered to be bad because side effects can lead to unexpected failures and make it hard to recover from disaster. For example, one way to achieve immutability is by endeavoring to treat policy updates as new deployments and validating them in the same way you would for a code change. This is extreme, but very robust.

The traditional deployment techniques from "Deploying multiple agents" on page 324 can also help limit user-facing problems by treating each new instantiation of a policy, as defined by the policy parameters, as a separate deployment. Automated A/B testing can ensure that the new parameters do not adversely affect users.

Safety, Security, and Ethics

RL agents can sometimes control hazardous equipment, like robots or cars, which increases the jeopardy of making incorrect choices. A subfield called *safe RL* attempts to deal with this risk. RL agents are also at risk from attack, like any connected system. But RL adds a few new attack vectors over and above traditional software and machine learning exploits. And I think that engineers are the first line of defense against ethical concerns and that they should be considered proactively, so I think it's important to talk about it here.

Safe RL

The goal of safe RL is to learn a policy that maximizes rewards while operating within predefined safety constraints. These constraints may or may not exist during training and operation. The problem with this definition is that it includes ideas about preventing catastrophic updates, in the reward sense. Algorithms have been designed to solve this problem intrinsically, like trust region methods (see "Trust Region Methods" on page 163), for example. Another form of research involves extrinsic methods that prevent certain actions from causing physical harm, monetary loss, or any other behavior that leads to damaging outcomes and it is this that I will summarize here. The obvious place to start is with techniques that have already been described in this book.[34]

If your problem has safety concerns that can be naturally described as a constraint, then you can use any algorithm that performs constrained optimization. TRPO and PPO are good choices, where you can adapt the optimization function to incorporate your problem's constraints. For example, if you are training an algorithm to deploy replicas of a web service to meet demand, it shouldn't deploy more than the available capacity of the infrastructure. This information could be provided as a constraint to the optimization function. Ha et al. present a good example of training a robot to prevent falling over using a constrained version of SAC.[35]

Similarly, you could shape the reward to penalize certain behaviors. For example, a robotic arm will undergo significant stress when fully extended. To prolong the life of the robot you should prevent extensions that might cause metal fatigue. You could incorporate an element that penalizes extension into the reward function.

The problem with these two approaches is that they are hardcoded and likely to be suboptimal in more complex problems. A better approach could be to use imitation or inverse RL to learn optimal constrained actions from an expert.

However, all of the previous approaches do not guarantee safety, especially during learning. Safety is only approximately guaranteed after a sufficient amount of training. Fundamentally, these approaches learn how to act safely by performing unsafe acts, like a child—or an adult—touching a hot cup, despite telling them that the cup is hot.

A more recent set of approaches use an external definition of safety by defining a super-level *safe set* of states. For example, you could define a maximum range in which a robot is allowed to operate or the minimum allowable distance between vehicles in a follow-that-car algorithm. Given this definition, an external filter can evaluate whether actions are safe or not and prevent them.

A crude filter could prevent the action entirely and penalize the agent for taking an action, which is basically the same as reward shaping, except you prevent the dangerous action taking place. But that doesn't incorporate the knowledge of the safe set into the optimization process. With this approach, for example, you would have to jump out of a tree at every height before you know for sure that certain actions are unsafe—may I suggest a safety rope.

A more pragmatic approach is to build models that are able to abort and safely reset agents. You can often design your training to avoid unsafe actions by definition. For example, Eysenbach et al. built a legged robot and trained it to walk by changing the goal to be far away from unsafe states. For example, if it moves too far to the left, then the goal is changed to be on the right. They also learn a reset controller to provide an automated method to get back to a safe state.[36]

Researchers have looked at a variety of ways to incorporate this information. One suggestion is to use rollouts to predict the probability of an unsafe event and prefer actions that lead to safe trajectories.[37] This can be incorporated into value-based RL algorithms by pushing the value approximation parameters toward safe states and into policy gradient methods by directing the gradient steps toward safe states, with a correction that accounts for the biased policy generation.[38]

Another set of suggestions called *formally constrained RL* attempt to mathematically define and therefore guarantee safety, but these methods tend to rely on perfect, symbolic representations of unsafe states that are only possible in toy examples. One practical implementation from Hunt et al. resorts to using a model-driven action filtering technique.[39] Without doubt, this remains an open problem and I anticipate many more improvements to come.

Secure RL

If an attacker could alter the source code of an application they could inject malicious code. This is called a *white box* attack. Software deployments mitigate this risk with strict access control mechanisms on the codebase. But if the developer exposes the software to the public internet, then they run the risk that the attacker might be able to probe and find a weakness that allows them to alter the running of the application. This external approach is called a *black box* attack.

Machine learning, or any data-driven process, is also vulnerable to attack. These are broadly classified as attacks targeting either the *training phase* or the *prediction phase*. In the training phase, the attacker may be able to alter or manipulate the training data so that the attacker can exploit this data to produce a known result. This is commonly known as *poisoning*. For example, if an attacker could introduce a spam email with an incorrect label into a public spam dataset then the attacker might be able to reuse a similar email to sell pills that apparently enhance your libido, which would be classified as not spam by any model trained upon that data. Prediction attacks provide or augment the input data to produce invalid results. Many methods are white hat techniques and assume knowledge of the underlying model.[40] But more recently researchers have found black box techniques, like where the attacker can create a second model, similar to the first. Once trained, the attacker can generate white hat attacks for the second model and use them to attack the first. This approach shows that attacks are transferable.[41] Together, these are known as *adversarial attacks*.

RL agents can also be attacked, in all the same ways. Your first step should be to fix the basics. An attacker is not going to go to the trouble of creating a trained replica if they can find an open SSH port on one of your servers or someone's GitHub credentials have been phished and you don't have multifactor authentication enabled. Next, make sure you have robust data integrity testing and monitoring in place; use rate limiting and denial-of-service protection to limit how much of the model a black-box attacker can explore. Ensure your models are simple and robust, as much as practicable. Consider a research spike to investigate how you could improve the countermeasures put in place for your ML models.

RL poses greater risks because of the increased attack surface. ML models generally have a single entry point, the input, and a single response, the output. In RL, attackers could target the environment, the observation of the environment, the rewards, or the actions. Successfully altering any of these could cause the policy to tend toward a different result. If the attacker has access to internal systems then they could also target ancillary services like the experience replay buffer or the parameter server.

Ways to prevent or mitigate these types of attacks are under active research. One branch reminds us that model robustness is at the heart of a security strategy and is strongly related to safe RL. If you have a model or a policy that works well under adverse conditions then it is less likely to succumb to an external attack. Behzadan and Munir suggest perturbing agents during training to teach them to be more robust to prediction attacks, which is a common strategy to harden ML models.[42]

Another approach proposed by Liu et al. is to try to detect an adversarial attack and stop it before it does any damage. RL is sequential and often correlated over time, so you could build a model to predict the next state given the current observation. If you calculate the divergence between the prediction and what actually happened, then compare that to "normal" behavior (a model of the typical distribution of divergences), you could build an algorithm to warn you when large divergences are observed.[43]

You could consider guiding exploration by directing agents' actions to states that would cause maximum adversarial gain.[44] Or even mitigate adversarial training examples by considering the problem to be hierarchical; adversarial poisoning is likely to "look" very different from normal interaction, so hierarchical RL should be able to consider this a subpolicy. The subpolicies could then be analyzed to ensure legitimacy and that the poisoned data is removed.[45]

As you can see there are many ideas to tackle the many potential attack vectors. But therein lies the problem: potential. Investing time, energy, and money into mitigating these attacks has to be weighed against the probability of them occurring in the first place. For example, if you have an agent that runs on an internal network and is never exposed to the public internet, then I would consider this level of mitigation to be a poor use of time, given the probability of attack being so low. This is why you have to perform a risk analysis for your particular situation.

Attack mitigation also has diminishing returns, because the knowledge and resources to perform an attack increases exponentially. According to Symantec's 2019 Internet Security Threat Report, a whopping 65% of all targeted hacks were caused by phishing, 23% by unpatched software, and 5% by bogus software updates. Only when you get to the bottom do you find exploits that directly relate to an exposed RL agent: 2% web server exploits and 1% data storage exploits. These statistics demonstrate that basic security practices are more valuable to a company than RL or possibly even ML attack mitigation techniques. To be clear, I'm not suggesting that RL security is unimportant, just get the basics right first.[46]

Ethical RL

It's probably not quite the dictionary definition of the term, but I like to think of *ethics* as a professional consensus of individual morality. This is an important distinction, because what you believe is right and wrong is not necessarily what I believe. But I would like to think that there is a compromise that we can both accept. So morals represent a distribution of beliefs and the mean represents the ethical standards. Engineers, in general, don't have a single unified way or place to define the ethical means, so it is important that you are aware that they exist, on a conceptual level at least, and that your perspective is but one of many.

I say this not to preach philosophy or religion, but to remind you that you are in a position of power. You have the power and the authority to not only automate decisions (machine learning) but also entire strategies (RL). Whenever you enact these techniques, you are effectively removing the opportunity for a human to make decisions. This could be a good thing, if the decision is trivial or burdensome, but sometimes it is not. Sometimes the decision is so important that it *has* to be made by a human, so that they can take responsibility for that decision, right or wrong. They are free to use the information provided by an algorithm, but this does not remove that responsibility. Other times the decision might not be so important on a global scale, but it might be important on a human scale; a person may feel a sense of loss or disempowerment if they lose the ability to make a decision.

Unfortunately, the stakeholders (both users and owners) of your systems are generally not able or not in a position to independently assess impact. They may lack the authority or opportunity to protest or they are prevented from understanding the technical intricacies. You are in a position to prevent this from happening. You can explain, in simple terms, what the pros and cons of your solution are in a way that relates to them personally. You can listen to their questions and address their concerns. You can explain when your system works and when it doesn't and all the assumptions that you have made along the way.

As for you, you are probably lucky enough to be able to choose what work you do, or at least actively decide not to work on something or for someone that violates your moral principles. This is an unspoken benefit of opportunity, education, and engineering. The fact that you are in a position to read this book is a truly remarkable achievement. You can repay this debt by actively considering what is important to you and how your work affects the world. The following is a list of items that may or may not be important to you. Whenever you are developing an application, ask yourself:

Bias

Does this solution affect certain groups of people more than others? Are there aspects of your data that could accidentally add bias?

Personal impact

How does this affect individuals? What will they feel like when they see/use your solution? If people will be impacted, is there a way to mitigate this? Can you include humans in the decision loop?

Climate

How does your solution affect the climate? Is the application valuable enough to be worth the cost in energy?

Unintended use

How else could your application be used? Would you be uncomfortable if it was used in certain industries? Can you prevent that from happening?

Nefarious use

Is your solution, directly or indirectly, going to be used for an activity that you do not agree with?

Legality
> Is it legal? Could it be deemed illegal in certain juristrictions or countries?

Human rights
> Could your solution violate legal or your definition of human rights? For example, could it affect the privacy of individuals?

Justification and explainability
> How can you justify the actions of your algorithm? How much explanation do they need to provide to be deemed trustworthy?

Performance misinformation
> Have you explained effects of your algorithm or potential performance in the clearest, most independent way possible? Is there a chance that others could misinterpret your results and be unduly penalized?

On a technical front, there are efforts to attempt to incorporate some of these ideas into machine learning and RL directly. For example, ML-fairness-gym (*https://oreil.ly/n3edb*) is a set of components that build simple simulations that assess the long-term impacts of decision systems in social environments. For example, in countries around the world credit scores are used to rate how likely individuals are to repay debt. But the fact that companies use this measure encourages individuals to artificially inflate their credit scores through techniques such as credit utilization and even overstating affordability measures on applications. In turn, this makes it harder for people who don't engage in these tactics, those who don't have the capability or opportunity to access such information, to access credit when they need it.[47]

The long-term consequences are so hard to predict that you might consider not doing it at all. But wait, you have access to a framework that is able to monitor and optimize for long-term sequential rewards. Yes, RL. Researchers have gone so far as to suggest that you can use RL to optimize and make ethical decisions, and even consider using reward shaping as a proxy for *ethics shaping*.[48,49] Maybe RL will save the world?

Summary

To the best of my knowledge, this chapter is the first to provide cohesive and comprehensive advice on how to implement and deploy RL agents. There are many tidbits scattered throughout the research papers, but engineers, on average, have simply not had enough experience with RL in production. My hope is that this chapter, and indeed this book, will begin to change that.

Of course this also means that I am writing from the perspective of my experience and what I think is important. Feel free to take this advice and adapt, change, or totally ignore it as you see fit. The sheer breadth of applications means that the circumstances of a project should dictate how these ideas can be applied and the value of doing so.

Despite the lack of production use (compared to machine learning, for example), there are already a wide range of frameworks to help you get started quickly. These range from algorithmic through to operational frameworks and also include specialized ancillary frameworks to implement a specific part of the RL problem. But it is likely, especially if going into production, that you will still need a lot of custom code, since RL is still young. Scaling RL is similarly supported on the training side by frameworks, and traditional software stacks and orchestrators should help you scale into production.

Evaluating agents is crucial, and could have been included in Chapter 9. But I left it to here since it only really becomes crucial when you are looking to deploy your first agent. While you're in the proof-of-concept phase, you can usually get away with ad hoc evaluation with standard metrics and environment-specific debugging.

When you do find yourself wanting to deploy a project into a setting where other people can use it, you should take a step back and consider the operational aspects of running RL. Take the time to consider what you are trying to achieve and build an architecture that supports those goals. Don't be afraid to say that certain aspects are not important to save time, but do so only when considering the risks. To support the deployment you will need to leverage a wide range of software engineering and machine learning tooling. Take advantage of these and adapt them to your RL process.

Safe RL is an important topic for agents that interact with the real world and can directly affect algorithm implementations. Try to catch this requirement as early as you can, since popular algorithms may appear to work well, but could be unsafe. Securing your application is important here as it is in any project and there are RL-specific attack vectors to be aware of. But basic security practices should take priority, since these are the focus of most attacks.

And finally, consider how your application impacts ethical concerns, from an industry perspective, and moral concerns, from a personal perspective. This becomes more important and harder to do the higher you go in the decision stack. Ethical machine learning is hard enough to get right, but since RL is automating whole strategies, there is potential for long-term and wide-reaching consequences.

Further Reading

- Software engineering:
  - Martin, Robert C. 2008. *Clean Code: A Handbook of Agile Software Craftsmanship*. Pearson Education.

— McConnell, Steve. 2004. *Code Complete*. Pearson Education.

— Hunt, Andrew, and David Thomas. 1999. *The Pragmatic Programmer: From Journeyman to Master*. Addison-Wesley Professional.

- Psychology:

  — Kahneman, Daniel. 2012. *Thinking, Fast and Slow*. Penguin UK.

  — Baumeister, Roy F., and John Tierney. 2012. *Willpower: Rediscovering Our Greatest Strength*. Penguin UK.

- Evaluation:

  — Provost, F., and T. Fawcett. 2013. *Data Science for Business: What You Need to Know about Data Mining and Data-Analytic Thinking* (*https://oreil.ly/xh5ya*). O'Reilly Media.

  — I found this old paper to be a useful resource on traditional RL evaluation methods.[50]

- Explainability:

  — A good review of explainability, although biased toward medicine.[51]

  — Check out the PyTorch Captum (*https://oreil.ly/AsYTe*) and TensorFlow tf-explain (*https://oreil.ly/lUpRf*) projects for black-box explainability implementations.

  — Recent survey on explainability in RL.[52]

- Microservices and deployment strategies:

  — Newman, Sam. 2021. *Building Microservices: Designing Fine-Grained Systems* (*https://oreil.ly/96Tc1*). O'Reilly.

- Continuous integration and deployment:

  — Duvall, Paul M., Steve Matyas, and Andrew Glover. 2007. *Continuous Integration: Improving Software Quality and Reducing Risk*. Pearson Education.

  — Humble, Jez, and David Farley. 2010. *Continuous Delivery: Reliable Software Releases through Build, Test, and Deployment Automation*. Pearson Education.

- Safe RL:

  — A thorough survey, but a bit outdated.[53]

  — Pfleeger, Charles P., and Shari Lawrence Pfleeger. 2012. *Analyzing Computer Security: A Threat/Vulnerability/Countermeasure Approach*. Prentice Hall Professional.

  — Excellent thesis on the subject by Vahid Behzadan.[54]

- Ethics:

  — Nielsen, Aileen. 2020. *Practical Fairness* (*https://oreil.ly/yjc_K*). O'Reilly.

— The Institute for Ethical AI & ML (*https://ethical.institute*) is pioneering work in this area.

— I was really inspired by this paper on how ML can be used to tackle climate change.[55]

References

[1] GitHub Archive Program (*https://oreil.ly/GzE9T*). n.d. GitHub Archive Program. Accessed 26 July 2020.

[2] Dhariwal, Prafulla, Christopher Hesse, Oleg Klimov, Alex Nichol, Matthias Plappert, Alec Radford, John Schulman, Szymon Sidor, Yuhuai Wu, and Peter Zhokhov. 2017. OpenAI Baselines. GitHub Repository. GitHub.

[3] Hill, Ashley, Antonin Raffin, Maximilian Ernestus, Adam Gleave, Anssi Kanervisto, Rene Traore, Prafulla Dhariwal, et al. 2018. Stable Baselines. GitHub Repository. GitHub.

[4] Albin Cassirer, Gabriel Barth-Maron, Thibault Sottiaux, Manuel Kroiss, Eugene Brevdo. 2020. Reverb: An Efficient Data Storage and Transport System for ML Research.

[5] Espeholt, Lasse, Raphaël Marinier, Piotr Stanczyk, Ke Wang, and Marcin Michalski. 2020. "SEED RL: Scalable and Efficient Deep-RL with Accelerated Central Inference" (*https://oreil.ly/6wbbU*). ArXiv:1910.06591, February.

[6] Nair, Arun, Praveen Srinivasan, Sam Blackwell, Cagdas Alcicek, Rory Fearon, Alessandro De Maria, Vedavyas Panneershelvam, et al. 2015. "Massively Parallel Methods for Deep Reinforcement Learning" (*https://oreil.ly/pviAX*). ArXiv: 1507.04296, July.

[7] Dean, Jeffrey, Greg Corrado, Rajat Monga, Kai Chen, Matthieu Devin, Mark Mao, Marc'aurelio Ranzato, et al. 2012. "Large Scale Distributed Deep Networks" (*https://oreil.ly/RRh-I*). *Advances in Neural Information Processing Systems* 25, edited by F. Pereira, C. J. C. Burges, L. Bottou, and K. Q. Weinberger, 1223–1231. Curran Associates, Inc.

[8] Mnih, Volodymyr, Adrià Puigdomènech Badia, Mehdi Mirza, Alex Graves, Timothy P. Lillicrap, Tim Harley, David Silver, and Koray Kavukcuoglu. 2016. "Asynchronous Methods for Deep Reinforcement Learning" (*https://oreil.ly/wplVP*). ArXiv: 1602.01783, June.

[9] Niu, Feng, Benjamin Recht, Christopher Re, and Stephen J. Wright. 2011. "HOGWILD!: A Lock-Free Approach to Parallelizing Stochastic Gradient Descent." (*https://oreil.ly/fbJ_i*) ArXiv:1106.5730, November.

[10] Clemente, Alfredo V., Humberto N. Castejón, and Arjun Chandra. 2017. "Efficient Parallel Methods for Deep Reinforcement Learning" (*https://oreil.ly/gHuxR*). ArXiv:1705.04862, May.

[11] Horgan, Dan, John Quan, David Budden, Gabriel Barth-Maron, Matteo Hessel, Hado van Hasselt, and David Silver. 2018. "Distributed Prioritized Experience Replay" (*https://oreil.ly/nR8_I*). ArXiv:1803.00933, March.

[12] Wijmans, Erik, Abhishek Kadian, Ari Morcos, Stefan Lee, Irfan Essa, Devi Parikh, Manolis Savva, and Dhruv Batra. 2020. "DD-PPO: Learning Near-Perfect Point-Goal Navigators from 2.5 Billion Frames." (*https://oreil.ly/sHcgQ*) ArXiv:1911.00357, January.

[13] Stooke, Adam, and Pieter Abbeel. 2019. "Accelerated Methods for Deep Reinforcement Learning" (*https://oreil.ly/Id0xg*). ArXiv:1803.02811, January.

[14] OpenAI. 2018. "OpenAI Five" (*https://oreil.ly/k8Zwo*) 2018.

[15] Espeholt, Lasse, Hubert Soyer, Remi Munos, Karen Simonyan, Volodymir Mnih, Tom Ward, Yotam Doron, et al. 2018. "IMPALA: Scalable Distributed Deep-RL with Importance Weighted Actor-Learner Architectures" (*https://oreil.ly/IU2-T*). ArXiv: 1802.01561, June.

[16] Espeholt, Lasse, Raphaël Marinier, Piotr Stanczyk, Ke Wang, and Marcin Michalski. 2020. "SEED RL: Scalable and Efficient Deep-RL with Accelerated Central Inference" (*https://oreil.ly/2CMLU*) ArXiv:1910.06591, February.

[17] Hung, Chia-Chun, Timothy Lillicrap, Josh Abramson, Yan Wu, Mehdi Mirza, Federico Carnevale, Arun Ahuja, and Greg Wayne. 2019. "Optimizing Agent Behavior over Long Time Scales by Transporting Value" (*https://oreil.ly/hX1ep*). *Nature Communications* 10(1): 5223.

[18] Colas, Cédric, Olivier Sigaud, and Pierre-Yves Oudeyer. 2019. "A Hitchhiker's Guide to Statistical Comparisons of Reinforcement Learning Algorithms" (*https://oreil.ly/f-_z0*). ArXiv:1904.06979, April.

[19] Colas, Cédric, Olivier Sigaud, and Pierre-Yves Oudeyer. 2018. "How Many Random Seeds? Statistical Power Analysis in Deep Reinforcement Learning Experiments" (*https://oreil.ly/49cDY*). ArXiv:1806.08295, July.

[20] Lee, Xian Yeow, Aaron Havens, Girish Chowdhary, and Soumik Sarkar. 2019. "Learning to Cope with Adversarial Attacks" (*https://oreil.ly/0vN_I*). ArXiv: 1906.12061, June.

[21] Osband, Ian, Yotam Doron, Matteo Hessel, John Aslanides, Eren Sezener, Andre Saraiva, Katrina McKinney, et al. 2020. "Behaviour Suite for Reinforcement Learning" (*https://oreil.ly/Lfqfj*). ArXiv:1908.03568, February.

[22] Gulcehre, Caglar, Ziyu Wang, Alexander Novikov, Tom Le Paine, Sergio Gomez Colmenarejo, Konrad Zolna, Rishabh Agarwal, et al. 2020. "RL Unplugged: Benchmarks for Offline Reinforcement Learning" (*https://oreil.ly/F3PKn*). ArXiv: 2006.13888, July.

[23] James, Stephen, Zicong Ma, David Rovick Arrojo, and Andrew J. Davison. 2019. "RLBench: The Robot Learning Benchmark & Learning Environment." (*https://oreil.ly/N8ubF*) ArXiv:1909.12271, September.

[24] Leike, Jan, Miljan Martic, Victoria Krakovna, Pedro A. Ortega, Tom Everitt, Andrew Lefrancq, Laurent Orseau, and Shane Legg. 2017. "AI Safety Gridworlds" (*https://oreil.ly/HfuRk*). ArXiv:1711.09883, November.

[25] Liu, Guiliang, Oliver Schulte, Wang Zhu, and Qingcan Li. 2018. "Toward Interpretable Deep Reinforcement Learning with Linear Model U-Trees" (*https://oreil.ly/2ck-z*). ArXiv:1807.05887, July.

[26] Yoon, Jinsung, Sercan O. Arik, and Tomas Pfister. 2019. "RL-LIM: Reinforcement Learning-Based Locally Interpretable Modeling." (*https://oreil.ly/fDoKK*) ArXiv: 1909.12367, September.

[27] Madumal, Prashan, Tim Miller, Liz Sonenberg, and Frank Vetere. 2019. "Explainable Reinforcement Learning Through a Causal Lens" (*https://oreil.ly/-4imX*). ArXiv:1905.10958, November.

[28] Atrey, Akanksha, Kaleigh Clary, and David Jensen. 2020. "Exploratory Not Explanatory: Counterfactual Analysis of Saliency Maps for Deep Reinforcement Learning" (*https://oreil.ly/eo4mI*). ArXiv:1912.05743, February.

[29] Agarwal, Alekh, Sarah Bird, Markus Cozowicz, Luong Hoang, John Langford, Stephen Lee, Jiaji Li, et al. 2017. "Making Contextual Decisions with Low Technical Debt" (*https://oreil.ly/0Xj1M*). ArXiv:1606.03966, May.

[30] Merentitis, Andreas, Kashif Rasul, Roland Vollgraf, Abdul-Saboor Sheikh, and Urs Bergmann. 2019. "A Bandit Framework for Optimal Selection of Reinforcement Learning Agents" (*https://oreil.ly/V5Afb*). ArXiv:1902.03657, February.

[31] Lee, Kimin, Michael Laskin, Aravind Srinivas, and Pieter Abbeel. 2020. "SUNRISE: A Simple Unified Framework for Ensemble Learning in Deep Reinforcement Learning" (*https://oreil.ly/GncZJ*). ArXiv:2007.04938, July.

[32] Matsushima, Tatsuya, Hiroki Furuta, Yutaka Matsuo, Ofir Nachum, and Shixiang Gu. 2020. "Deployment-Efficient Reinforcement Learning via Model-Based Offline Optimization" (*https://oreil.ly/nUg_v*). ArXiv:2006.03647, June.

[33] Tian, Huangshi, Minchen Yu, and Wei Wang. 2018. "Continuum: A Platform for Cost-Aware, Low-Latency Continual Learning." (*https://oreil.ly/weHtP*) *Proceedings of*

the ACM Symposium on Cloud Computing, 26–40. SoCC '18. New York, NY, USA: Association for Computing Machinery.

[34] García, Javier, and Fernando Fernández. 2015. "A Comprehensive Survey on Safe Reinforcement Learning." *The Journal of Machine Learning Research* 16(1): 1437–1480.

[35] Ha, Sehoon, Peng Xu, Zhenyu Tan, Sergey Levine, and Jie Tan. 2020. "Learning to Walk in the Real World with Minimal Human Effort" (*https://oreil.ly/Ezr_4*). ArXiv:2002.08550, February.

[36] Eysenbach, Benjamin, Shixiang Gu, Julian Ibarz, and Sergey Levine. 2017. "Leave No Trace: Learning to Reset for Safe and Autonomous Reinforcement Learning." (*https://oreil.ly/JfDIW*) ArXiv:1711.06782, November.

[37] Wabersich, Kim P., Lukas Hewing, Andrea Carron, and Melanie N. Zeilinger. 2019. "Probabilistic Model Predictive Safety Certification for Learning-Based Control." (*https://oreil.ly/dmjmF*) ArXiv:1906.10417, June.

[38] Gros, Sebastien, Mario Zanon, and Alberto Bemporad. 2020. "Safe Reinforcement Learning via Projection on a Safe Set: How to Achieve Optimality?" (*https://oreil.ly/6vaDf*). ArXiv:2004.00915, April.

[39] Hunt, Nathan, Nathan Fulton, Sara Magliacane, Nghia Hoang, Subhro Das, and Armando Solar-Lezama. 2020. "Verifiably Safe Exploration for End-to-End Reinforcement Learning" (*https://oreil.ly/lKX7i*). ArXiv:2007.01223, July.

[40] Goodfellow, Ian J., Jonathon Shlens, and Christian Szegedy. 2015. "Explaining and Harnessing Adversarial Examples." (*https://oreil.ly/6dXk-*) ArXiv:1412.6572, March.

[41] Papernot, Nicolas, Patrick McDaniel, Ian Goodfellow, Somesh Jha, Z. Berkay Celik, and Ananthram Swami. 2017. "Practical Black-Box Attacks against Machine Learning" (*https://oreil.ly/dnIgv*). ArXiv:1602.02697, March.

[42] Behzadan, Vahid, and Arslan Munir. 2017. "Whatever Does Not Kill Deep Reinforcement Learning, Makes It Stronger" (*https://oreil.ly/WcQ8j*). ArXiv:1712.09344, December.

[43] Lin, Yen-Chen, Ming-Yu Liu, Min Sun, and Jia-Bin Huang. 2017. "Detecting Adversarial Attacks on Neural Network Policies with Visual Foresight" (*https://oreil.ly/haYxX*). ArXiv:1710.00814, October.

[44] Behzadan, Vahid, and William Hsu. 2019. "Analysis and Improvement of Adversarial Training in DQN Agents With Adversarially-Guided Exploration (AGE)" (*https://oreil.ly/PHjCj*). ArXiv:1906.01119, June.

[45] Havens, Aaron J., Zhanhong Jiang, and Soumik Sarkar. 2018. "Online Robust Policy Learning in the Presence of Unknown Adversaries" (*http://arxiv.org/abs/1807.06064*). ArXiv:1807.06064, July.

[46] *Internet Security Threat Report* (*https://oreil.ly/rdW_8*) (Volume 24). 2019. Symantec.

[47] Milli, Smitha, John Miller, Anca D. Dragan, and Moritz Hardt. 2018. "The Social Cost of Strategic Classification." (*http://arxiv.org/abs/1808.08460*) ArXiv:1808.08460, November.

[48] Abel, David, James MacGlashan, and Michael L Littman. 2016. "Reinforcement Learning as a Framework for Ethical Decision Making." *Workshops at the Thirtieth AAAI Conference on Artificial Intelligence.*

[49] Yu, Han, Zhiqi Shen, Chunyan Miao, Cyril Leung, Victor R. Lesser, and Qiang Yang. 2018. "Building Ethics into Artificial Intelligence" (*https://oreil.ly/Xw5D1*). ArXiv:1812.02953, December.

[50] Kaelbling, L. P., M. L. Littman, and A. W. Moore. 1996. "Reinforcement Learning: A Survey" (*https://oreil.ly/w6Ffn*). ArXiv:Cs/9605103, April.

[51] Tjoa, Erico, and Cuntai Guan. 2020. "A Survey on Explainable Artificial Intelligence (XAI): Towards Medical XAI" (*https://oreil.ly/1Az_5*). ArXiv:1907.07374, June.

[52] Puiutta, Erika, and Eric MSP Veith. 2020. "Explainable Reinforcement Learning: A Survey" (*https://oreil.ly/CIh1I*). ArXiv:2005.06247, May.

[53] García, Javier, and Fernando Fernández. 2015. "A Comprehensive Survey on Safe Reinforcement Learning." The Journal of Machine Learning Research 16(1): 1437–1480.

[54] Behzadan, Vahid. 2019. "Security of Deep Reinforcement Learning." (*https://oreil.ly/gS4WB*) Manhattan, Kansas: Kansas State University.

[55] Rolnick, David, Priya L. Donti, Lynn H. Kaack, Kelly Kochanski, Alexandre Lacoste, Kris Sankaran, Andrew Slavin Ross, et al. 2019. "Tackling Climate Change with Machine Learning." (*https://oreil.ly/VIeiJ*) ArXiv:1906.05433, November.

CHAPTER 11

Conclusions and the Future

At this point you might be expecting (and be glad) that this is the end of the book. Not quite, because during my time writing this book I collected a smorgasbord of tidbits and ideas for future work. In the first half, I delve into some tips and tricks that I have accumulated that didn't fit into other parts of the book. In the second half I outline the current challenges and provide direction for future research.

Tips and Tricks

I've said this a few times now: RL is hard in real life because of the underlying dependencies on machine learning and software engineering. But the sequential stochasticity adds another dimension by delaying and hiding issues.

Framing the Problem

Often you will have a new industrial problem where the components of the Markov decision process are fuzzy at best. Your goal should be to refine the concept and prove (at least conceptually) the viability using RL for this problem.

To start, try visualizing a random policy acting upon a notional environment. Where does it go? What does it interact with? When does it do the right thing? How quickly does it find the right thing to do? If your random policy never does the right thing, then RL is unlikely to help.

After trying a random policy, try to solve the problem yourself. Imagine *you* are the agent. Could you make the right decisions after exploring every state? Can you use the observations to guide your decisions? What would make your job easier or harder? What features could you generate from these observations? Again, if you can't notionally come up with viable strategies, then RL (or machine learning, for that matter) is unlikely to work.

Use baselines to frame performance. Start with a random agent. Then use a cross-entropy method (which is a simple algorithm that recalls the best previous rollout from random exploration). Then try a simple Q-learning or policy gradient algorithm. Each time you implement a new algorithm, treat it like a scientific experiment: have a theory, test that theory, learn from the experiment, and use it to guide future implementations.

Simplify the task as much as humanly possible, then solve that first. Go for the quick wins. By *simplify*, I mean reducing the state and action space as much as practicable. You can hand engineer features for this or use your domain knowledge to chop out parts of the state that don't make sense. And simplify the goal or the problem definition. For example, rather than trying to pick up an object with a robot, try training it to move to a position first. And simplify the rewards, too. Always try to remove the sparsity by using metrics like the distance to the goal, rather than a positive reward when the agent reaches the goal. Try to make the reward smooth. Remove any outliers or discontinuities; these will make it harder for your model to approximate.

Ask yourself whether you need to remember previous actions to make new ones. For example, if you need a key to open a door, then you need to remember that you have picked up a key. If you want to place an item in a box, you need to pick it up first. These situations have states that must be visited in a specific order. To provide this capability you should incorporate a working memory, and one common implementation is via recurrent neural networks.

Don't confuse this with two actions, though. It's easy to fall into the trap of thinking that you need memory, but in fact you have actions to reach these states directly. For example, you would imagine that before moving forward in a car you need to turn the engine on. This sounds like ordered tasks again, but it is not, because you probably have separate actions to turn the car on and move forward. An agent without memory is fully capable of learning to keep the car turned on in order to move forward. This highlights a way of removing the need for memory, too. If you can find an action that provides a shortcut to this state, then you might be able to do away with the working memory.

Also remember hierarchical policies at this point. Consider if your application has disparate "skills" that could be learned to solve the problem. Consider solving them independently if you can, which is conceptually and practically simpler than using hierarchical RL and the end result may the same.

Your Data

I think the vast majority of development time is spent retraining models after tweaking some hyperparameter or altering features, for example. For this reason, and this almost goes without saying, you should try to do things right the first time. This only comes with experience: experience with RL in general, in your domain, and with your problem. But here are a few tips that should provide a bit of a shortcut.

Like in machine learning, scale and correlation is really important. Not all algorithms *need* rescaling (trees, for example), but most do, and most expect normally distributed data. So in general you should always rescale your observations to have a mean of zero and a standard deviation of one. You can do this with something as simple as a rolling mean and standard deviation, or if your input is stationary or bounded, you can use those observed limits. Be aware that the statistics of your data may change over time and make your problem nonstationary.

Also try to decorrelate and clean your observations. Models don't like correlation in time or across features, because they represent complex biases and duplicate information. You can use the z-transform, principal component analysis, or even a simple diff between observations to decorrelate single features. You use your data analysis skills to find and remove correlations between observations.

Monitor all aspects of your data. Look at the reward distributions; make sure there are no outliers. Look at the input data, again, plot distributions or visualizations, and make sure the input data isn't wild. Look at the predictions being made by various parts of the model. Is the value function predicting well? What about the gradients? Are they too big? Look at the entropy of the action space: is it exploring well, or is it stuck on certain actions? Look at the Kullback–Liebler divergence: is it too big or too small?

Think about increasing increasing the amount of discretization, in other words, increase the time between actions. This can make training more stable, because it's less affected by random noise, and speed it up, because there are fewer actions to compute. The de facto frame skipping in the Atari environments is an example of this. A good rule of thumb is to imagine yourself picking actions; at what rate do you need to make decisions to produce a viable policy?

Training

Training can be quite a demoralizing process. You think you have a good idea only to find that it doesn't make any difference and it took you a day to implement and retrain. But at least this is visible. One of the biggest issues in RL right now is that it is easy to overfit the development of an algorithm to your specific environment and therefore produce a policy that doesn't generalize well.

Try to develop your algorithm against a range of environments. It is very easy to overfit your development to the environment you use for ad hoc testing. This takes discipline, but try to maintain a set of representative environments, from simple to realistic, that also have different setups, like larger or smaller, easier or harder, or fully observable or partially observable. If your algorithm works well across all of them, then that gives you confidence that it is able to generalize.

Use different seeds. I've sometimes thought I was doing well in an environment, but it turned out that one specific seed was massively overfitting and happened to stumble across a viable policy purely by chance. When you use different seeds, this forces your agent to explore in a slightly different way than it did before. Of course, your algorithm should perform similarly irrespective of the seed value, but don't be surprised if it doesn't.

Test the sensitivity of your hyperparameters. Again, you should be aiming for an algorithm that is robust and degrades gracefully. If it works only with a very specific set of hyperparameters then this is an indication of overfitting again.

Play with the learning rate schedules. A fixed value rarely works well because it encourages the policy to change, even when it is doing well. This can have the effect of knocking the agent away from an optimal policy.

Evaluation

Evaluation tends to be one of the least problematic phases because you should already have a good idea of how well things are going from all the monitoring you did during training. But there is still enough fuel left to get burnt.

Be very careful drawing conclusions when comparing algorithms. You can use statistics to quantify improvement (see "Statistical policy comparisons" on page 310) but I find that I make fewer mistakes when visualizing performance. The basic idea is that if you can see a significant performance increase, where there is clear space between the performance curves over many different seeds, then it's quite likely to be better. If you don't see a gap, then run more trials with more seeds or simply don't trust it. This sounds simple enough but in really complex environments it is not. Often, through no fault of your algorithm, you can end up with a really bad run. This can happen in a complex environment where a bad initial exploration led to states that are really hard to get out of. Take a look at the states that your agent is choosing to explore; you might want to alter the exploration strategy.

No one measure or plot can truly prove performance. I find that a holistic combination of experience with that domain and environment and intuition about how an algorithm *should* behave dictates whether I believe there to be a change in performance. This is why it is important to have baselines to compare yourself against, because it provides another piece of evidence.

Remember that some policies are stochastic by default—many policy gradient algorithms, for example—so evaluate using deterministic versions of these policies if you want a pure performance measure. Similarly, if you have any random exploration in your policy—ϵ-greedy, for example—make sure you disable it. Even though you might disable it during evaluation, consider retaining the stochasticity in the real environment if there is a chance that the optimal policy could change over time.

Deployment

I think the key to quickly developing successful applications is defined by the ability to combine off-the-shelf components and modules to solve a particular problem. This necessitates a certain amount of composability, which is primarily driven at the software level through good coding practices. The idea is that you look at your problem, pick the components that would help—intrinsic motivation or a replay buffer for example—stick them all together through nicely encapsulated interfaces, and deploy them in unison. At the moment, unfortunately, this dream is a long way away. Any production deployment will involve significant software engineering and DevOps expertise.

Frameworks help here, too, because many of them have the desire to be composable. But that usually means that they are composable within the bounds of their codebase. Frameworks often struggle to interact with external components because of a lack of standards. OpenAI's Gym is an obvious exception to this.

So think hard about your architecture, because I think this is the key to successful deployment and operation of a real-life product.

Debugging

Despite RL algorithms fueling much of the publicity surrounding artificial intelligence, deep RL methods are "brittle, hard to reproduce, unreliable across runs, and sometimes outperformed by simple baselines."[1] The main reason for this is that the constituent parts of an algorithm are not well understood: how do the various parts of an implementation impact behavior and performance?

Implementation details are incredibly important. Engstrom et al. find that seemingly small modifications like code-level optimizations can explain the bulk of performance in many popular algorithms. For example, despite the claim that PPO is performant due to update clipping or constraints, these researchers proved that the code-level optimizations improved performance *more* than the choice of algorithm (they compared TRPO to PPO).[2]

This leads to the obvious conclusion that bugs impact performance. For example, during OpenAI's random network distillation research (see "Random embeddings (random distillation networks)" on page 280), Cobbe et al. noticed that seemingly small details made the difference between an agent that gets stuck and one that can solve a difficult Atari game. They noticed one issue where the value function approximation, which should be stable after enough training, was oscillating. It turned out that they were accidentally zeroing an array that was used to produce the curiosity bonus, which meant that the value function was pulled lower at the start of each episode. This explained the oscillation and, once fixed, dramatically improved performance due to the stable value estimates.[3]

So the question is, how do you prevent these bugs? Well, every single line of code introduces a possibility of a bug, so the only way to eliminate all bugs is to have no code at all. I preach this mantra a lot during my productization projects with Winder Research, which also has the added benefit of reducing the operational burden. Obviously you need code, but the point I'm making is that less is better. If you have an option of using an off-the-shelf library or component, then use it, even if it doesn't quite meet all your requirements. Similarly, if you are writing code or developing a framework, prefer less code over fancy design. This is why I love languages like Go or Python. They actively promote simplicity because they don't have all the so-called sophistication of a language like C++ or Java.

Beyond this, the normal debugging practices of tracing, visualizing your data, testing, and `print` statements will become your day-to-day experience of RL. At its heart, debugging is just a manifestation of the scientific method: you observe something strange (visualizations are really important), you develop a theory to explain the behavior, you develop ways to test that theory (`print` statements), and you evaluate the results. If you want to learn more, pick up a book on debugging software; some recommendations are in "Further Reading" on page 355.

RL is sequential, which means that bugs might not manifest for some time, and RL is stochastic, which means that bugs can be hidden by the noise of the learning process. Combine this with the underlying dependencies of machine learning and software engineering and you end up with a volatile witch's cauldron of bubbling bugs.

If you were to speak to your project manager and estimate how long you would spend developing an algorithm for a new problem, you would estimate something like the top part of Figure 11-1; most of the time is spent on research and implementation, right? No. The vast majority of time is spent debugging, attempting to figure out why your agent can't solve the simplest thing. The bottom part of Figure 11-1 shows something more representative, with the added time that is required to reimplement your code properly, with clean code and tests. The measurements I picked are arbitrary, but they are representative, in my experience.

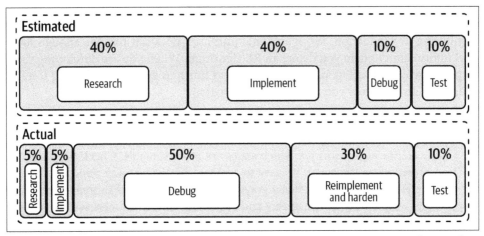

Figure 11-1. A comparison of expected versus actual time spent on activities during algorithm development. Inspired by Matthew Rahtz.[4]

${ALGORITHM_NAME} Can't Solve ${ENVIRONMENT}!

Even though these algorithms can achieve amazing feats, with examples that you might even consider intelligent, it is important to remember that they are not magic. They cannot solve every problem and they certainly don't do it automatically.

If you are using RL in industry, you must take a holistic view. It is very likely that you can do something to dramatically simplify the problem. The main reason why RL methods fail is not because the algorithm isn't good enough, but because the problem isn't suited to being solved in this way. For example, the `MountainCar-v0` environment is notoriously difficult for RL algorithms to solve, despite being conceptually simple. This is not a problem with the algorithm; the value function is surprisingly simple. This is an exploration and a credit assignment problem. If you developed a better way to explore or changed the reward to encourage movement up the hill, any of these algorithms can solve the problem in no time.

There is no single solution to solving environments either. Sometimes the problem lies with the observation space, sometimes the exploration, sometimes a hyperparameter. Welcome to RL, where intelligent agents automate complex strategic goals, sometimes. My only recommendation is to use this book to guide you, one experiment at a time, toward a tractable problem. If you forced me to pick one, I'd start with a simplification of the problem or observation space. Get it simple enough so you can visualize what is going on and then solve that simple problem. With that in your bag, you'll probably have enough domain knowledge to know the issues with the more complex version.

Monitoring for Debugging

Monitoring in production, for operational purposes, does not provide enough low-level information to help you debug an RL algorithm. When you are developing your agent you will want to log, plot, and visualize as much as you can. Following is a list of tips to help you when you need more information:

- Log and visualize observations, actions, and rewards. Actions should have high entropy to encourage exploration. The rewards for states should not be the same; if they are the agent can't tell which states are more valuable. Check the observation presented to the agent; it's easy to accidentally throw away important information. For example, check that a grayscale transformation of an image preserves features within that image; green and red traffic lights are clearly different in color, but not so much in grayscale.

- Evaluate the value function for different parts of your state space. If you can, visualize the whole space. If not, pick some representative states and plot them. Is it overfitting?

- Plot the value function over time (for a reasonable number of states). How does it change? Does it get stuck? Does it oscillate? What is the variance during a run? What is the variance over several runs? The estimate should alter over time and then stabilize. Remember that when the policy changes, the perfect value function changes, too. The value function approximation should remain stable enough to cope with the nonstationarity, but flexible enough to react to changes.

- Poor or buggy neural network implementations make RL look bad. Start with something simple, a linear approximator or equivalent single-layer neural network. Make sure everything works as expected before trying more complex networks. Look at a good practical deep learning book for help with this (see "Further Reading" on page 355).

- Make sure everything works with fixed seeds and single threading, before you scale up to multiple seeds or multithreading/multinode runs.

- Start with hyperparameters that are known to work well from your past experience with other implementations.

The Future of Reinforcement Learning

What is the current opinion of RL right now? This makes me think of Andrew Ng's almost seminal talk on practical deep learning, where he manages to perfectly balance a healthy dose of short-term cynicism with long-term optimism.[5] This left me appreciating the complexities of the subject, especially when it comes to industrial implementations, but at the same time the optimism made these issues feel like it was just part of the process. The challenges are there, so accept them, deal with them in the best way you can, and move on. Sometimes deep learning doesn't make sense, and that's OK. But when it does, the confluence of model and data are a beauty to behold.

I think RL is in this position right now. We're on the cusp of where industrial productization and operationalization are possible, but tricky. There are still many cases where simpler algorithms outperform RL; for example, if you are able to play your environment offline, then you could just use a Monte Carlo tree search (MCTS) algorithm, like AlphaGo, to evaluate your possible moves. For example, an experiment in 2014 smashed the performance of DQN using MCTS and it took some time before RL methods could catch up.[6] But this is OK. RL isn't a silver bullet, just like machine learning hasn't had babies and created artificial intelligence yet. It's just a tool. And like a carpenter, you should use the best tool for your job.

RL Market Opportunities

Deep learning has become mainstream, so even my enterprise clients are investing in operationalization. I believe that RL will follow within the next few years. This opens up new markets and opportunities. Unfortunately, like machine learning, RL is a cross-industry technique, not a solution. You will need domain expertise, industry-specific market awareness, and a dollop of inspiration to exploit RL.

There are already signs that RL is especially well suited to specific domains, however. Robotics is one obvious one. But automated bidding and recommendations are others that could overtake robotics in terms of global revenue. There hasn't been any industry-wide research specific to RL yet, but that will come if RL is successful.

The market research firm Gartner reckons that RL is still on the rise of the hype curve and that a third of enterprises are looking to automate strategic decision making (which they call decision intelligence) by 2023.[7,8] They are suitably vague about market values, especially when it comes to quantifying the impact of specific technologies, but the worldwide value to business is reported to be many trillions of dollars per year.[9] Interestingly, in some of Gartner's visualizations, they are beginning to separate "agents" and "decision automation" from other forms of more traditional machine learning, which they call "decision support/augmentation," so they can clearly see the emerging value of optimizing sequential decisions.

This promise means that there is value and opportunity in the operational space. Companies won't be able to use the current crop of machine-learning-as-a-service offerings because most are not well suited toward continuous learning and sequential decision making. Some will adapt, of course, but there are opportunities for companies to fill this space.

Open source projects won't be far behind, either, and could even be in front in many cases. There is an argument to be made that only open source projects can be truly successful because, like machine learning, global adoption needs open collaboration.

Otherwise your needs and challenges might conflict with proprietary processes and opinions. If you are considering this, make sure you position your product some distance away from what large vendors might be interested in. And make sure you reflect on how you and the global community can mutually gain from open source development.

This also means that companies will need RL support and expertise for a long time into the future. It could be as much as 10 years before RL is a commodity. So consultants and engineers with demonstrable RL expertise, like those from my company, will be sought after. If you are thinking about specializing in RL as a career, this would not be a bad decision, I don't think, because of the obvious opportunities and projections just discussed. But don't let this lull you into a false sense of security. RL, ML, and software engineering is hard, especially when you try to move these things into production. And like in any knowledge-based industry, the goal posts are constantly moving. You have to accept this and move with them to assure a long-term position in this highly competitive field. To put in this much effort you really have to love it. You have to enjoy the craft and the challenge of adversity, the challenge of being met with a specific industrial situation that nobody, ever, has dealt with before.

Future RL and Research Directions

RL has many challenges, as I have discussed throughout the book. Don't let these prevent you from exploring the potential of RL, because I truly believe that the next level of artificial intelligence is going to be driven by these ideas; they are just waiting for breakthrough applications. But hopefully I have clearly marked which parts of RL can slow you down or cause you to stumble when working on an industrial problem. These problems mostly translate into future research opportunities.

The research directions can be broadly split in two: industrial and academic research. Industrial research is comprised of ways to improve the development and operational efficiency and is driven by business needs. Academic research focuses more on improving or redefining fundamental understanding and is driven by a theoretical notion of novelty or advancement, as defined by their peers. This means that academic researchers are not going to invest their time in improving their code's readability, for example. Likewise, industrial researchers are unlikely to stumble across anything truly groundbreaking. But of course, there are people that sit in between.

I believe that there is a problem in the academic machine learning community at the moment. The primary venues for academic success are conferences and journals. The most popular can afford to pick and choose, so reviewers have a lot of power to direct current and future content. And unfortunately, applications are deemed to be of lesser value than, for example, a novel algorithmic improvement. For example, Hannah Kerner has recently spoken about her experience trying to push application-focused papers to conferences, only to find that "the significance seems limited for the machine-learning community."[10] Of course, fundamental improvement is the primary goal for academia and scientific discovery in general, but I feel like the scale has tipped too far.

Research in industry

Starting from an industrial perspective, these are the areas in which I think there are research opportunities and momentum:

Operationalization and architecture

RL is being used more and soon there will be a glut of applications moving into production. I don't think that any of the current machine learning frameworks have the capability and the RL frameworks tend to focus on development, not production. Of course, there are a few exceptions, but there is a lot of room for improvement, particularly on the architecture side.

RL design and implementation

There is already a lot of work in this area—see all the RL frameworks for an example—but many of them tend to focus on the wrong problem. Many of them are attempting to implement RL algorithms, but this is not the goal for an industrial problem. The goal is to find, refine, and build an RL solution to a business challenge. This means that things like feature engineering, reward shaping, and everything else listed in the previous two chapters are also important, possibly more so, than the algorithm. The frameworks need to shift their focus away from algorithm development and toward application development.

Environment curation and simulation

Simulators are obviously crucial for initial development. Accurate simulations provide the ability to transfer knowledge to the real world. As more complex industrial problems are attempted, these will benefit from more realistic simulations. This is already the case for 3D simulation engines, which are capable of simulating scarily good representations of the real world. But for all the other domains, decent, realistic simulators are hard to come by. One reason for this is that they contain a lot of proprietary information. The models that drive the simulations are often built from data that the company owns, so they know that this represents a competitive advantage. One way research could help here is to improve the curation and development process of an environment. This side-steps the data issue but will still help this crucial phase of development.

Monitoring and explainability

The tooling and support surrounding monitoring RL agents is lacking and can be attributed to the lack of operationalization. When in production you need to be certain that your policy is robust and the only way to be sure of that is through adequate oversight. Some applications may even demand explainability, which is quite tricky at the moment, especially in production settings. But more than that, you need tools to help debug the development of applications, tools that give you a view of what is happening inside the agent. The problem with this is that it tends to be algorithm and domain specific, but it is still a worthwhile challenge.

Safety and robustness

This is a hot topic in academic research, too, but the impact of the research is only felt when it is applied to a real-life application. Proving the robustness of your model is important for every application, so I envisage libraries and tools to help solve that problem. Safety is a much bigger concern. I'm less worried about the technical aspects, because I'm confident that engineers can create solutions that are safe by design. I'm concerned about the legal and regulatory impacts, because at this point it becomes more of an ethical problem. Who is liable? How safe does it need to be? How do you test how safe it is?

Applications

And of course, businesses are paying for the application of RL. The research directions discussed here help in delivering that application. There will be a lot of interest and therefore research in applying RL to business challenges. The hard part, like with any technology, is mapping the technology to a business challenge. This is a lot harder than it sounds, because RL is so general; there are many possible applications. So use the suggestions presented in "Problem Definition: What Is an RL Project?" on page 254 to find a viable RL problem and then prioritize by business value.

Research in academia

From an academic perspective, RL is really exciting, because it feels like we're only a few steps away from something truly revolutionary: an agent that can learn any task as well as a human. This moment is like a bulkhead; once it is breached, this opens up a whole world of possibilities, mostly good, some scary.

Current applications of machine learning and, to a lesser extent, RL, are limited by their inability to utilize the scientific method and retain that knowledge in an intelligent way. If an agent was capable of developing its own theories, testing its own beliefs, and can apply that knowledge to discover new theories, then I think that is the moment where we can generalize RL to solve any sequential problem on any data.

And I feel like we're almost there. But to be specific, the challenges that are preventing this goal, from an application perspective, are:

Offline learning

This is probably the biggest challenge. The primary reason why we need simulators is because the agent must test an action to learn a policy. If we can move away from this regime, training a policy without that interaction, this means we can remove the simulator entirely. Just capture log data and train upon that, just like in machine learning. Researchers have already begun to improve this process; look back at Chapter 8, for example. But there is a lot left to be desired. Intuitively, I don't think it is unreasonable to imagine an algorithm that is capable of understanding the stochasticity of an environment, observing examples of an optimal trajectory, then applying a model to fit a generalized trajectory to the data. This should provide a compromise between finding an optimal policy and retaining enough uncertainty about the states not observed from the log.

Sample efficiency

Improving the sample efficiency of algorithms is desirable because applications generally want an optimal policy in the shortest number of interactions. Consider the shopping cart example: I really don't want to get bags of dog and cat food delivered when I don't have any pets. The faster it can learn this preference, the less upset I'm going to be. Again, there are a range of research directions here, from improving exploration to consolidating knowledge, like ensembles, but these are often driven by the domain. It would be great if there was some universal, theoretical efficiency guarantee that algorithms could work toward.

High-dimensional efficiency

Large state and action spaces are still problematic. The large state spaces are awkward because of the amount of computational energy required to reduce it to something useful. I imagine that for certain domains pretrained transformers or embeddings could be used to simplify the state space without having to train the reduction. A large action space is more problematic because agents have to actively sample all available actions at all times to ensure they have an optimal policy. This is easier when actions are related. For example, a single continuous action is infinite, but it is quite easy to solve because you can model the action with a distribution. But many distinct actions cause more of a problem, mainly because this yields a more difficult exploration problem.

Reward function sensitivity

Supervised machine learning is easy because you know what the goal is. I would *love* to have such a simple way of defining goals in RL. RL rewards are often sparse, have multiple objectives, and are highly multidimensional. To this day defining a reward function is largely an exhaustive manual process, even with techniques such as intrinsic rewards. In the future I still expect some manual intervention to define the high-level goals, but I expect to do this in a less invasive way; I shouldn't need to shape the reward. This becomes even more important when rewards are delayed.

Combining different types of learning

Is there a way to combine the exploratory benefits of multi-agent RL, the generalization of hierarchical RL, and expert guidance? Could you combine evolutionary or genetic learning with these RL techniques?

Pretrained agents and improving curriculum learning

I once read, I can't remember where, that learning is only possible when the gap between knowing and not knowing is small. I believe this to be true in RL, too. I don't expect a child to be able to drive a car; similarly, you should not expect an untrained agent to either. And overfitting the training to that one task is not the solution, since driving a car is more than just learning how to incorporate complex stereo vision and move a wheel. The agent needs a breadth of knowledge that can be provided by agents pretrained on specified curricula. You could even give them a grade at the end of it if you like.

Increased focus on real-life applications and benchmarks

I think that academia understands that real-life applicability is desirable, but I would like to see more emphasis placed on this. I can see algorithms that are overfitting the Atari benchmarks and that is by design, to be able to claim state-of-the-art performance.

Ethical standards

Ethical or moral machine learning and RL crosses into both industry and academia. There seems to be a melting pot of desire for advancing the discussion, but this is proving difficult. Maybe because it always turns into a philosophical debate or maybe because everyone has a different set of morals or contexts that makes it difficult to agree on what ethical conclusions to make. It's a really sensitive subject that I don't feel qualified to comment on. But that doesn't mean that you shouldn't consider it; you should. In everything you do.

Regarding the future, I don't feel like there has been a flood of support for even attempting to define ethical standards, let alone solving them. The General Data Protection Regulation (GDPR) is one example of a governmental attempt to define the ethical use of someone's data. And although I totally agree with the idea, in practice it is too vague and has too much legal jargon to be useful. For example, article 7, conditions for consent of the GDPR, states:

> Consent shall be presented in a manner which is clearly distinguishable from the other matters, in an intelligible and easily accessible form, using clear and plain language.

Fair enough. But in that same exact page, point 4 reads:

> When assessing whether consent is freely given, utmost account shall be taken of whether, inter alia, the performance of a contract, including the provision of a service, is conditional on consent to the processing of personal data that is not necessary for the performance of that contract.

Clear and plain language? And as evidence of the complete disregard for the letter of this law, the clarifying recital number 32, conditions for consent, states "pre-ticked boxes or inactivity should not therefore constitute consent." I would hazard a guess at suggesting that nearly all GDPR opt-in forms on a website provide an "accept all" box, which of course, checks all the boxes before you've had chance to read what they are for.

This pseudosafety comes at a cost, too. I'm constantly annoyed at having to find a cross to remove the pop-up (what does the close button do, by the way, accept all or reject all?). It's like being back in the '90s with GeoCities websites filled to the brim with pop-ups.

So what has the GDPR got to do with machine learning and RL ethical standards? It represents the first and largest government-led attempt to rein in a practice, related to data, which it deemed to be unethical. Has it worked? A bit, maybe. It has curtailed some of the exploits of some large companies or governments that were attempting to steer important conversations about democracy and freedom. But at what cost? Is there a better way? Probably, but I don't think there is a single right answer.

For more general applications of machine learning and RL, I feel like this will be a slow burner; it won't become important until it smacks people in the face, a bit like climate change. I think there will be success at a grassroots level, however, a bit like how ethical hacking is forcing companies to invest in digital security. All businesses want to be safe and secure, but it takes the challenge to actually do anything about it. The same will be true for data and the models derived from it. Individuals or groups of loosely affiliated individuals will be passionate enough to attempt to hold businesses or governments to account.

And then there are people like you. The practitioners. The engineers. The people building these solutions. You are first in line to observe the impact of your work, so there is a great responsibility placed upon you to decide whether your algorithm is ethical. This is the burden of knowledge; use it wisely and make good decisions.

Concluding Remarks

I find it ironic that I finish a book about optimizing sequential decision making with a remark asking you to make good decisions. Who knows, maybe in the future we can use RL to make the ethical decisions for us.

Until recently, RL has been primarily a subject of academic interest. The aim of this book was to try to bring some of that knowledge to industry and business, to continue the journey of improving productivity through automation. RL has the potential to optimize strategic-level decision processes using goals directly derived from business metrics. This means that RL could impact entire business structures, from factory floor workers to CEOs.

This poses unique technical and ethical challenges. Like how decisions can have long-lasting consequences that are not known at the time and how an automatic strategy can impact people. But this shouldn't prevent you from experimenting to see how RL can help you in your situation. It really is just a tool; how you use it is what counts.

Next Steps

You've probably got lots of questions. That's good. Collate those questions and send them to me (see About the Author for contact details). But in general I recommend that you don't stop here. Try to find a practical problem to solve, ideally at work. If you can persuade your business to support your research, maybe in your 20% time or maybe as a fully fledged time-boxed proof of concept, this gives you the time and the impetus to deal with the real-life challenges that you will face. If you stick to toy examples, I'm afraid that it will be too easy for you. If you can't do this in work time, then find a problem that is interesting to you, maybe related to another hobby. You probably won't get any dedicated time to do this, because life gets in the way, but hopefully it is rewarding and gives you some practical experience.

Beyond practical experience, I recommend you keep reading. Obviously RL is hugely dependent on machine learning, so any books on data science or machine learning are useful. There are some other RL books out there, too, which are very good, and should provide another perspective. And if you want to go full stack, then improve your general software and engineering skills.

To help cement everything you have learned, you need to use it. Experience is one way I've already mentioned, but mentorship, teaching, and general presenting is another great way to learn. If you have to explain something to someone else, especially when the format is formal, like a presentation, it forces you to consolidate your ideas and commit your models and generalizations to memory. Don't fall into the trap of thinking that you are not experienced enough to talk about it. You are; you are an expert in the experiences you have had. It is very likely that some of your experiences can generalize to RL to help apply, explain, or teach these concepts in a way that nobody else could. Give it a go!

Now It's Your Turn

With that, I'll hand it over to you.

As you know, you can find more resources on the accompanying website (*https://rl-book.com*). But I also want to hear from you. I want to hear about the projects that you are working on, your challenges, your tips and tricks, and your ideas for the future of RL. I especially want to talk to you if you are thinking about applying RL in industry or you are struggling with a problem. I can make your life easier with solutions, tips, and assessments to reduce effort, reduce risks, and improve performance. My full contact details are printed in About the Author.

Good luck!

Further Reading

- Debugging:
  - — Agans, David J. 2002. *Debugging: The 9 Indispensable Rules for Finding Even the Most Elusive Software and Hardware Problems*. AMACOM.
  - — Fowler, Martin. 2018. *Refactoring: Improving the Design of Existing Code*. Addison-Wesley Professional.
  - — Feathers, Michael C. 2004. *Working Effectively with Legacy Code*. Prentice Hall PTR.
- Deep learning debugging:
  - — Goodfellow, Ian, Yoshua Bengio, and Aaron Courville. 2016. *Deep Learning*. MIT Press.
- RL debugging:
  - — Excellent Reddit thread, which led to a lot of this information.[11]
  - — John Schulman's fantastic nuts and bolts presentation.[12]
  - — Representative experience from Matthew Rahtz.[13]
- Research directions:
  - — Many of the ideas were inspired by the paper by Dulac-Arnold et al.[14]
  - — Offline RL.[15]
  - — I personally loved Max Tegmark's book on the future for AI.[16]

References

[1] Engstrom, Logan, Andrew Ilyas, Shibani Santurkar, Dimitris Tsipras, Firdaus Janoos, Larry Rudolph, and Aleksander Madry. 2020. "Implementation Matters in Deep Policy Gradients: A Case Study on PPO and TRPO" (*https://oreil.ly/8DR7T*). ArXiv:2005.12729, May.

[2] Ibid.

[3] Cobbe, Karl et al. "Reinforcement Learning with Prediction-Based Rewards." (*https://oreil.ly/9VV5z*) OpenAI. 31 October 2018.

[4] "Lessons Learned Reproducing a Deep Reinforcement Learning Paper" (*https://oreil.ly/OPnQm*). n.d. Accessed 17 August 2020.

[5] Ng, Andrew. "Nuts and Bolts of Applying Deep Learning" (*https://oreil.ly/qEz3Z*). 2016.

[6] Guo, Xiaoxiao, Satinder Singh, Honglak Lee, Richard L Lewis, and Xiaoshi Wang. 2014. "Deep Learning for Real-Time Atari Game Play Using Offline Monte-Carlo Tree Search Planning" (*https://oreil.ly/dl-az*). *Advances in Neural Information Processing Systems* 27, edited by Z. Ghahramani, M. Welling, C. Cortes, N. D. Lawrence, and K. Q. Weinberger, 3338–3346. Curran Associates, Inc.

[7] "Hype Cycle for Data Science and Machine Learning, 2019" (*https://oreil.ly/s7kEo*). n.d. Gartner. Accessed 17 August 2020.

[8] "Gartner Top 10 Trends in Data and Analytics for 2020" (*https://oreil.ly/nYjE_*). n.d. Accessed 17 August 2020.

[9] "Gartner Says AI Augmentation Will Create $2.9 Trillion of Business Value in 2021" (*https://oreil.ly/OjbkG*). n.d. Gartner. Accessed 17 August 2020.

[10] "Too Many AI Researchers Think Real-World Problems Are Not Relevant" (*https://oreil.ly/B0k1N*). n.d. *MIT Technology Review*. Accessed 20 August 2020.

[11] "Deep Reinforcement Learning Practical Tips" (*https://oreil.ly/rSrgg*). R/Reinforcementlearning, n.d., Reddit. Accessed 17 August 2020.

[12] "Deep RL Bootcamp Lecture 6: Nuts and Bolts of Deep RL Experimentation" (*https://oreil.ly/PjuAc*). 2017.

[13] "Lessons Learned Reproducing a Deep Reinforcement Learning Paper" (*https://oreil.ly/SNSVk*). n.d. Accessed 17 August 2020.

[14] Dulac-Arnold, Gabriel, Daniel Mankowitz, and Todd Hester. 2019. "Challenges of Real-World Reinforcement Learning" (*https://oreil.ly/WKoG5*). ArXiv:1904.12901, April.

[15] Levine, Sergey, Aviral Kumar, George Tucker, and Justin Fu. 2020. "Offline Reinforcement Learning: Tutorial, Review, and Perspectives on Open Problems" (*https://oreil.ly/Kae6m*). ArXiv:2005.01643, May.

[16] Tegmark, Max. 2017. *Life 3.0: Being Human in the Age of Artificial Intelligence.* Penguin UK.

The Gradient of a Logistic Policy for Two Actions

Equation 5-6 is a policy for two actions. To update the policies I need to calculate the gradient of the natural logarithm of the policy (see Equation 5-4). I present this in Equation A-1. You can perform the differentiation in a few different ways depending on how you refactor it, so the result can look different, even though it provides the same result.

Equation A-1. Logistic policy gradient for two actions

$$
\nabla \ln \pi(a \mid s, \theta) =
\begin{pmatrix}
\dfrac{\delta}{\delta\theta_0} \ln \left(\dfrac{1}{1 + e^{-\theta_0^{\mathsf{T}} s}} \right) \\[4ex]
\dfrac{\delta}{\delta\theta_1} \ln \left(1 - \dfrac{1}{1 + e^{-\theta_1^{\mathsf{T}} s}} \right)
\end{pmatrix}
$$

I calculate the gradients of each action independently and I find it easier if I refactor the logistic function like in Equation A-2.

Equation A-2. Refactoring the logistic function

$$\pi(x) \doteq \frac{1}{1 + e^{-x}} = \frac{e^x}{e^x(1 + e^{-x})}$$

$$= \frac{e^x}{e^x(1 + e^{-x})}$$

$$= \frac{e^x}{e^x + e^x e^{-x}}$$

$$= \frac{e^x}{e^x + e^{x-x}}$$

$$= \frac{e^x}{e^x + e^0}$$

$$= \frac{e^x}{e^x + 1}$$

$$= \frac{e^x}{1 + e^x}$$

The derivative of the refactored logistic function, for action 0, is shown in Equation A-3.

Equation A-3. Differentiation of action 0

$$\frac{\delta}{\delta\theta_0} \ln \pi_0(\theta_0^\mathsf{T} s) = \frac{\delta}{\delta\theta_0} \ln\left(\frac{e^{\theta_0^\mathsf{T} s}}{1 + e^{\theta_0^\mathsf{T} s}}\right)$$

$$= \frac{\delta}{\delta\theta_0} \ln e^{\theta_0^\mathsf{T} s} - \frac{\delta}{\delta\theta_0} \ln\left(1 + e^{\theta_0^\mathsf{T} s}\right)$$

$$= \frac{\delta}{\delta\theta_0}\theta_0^\mathsf{T} s - \frac{\delta}{\delta\theta_0} \ln\left(1 + e^{\theta_0^\mathsf{T} s}\right)$$

$$= s - \frac{\delta}{\delta\theta_0} \ln\left(1 + e^{\theta_0^\mathsf{T} s}\right)$$

$$= s - \frac{\delta}{\delta\theta_0} \ln u \quad \text{where } u = 1 + e^{\theta_0^\mathsf{T} s}$$

$$= s - \frac{1}{u}\frac{\delta}{\delta\theta_0}u$$

$$= s - \frac{1}{1 + e^{\theta_0^\mathsf{T} s}}\frac{\delta}{\delta\theta_0}\left(1 + e^{\theta_0^\mathsf{T} s}\right)$$

$$= s - \frac{1}{1 + e^{\theta_0^\mathsf{T} s}}\frac{\delta}{\delta v}(e^v)\frac{\delta}{\delta\theta_0}v \quad \text{where } v = \theta_0^\mathsf{T} s$$

$$= s - \frac{1}{1 + e^{\theta_0^\mathsf{T} s}}e^{\theta_0^\mathsf{T} s}s$$

$$= s - \frac{se^{\theta_0^\mathsf{T} s}}{1 + e^{\theta_0^\mathsf{T} s}}$$

$$= s - s\pi(\theta_0^\mathsf{T} s)$$

The method to calculate the derivative of the policy for action 1 is shown in Equation A-4. Note that the derivation towards the end is the same as Equation A-3.

Equation A-4. Differentiation of action 1

$$\frac{\delta}{\delta\theta_1} \ln \pi_1(\theta_1^\mathsf{T} s) = \frac{\delta}{\delta\theta_1} \ln\left(1 - \frac{e^{\theta_1^\mathsf{T} s}}{1 + e^{\theta_1^\mathsf{T} s}}\right)$$

$$= \frac{\delta}{\delta\theta_1} \ln\left(\frac{1 + e^{\theta_1^\mathsf{T} s}}{1 + e^{\theta_1^\mathsf{T} s}} - \frac{e^{\theta_1^\mathsf{T} s}}{1 + e^{\theta_1^\mathsf{T} s}}\right)$$

$$= \frac{\delta}{\delta\theta_1} \ln\left(\frac{1 + e^{\theta_1^\mathsf{T} s} - e^{\theta_1^\mathsf{T} s}}{1 + e^{\theta_1^\mathsf{T} s}}\right)$$

$$= \frac{\delta}{\delta\theta_1} \ln\left(\frac{1}{1 + e^{\theta_1^\mathsf{T} s}}\right)$$

$$= \frac{\delta}{\delta\theta_1} \ln 1 - \frac{\delta}{\delta\theta_1} \ln\left(1 + e^{\theta_1^\mathsf{T} s}\right)$$

$$= -\frac{\delta}{\delta\theta_1} \ln\left(1 + e^{\theta_1^\mathsf{T} s}\right)$$

$$= \cdots \quad \text{same as the derivative of } \pi_0$$

$$= -s\pi(\theta_1^\mathsf{T} s)$$

These result in the gradient shown in Equation A-5.

Equation A-5. Logistic policy

$$\nabla \ln \pi(a \mid s, \theta) = \begin{pmatrix} s - s\pi(\theta_0^\mathsf{T} s) \\ -s\pi(\theta_1^\mathsf{T} s) \end{pmatrix}$$

The Gradient of a Softmax Policy

The derivation of the gradient of a softmax policy is shown in Equation B-1. Note how this is a similar form to the logistic gradients in Appendix A.

Equation B-1. Gradient of a softmax policy

$$\nabla_\theta \ln \pi(\theta^\mathsf{T} s) = \nabla_\theta \ln \frac{e^{\theta^\mathsf{T} s}}{\Sigma_a e^{\theta_a^\mathsf{T} s}}$$

$$= \nabla_\theta \ln e^{\theta^\mathsf{T} s} - \nabla_\theta \ln \sum_a e^{\theta_a^\mathsf{T} s}$$

$$= \nabla_\theta \theta^\mathsf{T} s - \nabla_\theta \ln \sum_a e^{\theta_a^\mathsf{T} s}$$

$$= s - \nabla_\theta \ln \sum_a e^{\theta_a^\mathsf{T} s}$$

$$= s - \nabla_\theta \ln \sum_a e^{\theta_a^\mathsf{T} s}$$

$$= s - \frac{\nabla_\theta \Sigma_a e^{\theta_a^\mathsf{T} s}}{\Sigma_a e^{\theta_a^\mathsf{T} s}}$$

$$= s - \frac{\Sigma_a s e^{\theta_a^\mathsf{T} s}}{\Sigma_a e^{\theta_a^\mathsf{T} s}}$$

$$= s - \sum_a s\pi(\theta^\mathsf{T} s)$$

Glossary

Acronyms and Common Terms

ACER
Actor-critic with experience replay

ACKTR
Actor-critic using Kronecker-factored trust region

AGE
Adversarially guided exploration

Agent
An instantiation of an RL algorithm that interacts with the environment

AGI
Artificial general intelligence

AI
Artificial intelligence

ANN
Artificial neural network

API
Application programming interface

AWS
Amazon Web Services

BAIL
Best-action imitation learning

BCQ
Batch-constrained deep Q-learning

BDQN
Bootstrapped deep Q-network

CAQL
Continuous action Q-learning

CDQ
Clipped double Q-learning

CI/CD
Continuous integration/continuous delivery

CNN
Convolutional neural network

CORA
Conditioned reflex analog (an early robot)

CPU
Central processing unit

CRISP-DM
Cross-industry process for data mining

CTR
Click-through rate

CVAE
Convolutional variational autoencoder

DAG
Directed acyclic graph

DBN
Deep belief network

DDPG
Deep deterministic policy gradient

Dec-HDRQN
Hysteretic Deep Recurrent Q-networks

DEC-MDP
Decentralized Markov decision process

Deep
A method that uses multilayer neural networks

Deterministic policy
Maps each state to a single specific action

DIAYN
Diversity is all you need

DL
Deep learning

DP
Dynamic programming

DPG
Deterministic policy gradient

DQN
Deep Q-network

DRL
Deep reinforcement learning

EFG
Extensive-form game

Environment
Abstraction of real life, often simulated

ESN
Echo state network

FIFO
First in, first out

Fully observable
Agents can observe the complete state of the environment

GAIL
Generative adversarial imitation learning

GAN
Generative adversarial network

GDPR
General data protection regulation

GQ and Greedy-GQ
Generalized gradient algorithms for temporal-difference prediction

GPI
Generalized policy iteration

GPT-3
Generative Pre-trained Transformer 3

GPU
Graphics processing unit

GRU
Gated recurrent unit

GTD
Gradient temporal difference

HAAR
HRL with advantage-based rewards

HIRO
Hierarchies with intrinsic rewards

HRL
Hierarchical reinforcement learning

IID
Independent and identically distributed

IMPALA
Importance weighted actor-learner architecture

IRIS
Implicit reinforcement without interaction at scale

IRL
Inverse reinforcement learning

KPI
Key performance indicator

KL
Kullback–Leibler (divergence)

LSTM
Long short-term memory

MADDPG

Multi-agent deep deterministic policy gradient

MARL

Multi-agent reinforcement learning

MC

Monte Carlo

MCTS

Monte Carlo tree search

MDP

Markov decision process

MG

Markov game

ML

Machine learning

MLP

Multilayer perceptron

Model

Understand phenomena through a mathematical representation

Model-based

Literal, based on a model

Model-free

Literal, no model assumed

MSE

Mean squared error

NN

Neural network

Nonstationary

Not stable, in a statistical sense; chaotic, not predictable

NPG

Natural policy gradient

Observation

Externally observed features of an environment

Off-policy

Algorithms that learn an optimal policy while another policy makes decisions

Offline

In the ML sense, training without inferencing

On-policy

Algorithms that improve a policy that is being used to make decisions

Online

In the ML sense, training at the same time as inferencing

PAAC

Parallel advantage actor-critic

PAC

Probably approximately correct

Partially observable

Agents can observe a limited view of the environment

PCL

Path consistency learning

PG

Policy gradient

Policy

Rules that define how to act

POMDP

Partially observable Markov decision process

PPO

Proximal policy optimization

QMIX

Monotonic value function factorization for deep multi-agent reinforcement learning

RAM

Random access memory

RBM

Restricted Boltzmann machine

REINFORCE

A Monte Carlo–inspired policy gradient algorithm

Reward

> A numeric value given to agents to signify success or failure

RL

> Reinforcement learning

RNN

> Recurrent neural network

ROBEL

> Robotics Benchmarks for Learning

RTB

> Real-time bidding

SAC

> Soft actor-critic

SARSA

> Exhaustive version of Q-learning

SAS

> Stochastic action set

SEED

> Scalable and efficient deep RL

State

> The fully observable internal state of an environment, often a misnomer for observation

Stationary

> Stable, in a statistical sense; implies predictability

Stochastic policy

> Maps states to a probability distribution over actions

Strategy

> Long-term sequential decision making; see policy

SQIL

> Soft Q imitation learning

SQL

> Soft Q-learning

TD

> Temporal difference

TRPO

> Trust region policy optimization

UAV

> Unmanned aerial vehicle

UCB

> Upper confidence bound

VAE

> Variational autoencoder

VIME

> Variational information maximizing exploration

XAI

> Explainable artificial intelligence

Symbols and Notation

$\|$

> Divergence between two distributions, typically KL divergence

α

> Typically a learning rate parameter

β

> The behavior policy, also a second learning rate parameter in some algorithms

γ

> Discount factor

∇

> Gradient operator

π

> A policy, or a target policy, often used in a subscript to denote following a policy

θ

> Parameters of a model or policy

φ

> A function that maps from one dimensionality to another

$\mathcal{A}$

> All possible actions, a set

a

> A specific state, a member of $\mathcal{A}$

E
Expectation operator

G
The return (sum of all rewards between two points on a trajectory)

$\mathcal{H}$
Entropy operator

J
The objective function for a policy gradient algorithm

Q
Action-value function, also known as the Q-function, the expected return for a given state and action

$\mathcal{R}$
All possible rewards, a set

r
A specific reward, a member of $\mathcal{R}$

$\mathcal{S}$
All possible states, a set

s
A specific state, a member of $\mathcal{S}$

V
The state-value function, the expected return for a given state

Z
Distributional action-value function

Index

A

A/B testing, 324
academic pseudocode, xxi
acronyms and common terms, 363
action-value function, 47
actions
    bonuses added to, 34
    discrete or continuous, 10
    mapping policies to action spaces, 273-277
    in Markov decision process, 35
    role in reinforcement learning, 4
    stochastic action set (SAS), 219
activation functions, 88
actor-critic algorithms
    actor-critic using Kronecker-factored trust
        regions (ACKTR), 183
    actor-critic with experience replay (ACER),
        182
    advantage actor-critic (A2C), 129-134, 301
    asynchronous advantage actor-critic (A3C),
        301
    development of, 18
    eligibility traces actor-critic, 134
    n-step actor-critic, 129-134
    on- and off-policy, 151
    parallel advantage actor critic (PAAC), 302
    soft actor-critic (SAC), 193-196, 198
advantage function, 102
adversarial attacks, 328
advertising, real-time bidding in, 70-73
agents
    deploying multiple, 324
    effect of policies on, 40
    how agents use and update strategy, 9

improving learning in
    expert guidance, 235-239
    further reading on, 242
    hierarchical RL, 220-225
    multi-agent RL, 225-235
    other paradigms, 240
    overview of, 215
    rethinking MDP, 216-220
in Markov decision process, 35
on- and off-policy agents, 9, 64-65, 145
pretrained, 352
role in reinforcement learning, 5
tracing trajectory of, 38
algorithms
    actor-critic, 18, 151
    advantage actor-critic (A2C), 129-134, 301
    Ape-X, 303
    asynchronous advantage actor-critic (A3C),
        301
    comparison of basic policy gradient algo-
        rithms, 135
    debugging, 343-346, 355
    eligibility traces actor-critic, 134
    experience replay buffers, 77
    first RL algorithm, 12
    generalizing, 45
    gradient-temporal-difference (GTD), 151
    imitation-based, 11
    improving sample efficiency of, 351
    maximizing rewards, 57
    model-based, 8
    model-free, 9
    Monte Carlo (MC), 50-52, 58
    multi-agent DDPG (MADDPG), 231

n-step actor-critic, 129-134
n-step algorithms, 76-79, 85
off-policy, 145-152
parallel advantage actor critic (PAAC), 302
performance measures, 313
policy-based, 11
Q-learning, 62-64
REINFORCE, 122-127
Retrace(λ), 182
sampling efficiency of, 56
selecting, 185
single-agent, 229
soft actor-critic (SAC), 193-196, 198
value-based, 11
ϵ-greedy, 33
Ape-X algorithm, 303
application containers, scaling, 68-70
arbitrary policies, 122
artificial intelligence (AI), 3
artificial neural networks (ANNs), 88
artificial neurons, 16
asynchronous advantage actor-critic (A3C), 301
asynchronous methods, 185
attack mitigation, 329
autoencoders, 89, 267
autonomous vehicles, using POMDPs in, 218
average-reward model, 308

B
backup diagrams, 53
batch RL, 109-110, 258
batch-constrained deep Q-learning (BCQ), 110
behavior cloning, 236
behavior policy, 148
behavior suite, 313
Bellman optimality equation, 49
Bellman, Richard, 18
best practices
    flexibility, 317
    reliability, 317
    scalability, 317
bidding, real-time in advertising, 70-73
binary actions, 10, 274
binning, 272
black box attacks, 328
black-box approaches, 314
bootstrap confidence interval test, 311
bootstrapping, 59

C
canary deployment strategy, 324
CartPole environment, 94-98
case studies (see also industrial examples)
    automated traffic management, 195
    POMDPs in autonomous vehicles, 218
    recommendations using reviews, 161
    reducing energy usage in buildings, 98
    scaling application containers, 68-70
    single-agent decentralized learning in UAVs, 230
catastrophic forgetting, 197
centralized learning, 228, 231
chess programming, 2
clipped double Q-learning (CDQ), 158
CNTK, 90
code examples, obtaining and using, xvi, xix, xxi
cold start problem, 278
comments and questions, xxii
concurrent learning, 260
conditional variational autoencoders, 110
constraints, 169, 267
contact information, xxii
contextual MDP (CMDP), 219
continuous actions, 274
continuous features, 270
continuous integration/continuous delivery (CI/CD), 322, 333
continuous learning, 219
continuous states, 270-272
control, 15
convolutional NNs (CNNs), 89
counterfactual actions, 97
counterfactual reasoning, 183, 315
curiosity, 279
curriculum learning, 238, 352

D
data science, 3
debugging, 343-346, 355
decay rates, 133
decentralized distributed proximal policy optimization (DD-PPO), 303
decentralized learning, 228, 232
decisions, 36
deep artificial neural networks, 88
deep belief networks (DBNs), 89

About the Author

Dr. Phil Winder is a multidisciplinary software engineer, data scientist, and CEO of Winder Research (*https://WinderResearch.com/?utm_source=oreilly&utm_medium =book&utm_campaign=rl*), a cloud native data science consultancy. He helps startups and enterprises improve their data-based processes, platforms, and products. Phil specializes in implementing production-grade cloud native machine learning and was an early champion of the MLOps movement.

He has thrilled thousands of engineers with his data science training courses in public, private, and on the O'Reilly online learning platform. Phil's courses focus on using data science in industry and cover a wide range of hot yet practical topics, from cleaning data to deep reinforcement learning. He is a regular speaker and is active in the data science community.

Phil holds a Ph.D. and M.Eng. in electronic engineering from the University of Hull and lives in Yorkshire, UK, with his brewing equipment and family.

Contact Details

For any support or advice, please get in touch with Phil using the following details:

- *Website*: *https://WinderResearch.com*
- *Email*: *phil@winderresearch.com*
- *LinkedIn*: *DrPhilWinder* (*https://www.linkedin.com/in/DrPhilWinder/*)
- *Twitter*: *@DrPhilWinder* (*https://twitter.com/DrPhilWinder*)

Colophon

The animal on the cover of *Reinforcement Learning* is an African penguin (*Spheniscus demersus*). The four species in the *Spheniscus* genus are known as banded penguins due to the band of black that runs around their bodies. These penguins also have black dorsal coloring, black beaks with a small vertical white band, spots on their bellies, and a patch of unfeathered or thinly feathered skin around their eyes.

The penguins live in colonies along the southwestern coast of Africa, mainly across 24 islands, with only a few colonies on the mainland.

At the beginning of the nineteenth century there were roughly 4 million African penguins. Today, the population has declined by 95%. Some estimate that the penguins will be extinct by the end of the decade. The penguins face many threats, including declining food sources because the fish they eat are sensitive to rising water temperatures.

The African penguin's conservation status is endangered. Many of the animals on O'Reilly covers are endangered; all of them are important to the world.

The cover illustration is by Karen Montgomery, based on a black and white engraving from *Lydekker's Royal Natural History*. The cover fonts are Gilroy Semibold and Guardian Sans. The text font is Adobe Minion Pro; the heading font is Adobe Myriad Condensed; and the code font is Dalton Maag's Ubuntu Mono.